The Skittle Craze

The Skiffle Craze

Mike Dewe

Foreword by Chris Barber

Planet

First published in Wales in 1998
by Planet

PO Box 44
Aberystwyth
Ceredigion SY23 3ZZ
Cymru/Wales

Designed by Glyn Rees

Cover photo by Jonathan Clements

Printed by Gwasg Gomer
Llandysul, Ceredigion

Supported by an Arts for All
Lottery grant from the Arts Council
of Wales

CRONFA LOTERI
LOTTERY FUND

CYNGOR
CELFYDDYDAU
CYMRU

THE ARTS
COUNCIL
OF WALES

ISBN 0 9505188 5 9

Contents

Foreword by Chris Barber   i

Preface   iii

1. Get Your Ticket at the Station — Skiffle Arrives   1

2. Black, Brown and White — Skiffle Origins   26

3. Puttin' on the Style — Britain and its Young
   People in the Fifties   49

4. The Big Four — Skiffle in the Hit Parade   75

5. Listen to the Song I Sing — Groups Galore   108

6. Mama Don't Allow — Grassroots Skiffle   133

7. Over the Points — Skiffle Takes to the Airwaves   159

8. Oh Boy! — Skiffle Goes Pop   181

9. I'm Alabamy Bound — Skiffle Today   205

Notes   227

Bibliography   235

Discography by Paul Redmond Drew   239

Index   261

To the memory of my brother-in-law, Michael Redding

— one-time skiffler

Foreword by Chris Barber

My reaction to this book is perhaps best explained metaphorically. In the popular motion picture Star Trek Generations *(yes, you've guessed it, I'm a science-fiction fan of more than forty years!) a scientific mistake finds two* Star Trek *Captains from different centuries fighting together against a nasty person played with great gusto by Roddy McDowell in order to save the world, the universe as we know it, from destruction. They indulge in serious hand-to-hand fighting — it's very rough even for hand-to-hand fighting — and at the end of it all McDowell is beaten, the galaxy is saved and Captain Kirk, alias William Shatner, lies dying. He says to Jean-Luc Picard, in the form of Patrick Stewart, "Did we make a difference?" How he hasn't noticed that they've just saved the universe I can't imagine, but undoubtedly it's possible to miss things — just as I did back in the '50s.*

When Lonnie was playing in my amateur band in 1952, we thought we'd like to do a couple of numbers which we vaguely identified as "skiffle", because we had a 78rpm record called "Hometown Skiffle" from the 1920s which was a sampler of blues artists on the Paramount label in America. We were just doing what we liked. Indeed, our whole objective in playing jazz and blues was to attempt to bring to people's notice a music which was largely forgotten and ignored both in its home country and in Europe. We performed a few numbers by Blind Blake and Big Bill Broonzy and so on — I remember doing "Midnight Special" , for example — and didn't think much more of it. We didn't call ourselves a skiffle group at that time, but we did refer to the music as skiffle. Usually I played bass, Alec Revell played clarinet, and Lonnie played banjo and sang.

Later that same year in September '52, Lonnie and I, together with Monty Sunshine, Jim Bray and Ron Bowden decided to form a professional band. We wanted to play the music better, and to do that we had to play much more often than we were doing with our amateur band. It meant playing as if our lives depended on it — which it did.

So we rehearsed. Now, our rehearsals were not like public performances, they didn't need any variety, we just tried to practice the jazz music which we were most keen on, and at this point we didn't play much of what you might call skiffle, although my amateur band was still in existence and Lonnie and I did the odd number with it. The professional band with Monty Sunshine, Lonnie, myself and the others began playing in public in Denmark in 1953 after we'd been joined by the late, sadly missed Ken Colyer who was as fond of the music of Lead Belly, the Memphis Jug Band, and so on, as we were. So Ken, Lonnie and myself began playing and singing these bluesy numbers. We still didn't call ourselves a skiffle group, though, as I say, we referred to the music as skiffle. When the band returned to play in Britain, opening the

Jazz Club in Bryanston Street, Marble Arch at the end of March 1953, we took to including a session by this little group each time we played. At this time, Ken's brother Bill joined in on washboard, and I played a string bass (in fact we never used a tea-chest bass). Our concern was simply to play the music — it wasn't a question of what we played — what instruments there were — but of the fact, as I say, that we loved this music.

A year later we split up with Ken, who tried to throw half the band out while allowing Monty and me to stay. We said we'd rather stay with them than with you, sorry about that! So we did and I became leader of the band. At this time we made our first album and agreed that we ought to include a couple of skiffle numbers. Lonnie was doing "Rock Island Line", so we included that with Beryl Bryden joining in on washboard. We hadn't considered adding drums to the group at this point, but it was now called a skiffle group. "Rock Island Line" was recorded in June '54, though the album didn't appear until the end of '54 or the beginning of '55, and wasn't released as a single until almost a year after that. Decca wasn't exactly quick off the mark in noticing what was going on! In the meantime we'd recorded things for other people. We'd recorded, with Lonnie singing, "On a Christmas Day", a Huddie Ledbetter song, at the end of '54 which was released for Christmas of that year. In January '55 we signed up for a contract with Dennis Preston's Landsdown series for the new Nixa label, which eventually became Pye. We recorded two EPs — Backstairs Session *and* Skiffle Session *— for that label which were very successful. Lonnie achieved tremendous success, with all these records selling enormously well within the next year or so.*

This group was of course called The Skiffle Group, which now included drums played by the band's drummer Ron Bowden. The interesting thing is that the people who listened to the skiffle group and loved the music most — the fans you might say, a whole generation of young people in Britain — really did not pick up on the origins of the music, about which we were so careful and sincere, but more on the fact that here was a music which you could play and sing yourself.

Up to that time, music had really been something that other people did — you paid to see a group or you bought records by them — and the idea that virtually anybody could easily obtain or make instruments and play the music for themselves, was unheard of. Indeed this was the beginning of a cultural revolution in England, in that music was now played rather than merely listened to. As a result many youngsters began playing instruments in skiffle or rock 'n' roll groups, a number of which had more than a modicum of success. John Lennon and Paul McCartney, for example, got into skiffle and by this means found their way into music. Quite arguably, without skiffle, people like that might never have been led into playing music at all.

Had you asked me at the time, I certainly would not have realized that we were in the process of having such an impact. In The Skiffle Craze, *however, Mike makes it quite clear that we did — and I'm very happy to be told this, it's very flattering to feel one has done something, and odd to reflect that we did it without knowing. All I can add is that this book told me a great deal I didn't realise, and I commend it to all readers with an interest in popular music for information and enjoyment.*

Preface

If I were to ask people of a certain age what they remembered about skiffle music of the Fifties, what would they come up with? Lonnie Donegan, of course... Spanish guitars... the Vipers Skiffle Group... washboards... "Freight Train"... tea-chest basses... *Saturday Skiffle Club*... "Cumberland Gap"... the list would go on. Gradually the story would emerge of a popular music genre that enjoyed some commercial success in the Fifties but more importantly, perhaps, inspired hundreds of young people to form groups to play skiffle. This book sets out to tell that story.

Any special insight that I may bring to my task of telling the story of skiffle, however, rests largely on the fact that I was around in the Fifties. Born in 1940, the Fifties encompassed my teenage years exactly. Not only was I there, but I was also a member of a London skiffle group. My own personal history, therefore, forms part of the story of the times I am chronicling, illustrating the attraction of skiffle (and rock 'n' roll) for one of Britain's young people, newly identified as "teenagers".

Until about 1956-57 music largely meant church music to me, as since the late 1940s, I had sung in the church choir of Holy Trinity, Roehampton. My musical education was further extended by the choruses that were sung at Sefton Hall Mission where my brothers and I attended on a Sunday afternoon. At secondary school, in the first half of the Fifties, music lessons consisted of playing (or more rightly attempting to play) disinfectant-drenched plastic recorders and singing jolly traditional tunes or wistful folk songs. At home, there was no family music-making, but there was a radio (wireless, we called it then), not used much by me in my early teens for listening to music but for the *Goon Show*. But no radiogram, that large and splendid item of furniture that combined wireless and gramophone. A friend's family had such a contraption that introduced me to singers like Al Jolson, Doris Day and Billy Eckstine. At school, I don't think we discussed popular music much (if at all) as teenagers do today, but there was a great deal of imitating the Goons (especially Bluebottle and Eccles). I heard some older boys rehearsing once and claiming to be the school jazz band.

Then, when I left school in the summer of 1956, the relative absence of popular music began to be remedied. At parties I heard records of Elvis Presley, singing "Heartbreak Hotel", for example, and Fats Domino playing and singing "Blueberry Hill" — this was exciting, attention-grabbing music that was different to other kinds. Equally powerful was the music played by the Lonnie Donegan Skiffle Group — experienced live at the Chiswick Empire. Not only powerful but capable of imitation, as proved by a teenager playing guitar and singing Lonnie Donegan numbers at a youth club I attended. Like thousands of other young people in the late 1950s I became a member of a skiffle group. There seemed to be an uncontrollable urge abroad for teenagers to make music. We may not have properly understood in the beginning what it was that was being imitated, nor the urge to do so, but we responded to it.

When I agreed to the suggestion, therefore, to write this book on skiffle, I decided almost immediately that it should be called *The Skiffle Craze*, reflecting accurately what took place and indeed how this particular popular musical phenomenon was seen by many in the Fifties and later. Unlike other crazes, however, which are usually short-lived and have little or no after-effects, skiffle turned out to be different, both as regards its duration (1956-58 as a commercial music) and long-term consequences for popular music — members of the Shadows and the Beatles, amongst many others, began in skiffle groups.

Since my skiffle group days in the late Fifties, I have looked back from time to time and realised the importance of the skiffle experience to me personally in terms of the development of my interest in popular music, particularly jazz. Likewise, it is only with hindsight that I could see the significance of skiffle as a transitional stage in the development of popular music in Britain. From reading, it was clear that others felt similarly about the significance of the skiffle craze, but nobody had attempted to fully document the phenomenon. This book gives me the opportunity to do so.

The only full-length work on the subject (until Chas McDevitt's book published in 1997 [1]) was the contemporary account written by Brian Bird, an Essex clergyman and skiffle enthusiast, and published in 1958,[2] who, while seeing a future for skiffle — "the music of the people" — could only hint at its subsequent far-reaching and diverse impact on popular music.

To demonstrate the importance of skiffle, not just for those who were to become established and well known performers, but for others, like myself, who became involved in the music, this book includes extracts from the reminiscences of Fifties grassroots skifflers. These extracts — displayed in shaded boxes in the text — help to exemplify many of the points made in the book but at the same time show the uniqueness of each Fifties skiffler's story and of their subsequent musical development. Written nearly forty years after the events they describe, and in most cases relying on memory, there are bound to be some errors of detail and chronology. Nevertheless, regardless of such possible faults, they provide a lasting testimony to the importance and significance of the skiffle craze.

Although largely identified with the Fifties, skiffle is still performed today, however, and there is some evidence — of which this book forms part — of a renewed interest in the music of the Fifties and of a skiffle revival. Consequently readers will also find here an account of the current skiffle scene. This follows a full and detailed story of the skiffle phenomenon, placing it in the context from which it emerged, as well as giving some description of its long-term influence.

Writing about popular culture, however, is notoriously difficult, and I would, therefore, be grateful to hear from any reader with corrections, comments, or further information that might help with my continuing research into the subject, and be incorporated into any future edition.

Many people and organisations have helped to make the writing of this book possible. I would particularly like to thank the following individuals: John Badham, Al Boden, Bob Brooks, Shirley Collins, John Cumming, Paul Drew, Mrs D. Ellis, Gil Fish, Norman Froggatt, John Gill, John Harper, Geoff Harris, Mike Hart, Hans Heunks, Dave Illingworth, Sean Killeen, Paul Leegan, Holger Lührig, Phil Malik, Tim Mallinson, Derek Mason, Gwenda Morris, Terry Pamplin, Terry Potter, Duffy Power, Mike Raftery, Peter Rice, Brian Smith, Mike Waites, John Wall, Ian Whitcomb, Jen Wilson and Basil Wright. Some of these people kindly agreed to contribute their memories to *The Skiffle Craze*.

I am also grateful to Chris Barber for agreeing to write the foreword to this book and in doing so providing his own short account of those early, exciting days. Talking to Chris, there seems to be a query as to Lonnie Donegan's involvement with his band prior to 1952. Various sources seem to indicate that Lonnie played with Chris Barber in some capacity prior to that date and so I have retained the information in my story of skiffle.

Thanks are also owed to a number of organisations, and to the many librarians, archivists and curators who responded to my letter of enquiry about print and non-print material on skiffle in their care. Even if they could not help directly they often gave useful advice on potential lines of enquiry. Special thanks for help and information, however, must be paid to: Bradford Libraries (E.M. Willmot), Center for Black Music Research (Suzanne Flandreau), Cromwell Management (Vic Gibbons), Exeter University Library (Julie Crawley), *Folk Roots*, Folk South West (Eddie Upton), Hogan Jazz Archive (New Orleans, Bruce Boyd Raeburn), Inside Sounds (Memphis, Jeff Cargerman), Jazz North West Ltd (Nick Purnell), *Jazz UK* (Jed Williams), *Juke Blues* (Cilla Huggins), Lead Belly Society (John Reynolds), Marion Löffler, Music Industries Association (Linda Mitchell), National Jazz Federation Archive (Ken Jones and David Nathan), National Library of Australia (Richard Stone), National Sound Archive (Andrew Simons), Railroad Bill, Red Lick Records (Ann and Ken Smith), School of Scottish Studies (Rhona Talbot), Salvation Army (John K. Hughes), Scottish Music Information Centre (Catherine Owen), City of Westminster Archives Centre (Jill Barber), and the BBC Written Archive Centre. My special thanks must also go to the National Library of Wales, including its Sound and Moving Image Collection, whose staff have seen rather more of me than they might wish, and have fetched numerous books, periodicals and other material for me to consult. Thanks as well to Marian Delyth for the photographs of record sleeves and 78 rpm roundels.

Finally, thanks are due to John Barnie, the editor at Planet — this book was his idea — whose stimulating, friendly and ever-ready assistance was much appreciated, and to his staff, Helle Michelsen and Angharad James, for their interest, practical support and encouragement; to my wife Kathy, who assisted me in my research and did much of the donkey work of reading microfilm and photocopying, and to Ann Hill who typed much of my correspondence.

I should also like to express my appreciation of all those editors and compilers of guides, listings, dictionaries, encyclopedias, discographies and histories of popular music that provided the clues and basic information to develop and write this book.

1 Get Your Ticket at the Station — Skiffle Arrives

The Royal Variety Performance of May 1960 at the Victoria Palace, London was dubbed by the *Melody Maker* as "a dish fit to set before the Queen".[1] The bill of this Sing-a-Song-of-Sixpence royal show featured big American names like Sammy Davis Jnr, Nat King Cole and Liberace, as well as a lengthy list of homegrown talent, such as Bruce Forsyth, Charlie Drake, Max Bygraves, Benny Hill, Billy Cotton, Harry Worth and Diana Dors, in starring or walk-on roles.

The "Focus on Youth" spot in the show was opened by the Vernon Girls and then presented the John Barry Seven, a nervous and subdued Adam Faith, Cliff Richard, and Lonnie Donegan, whose early 1960 hit, "My Old Man's a Dustman" was well received by the audience. Donegan — at twenty-nine and not really in the youth category — was still a very popular performer after just over four years of phenomenal success as a variety and recording artist, that included making the charts in the USA, almost unheard of for a British musician.

Both Richard and Faith owed something to the skiffle craze that Donegan and his fellow jazz musicians and others had set in train earlier in the Fifties. Indeed, along with the mid-Fifties advent of rock 'n' roll, Donegan and skiffle came to be major influences on the development of popular music in Britain. In April 1960, the month before the royal show, the *Melody Maker* reported that every Donegan record went straight into the charts and that his total sales were the highest in Britain.[2] Yet, prior to the few years of success and fame that resulted in an appearance before royalty, Lonnie Donegan had been an obscure banjo player in a jazz band. A mixture of talent and luck, however, had changed all that.

It all began when the Lonnie Donegan Skiffle Group's recording of the American railroad song, "Rock Island Line", featured unexpectedly and unlooked for in the British hit parade in January 1956 and, by April 1956, in the USA charts, eventually going on to become a million-seller. While a remarkable achievement in itself, the record's success — for what was a section of a jazz band — catapulted a minor feature of the early Fifties jazz scene — skiffle music — into the popular music consciousness of the general public and encouraged many groups of imitators of the genre from among young people of the day. Unforeseen, although not entirely unheralded, the skiffle craze had arrived. Popular music would never be the same again.

By May 1956, Glasgow-born and London-bred Lonnie Donegan had set off on what was to be his first American tour, for which (presumably because of his name), he was quaintly dubbed by the Americans the "Irish hillbilly". He was now no longer "an obscure banjo player in a jazz band" — the band being the well-regarded Chris Barber Jazz Band, where Donegan had been part of the rhythm section. However, Donegan's success was to be essentially with British audiences and his American tour attracted little attention across the Atlantic. Nevertheless, because of his record sales he was offered a ten-week extension of his tour and a $30,000 advance to record for a big USA label. Because of prior commitments in Britain, Donegan was obliged to refuse both offers.

The emergence of skiffle in early 1956 to become, by 1957, a vibrant part of the popular music scene, may have occurred almost accidentally and overnight, but skiffle had been around in jazz for a good number of Britain's post-war years and had an even longer history if its American antecedents are taken into account. Although Lonnie Donegan is popularly associated with getting skiffle off the ground in Britain, this is not the full story. The names of at least three other jazz men must be taken into account when telling its early history: Ken Colyer, Chris Barber and Alexis Korner. Of these three, Korner is perhaps the less important, as far as skiffle is concerned, but he is inextricably linked with both Colyer and Barber. His special significance is connected with the later development of rhythm and blues in Britain, for which his skiffle involvement could be seen as a meaningful preparation.

However, the emergence of skiffle, and the part played by musicians such as Colyer and Donegan, must be placed in the context of the development of jazz in Britain in the late Forties and early Fifties, when jazz was still a relatively young art form — forty or so years old — and many of its early American practitioners still living.

Even though a relatively young music, jazz was already split into different camps and styles from traditional through swing to modern jazz. British jazz had its modern jazz players in the late Forties and Fifties, as evidenced by such artists as Johnny Dankworth, Ronnie Scott, Don Rendell, Victor Feldman, Tubby Hayes and Tony Kinsey — musicians following in the footsteps of the great black American innovators in modern jazz, such as Charlie Parker, Dizzy Gillespie, Miles Davies and Charlie Christian.

At the same time as jazz was finding new directions, it was also going through a New Orleans revival movement — a renewed interest in the earliest jazz and pioneering jazzmen like Kid Ory and Bunk Johnson, who were often persuaded to play again in the early 1940s. The music was thus both looking forward and backward at the same time. Although having its beginnings in America in the late Thirties, notably with Lu Watters and his Yerba Buena Jazz Band in San Francisco, revivalism was to become a very strong movement in Britain. This revival of the founding jazz of New Orleans was characterised by young, amateur white players emulating black musicians like Oliver, Armstrong, Ory and Morton, rather than the major white jazz musicians of the Twenties and Thirties. In Britain, revivalist jazz was promoted by bands with such leaders as George Webb, Humphrey Lyttleton, Chris Barber and Ken Colyer.

The British trumpeter, Freddie Randall, was the leading light in another, but lesser jazz revival movement that took place alongside that of the New Orleans revival; it was one which used as its models white musicians like Muggsy Spanier for its Chicago-style music.

The New Orleans jazz revivalist climate was one in which skiffle, seeking, amongst other things, to emulate in performance the blues and folksongs of American blacks, and relying particularly on the recordings of the Twenties and Thirties, would come to have a place. Like jazz itself, skiffle too would attract disagreement amongst performers and critics about what was, and what was not to be properly called skiffle, and its practitioners were condemned for succumbing to commercialism.

The New Orleans revivalist movement in Britain began with the formation of George Webb's Dixielanders in 1943 at Bexleyheath. Webb, a pianist, led a band with a two-cornet lead in the best traditional fashion and which was to make many recordings. By 1945 the Dixielanders had fans nationwide. In April 1947 Humphrey Lyttleton joined them, replacing the two-cornet lead, but left in November that year to set up his own band, which played at the Leicester Square Jazz Club. Humph alternated with the Australian Graeme Bell's Jazz Band, which got people dancing to jazz once more. Jazz and dancing "made for a unique atmosphere infinitely healthier than the previous solemnity of the rhythm-club procedure."[3] Bell's band was on a visit to Britain as part of a European tour during 1947-48; he was later to establish a skiffle group in Australia.

The Dixielanders disbanded in early 1948 and, in autumn that year, George Webb joined the Lyttleton band but subsequently made infrequent appearances as a pianist. In London and the provinces many young whites from all classes formed jazz bands in imitation of Webb and Lyttleton, many of whom recorded. Of such bands the Crane River Jazz Band and the Colyer and Barber bands were to be important for the development and promotion of skiffle in the early Fifties.

Prior to the emergence of skiffle in Britain, it is worth noting that a spasm band called the Original London Blue Blowers — sometimes seen as a harbinger of the skiffle movement — was formed in 1945 but disbanded three years later. Clearly influenced by the Mound City Blue Blowers, and led by kazooist-vocalist, Bill Bailey, it used a strictly jazz repertoire: "its music was crude and commercially unsuccessful."[4] It was to re-emerge as the Bill Bailey Skiffle Group in 1957.

Some idea of the growing appeal of jazz in Britain might be seen in the first inter-university jazz contest held in Liverpool in 1955, featuring both traditional and modern groups. Won by the local Liverpool University Jazz Band, a hit of the night was the bass-player of Bangor's Straits Jazzmen playing a home-made, one-string, soap-box bass.[5] A foretaste of what was to come in the ensuing skiffle craze.

In British jazz historian, Jim Godbolt's opinion: "The first British band wholly to embrace the spirit and style and certainly the guts of the New Orleans stay-at-homes emerged in 1949. This was the Crane River Jazz Band, based at Cranford, then a semi-rural town in Middlesex."[6] Originally known as the Crane River Brass Band, it changed its name when Monty Sunshine joined it later in its founding year. The other personnel consisted of Ken Colyer (trumpet, and an admirer of the sound made by George Webb's Dixielanders), his brother Bill Colyer (vocalist), Sonny Morris (second cornet), John Davies (trombone), Ben Marshall (banjo and guitar), Julian Davies (sousaphone, later bass) and Ron Bowden (drums). When Bowden left "to try his hand at modern drumming", the band was unable to find a replacement and so Bill Colyer played washboard.[7]

The band was soon recording, cutting, for example, four sides in London in August 1950 (apparently without benefit of either drums or washboard but with the addition of Pat Hawes on piano), which included, "My Old Kentucky Home" and "If I Ever Cease to Love". The Crane River Jazz Club was held weekly at Great Newport Street, near Leicester Square, around late 1950 to mid-1951 and promised London's greatest New Orleans-style sessions. The Cranes' 1951 recording of "I'm Travelling" was played at the Ken Colyer Thanksgiving Service following his death in 1988.

According to Colyer, himself, the first skiffle group in Britain was formed within the Crane River Jazz Band in the early part of 1949. However, the skiffle group played chiefly at parties and for the amusement of its own members. It consisted of Ken Colyer (guitar), Ben Marshall (guitar), Pat Hawes (washboard) and Julian Davies (bass). It seems at this stage not to have been called skiffle and was performed by the group to illustrate aspects of the roots of jazz and to add variety to a programme. The group's main influences were Huddie Ledbetter ("Lead Belly"), Brownie McGhee and various blues and folk artists but, outside the band, little interest was shown in this type of music at that time.[8]

The Crane River Jazz Band is said to have "inspired many others throughout the country to play in a similarly earthy manner, and was the blueprint for the bands Ken Colyer was later to lead."[9] It might be argued that much the same could be said for skiffle — Colyer inspired others to play skiffle and the skiffle group concept he began with the Cranes was to be reflected in later Colyer bands. But who was Ken Colyer and what made him so special and inspirational?

Ken Colyer, born in Great Yarmouth in 1928, passed his childhood in Soho before the family moved to Cranford, Middlesex in 1936. He left school at fourteen and joined the merchant navy in 1945. Colyer had developed an interest in jazz and began playing the harmonica, later switching to the trumpet, taking it with him into the merchant navy. Ken, together with his brother Bill (a suitcase "drummer"), who had joined him at sea, returned to Cranford in 1948. Ken had bought a guitar during a trip to Canada in 1947 and also acquired a collection of Lead Belly 78s in New York. The origins of British skiffle might be said to stem from these milestone actions. There is a great deal of truth in what was said many years later that, without Lead Belly, there would have been no skiffle boom — nor rhythm and blues or folk revivals.

Ken Colyer (left) with l. to r. Bruce Turner, Micky Ashman, the folklorist A.L. Lloyd, and Alexis Korner, c. mid-1950s. (Courtesy Max Jones Archive.)

In his autobiography, Colyer gives an account of his early days learning the guitar on board ship: "Ken, the chippy, had bought a nice guitar in Montreal and I had a cheap one that cost considerably less. Though Ken had also bought a very good chord tutor, it was too advanced for us and we weren't getting anywhere. We were both left-handed and had struggled to learn right-handed as it saved changing the strings round. But finally we both agreed that our left-hand instinct was too strong and laboriously changed the strings round. Sea air plays havoc with strings. When we were at sea and had no spares we would tie knots in them when they broke. As long as there was enough string to tie the knot above the nut. This works with the wound strings but not the first and second. Ken worked on this and devised a knot of his own that would grip and not slip."[10]

How many would-be skiffle players a decade later would encounter similar problems of finding the right tutor, left-handedness, and broken strings? They would probably not have to contend with being at sea, however.

What made Ken Colyer inspirational for many people, both musicians and fans, yet at the same time antagonised others, was his purist approach to his music and his self-proclaimed abhorrence of the commercial dimension to jazz and popular music. His beliefs and musical ability carried others along with him but the apparent desire to lead, rather than be led, inevitably made for difficulties. He became known as the Guv'nor and was clearly loved by his fans for his devotion and single-mindedness. Towards those who had crossed him, however, his autobiography makes him seem to be unforgiving at times.

Colyer left the Crane River Jazz Band in July 1951 and helped form the Christie Brothers Stompers with Keith and Ian Christie, who played trombone and clarinet respectively. Following musical differences, Colyer split from the Stompers and rejoined the merchant navy in November 1951 in order to be able to travel to New Orleans, the birthplace of jazz. He jumped ship in Mobile, Alabama and then went by Greyhound bus to New Orleans, arriving in October 1952. While there he sat in with people like George Lewis and recorded with Emile Barnes and others. George Lewis was so impressed with Ken Colyer that he offered him a tour with his band.[11] At a thanksgiving service for Colyer in 1988, Kevin Sheldon reflected on "how a young white musician had gone to New Orleans and had been accepted as part of their jazz scene by coloured musicians, some living legends, who admitted that not only did Ken fit in to their music but added to it."[12]

Eventually, after thirty-eight days imprisonment, Colyer was deported from the States for overstaying his visa. He was also in trouble for playing with black musicians. So he was sent home, repatriated as a passenger on the *United States*. While on the way back, he resisted the invitation of a fellow boat passenger and former Bowery bum to form a guitar and spoons duo and, on their return to England, tour the Liverpool pubs.[13] On arrival in Southampton, flat broke, Ken was met by brother Bill and Chris Barber.

In early 1953, on Colyer's return to England, he joined an existing co-operative band, soon to be known, however, as Ken Colyer's Jazzmen. During his American sojourn, brother Bill had written to say that Chris Barber had agreed to Ken taking over the lead from Pat Halcox, to whom it had been offered, but who declined it, not wishing to continue with a jazz career. "It sounded fine to me as my sole intention was to carry on playing somehow or other."[14] The band, now led by Colyer (trumpet), consisted of Chris Barber (trombone), Monty Sunshine (clarinet), with a rhythm section of Lonnie Donegan (banjo), Jim Bray (bass) and Ron Bowden (drums). Bowden and Sunshine were, of course, ex-Crane River musicians and Barber, Sunshine and Donegan had themselves all led amateur bands and believed it was now time to become full-time professionals if jazz was to get anywhere.

The first *regular* UK skiffle group, according to Alexis Korner, was established within the Jazzmen and consisted of Colyer, Donegan and Alexis Korner (guitars), Bill Colyer (washboard) and Chris Barber or Jim Bray (bass).[15] The idea for this group had come from Korner and Ken Colyer and had been suggested before Ken left for New Orleans.[16] Bill Colyer, it was though, who claimed to have come up with the skiffle label: "One day after my brother Ken's band had had a blow, I said: 'Now the skiffle group takes over.' And it stuck." [17]

The Colyer Jazzmen generated a following, secured a residency at the London Jazz Club, Bryanston Street, undertook a successful Danish tour, and then recorded an album, *New Orleans to London*. The album included a version of the Thirties song, "Isle of Capri", which briefly appeared in the lower reaches of the charts when released as a single.

Following disagreement, Chris Barber assumed leadership of the Jazzmen and Ken Colyer left in May 1954 to form a band of his own. The reasons for the split were a mixture of a challenge to Colyer's status as band leader, a sense of being used (because of the reputation gained from his New Orleans visit), and musical incompatibility. Colyer thought that Barber "still considered hisself [sic] the leader", that he was wanted until the reflected glory from his "novelty wore off", and that Barber's preference for arranged numbers was opposed to Colyer's interest "in developing the important things that make New Orleans music unique. The free interplay on the three part counterpoint harmony. A rhythm section that lays down the right beat, that swings right whatever the tempo."[18]

Suspicious of Barber, critical of Ron Bowden's supposed modernistic drumming, Colyer thought Lonnie Donegan was unreliable: "He would be sitting at home when he should have been at the station waiting for a train. He missed a ferry boat in Denmark through his own ineptitude. It was only through a reporter paying the captain that he turned back for him, he had a good story. He would be sick and miss jobs through a broken toe nail, or whatever."[19]

In making the split, Ken Colyer tried to take Jim Bray and Monty Sunshine with him: "But they knew which side their bread was buttered so I left on my own when Barber tried to dictate ridiculous terms to me in Harold Pendleton's presence. I told them what they could do with their terms and Pat Halcox rejoined the band."[20] The LP made for Decca for a flat fee, before the band split up, also occasioned comment. Colyer received £12. He thought it ironic that Monty Sunshine had received £50 for designing the LP's cover.[21]

Putting it mildly, Ken Colyer did not come to have much regard for his former colleagues, such as Donegan, Barber and Dick Smith. He knocked Dick Smith down (after Smith had left Colyer's new band for the Barber outfit) following an exchange of words at Wimbledon Palais.[22]

After what he considered to be a year's wasted effort, Ken Colyer formed his new band in mid-1954. In addition to himself, this was made up of Eddie O'Donnell (trombone), Acker Bilk (clarinet, who was to become famous in his own right), Diz Disley (banjo, whose more recent reputation is as a guitarist in the Django Reinhardt mould), Dick Smith (bass) and Stan Greig (drums). At the new band's recording debut in November 1954, three skiffle numbers were added to its Decca LP, *Back to the Delta* — "Midnight Special", "Casey Jones" and "K.C. Moan" — which, however, went virtually unnoticed. These very first recorded skiffle numbers — leaving aside some earlier, unissued Colyer tracks — had been made in June 1954, probably prior to the formation of the new band, with Colyer (guitar and vocals), Alexis Korner (guitar and mandolin), Micky Ashman (bass) and brother Bill (washboard). Significantly these recordings predate the "Rock Island Line" and "John Henry" sides, recorded by Donegan, by just over two weeks.

Prior to skiffle coming to popular attention, Ken Colyer made a further recording of four songs in July 1955. This time the group consisted of the two Colyers and Korner with John Bastable (banjo and guitar) and Dick Smith (bass); numbers included "Take This Hammer" and "Streamline Train".

With his latest band Ken Colyer had a regular night at the Studio 51 jazz club, and, with replacements for Bilk (Ian Wheeler) and O'Donnell (Mac Duncan), went over to Germany and played in Düsseldorf, then Hamburg and a financially disastrous three days in Lüneburg. The skiffle group in this amended line-up consisted of the two Colyers, Ian Wheeler and Diz Disley (guitars) and Stan Greig (piano).

Alexis Korner's name has occurred several times in connection with Colyer and skiffle and will also weave in and out of the Barber part of this narrative. Of mixed parentage, a Greek mother and Austrian father, and with a distinctive appearance, Alexis was born in Paris in 1928. His parents left France in 1940 and eventually came to live in Ealing, west London; Alexis became a pupil of St Paul's School, Hammersmith. He had studied piano from a young age and, in the early Forties, discovered jazz and blues, attempting to play boogie-woogie piano much to his father's distaste. His initiation into jazz had come from a 78rpm recording of Jimmy Yancey's "Slow and Easy Blues" stolen by Alexis from a stall in Shepherd's Bush Market. Alexis also became a self-taught guitarist but again suffered from his father's intolerance, as his father considered it to be a woman's instrument.

Called up in 1947, Korner served in the British Army in Germany, working as record librarian for the British Forces Network. He also presented a jazz records programme for Nord-West Deutsche Rundfunk and had access to swing, jazz, and other types of black music, through the American Forces Network. Rather perversely, for those who like pigeon-

holes Alexis came to admire both traditional and modern jazz. In 1949 he returned to England to work in a shipping firm owned by his Greek mother's family.

In 1949 Korner joined the Chris Barber Band, playing a semi-acoustic Hofner guitar, acting as a replacement for Donegan, called up for national service. In addition, Korner recalled in a radio interview: "We used to do a half-hour set of R&B — 'race blues' it was called then — a piano [Dave Stevens], guitar [Alexis], bass [Chris], drums [Brian Lawes] set-up — like the Tampa Red and Bill Broonzy Chicago sessions on Bluebird in the late Thirties and early Forties. I was given the mike and I used to do single string and people would say, 'What's that funny stuff you played in the middle?'" [23]

On his departure from the Barber Band, Alexis later joined a band led by the former Yorkshire Jazz Band trumpeter, Dick Hawdon, in the very early Fifties.

After the founding of the Crane River Jazz Band in 1949, Alexis met Ken Colyer on the jazz circuit and Ken and brother Bill often went to Alexis' Norfolk Crescent flat to play and talk. Alexis and Ken played acoustic guitars and Bill "swished brushes across a suitcase to keep the noise down." [24] They were joined in their sessions by the American painter, Ralston Crawford. The song that they most often played and sang together was "Midnight Special" and this started Alexis' "lifelong interest in the history of train songs in American folk music." [25] The style they played in

Alexis Korner (guitar) in an early skiffle group c. 1950. The pianist is Roy Sturgess. Drummer not identified. (Courtesy Max Jones Archive.)

9

— voice accompanied by a strong rhythm — was to become known later as skiffle, although at that time, as Korner's biographer adds: "it is unclear if that was the name used by Ken Colyer."[26] Later, when Colyer was leading the band with Barber and the others, it was decided to introduce skiffle — this was probably 1953 — and Korner, playing guitar, mandolin (and briefly a poor harmonica) was, as noted earlier, part of the group line-up, together with Barber, both Colyers and Lonnie Donegan, though Donegan is convinced he never performed publicly with Korner. "Alexis claimed he soon dropped the Chris Barber version of skiffle altogether because he couldn't stand Lonnie Donegan shifting the music towards 'country weepies' as he called them, in the style of the Carter Family."[27]

Following the split with Barber and the others, described earlier, Korner left with Colyer and was included in his new band's skiffle section, playing guitar and mandolin on the seven Decca tracks recorded in June 1954 and July 1955. However, Korner began to drift away from skiffle because he wanted to be a solo country-blues artist, although that required him to do away with his open-tuned guitar and learn to play it "correctly". This he did with the help and encouragement of his wife, Bobbie. Nonetheless, it would be a little while before he would be able to fully lose the skiffle tag.

Chris Barber, linked musically to both Colyer and Korner, was born in 1930 in Hertfordshire, and studied trombone and bass at the Guildhall School of Music. He formed his first band in 1949. One member of that band was Tony Donegan, who was eventually obliged to leave Barber to do his national service. By 1951 the band was featuring the two trumpeters, Ben Cohen and Dick Hawdon. In that year it also recorded "Everybody Loves My Baby" and "Whoop It Up" as Chris Barber's Washboard Wonders, with Brian Lawes on washboard. These were like the earlier Korner rhythm and blues half-hours, not skiffle, but steps in that direction. However, Chris Barber claimed that he was featuring skiffle from 1952 onwards: "when we'd do part of the set using songs like 'Midnight Special', we called it skiffle."[28] Barber confirmed this claim in a recent radio broadcast, recounting that he and Lonnie Donegan were devotees of original black blues music, though not all the records that they copied were of a blues singer and guitar, some were of small groups. So they presented numbers with Donegan singing and playing guitar, Barber on bass, and a clarinet and washboard. And this they called skiffle.

Following the unsuccessful union with Ken Colyer in 1953-54, Barber took on the trumpeter Pat Halcox as his replacement and he has stayed ever since. In July 1954, Decca recorded an LP of the Barber band consisting of six jazz tunes and two skiffle numbers (the all-important "Rock Island Line" and "John Henry") by the Lonnie Donegan Skiffle Group. This consisted of Donegan (guitar and vocal), Chris Barber (bass) and Beryl Bryden (washboard).

In March 1955, a review of a Columbia disc of four spirituals by the

Barber band, recorded in November 1954, commented on the standard of musicianship and enthusiasm. The reviewer confessed to not being an admirer of Donegan's singing but admitted he was not offensive on "Precious Lord". The rhythm section, of which Donegan was part, was seen as "quite fair for a British band." Overall, the record was recommended "as one of the best of those by revivalist bands."[29] Donegan's banjo playing was discussed with that of others in an article in *Jazz Journal* some years later. As a banjoist he was not to be compared with a "fully fledged" player, but he was regarded as superior to most of the trad-boom "clankers". Although not a soloist, he was considered to provide a useful and dependable rhythmic accompaniment, was aware of dynamics, and could successfully back the band's vocalist, Ottilie Patterson, "with accurate passing chords."[30] Ottilie Patterson had made her debut with the band in January 1955, in a concert at the Royal Festival Hall.

The Chris Barber Jazz Band, c. 1955-56. L. to r. Micky Ashman, Monty Sunshine, Ron Bowden, Pat Halcox, Chris Barber. Front: Ottilie Patterson, Lonnie Donegan. Photo by John Chown (courtesy Cromwell Management).

Although Chris Barber did not really jump on the commercial skiffle bandwagon, he was its keen supporter. In his foreword to David Boulton's book, *Jazz in Britain*, he commented that the author did "not... condemn skiffle as something either worthless or horrible." And wrote further: "I personally must confess to having had a considerable hand in the establishing of skiffle on the English popular scene and I do not regret it. I cannot see the appearance of such wonderful material as 'Bring a Little Water, Sylvie', or 'John Henry' and 'Lost John' on the Hit Parade as

11

L. to r. Dickie Bishop, Lonnie Donegan, Chris Barber, c. 1955-56. Photo by John Chown (courtesy Cromwell Management).

anything short of a miracle — and a very pleasant one at that!"[31]

After Donegan left for a solo career, the Chris Barber Skiffle Group recorded four numbers — "Doin' My Time", "Where Could I go?", "Gypsy Davy", and "Can't You Line 'Em" — in September 1956 with Dickie Bishop and Johnny Duncan. Bishop had been brought in to augment the band's skiffle line-up (and then also took over Donegan's vacant banjo chair), Duncan to replace Donegan. When both Bishop and Duncan left Barber, forming their own groups, Chris gave up presenting skiffle. Losing one skiffler could be endured, perhaps, loosing three must have been downright disheartening.

Even more disheartening, perhaps, was the accusation that Chris had "calculatingly built up the Skiffle gimmick in a quest for commercial success." He replied that the band "regarded the Skiffle group as a legitimate part of a jazz band's scope. There were boos when we first introduced it; we ignored them." He felt that the band would go on featuring skiffle after the vogue had passed because it had a place in jazz.[32] However, this was not to be the case, and a different direction was chosen.

Along with acting as a springboard for skiffle, the Barber band

12

1956 And All That: Skiffle Reminiscences

Influenced by Lonnie Donegan, and in particular his recording of "Rock Island Line", four of us formed a skiffle group in our home town of Warrington. This was towards the end of 1956, and, though our musical ability was not apparent at first, we found we could sing in tune and harmonise. But above all we were enthusiastic.

I played the tea-chest bass to start with and my twin brother Jack played guitar. He hit the ground running, since he had taken a course of eight lessons which cost him two guineas and taught him three chords (C, F, G7), the scale of C major and a few exercises. Jack's guitar was a cheap steel-strung, round-hole instrument with a tail-piece, not a fixed bridge, and was of Italian origin. Our lead singer and drummer was Tom Gorman, and, at twenty-two, was a year younger than Jack and me. His kit comprised an old snare drum on a stand and he always stood to perform, beating out the rhythm of the songs with brushes in preference to sticks. Later, we were joined by thirty-two year-old bus-driver, Bob McLennon, as lead guitarist. His instrument was a Hofner Senator, but, more importantly, he also had a small Selmer amplifier, bought from Hessy's in Liverpool. This gave us use of a microphone and, using pick-ups, amplified guitars, boosting not only our volume but also our confidence.

We called ourselves the Livewires, reflecting Warrington's major industry — the manufacture of wire. Other groups were also forming in the area at the same time. The Blackcaps took their name from the Fleet Air Arm base in the village of Stretton where they lived, five miles outside the town. Another bunch of lads called themselves the Costers, since they were clerks in Crosfields cost office, the company famous for making Persil.

Norman Froggatt

endeavoured to showcase blues artists like Big Bill Broonzy, Lonnie Johnson, Sonny Terry and Brownie McGhee, and Muddy Waters, as well as gospel singers such as John Sellers and Rosetta Tharpe, and other bluesmen like Champion Jack Dupree and Memphis Slim who had settled in Europe. Because of the union ban on American musicians performing in Britain, they were described as entertainers, as there was a different ruling for this category which included people who sang.[33] This policy allowed both jazz and skiffle fans to experience their work and to come under the influence of such original performers; it helped pave the way for the later blues revival. Indeed Barber moved on from the skiffle to the blues cause, while, of course, still maintaining a successful jazz band.

Born Anthony James Donegan in Glasgow in 1931, Tony Donegan was brought up in East Ham, London — he was later to be described by a journalist as a Scots-born Irish Hillbilly from London. His father played the violin and had performed with the National Scottish Orchestra. At the age of fifteen Donegan bought a second-hand guitar from a workmate at the stockbroker's office where he was employed.

Having no success at teaching himself to play, Tony took a few lessons and began to busk with a friend who had bought a trumpet. Together they started to go to jazz clubs. He was then asked to join an amateur jazz band in Ilford as their guitarist and, in spite of admitting to a lack of ability, was given the guitar chords and a week to learn them. After about six weeks rehearsal the band gave its first public performance.

Tony left his job at the stockbrokers and became in turn a laboratory assistant, an assistant in a menswear shop and a builder's labourer. He continued to play jazz in the evenings.

From 1949-51 Tony Donegan did his national service in the army. In the middle of his training, he got appendicitis and was sent off to Southampton to recuperate after the operation. There, although no drummer, he took over that role in a local jazz band and stayed in Southampton as long as possible, returning to Aldershot to continue training. Sent to Woolwich on a special training course, he was able to renew his contact with Chris Barber — Chris had been the trombonist in the Ilford group — and play with his band. "I used to creep back to the barracks half dead. And I learned that the whole object of the course was overseas service, so I failed the examination deliberately. But they rumbled that and sent me anyway."[34] Tony had wanted to stay on in the area to continue playing with Barber and the band.

Dispatched to Austria as a medical orderly in Vienna, Donegan played guitar and sang folk songs in the barrack room and sang to his own guitar accompaniment at troop concerts. He was to say later that his favourite singing stars were Hank Williams, Woody Guthrie, Lead Belly, Lonnie Johnson and Jimmy Rushing[35] — more recently he added Josh White and Big Bill Broonzy to the list. Looking back to those early days from success in 1957, Donegan is reported as feeling that: "Inside was the stubborn conviction that he would become an entertainer — and that's the way it turned out."[36]

Things did not always go well on the way, however. James Asman recalls booking the first Barber band for a south-east London jazz club at the end of the Forties and that Donegan was asked to sing during the band's break. According to Asman "This was the very first time Lonnie Donegan ever performed in public and I regret to say that the small audience joined the boys at the bar and turned their back on a musical act which, a few years afterwards, was responsible for the 'Skiffle' explosion which took over the Top Twenty charts..."[37]

After his demob in 1951 Donegan formed his own band, a New Orleans group, which played in clubs such as the Abbey Wood Jazz Club in south London, the Wood Green Jazz Club and the Freddie Randall Club, Tottenham. Along with Donegan, the members of the band were: Bill Brunskill (cornet), Gordon Blundy (trombone), Geoff Kemp (clarinet), Bill Wren (piano), Jim Bray (tuba) and Arthur Fryatt (drums).[38]

The year 1952 was a good one for the Donegan band. It got in on the Jazz Saturday series at Battersea Pleasure Gardens and in July it was one of the substitute supporting groups, along with George Webb's Dixieland-ers, for a concert by Lonnie Johnson and pianist Ralph Sutton at the Royal Festival Hall. Donegan was able to get Lonnie Johnson — one of his jazz heroes, whose name he adopted in place of the more mundane, Tony — to autograph his banjo.[39] Apparently at the concert the compère introduced Donegan as Lonnie Johnson and Lonnie Johnson as Donegan. The original supporting bands had withdrawn at the behest of the Musicians Union who had tried to stop the visiting Americans playing in Britain.[40] The Musicians Union 1935 ban on American musicians performing in Britain, imposed in retaliation for the American Federation of Musicians ban on British musicians performing in America, was not lifted until 1956.

Subsequently Donegan parted from the band, following a clash of temperament and opinions — about turning full-time professional — and performed at a few concerts as a solo artist. To take one example, at the Jazz Big Show at the Royal Albert Hall in June 1952, featuring various jazz bands, Lonnie Donegan appeared as a guest solo singer along with George Melly, Beryl Bryden and Denny Dennis. (The *Melody Maker* critic was not appreciative of Lonnie as a solo singer.) Around the same time he joined Chris Barber, Monty Sunshine and two others to form a jazz quintet and this later became the co-operative band that featured a skiffle group, and welcomed Ken Colyer on his return from New Orleans in 1953. In

Lonnie Donegan c. 1955-56. Photo by John Chown (courtesy Cromwell Management).

that year some skiffle numbers were recorded during the band's first studio session but were not used.[41] While with Colyer, Lonnie went on a month's tour of Denmark, his first full-time professional job as musician. On the band's return it landed a good job at the London Jazz Club, playing to packed crowds of a weekend.

Colyer's subsequent departure from the band left Lonnie Donegan to front the skiffle group in what was now the Chris Barber Jazz Band. The skiffle group, usually composed of Donegan, Barber on bass, a drummer and sometimes a washboard player, was to become quite a feature of the band. Donegan became so popular in his own right — with teenage girls and gate-crashing Teddy Boys at London's 100 Club, for example — that at that venue Barber usually held back his featured numbers until the second set. Because of skiffle's popularity, an additional guitarist and singer, Dick Bishop, was eventually hired to play in the skiffle group. But this is getting a little ahead of events.

In July 1954 the Barber band released an LP for Decca called *New Orleans Joys* that featured tunes such as "Bobby Shaftoe", "Chimes Blues" and "The Martinique" and also included two skiffle tracks, "Rock Island Line" and "John Henry" , billed as by the Lonnie Donegan Skiffle Group. Beryl Bryden, the washboard player on "Rock Island Line", began singing with George Webb's pioneer revivalist band in 1945 and later with Freddy Randall. She also appeared with Graeme Bell and, largely at the suggestion of its band members, formed Beryl's Backroom Boys in which she sang

1956 And All That: Skiffle Reminiscences

The Avon Cities Jazz Band was formed in 1949. It became a semi-professional band, had its own club and large local following. The band members, each with a good "day job", consisted of school master, Geoff Nichols (trumpet), car salesman, Ray Bush (clarinet), architect, Mike Hitchins (trombone), managing director, John Ridd (piano), and Woolworths manager, Wayne Chandler (banjo and guitar). My brother, Malcolm Wright, a technical illustrator, was the bassist in the band and I, a technical officer with the Admiralty, was its drummer. Periodically the band would throw a party at the club for its members.

I think it was in 1955 that Ray Bush holidayed in Spain and brought back a guitar, which he taught himself to play. Ray bought the guitar to one of the club parties and, during the evening, began to strum it and sing. Wayne joined him on guitar, I upended a drum case and used brushes, Geoff picked up an earthenware jug and began blowing across the top, and Mike Hitchins ran to his home, which was next door to the club, and brought back his mandolin. As a spasm band we got a terrific reception that evening. I then bought a washboard and thimbles and Geoff practiced on my brother's bass. However, we still only performed at club parties.

The band wanted a recording contract and so we rehearsed a selection of band numbers and made a demo tape. As there was some tape left at the end of the recording, someone suggested that we fill it with a couple of skiffle numbers. When Decca heard the tape in 1956 they immediately issued a contract, mainly for the skiffle but included the band on it. After that we were on our way. We recorded for Decca's Tempo Records label and on the strength of the skiffle group's "Green Corn" (the most monotonous number that we played) and the band being in the Irish Hit Parade with both it and "Hawaiian War Chant", we undertook tours of Ireland and Denmark apart from gigs all over England and Wales.

In 1956 the Harold Davidson Agency put us on their books and wanted us to turn professional. We all realised that being pro musicians was a precarious way of life when we all had young families to bring up and so we turned the offer down. The agency then pushed the Acker Bilk Band and look how far it went!

As a skiffle group, Ray always kept us clear of other groups' numbers. He had made a fairly comprehensive study of American, particularly black folk music, and so we had a good, wide range from which to choose to play. We never accepted skiffle group only bookings; the group was part of the band's performance and not a separate show. My one memory as a washboard player is of the pain and cuts sustained by my cuticles through the constant rubbing of the thimbles.

Basil Wright

and played washboard.[42] Beryl appeared with many of Britain's jazz bands of the Forties and Fifties but her contribution to "Rock Island Line" and "John Henry" was apparently unplanned and never repeated on later Donegan discs. Drums were to replace the washboard in the Barber band skiffle line-up.

New Orleans Joys was Donegan's recording debut as a featured artist

and the band deal was based on a fee — its amount changes with every retelling — but no royalties, as large sales were not expected. However, *New Orleans Joys* sold an unexpected 10,000 copies. At Christmas-time 1955 the LP was split up and reissued in pairs of titles on 78s in order to generate further sales. "Rock Island Line" was played by two disc jockeys of the day, Chappie d'Amato and Jack Payne, who were both swamped with requests for details about the song and its performer and asked to play it again: "for the first time, British teenage taste (or, as many would have it, lack of taste) followed the American pattern and became a force in the entertainment industry."[43] George Melly had recorded the song a couple of years early and had provoked no such interest.

Because of its success, eight American artists recorded "Rock Island Line", including a take-off by the satirist, Stan Freberg. This was the first time a British performer had merited the attention of Freberg's biting humour. What was this song that aroused such interest, turning Donegan and the Barber band into well-known performers, and marking the beginning of the British skiffle craze? It has been neatly summed up as: "an off-beat little recitative about a branch railway line that 'run down to Noo Orlean' and the stratagems adopted by its drivers to avoid toll payments on a certain section."[44] The song was associated with the black American songster, Huddie "Lead Belly" Ledbetter, and was one he had recorded three times; the last, in 1944, was the model for Donegan's rendition. Lead Belly died in 1949 and it is unlikely that his recordings outsold those of Donegan; his widow belatedly received some royalties.

"Rock Island Line", as Donegan was to admit some twenty years later, "was a complete accident. It was only done as a track on a jazz LP and wasn't put out as a pop effort at all. And when it went pop we all thought it was a huge joke, y'know? It was all very weird. And then, when it hit in the States, we laughed for a week."[45] As has often been remarked in respect of this record and Donegan's subsequent American tour, it was a case of coals to Newcastle — selling Americans their own music.

Donegan was with the Chris Barber band until March 1956, but on leaving Barber and having signed up with the agents Lynn Dutton and Denis Preston, he set off two months later on his ten-week American club, theatre, concert and television tour aimed at cashing in on his success in the American charts. Donegan's tour began with an appearance on the Perry Como Show on television. Then from New York he went to the mid-west and on to Charleston, South Carolina. Donegan and skiffle had come into their own and he was able to buy a blue 2½ litre Daimler convertible on his return.

Before setting off, however, Donegan was persuaded by his agents to record "Lost John" backed by "Stewball" under his own name on the new Pye Nixa label. Accompanied by Dick Bishop (vocal and guitar) and Barber and Bowden on bass and drums, these sides were recorded in late February 1956. The same musicians had also recorded three songs in early January

Opposite: Sheet music for "The Skiffle Galaxy", a medley of skiffle hits.

19

and one in early April. Dick "Cisco" Bishop sang the Woody Guthrie version of "Stackolee", while Donegan sang the other bad-man ballad, "Jesse James", the song about the infamous railroad bum, "Railroad Bill", and the Lead Belly chain gang song about the escapee "Ol Riley" and the bloodhound Rattler. Issued as an EP (the *Lonnie Donegan Skiffle Session*), it was the first EP by a British performer to reach the singles-dominated UK top twenty, which it did in June 1956. It is interesting to note that the EP — as are other recordings at the time — is credited with being recorded under the supervision of Donegan's agent, Denis Preston.

Backstairs Session, featuring the Lonnie Donegan Skiffle Group, was a retrospective EP issued in 1956. It consisted of four songs recorded in May 1955 when Donegan was a little known member of the Chris Barber band — Barber played harmonica. The vocals and guitar work were shared with Dick Bishop, with the addition of Bob Watson (voice), while the other instrumentalists were Jim Bray (bass) and Pete Korrison (mandolin). The songs included two that were to become skiffle standards: "Midnight

Special" about the train whose headlights shone through the Texas State Prison near Huntsville, and "Worried Man Blues" a story in which prison features once again. The other two songs were "When the Sun Goes Down", a Leroy Carr blues learned from Big Bill Broonzy, and a worksong, "New Burying Ground", transcribed by Alan Lomax for the Library of Congress.

The "Lost John"/"Stewball" disc reached number two in the charts in Britain in June 1956, selling over 200,000 copies in its first three months, but got nowhere in the States, as with Donegan's other recordings until 1961. This single was followed by "Bring a Little Water, Sylvie", backed by "Dead or Alive" which entered the UK charts at number eleven in September 1956. Recorded early the previous month, these sides featured an independent Donegan's new line-up of Denny Wright (guitar), Micky Ashman (bass) and Nick Nicholls (drums).

It has been suggested that Lonnie Donegan was the first of the young pop stars of the Fifties — young people who became successes over night following a single hit record, rather than working their way up in variety as was usual. However, while Donegan (and skiffle) was certainly launched by a hit record, Donegan already had a few years of performing experience, albeit in jazz rather than pop music, and, as someone in his mid-twenties, he was a few years older than the other new recording stars to emerge in the late Fifties, such as Tommy Steele, Cliff Richard and young rockers in the Larry Parnes stable.

As early as May 1956, Donegan was being identified in a *Melody Maker* profile as "the phenomenon of 1956."[46] He had achieved a breakthrough in popular music and now needed to consolidate and build on this in order to ensure his continuing commercial success. How this was brought about will be recounted later. Suffice it to say here, that The *New Musical Express* poll of late 1956 for the Outstanding British Music Personality placed Donegan second, with a few votes more than Ted Heath. The winner, however, who, it must be said, received substantially more votes than either Donegan or Heath, was Dickie Valentine. Not a bad result though for someone who had started the year as an unknown banjo player.

The chart success of "Rock Island Line" in early 1956 thrust skiffle before the general public as a new musical genre but the story of jazz in Britain in the early Fifties has shown that this had been preceded by a short gestatory period involving certain key figures in the London revivalist jazz world. As to which of these figures "started" skiffle, it is difficult and probably impossible now to decide. What is clear is that Colyer, Korner and Donegan as guitarists and singers were developing along the same lines at the same time and often in each other's company. The bands of Colyer and Barber provided much of the context in which this interplay could take place and from which skiffle emerged. As to when it began to be called skiffle *publicly*, 1953 seems as good a bet as any.

In pre-1956 adverts in the music press both Colyer and Barber drew attention to the fact that their respective bands featured a skiffle group. On one occasion in 1953, Colyer advertised a "skiffle party", while Barber proposed a "good-time skiffle session" in a 1955 announcement. How was this party or good-time music received by the jazz public and viewed by jazz commentators of the time? Some short reviews of Colyer performances in 1953 and 1954 — the old and the new bands — give some idea of this reception.

Under the heading of "The New Sound", the *Jazz Journal's* diarist expressed his approval in July 1953 at the unexpected success of the skiffle group which played during the London Jazz Club intervals, attracting more people than the rest of the session. The writer acknowledged that the group's personnel could change "but is always based on the guitars, banjos and vocals of Ken Colyer, Alexis Korner and Lonnie Donegan." The journal's diarist concludes: "If you don't believe that this kind of music could draw in London... drop in and feel the electric atmosphere that builds up... Any time now the Library of Congress will be coming across from Grosvenor Square, to take the whole thing down on tape for Alan Lomax."[47]

In September that year a visiting black jazz pianist, Mary Lou Williams, recorded her views in *Jazz Journal* about the Colyer skiffle group and, while expressing general approval, suggested something be done about the awful amplification made worse by bad diction![48]

1956 And All That: Skiffle Reminiscences

In typical fashion, our skiffle group was part of a trad jazz band at Northampton Grammar School, organised by one of the masters, who played piano. A mate of mine, Billy Walker, and myself volunteered to play rhythm guitars on the condition we could have a skiffle group within the band. This was 1956 and I was sixteen years old.

The jazz band numbers were mainly in Bb or F, and so, only knowing rudimentary chords in the keys of C and G (and not having heard of capos), we tuned down a tone. The rest of the rhythm section (and skiffle group) comprised two second-years on washboards and a sixth-former playing a home-made electric bass, which was a plank of wood with strings made of different thicknesses of string or rope and a home-made pick-up embedded in the body of the bass. This guy was more of a technical whiz-kid than a musician; I think the bass must have sounded awful. Occasionally, he could not make the gigs, so we constructed a tea-chest bass, which I played.

Our first gig was a school dance (as part of the jazz band) but we also played a few things, just as a skiffle group, at youth club events. The one paid gig we ever did was at a pub called the County Tavern, close to the old Northampton Town Football Ground.

Moving to Morden in south-west London in 1957, I joined the Amazon Skiffle Group, comprising myself (lead vocal/guitar), Ray Hayhurst (guitar), Grant Peet (tea-chest bass) and Eddie Philips (leader/washboard/vocal). We were all about the same age, give or take a year or two. Eddie's real name was Phil Cunliffe but he didn't think that sounded very "skiffly". Before I joined, the group was called Eddie Philips and his Amazon Skiffle Group, but the name was shortened when I took over lead vocals. Ray and Grant were both ladies hairdressers.

Dave Illingworth

In August 1954, the *Jazz Journal* diarist reviewed a recent concert by Ken Colyer's new band given in the packed recital room at the Royal Festival Hall in the National Jazz Federation's New Orleans Encore Series. The band's line-up included Bilk, O'Donnell, Bastable, Eric Skinner (drums) and Mickey Ashman, not a permanent member, on bass. As Bill Colyer played a little washboard and Alexis Korner and Johnny Parker (piano) were guest stars, it is likely some skiffle was played. While accepting the sincerity of the band, the reviewer felt its standard of musicianship had not progressed, the technical command of the players (with the exception of Ashman) was lacking, and that the band did not swing. The fans, however, probably loved every moment of it.

Writing about the Ballads and Blues Concert of July 1954 in the same article, the diarist considered that: "A more unlikely collection of participants never graced the Festival Hall..." The programme ranged through Colyer's Jazzmen and Skiffle Group, an Irish street singer, a specially formed folk band, and folk singers Al Lloyd, Isla Cameron and Ewan MacColl. The diarist reckoned the skiffle group acquitted itself well but was outdone by the applause for a fiddle and flute duo performing Irish dance music: he thought the concert was carrying a practical joke too far but admitted it was a sell-out.[49] Skiffle not triumphant, but nearly so.

Given the attraction of the skiffle group idea, it was taken up by other jazz bands in Britain, the Avon Cities Jazz Band, for example. Jazz venues also advertised a skiffle group as part of a programme, although it is likely that such groups did not always come from within the featured jazz band. The bill for an Ealing pub venue in September 1955 included Bob Watson's Skiffle Group alongside the Southern Stompers and, in Leeds in December 1955, the Tuxedo Jazz Band were paired with Boland's Skiffle Group. As the skiffle craze took off in 1956, more bands — the Crane River Jazzband, the Eric Silk Southern Jazzband, the Bill Brunskill Jazzmen, the Mike Daniels Delta Jazzmen, the Cy Laurie Band, for example — announced the added attraction of a skiffle group at their advertised venue. Occasionally skiffle's role at a particular location — to fill the intermission — would be admitted to.

The concept of a "band within a band" of the jazz world was not, however, the only way skiffle evolved. Outside of the jazz environment it was developed in some of the pubs, clubs and coffee bars of London by groups that had no affiliation to a "parent" jazz band.

In 1954, for example, the City Ramblers, set up by Russell Quaye, played at Sunday lunchtime in the Perseverance pub off Tottenham Court Road. At the time it called itself a spasm band but was later to become well-known in the skiffle world. By 1956, the City Ramblers, with guests, were regular performers at the Princess Louise, a pub in High Holborn.

Around about the same time, John Hasted, who had a folk group called the Ramblers, decided to reorganise it as a skiffle and folk-song group after hearing Ken Colyer play. Redd Sullivan, a blues and work song singer, was to take most of the lead vocals in what then came to be called the John Hasted Skiffle and Folksong Group. Like the City Ramblers, who in 1957 were the mainstay of the Skiffle Cellar, Hasted's group had its own club in a Soho cellar at 44 Gerrard Street and offered regular club nights, with about three hours of singing, and some dancing. American songs were supplanted by British folk songs performed skiffle-fashion. The club became known as the 44 Skiffle Club and folk singer Shirley Collins, "the girl with the pure Sussex bell-like voice", worked with the Hasted group. Jack Elliott, who had spent a year with Woody Guthrie, was a visitor to the club and according to Hasted had a great influence on skiffle.

In late 1955 publicity was also given to "Europe's only Skiffle and Blues Club" at the Roundhouse, a pub in Wardour Street. This had been opened by Cyril Davies and Bob Watson, who also led a skiffle group. Cyril Davies would come to be an important music associate of Alexis Korner in their joint promotion of the blues.

In retrospect, it is difficult to say whether these other skiffle groups took their inspiration from the jazz-based ones — some, like Hasted's, clearly did — or whether they represented a different strand of popular

music development. As with jazz, this other strand of skiffle tended to be a feature of central London, particularly the Soho area, in these early years.

Soho was — and continues to be — a cosmopolitan community, which, in the post-War years, was moving away from being a place with a literary reputation, gained in the 1920s and 1930s, to one where music was all-important. A significant change was the spread of coffee houses in the district, the first modern one, the Moka, Frith Street, opening in 1953. Another feature of Soho life for four years, starting in July 1955, was the Soho Fair; the 1956 fair would prove to be an important event for the newly-formed Vipers Skiffle Group.

According to John Hasted, skiffle mushroomed from 1954 onwards and there was a lot of informal singing in London coffee houses, such as the Gyre and Gimble at Charing Cross, and the Nucleus near Seven Dials. "Some coffee houses were slow to realise the possibilities of guitar singing. Both the 2 I's and the Breadbasket ultimately cashed in and made money, but they could have done much better if they had been quicker off the mark."[50] Wally Whyton and others associated with the Vipers met up at the Breadbasket; the 2 I's (also to be important to the Vipers), would eventually assume an historical significance for its role in the development and spread of British skiffle and rock 'n' roll in the last part of the Fifties.

In 1956 skiffle arrived on the popular music scene via jazz club and coffee bar, but what of the American roots of the music, referred to only in passing so far?

2 Black, Brown and White — Skiffle Origins

Skiffle came to the fore in Britain in early 1956 and, as a form of popular music, would flourish until towards the end of 1958. While a number of individuals, such as Ken Colyer and Chris Barber, were involved in the emergence of skiffle in the first half of the Fifties, and other names, like the Vipers and Chas McDevitt skiffle groups, would be commercially successful during the craze, it is Lonnie Donegan who is best remembered, often to the exclusion of others. Donegan, it was, who was seen as representing all that skiffle stood for, so much so that, in his day, he was known as the "King (or Sultan) of Skiffle". Through his recordings, it was Donegan who largely defined the skiffle repertoire — often, as has been seen, with borrowings from the songster and blues singer, Lead Belly and the folk singer, Woody Guthrie.

Along with Lonnie Donegan, what people usually associate also with skiffle is the use of homemade and improvised instruments, such as the washboard and tea-chest bass. These were played in association with one or more acoustic guitars to provide a strong rhythmic accompaniment to a singer's delivery of a blues or folksong, usually of North American origin. In fact skiffle has been described by Brian Bird as "folk song with a jazz beat". Groups could also include other instruments such as the mandolin, kazoo and mouth organ, depending on the available talent.

Once successful, Donegan abandoned the washboard in favour of the drums and neither he nor other skiffle groups associated with jazz bands needed to resort to the tea-chest bass. Almost as a credential of authenticity, however, the washboard was employed by many skiffle groups, both professional and amateur, although drums could sometimes feature instead. Among the many amateur groups of the skiffle craze years, the tea-chest bass was virtually the only option, as young people generally could not afford a proper string bass. Some ambitious amateur groups did, nevertheless, progress from the humble tea-chest to the proper thing. Before long the availability of the electric bass guitar would solve the problem but, in the meantime, Bell Music were offering the two-string skiffle bassello in 1958 at twenty-nine guineas as just the job for skiffle, rock 'n' roll and hillbilly music.

Having abandoned improvised instrumentation for his post-"Rock Island Line" recordings, Donegan's later, independent group made use of the electric guitar, moving closer to a rhythm and blues or rock 'n' roll line-up and performance style. This was to happen in many a skiffle group as they moved towards the end of the skiffle craze. Donegan also included variety and other types of songs in his material, widening his repertoire, and his appeal, as skiffle's attraction faded. Other skifflers too would seek to expand their range of material to include spirituals, jazz, country music, and British songs, as well as rock 'n' roll.

For, strange as it may seem in retrospect, skiffle shared the popular music scene with rock 'n' roll. Both involved whites playing black music and both were deemed to be novelties that would soon be abandoned for newer musical forms — the calypso and cha-cha-cha were momentary contenders. However, with hindsight, the music critics of the 1950s can be seen to have got it completely wrong in respect of rock 'n' roll, which in one guise or another continues to pervade today's popular music scene. Skiffle probably lasted longer than its critics expected, or hoped, and was taken up in other countries including Australia, Sweden, the Netherlands and Germany, but there was no doubt about the finality of its commercial demise when it occurred. Skiffle served, perhaps, as a quick "foundation course" in American folk music for British teenagers, who could then progress to the UK beat, rock, blues and folk movements that followed.

The musical origins of British skiffle can be traced back to developments within black and white American cultures that would provide the foundations for jazz and popular music in the twentieth century. Blues, jazz and American folk music gave opportunities for group performance, generated a singable repertoire of material, and made use of non-standard instruments. Models that British skifflers would apparently draw on, as skiffle in Britain also encompassed the idea of the small musical group (of usually self-taught musicians), a common pool of songs, and the use of improvised instruments. Indeed, it was this use of improvised and homemade musical instruments that particularly characterised British skiffle, especially at the amateur, grassroots level.

The cover of the Christmas number of the *Illustrated London News* for 1957 reproduced in colour a painting by the seventeenth-century Dutch artist Jan Molenaer. Entitled the "Young Musicians", the painting shows a young lad playing a fiddle, another playing an improvised drum, and a girl tapping spoons on a metal helmet. Given the date of the periodical, it is not surprising perhaps that the *Illustrated London News* subtitled the painting "A 17th-Century 'Skiffle Group'".[1] What the painting demonstrates is not that skiffle originated in Holland in the seventeenth century but that there is a seemingly instinctive and long tradition of utilising improvised instruments as a part of music-making.

This was particularly well developed amongst black Americans since the early days of slavery. In part this was due to poverty and lack of permitted access to proper instruments but also to their view as to what

27

A home-made 1-string bass. Don Schofield of the contemporary Black Sheep Skiffle Group based in Leeds. (Photo Mike Dewe.)

are appropriate musical sounds. In her history of black folk music to the American Civil War, Dena Epstein quotes from a 1935 article on ex-slave reminiscences that mentions both non-standard and standard instruments: "Slaves usually amused themselves by... playing music on tin cans, Jew's harps, or any kind of instrument which they could get that would produce sound... a banjo... an accordion... fiddles, fifes and sometimes a drum. This same music was often carried to the home of the master when company came."[2]

Harold Courlander, author of *Negro Folk Music, U.S.A.*, rejects the customary view that such folk instruments were "inspired by irrepressible instincts to bang or twang on something." And goes on to add that: "Virtually every device used by the Negro in his folk music had its origin in European or African tradition, and very little was invented in the United States. What did happen is that substitutes were found for traditional instruments not easy, or impossible, to obtain."[3] Dena Epstein concluded on similar lines that: "Contemporary documents establish that [African musics and] African instruments were... transplanted, some as remembered aspects of a lost life, and some as tangible objects carried aboard slaving ships. Instruments common in Africa that were seen and described in the United States and other parts of the western hemisphere included drums of various kinds, rhythm sticks, banjos, musical bows, quills or panpipes, and a form of xylophone called the balafo."[4]

Amongst black people, performers would not only sing but also talk, whistle and yodel as part of music-making, and hands and feet could clap and dance. Black musicians brought a different view to the standard European one as to what was acceptable as music.

The three main improvised instruments involved in skiffle and its antecedents were the washtub bass, the washboard and the jug. The washtub bass was used instead of a proper string bass. In Britain in the 1950s, it was known as a tea-chest bass; tea-chests being presumably more readily and cheaply available than washtubs. Whether using a tub or chest as a resonator, fixed up with a single string attached to an upright, such as a broomstick, the general method of construction and use was the same. It has been suggested that the forerunner of this instrument is to be found in West and Central Africa and that it "was an apparent development of the spring snare, used for capturing small game. In its more primitive form, the resulting instrument was an earth bow."[5] In *Savannah Syncopators*, however, Paul Oliver also describes more complex string instruments in Africa — he mentions the "musical bow", the hunting bow plucked as a musical instrument, and belly-harps and belly-lyres, stringed bows with a gourd resonator, played by placing the cup of the resonator against the stomach and plucking or bowing.[6] The slapping and plucking used in playing the jazz double bass, and the skiffle washtub or tea-chest bass, as opposed to bowing in the European manner, possibly owes something to its African cousin.[7]

The washboard, known also as a rub board, made up for the absence of a more conventional rhythm instrument such as the drum. Held upright, sometimes secured in a frame, or laid across the knees, it was played by rhythmically scraping the corrugated metal centrepiece of the board. Modern washboard players might use a breastplate version of the instrument which is manufactured to be worn on the chest, rather like a piece of armour, and played in that position. Harold Courlander points out that

Washboard played in "breastplate" fashion by Dan Nichols of the contemporary Cardiff-based group Railroad Bill. (Courtesy Railroad Bill).

"scraping instruments are found everywhere in New World Negro cultures"; and that "The idea... is undoubtedly of African origin."[8] Dena Epstein contrasts black, European-style bands with a more primitive, more African combination, when referring to an 1830s report of an orchestra featuring a kind of mandolin, made of a gourd, and the teeth of a horse's jawbone scraped with a hollow stick.[9]

A jug could be used to create bass notes by blowing across the neck, and this instrument has been played in both black folk and white mountain music making. The jug takes the place of a tuba (in jazz) or the double bass in other bands.

A range of other improvised instruments were used from time to time by black folk musicians and by blues and jazz performers, such as gas-pipes, cooking hardware, wood blocks, tambourines, whistles, horns, suitcases, and paper-and-comb. The suitcase — used in place of the drums — was "stood on end, covered with paper and brushed with a clothes brush, while the foot beats time on the bottom of the suitcase like a big drum."[10] Along the way, other instruments manufactured commercially, such as the cigar-shaped kazoo, a "novelty" noise-maker (also known as the bazooka or blue blower) was used to make a noise when played rather like the paper-and-comb. This and the harmonica have been utilised to a greater or lesser degree by various black musicians.

In 1960, Frederic Ramsey published *Been Here and Gone*, based on field trips between 1951 and 1957 amongst southern blacks. In one chapter he illustrates in words and pictures the continuing use of standard and improvised instruments at "a place where... friends and neighbors like to come — to hear music, to dance or just to sit and watch and listen." In addition to the guitar and harmonica, the musicians use "The kazoo, jug, washboard, washtub, barrel and others of the humble household family of instruments [which] descend from an ancient lineage sprung from necessity. The need was to evoke rhythms and timbres from whatever lay close to hand."[11]

Although available as manufactured instruments, the banjo, fiddle and guitar were sometimes homemade, as ownership of a guitar, or any other musical instrument, especially for a youngster, could be difficult. The blues provides examples of the use of homemade instruments. The violinist Milton Roby made his first violin from a cigar box and Brownie McGhee learned the rudiments of music on "a small banjo with a marshmallow can for the head and a neck made of season poplar." He also learned piano and the guitar and, with guitar and kazoo, entertained at the Smokey Mountain summer resorts.[12] According to his autobiography, Big Bill Broonzy made a fiddle from a cigar box, around the age of ten, and also a guitar from goods boxes for a friend. The two played together for white people's picnics.[13]

Furry Lewis, a Memphis-based blues musician, says that I "made my own guitar. I taken a cigar box and cut a hole in the top of it and taken another little piece of thin wood like beaverboard and made the neck. And I taken some nails and nailed them in the end of the neck and bent them down and taken wire off a screen door. And that's just what I made my strings out of. Of course, I wasn't playing nothing, but that's just the way I got a start."[14] Lewis was six years old at the time; later W.C. Handy gave him his first good guitar — a Martin — which he wore out after twenty-five to thirty years.[15]

Any discussion of skiffle's roots needs to take into account the characteristics of both white and black music as regards instrumentation, as both

1956 And All That: Skiffle Reminiscences

As a teenager I wanted a guitar but could not afford one and so that was that. The advent of skiffle, however, was just the prod I needed to stop dreaming about owning a guitar and to do something about it. After all this was skiffle, the music of inventiveness.

Maybe I could not afford a guitar but I could use my ingenuity to make one. The one thing I did own (courtesy of a jumble sale at the local chapel) was a wind-up HMV console gramophone and a collection of Dixieland records like the "Saints" and the "Darktown Strutters Ball". At the time (after leaving school in 1955) I was a student at a college in Liverpool and only went home at weekends. Over two weekend visits home, the gramophone was dismantled for its timber and plywood and a "guitar" built from the proceeds. I guessed at the dimensions and built accordingly. The resultant instrument had the string length of a bass guitar, a 3"-wide fingerboard and a tone to match. So what if the fingerboard was hardboard stained with Indian ink and the frets made from Woolworth's valance rail sawn in half, it was all mine and it played in tune. An action of $^3/_8$" at the twelfth fret was neither here nor there when only three frets were in use. After about three weeks, I sawed the neck off at the fourth fret and screwed the head back on to get the string length to something like normal.

What owning a guitar did for me was to put me in touch with other players who had proper instruments. As a result, I was able to find out the guitar's correct dimensions and build a better one accordingly. The new one did have proper fretwire, even if the fingerboard was a Formica offcut with a woodgrain pattern. With this instrument I learned the whole of the skiffle repertoire.

By this time, early 1957, I was permanently home again from the college in Liverpool and very active at the local chapel youth club. At the youth club a skiffle group was a must. The breakthrough came when someone donated a banjo to the sports club raffle at my father's works. Despite spending a fair bit on tickets he did not win it, but he did get the winner to part with it for £2. I therefore became the owner of a 5-string G banjo. Rapidly Michael Braddock, one of my youth club friends was given lessons on my homemade guitar and, with two fretted instruments, it was all systems go. A tea-chest was obtained and converted to a bass, which Joe Wormald played, until he found a mandolin in his grandmother's attic, whereupon he became the mandolin player and James Lee took over as the bass player. Ronnie Turton, who had been a side-drummer in the Church Lad's Brigade Band volunteered his services as a washboard artist and we were away.

Bob Brooks

musics were drawn on by British skifflers. In its early days, country music had a simplicity, similar to the blues and early jazz, in its use of instruments and the three chord pattern of song accompaniment. Over the years, however, the music and its instrumentation have become more varied. The fiddle, banjo and guitar were the basic instruments of southern rural music but other instruments are associated with it, such as the mandolin, dulcimer, autoharp, dobro guitar (with a metal resonator for better amplification and often played across the knees with a steel bar or slide), string bass and the defining sound of the steel, or Hawaiian guitar, available from the 1930s onwards as an electric instrument.

As far as improvised and less orthodox musical instruments are concerned, these were not a major feature of country music. Jug bands, however, were popular in the 1920s and early 1930s — they were to be found in southern mountain districts since the early twentieth century — and appeared on shows such as the Grand Ole Opry. Rubbing a metal ice tray from an old-fashioned refrigerator to produce a subtler sound than a washboard was used in old-time country, Cajun and elsewhere. Bluegrass came to be strictly defined in the mid-Forties partly by its instrumentation of five unamplified string instruments — fiddle, banjo, guitar, mandolin and string bass. With its emphasis on string instruments, although not homemade and improvised ones, a considerable repertoire of songs, and its many bands, country music made a contribution to the skiffle idea if a lesser one than black music.

Various types of band employed non-standard instruments, such as wash-tub bass or jug, and can be seen as precursors of the British skiffle groups of the Fifties. Of these the spasm band is noted particularly for its line-up, which consisted of makeshift instruments, though it could include a conventional chord-playing one such as the guitar or ukulele. Perhaps because of its reliance on homemade and unorthodox instruments, the spasm band was particularly associated with children. During the skiffle craze in Britain, it was seen as a close relative if not sometimes synonymous with a skiffle group. The first known spasm band was Emile "Stale Bread" Lacoume's Razzy Dazzy Spasm Band in New Orleans in the late 1890s, which consisted of white youngsters, all newsboys, between twelve and

---

1956 And All That: Skiffle Reminiscences

In December 1956, I was demobbed from the RAF, and in 1957 I started listening to the new skiffle music. I bought, and learned to play, a guitar, autoharp, kazoo, washboard, drum brushes and my dad made me a solid string bass — a six feet high hardboard cutout with four strings. With vocals, our skiffle group (it didn't have a name, it was just a fun get-together) made a reasonable sound. Peter Baxter (who played in the group only a few times) was by far the best guitarist around Sussex but moved into jazz. However, with George Whetton (guitar/banjo), Tony Wales (guitar/vocals/drums), Lionel Bownton (guitar/vocals) and Ian Holder or Geoff Hedger on piano, we had fun at local venues. We played songs such as "Cumberland Gap", "Trouble in Mind", "2.19 Blues", "Mama Don't Allow", and "Hand Me Down My Walkin' Cane".

Terry Potter

fifteen. Its instrumental line-up was two zithers, a homemade guitar, a homemade bass fiddle, a harmonica and a mandolin. Spasm bands performed blues, ragtime and popular songs of the time and are said to have flourished in New Orleans in the first thirty years of this century.

In his autobiography, the black New Orleans jazz musician Danny Barker (guitar and banjo), recounts how he formed a spasm band in the early 1920s, at the time of another craze, the ukulele craze. He says that there were many such bands in New Orleans. George Picou, brother of the clarinetist, Alphonse, played kazoo in a spasm band called the Roody Doody Band — its base was the Roody Doody barrelhouse — in which Slow Drag Pavageau played a small homemade bass fiddle.[16]

Barker's band was called the Boozan Kings (Boozan is Creole for party), and consisted of six shoe-shine boys: Barker (ukulele-banjo) and five friends, of whom four played kazoo, drums, suitcase and ukulele respectively, while the fifth "played the harp and watched for the police". The band's object was to earn money in barrooms and elsewhere playing for both black and white audiences. Barker "would take the band where small combos were playing. They would watch us perform, glad for the recess."[17] Shades of British jazz club skiffle arrangements here.

If spasm music might be regarded as less than musically respectable, then hokum, with its faking and concern for musical effects and comedy vocals might be seen as a more sophisticated relation. One or two 1930s blues groups used hokum in their title — the Hokum Boys, the Hokum

---

1956 And All That: Skiffle Reminiscences

My early musical experiences, in the mid-Fifties, were, one way or another, largely skiffle based. About 1956, at the age of nine or ten, we had a Ukulele Club at Kelvedon Hatch County Primary School, Essex, at which eight to ten of us with ukes or uke-banjos were taught basic technique by Norman Howgego, the second master. He had a good working knowledge of playing guitar and similar instruments and so was able to get us off to a good start. The songs we played were mostly minstrel-type songs, "Campdown Races" and "Swanee River" for example, but some, such as "Tom Dooley" and "Worried Man", became the bread and butter of the skiffle and early folk groups. Even at the ripe old age of nine or ten, and just as skiffle was emerging, I found I was familiar with much of the material.

During this time, at weekends and summer evenings, we would try to get a skiffle group together. For those of us who had instruments — guitars, uke-banjos, ukes, penny whistles, harmonicas — there was no problem, but those without would borrow their mothers' washboards — plentiful and readily available then — or try to construct some sort of string bass. If anyone came by a tea-chest, it was quickly commandeered and a rake would soon be without a handle. We were all young, from nine to eleven at the most, and mainly played out-of-doors, but we had a lot of fun.

Geoff Harris

FAMOUS JUG BAND

Trio, for example — and Tampa Red (guitar) was accompanied by his Hokum Jug Band whose line-up made use of kazoo, jug and washboard.

Other groups of performers identified by historians of black music include the string, jug and washboard bands and these too can be seen as contributing to the British skiffle ethos. A string band is one that is made up completely or mainly of string instruments. A reliance on such was characteristic of blues ensembles, country and folk music. In its use of guitars and improvised instruments for bass and drum, the typical British skiffle group of the 1950s could be said to have its origins particularly in the spasm and string band traditions. The basic rock group that developed at the same time as skiffle was also essentially a string band.

Largely known from recordings of the 1920s and 1930s, jug bands date back to the beginnings of the twentieth century and provided entertainment at medicine shows and picnics. In addition to the jug, of which there was occasionally more than one, the band could consist of stringed instruments, such as the violin, guitar, and mandolin, as well as the harmonica or kazoo, and washboard.

Researching blues and jug bands in Memphis at the end of the 1960s, Bengt Olsson discovered that jug bands were enjoyed by white and blacks alike and that they played on the streets and at white parties — they, like Fifties skiffle groups, were seen as an amusing novelty. The Memphis bands, of which there were at least six by the early Thirties, played sentimental songs, popular hits, the blues and occasionally fast dance numbers, sometimes going further afield to Ohio or Colorado to perform.

The Memphis Jug Band (billed here as the Famous Jug Band). L. to r. Charlie Burse (gtr), Will Shade (jug), Wilfred "Birdbreath" Bell (kazoo), Robert Burse (percussion), early 1930s. (Photo: Jones-Purdy, Courtesy Delta Haze Corp.)

35

The Memphis Jug Band and the Beale Street Jug Band also visited New Orleans each year for Mardi Gras.[18] The Memphis Jug Band number, "K.C. Moan", a train blues, became part of the Ken Colyer skiffle repertoire.

Another Memphis band was Cannon's Jug Stompers, considered by Paul Oliver to have recorded "outstanding examples of the jug band idiom." A revived Gus Cannon composition "Walk Right In" by the Roof Top Singers "brought him unexpected royalties and recognition and in 1963 he made a number of concert appearances."[19]

There were jug bands in other American states and these included the Birmingham Jug Band, which recorded in the early Thirties and the Cincinnati Jug Band that recorded in 1929, possibly using two jugs. In the 1930s, Big Bill Broonzy made two sides with his "Jug Busters" and one further side accompanied by a jug band.

Although still to be heard, jug bands faded out in the early postwar years as the music changed, becoming amplified, aggressive and more powerful.[20] Today's jug band proponents, however, tend to be made up of white musicians: the revivalist Last Chance Jug Band from Memphis, dating from 1989, is led by David Evans on vocals, guitar and kazoo; the Juggernaut Jug Band, founded in 1965 and from Louisville, has a programme of cover songs and originals.

Of the three major black folk instruments, the washtub bass, jug and the washboard, the last-named came to be used most frequently in blues and in a small way in jazz. By the 1920s and 1930s a number of groups described themselves as "washboard bands". Amongst the recorded groups were James Cole's Washboard Band, Eddie Kelly's Washboard Band, the Nashville Washboard Band (which recorded in 1942 using mandolin, two guitars, tin can, bull fiddle and washboard), Red and his Washboard Band, and Joe William's Washboard Blues Singers.

In many ways the divisions between jug, washboard and string bands are rather artificial, since they played the same kind of music for the same kind of audience. Nevertheless, the divisions help to focus on the instrumentation of such groups and reflect groupings used both by music historians and others in attempting to describe the complexities of black music-making.

Jazz itself further legitimises the use of non-standard instruments in popular music. Well-known jazz groups of the 1920s and 1930s that featured improvised and less orthodox instruments were the Spirits of Rhythm, the Mound City Blue Blowers and bands involving Adrian Rollini, in particular the Goofus Five.

The Spirits of Rhythm, a 1930s string band, featured a drummer playing a paper-wrapped suitcase with a pair of whisk brooms, and using other homemade percussion instruments. Red (William) McKenzie, who played comb-and-paper, kazoo and sang, led the Mound City Blue Blowers formed in Chicago in 1924. This spasm-type jazz group included Eddie Lang on guitar and in its founding year had a hit record with "Arkansaw Blues". A 1958 *Gramophone* review of four reissued tracks on the *Blue Blowing Jazz* EP, described the Mound City Blue Blowers tunes as 1925 spasm-skiffle music played with "a crispness and swing that is rarely heard today and seems quite unknown in the so-called 'skiffle' groups."[21] But then *Gramophone* reviewers were never very appreciative of skiffle.

Adrian Rollini was a talented multi-instrumentalist who, in his early career, had a penchant for the more unusual or novelty musical instruments of the day — the goofus (a keyboard harmonica played using a mouthpiece or through a piece of flexible tubing) and the hot fountain pen (a small keyless instrument of the clarinet family). His other jazz instruments were the bass saxophone and the vibraphone. Rollini apparently concentrated on the vibraphone from the 1930s onwards, but he is best remembered as a master of the bass saxophone and a player of jazz on novelty instruments.

With some exceptions, would-be British jazz, folk and blues performers had to learn from recordings available in Britain. One source of loan for such recordings was the American Library of the United States Information Service at Grosvenor Square in London, and both Lonnie Donegan and Wally Whyton have testified to the importance to them of the availability of such loans. Donegan has even confessed to "losing" and paying for a recording by Muddy Waters in order to hang on to it.

However, in the early Fifties opportunities began to occur to learn from blues and other artists in the flesh through their visits to Britain. Lead Belly never made it to Britain, but was in Paris in 1949. Josh White visited Europe in 1950 — Britain in July — and was here again in 1956 and at

Lead Belly performing for school children at a Standard Oil Co. of California broadcast on 8 March, 1945, San Francisco (detail). (Courtesy Lead Belly Society Collection.)

dates in the Sixties; Lonnie Johnson was in Britain as part of a European tour in 1952. Big Bill Broonzy came to Europe in September 1951, visiting Paris and London. He returned again in 1952, 1955 and 1957. A few months prior to Big Bill's death in August 1958, Brownie McGhee and Sonny Terry visited London and, in autumn 1958, Muddy Waters and Otis Spann made their first UK visit. The blues provided the source for many skiffle songs, such as "2.19 Blues", "How Long Blues", "Good Morning Blues", "Trouble in Mind", and "Easy Rider". Of the blues singers, admired and copied by British musicians, Huddie Ledbetter (Lead Belly) provided much of the skiffle repertoire and Big Bill Broonzy's presence in Britain in the Fifties — with his seeming endorsement of skiffle — was a source of inspiration to young skifflers and blues fans.

Huddie Ledbetter, born in Louisiana in 1889 and raised in Texas, experienced prison sentences for murder, attempted homicide and assault. An association with the Lomaxes, begun in 1934, leading to club work and recordings (including prison songs for the Library of Congress) brought him recognition. Lead Belly sang to a 12-string guitar and at one time (around 1917) had teamed up with the blues singer Blind Lemon Jefferson. Lead Belly's "Goodnight Irene" was a hit song in the USA in 1950 after his death in 1949.

In Britain, Ken Colyer used Lead Belly material, but it was Lonnie Donegan's performances of his songs that made much of Lead Belly's unlikely material known to a wider popular music audience. These songs included: "Rock Island Line", "Alabama Bound", "Go Down Old Hannah", "Midnight Special", "Bring Me a Li'l Water Silvy", "John Henry", "Ol' Riley", and "Diggin' My Potatoes". Other skiffle groups trawled

Lead Belly's recordings that included work songs and spirituals and made their versions of "Ella Speed", "Pick a Bale of Cotton", "Mary Don't You Weep", "Green Corn", and "Good Morning Blues", although other singers than Lead Belly had recorded some of these songs.

Slightly younger than Lead Belly was the downhome blues performer, Big Bill Broonzy, born in Mississippi in 1893 or 1898. His childhood endeavours with a homemade fiddle have already been mentioned and his rent party performances as a singer and guitarist in the 1920s will be described later. Big Bill began recording in 1926 and in the 1930s gained a reputation as a top blues performer. None of these achievements brought him financial independence however, and he supported himself through various jobs. In the Fifties, though, he was to gain an international reputation through European tours, including visits to Britain, and enjoy some of the rewards that had eluded him.

In addition to Josh White, Broonzy and others, a number of white folk musicians, such as Rambling Jack Elliott, Derroll Adams, Peggy Seeger and Alan Lomax, were performing in Britain in the Fifties. Alan Lomax, son of the folk music scholar, John Lomax, was also broadcasting here on aspects of American folk music. The two Lomaxes were the force behind the Archive of American Folk Song at the Library of Congress, Washington. American folk songs that became part of the skiffle repertoire included songs like "Skip To My Lou", "Cumberland Gap", and "East Virginia" ("Greenback Dollar").

So far the origins of skiffle have been described largely in terms of the folk music, blues and jazz of black Americans mainly from the southern states. The roots of skiffle, as noted earlier in respect of instrumentation,

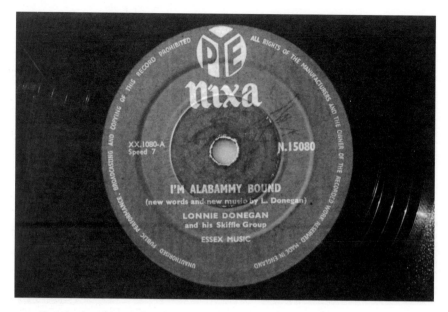

are also to be found in white country music, that shared a number of characteristics with black musical forms, and was also from the South. What is now called country music was originally dubbed hillbilly music when launched commercially in the 1920s, although generally known in the South among performers and their audiences as country or old-time music. It was a mixture of traditional folk music (with a strong British inheritance) from the southern Appalachian mountains and elsewhere in the south, the blues, and popular songs composed in America during the nineteenth-century.

Like the blues, country music's heroes (and more recently heroines) are singers, although it has its instrumental stars. Of greatest importance for skiffle was the itinerant, prolific songwriter, Woody Guthrie, born in Oklahoma in 1912. Guthrie came from a musical home and learnt many songs from his parents, at the same time becoming an able performer with the harmonica. By the age of sixteen he had begun a wandering way of life that was to take him over the USA, much of Canada and Mexico, learning to play the guitar in a Texas-based magic show. The songs he composed came from what he saw and experienced during his travelling and work. He also learned to play mandolin and fiddle. In 1935, Guthrie moved to California, appearing regularly on a Los Angeles radio station, going on to New York in the late Thirties.

Opposite: Rare photograph of Lead Belly and Woody Guthrie performing at a New York party, March 1944. The bit of white showing above Woody's right arm was a sign he kept attached to his guitar that read "This machine KILLS Fascists." (Courtesy Lead Belly Society Collection.)

A political activist and singer of protest songs, Guthrie appeared at union meetings and migrant labour camps, and scenes of Depression poverty motivated a number of his best songs, which included "Dust Bowl Refugees" and "This Land Is Your Land". His support for Roosevelt's New Deal is shown by songs such as "Grand Coolie Dam" — a hit for Donegan in mid-1958. Donegan also recorded Guthrie's "Sally Don't You

Grieve" and other skifflers recorded "New York Town", "Union Maid" and "This Land is Your Land".

In the late Thirties, Guthrie recorded for the Library of Congress, then, after meeting Pete Seeger in 1940, formed the Almanac Singers with Seeger and two others. In 1942 Guthrie joined the Headline Singers that brought together Lead Belly, Sonny Terry and Brownie McGhee for a short while. After war service in the merchant marine, Guthrie recorded for the Folkways label. His songwriting continued until the onset of Huntington's Chorea at the end of the Forties. Hospitalised in 1952, Guthrie died in 1967. A few years before his death Ray Lawless wrote: "Some singers, like Woody Guthrie for instance, defy any easy classification. Testily independent and sharply original, he colors any material he touches. He calls himself 'writer, composer, musician' and there are those who will hotly deny or stoutly defend him in all three categories. Folk composer he may well be, and a controversial one for sure."[22]

Of another significant group of musicians, the Carter Family, it was said: "This group was important because of its early recordings, but also for its longevity in performance and influence in country music."[23] The original Carter Family, consisting of A.P. Carter, his wife Sara, and sister-in-law, Maybelle, made its first recording in 1927. The women were instrumentalists, often playing guitar and autoharp, and also sang lead and middle voice, with A.P. singing bass. At the close of the Twenties, following further recordings, the group became known nationwide and their fame increased during the Thirties. Towards the end of that decade, children of the group's members were included in performances. From 1927 to 1941 the Carters made some 270 records. Songs associated with the family include, "The Titanic", "I Shall Not Be Moved", "Worried Man Blues", "Dixie Darling", "Wabash Cannonball", and "Jimmy Brown the Newsboy" — Donegan recorded some of these Carters' titles.

Another famous country name, whose material was sometimes drawn on by skifflers, was the songwriter/performer Hank Williams. Williams (a Donegan favourite), died aged twenty-nine in 1953 leaving many songs that continue to be sung.

As has been shown, British skiffle had diverse roots, but what is known about the source and use of the word "skiffle" itself, and does that information help to clarify further the nature and origins of the music? In mid-1956, Alexis Korner wrote that Big Bill Broonzy "mentioned that they had a regular dance on a Saturday night in his part of Mississippi which was called 'The Saturday Night Skiffle'".[24] This story — possibly an off-the-cuff remark by Big Bill, for which there is seemingly no other evidence — was probably the source of Brian Bird's statement about a free-and-easy party in Mississippi being known as a "skiffle".[25] A poor, elderly black man, the eponymous Bill Skiffle, has also seemingly been given credit for its origin in the Chicago of 1927.[26]

While of American derivation, the origin of the word "skiffle" is, essentially, unknown but its use in connection with the black American house-rent party is documented, if not particularly well, and it was this social custom that was usually referred to by British skifflers seeking to explain the music and its origins.

The house-rent party was a particular feature of the south side of Chicago and elsewhere, especially during the 1920s and 1930s, although it had flourished prior to prohibition coming into force in the USA in 1920. Its purpose was to collect money to pay the rent by charging those who attended an entrance fee and by the sale of food and drink. One jazz historian says that such a party was known on Chicago's south side as "pitchin' boogie", another that it was known as a "skiffle", "shake", or "percolator".[27] Other Chicago terms included "parlour social", "gouge", "struggle", or "too terrible party".

An important figure at the house-rent party was the pianist — such as Chicago's Jimmy Yancey — who was neither required to pay an entrance fee nor bring food and drink, where this was the practice. Pianists could maintain themselves from the benefits of playing at a number of such "skiffles", which might include a tip from the crap game winner. "It was in these parties that Montana Taylor, Romeo Briggs, Romeo Nelson, Charles Avery, Dan Burley, 'Mr Freddie' Shayne, Alex Channey and scores of other pianists, known and unknown, played."[28] In New York the rent party attracted the talents of pianists such as Duke Ellington, James P. Johnson, Willie "the Lion" Smith and Fats Waller. In their *Dictionary of Jazz*, Panassié and Gautier comment: "Much fine music has been played by some of the great pianists in these circumstances, and the phrase is used in the titles of various numbers: *Rent Party Blues, House Rent Stomp*."[29]

The house-rent pianists became associated with two types of blues piano-playing known as barrel-house and boogie-woogie. In *Shining Trumpets*, Rudi Blesh, writes — although not in the house-rent party context — that barrel-house pianists, whose style was often associated with singing and spoken monologues, could be accompanied by impromptu small groupings made up from string instruments (like the guitar and banjo), brass and woodwind instruments (such as cornet and the clarinet) that had seen better days, as well as drums, washboard, paper-covered suitcase, kazoo, harmonica, comb, jug, musical saw and accordion. As a piano style, boogie-woogie was not known as such until the late 1920s and in its early stages of development was usually associated with string bass, guitar, mandolin and kazoo.[30]

Big Bill Broonzy gives an account of his participation in house-rent parties, but, while naming other blues artists who played at such parties, does not mention other musical instruments and their players: "In 1920, I came to Chicago and the people there asked me to come to their house... they knew I could play and sing the blues. So I went every Saturday night...

"All of them was from some part of the South and had come to Chicago

to better their living... And those people started to give parties and some Saturday nights they would make enough money to pay the rent, and so they started to call them 'house rent parties', because they sold chicken, pig feet, home brew, chittlins, moonshine whisky. The musicians didn't have to buy nothing and would get a chance to meet some nice looking women and girls, too."[31]

Blesh records that the depression, beginning in the USA with the 1929 crash, seriously curtailed the "skiffle" institution but that the ending of prohibition in 1933 ensured its demise.

In spite of the use of the word "skiffle" to describe a house-rent party, it does not seem to have been used in America before the Second World War to describe the music played nor the groups of musicians who performed, as was to be the case in the UK in the 1950s. This is not to say that it was not used in that way, only that the evidence for it does not seem to be in place. Prior to the late Forties "skiffle music" as a genre would not appear to have attracted any critic's or historian's attention and no recorded jazz, blues or folk group appears to have included "skiffle" in its title.

According to the *Oxford English Dictionary*, the earliest documented use of the term was in the title of a piece of jazz music — "Chicago Skiffle" — in 1926. It was also used on a 1929 Paramount record, "Hometown Skiffle", (a blues medley which included Blind Lemon Jefferson and the Hokum Boys, amongst others) described in its advertising as a "big get-together party" and elsewhere as an "all-star affair which gives realistically a scene at a house party". It is similar to a Vocalion record of the period, "Jim Jackson's Jamboree".[32] In fact these are early sampler discs aimed at promoting the label's star bluesmen and probably bear little relation to a proper house-rent party atmosphere. It is no doubt this rent party background that led to the description of British skiffle by some of its exponents as good-time or party music.

The term "skiffle" is next used in 1946, when Dan Burley and his Skiffle Boys recorded eight titles, one of which was called "Skiffle Blues". Six of the titles — described as exciting rent party music — were issued on the *South Side Shake* album (Circle, 1947), where, in addition to Dan Burley (piano and vocal), the group consisted of two guitars and bass. "Skiffle Blues" (and "Chicken Shack Shuffle") neither of which was issued as part of the album, included a trombone and tenor saxophone in addition to Burley, two guitars (different players to the album) and bass. Dan Burley, described as a barrel-house pianist, and at one time business editor of the Harlem *Amsterdam News*, was noted as being the "master of more than two dozen basses and recalls the geographical origin of these as well as the complete sectional styles of which they were distinctive parts."[33] No improvised instruments were used by the Skiffle Boys, although two guitars is perhaps unusual in a jazz group of this kind, albeit not in a blues group.

By 1950, however, skiffle *was* being used as a term to describe a type

Opposite: (l. to r.) Little Bill Gaither, the pianist, Memphis Slim, Big Bill Broonzy, believed to be Chicago, 1940s. (Courtesy Lawrence Cohn/*Juke Blues Magazine*.)

An advert for Dan Burley and His Skiffle Boys, *Record Changer,* May 1947.

of music, as for a few months in that year the American magazine *Record Changer* ran a column called "Blues and Skiffle". Insofar as skiffle music was specifically mentioned, reference was made to the recordings of the Mississippi Jook Band, the Hokum Boys and Jane Lucas (using guitar, piano and drums), and Peetie Wheatstraw (featuring piano, guitar and bass). Earlier issues of the *Record Changer* had made reference in 1948 to Dan Burley, the skiffle man, and to Dan Burley and his skiffle music. Paul Oliver states that British skiffle took its name from the recordings of Dan Burley and his Skiffle Boys[34] — a suggestion that has its attraction as the recordings were quite close in date to the beginnings of British skiffle. At different times Chris Barber has admitted to both Dan Burley and the "Hometown Skiffle" recordings as the source of the "skiffle" label but seems to imply that, when adopted, the word had no special significance: "We'll call it skiffle, nice jolly name and at least people aren't going to say, 'Oh, I've heard that already'." Lonnie Donegan was clear in his mind that: "Skiffle was originally associated with rent-house [sic] parties... The kind of music they would play was very improvised, very folky and a bit jazzy. This was roughly parallel to what we were doing so we called it 'skiffle'."[35]

However, it is interesting to note that, in spite of an apparent small increase in the use of the term at the end of the Forties, Panassié and Gautier's *Dictionary of Jazz* published in 1956 has no entry for skiffle, which reinforces the view that it had not been a word in common usage in the field of jazz and blues. Nor indeed one that had much currency in the United States generally. Ron Goodwin's skiffle instrumental from the Fifties, "Skifflin' Strings", had to be re-titled when released on Capitol in

46

the States, where, as "Swinging Sweethearts", it went into the American top forty.

Clearly one much-accepted explanation of the origin of "skiffle" places it in the piano-centered blues and jazz music of the house-rent party, augmented by proper and improvised instruments depending on circumstances. However, as Alexis Korner noted in respect of Dan Burley and other performers, their "skiffle" was basically instrumental not vocal, and as Chas McDevitt pointed out in 1957: "British skiffle rarely uses the piano... Can you imagine a skiffle group pushing their grand piano along Old Compton Street?"[36] Virtually the only skiffle group to use a piano, was that of Ken Colyer, which featured Bob Kelly or Roy Foxley on some of its later tracks.

The rent party gave rise to the term "skiffle" and provides an example of music made by a combination of standard instruments and improvised and homemade ones. However, as has been seen, other models for British skiffle groups existed, such as the spasm, washboard, hillbilly and other bands of American folk music, blues and jazz. These usually featured string instruments, as well as improvised and homemade ones, and a large number were recorded in the Twenties and Thirties and to lesser extent in the Forties. British skiffle drew on the rent party tradition but it was the string bands, with their strong vocal input, that seem to have been more universally imitated, particularly by the amateur skifflers.

During the Fifties, many of these spasm, washboard and other groups were seen as coming under the skiffle umbrella, particularly where UK record reviewers and others were trying to put British skiffle in context and measure British performances up against similar but earlier American ones. The relating of skiffle to jug and washboard bands, for example, was endorsed by the 1954 publication by Decca of *Jazz on 78s*. Describing the listed records — by the Alabama Jug Band and State Street Ramblers — it said: "there is a sort of slap-happy atmosphere about these skiffle sessions, a complete absence of commercialism, that produces some of the most exciting and earthy jazz to be found on record."[37]

Possibly because of the popularity and publicity surrounding the British skiffle genre, this may have led American musicologists to apply the term "skiffle" retrospectively to some small-group aspects of their own popular music tradition. *American Skiffle Bands*, for example, recorded by Samuel B.Charters and issued by Folkway Records in 1957 uses the skiffle description. In an article in the November 1959 issue of the *New York Times*, Charters recounts stories associated with work begun in 1954 of finding, interviewing and recording obscure and forgotten black musicians and singers in the southern USA and there, too, uses the term, skiffle.[38]

Charters tells how, in July 1954, he bailed a washtub player, Tyler Jackson, who had spent the previous night in the drunk tank in Mobile, Alabama. Jackson sang and played in a three-piece, sidewalk skiffle band from Selma. Later, after equipping Jackson with a washtub bass, Charters recorded them in a living room, whose use had not been authorised by the returning owners. Moving on to Houston in November 1955, Charters finds the washboard player, Virgil Perkins and, after replacing his stolen rub board, records him singing and accompanying himself on washboard. Later, after too much beer, Charters joins in and plays the twelve-string guitar on a "wild" recording of "John Henry," which later (perhaps fraudulently) ends up on the Folkways set.

Having recounted his long and arduous search for skiffle bands — "noisy little groups that used to play on street corners in every Southern city" — Charters notes that the record was finally finished in Memphis in December 1956 and included contributions from the one-time members of the Memphis Jug Band and Cannon's Jug Stompers.

In Britain, the term "skiffle" may have been adopted fairly casually to describe the interval music played here at jazz band performances in the early Fifties. Although often associated by British skiffle performers with house-rent party music, its origins seem to be more diverse and the rent party attribution — apart from the word itself — even somewhat misleading, as British skiffle was not a piano-based music. Whatever skiffle's origins, the British product had a character all of its own and the recorded groups each had their individual sound. The use of the guitar and improvised instruments was usually part of that sound and of the special appeal of the music, particularly to the teenage amateur groups, and may be said to be defining features of the skiffle craze of the Fifties.

3 Puttin' on the Style — Britain and its Young People in the Fifties

Sandwiched between the Fighting Forties and the Swinging Sixties, the Fifties might be seen as a rather uneventful and dull decade in which to have lived. Yet images of Britain in the Fifties that challenge that supposed uneventfulness and dullness are plentiful: the Festival of Britain, the coronation of Queen Elizabeth II, the conquest of Everest, Brigitte Bardot films, *Eagle* comic, Angry Young Men, teddy boys, national service, bubble cars, the Comet jet airliner, the Suez Crisis, the Campaign for Nuclear Disarmament, Davy Crockett hats, the hula-hoop craze, television and skiffle and rock 'n' roll. Dull and uneventful it was not, and change, often for the better for the population as a whole, was in the air. However, a fuller snapshot of Fifties Britain than this is a necessary precursor to understanding how developments in popular culture, and in particular teenage culture, came about in that first post-war decade.

The Fifties may have begun with a continuation of Forties' austerity and with recovery from the shortages and destruction of the Second World War but, by the end of the decade, there had been considerable advances in living standards. Harold Macmillan's famous phrase from a 1957 Bedford speech told Britons: "Most of our people have never had it so good". Prosperity meant that the goods and pleasures of life began to be enjoyed by most people not just by a small, wealthy elite; for the Fifties witnessed the emergence of a financially better off working class, and working-class life and themes became the subject of painters, novelists, dramatists, and the film, the work of the playwrights being dubbed, somewhat dismissively, "kitchen sink" drama.

Affluence also affected Britain's young people, most of whom left school at 15 for relatively well-paid work, which gave them money to spend. This helped create a teenage market and culture that was to blossom even more in the Sixties. Young people, particularly young working-class people, started to express themselves in their own way and had the money to do so. Increasingly teenagers, as they became known, had more say in their own lives and impinged more on those around them. Those born in the Forties could easily appreciate the changes and benefits to teenagers that the Fifties, particularly the latter half of the decade, brought with them.

The Fifties was a period of great change, both nationally and internationally, and one with its share of wars, revolutions and refugees. It was a decade when the world became an even smaller place, for the press, the cinema newsreel, radio and, later in the decade, television, provided Britons with a constant view of the world and Britain's involvement in it. For a while, the names of certain foreign places and people became part of everyday life — Korea, Hungary, Malaya, Cyprus, Kenya and Suez; Jomo Kenyatta, Archbishop Makarios and Colonel Nasser.

It was a time of international political tension and of the "cold war", the confrontation between the West and Russia and its communist allies. Spying, defection and the creation of bigger nuclear deterrents by both sides replaced the battlefields of old.

European co-operation began very early in the Fifties but Britain held back. In March 1957, the Common Market — designed to abolish all trade barriers between member states — was established by the Treaty of Rome and the European Economic Community (now the European Union) came into existence in January 1958. Britain, committed to the Commonwealth, did not join until the Seventies.

In science and technology, the Fifties saw the developing use of nuclear power for both peaceful and warlike purposes, as well as the beginnings of automation and, more markedly, of the space age. As part of International Geophysical Year, 1957, a Commonwealth expedition led by Vivian Fuchs set out for the South Pole which it reached in January 1958. Brian Bird recounts that when Dr Fuchs arrived at Scott Base on Sunday 2 March 1958 after his trans-Antarctic journey, he and his colleagues were met by a pick-up skiffle group. Washboards, dustbin lids, tins and other improvised instruments, together with a trombonist, played all the group knew, including a skiffle version of "My Bonnie Lies Over the Ocean". According to Bird, " It was reported that Dr Fuchs, though disclaiming emotion, appeared close to tears!"[1]

It is impossible to think about Fifties Britain without taking into account the United States of America, which after the Second World War continued as a strong cultural influence on the rest of the world and became a major political influence in Europe and beyond. What America did one day was imitated the next elsewhere. Britons had experienced Americans and their way of life at first hand during the Second World War, when troops were stationed in their country, and this contact continued in a more limited way through the post-war American bases in Britain.

Affluent America, with its consumer society, built-in obsolescence, and teenagers who owned cars and went to drive-in movies, set the example for other countries like Britain to follow. However, Americanisation, particularly in areas of popular culture, like television and music, was not always welcomed and would be seen by some as a lowering of standards.

Perhaps giving people, especially young people, what they wanted rather than what was thought good for them (often the British attitude), was difficult for a still paternalistic and conservative establishment that directed Britain's affairs.

American influence came also via writers like Jack Kerouac (*On the Road*, 1957), whose work inspired the unconventional dress and behaviour of the beatniks of the Fifties and Sixties. Young people also identified with the Marlon Brando biker image (seen in *The Wild One*, 1954) and more particularly with the rebelliousness of James Dean portrayed in *Rebel Without a Cause* (1955).

The 1951 census showed a Britain with a population of just over fifty million where people were living longer, marrying earlier, divorcing more often, and drifting away from the traditional manufacturing industries. Some of these trends would accelerate in the coming decades. January 1955 saw the arrival of 400 Jamaicans in London looking for work; many more would come from the West Indies, Pakistan and elsewhere in the following years. Such immigration was to have considerable social, political and cultural implications for Britain. (The West Indian community would later bring reggae into the British popular music scene.)

Although there had been a post-war Labour government under Clement Attlee from 1945-51, for the rest of the Fifties (and until 1964) the Conservatives were in power. The Fifties was a decade that saw greater state involvement in people's lives and in industry. The Labour government nationalised industries, such as steel in early 1951, and increased social welfare. Under the 1946 National Insurance Act scheme, for example, which came into force in 1948, employees were provided for when sick or out of work, and would receive a state pension.

In February 1952 George VI died and his daughter succeeded to the throne as Queen Elizabeth II. The new monarch's coronation took place in June 1953 and, as the ceremony was to be televised, many people were encouraged to purchase a television set for the first time. There had been opposition to the televised coronation (fortunately overridden), which, looking back, perhaps marked the beginning of the demystification of the monarchy. Queen Elizabeth's accession was heralded as the beginning of a new Elizabethan age and, amongst other things, a children's magazine was renamed *The Elizabethan* to reflect this optimism.

In May 1959 Empire Day was renamed Commonwealth Day, recognising the changes that had taken place since, for example, India had been declared a republic within the Commonwealth in 1950. Ghana (formerly the Gold Coast) became the first independent black African colony in March 1957, while others, Malaya, Nigeria and Cyprus, followed soon after.

The optimism of a new Elizabethan Age, marked by the new queen's coronation, had been preceded by the morale-boosting Festival of Britain. Opened by King George VI in May 1951, it was visited by over eight million people. The festival, a celebration of Britain's progress and a symbol of future directions, offered the nation a different picture to the trials and tribulations of wartime and the austerity of the immediate post-war years. Features of the site were the Dome of Discovery, the Skylon, a cigar-shaped tube pointing

heavenwards and the symbol of the festival, and the Royal Festival Hall. A festival pleasure garden and fun fair were opened at Battersea in late May 1951. The Festival of Britain ended in September 1951 and most of its buildings were taken down. The Royal Festival Hall, however remained and provided a new venue for music of all kinds, including jazz and skiffle performances.

Work was easy to find in the Fifties; the idea that some kind of job would not be available was never really considered. New factories were lighter, cleaner and safer than the old ones, although working hours there and elsewhere were longer than today and holidays were usually two weeks. As regards weekly earnings and expenditure, Langley reports that: "In 1954, an average family with two children spent nearly three pounds each week on food... in the typical family only the father worked and his weekly earnings would not have been more than about ten pounds. Weekly rent for a three-bedroomed semi-detached house was between three and four pounds. Prices, wages and rents were higher in the south than in the north."[2] As to young people: "By the mid-1950s the average teenager's weekly *spending money* was over twice the *total* weekly wage he would have received in 1938."[3] By the end of the decade it was reckoned that the average manual worker was earning £13.2.11d and that the average weekly sum available for spending by young working men was around £5, by young women about £3. Between them in 1959, over four million young workers had roughly £17 million to dispose of each week.

Standards of living improved significantly in the post-war world. The National Health Service was launched in 1948 and provided free treatment from doctors, dentists and opticians but, although resented, charges were later introduced for spectacles and prescriptions. The health of children was improved by free school milk and other dietary supplements.

Because of war-time bombing, Britain needed many new schools, factories and, of course, houses, to replace those lost and to meet the requirements of a larger population with greater expectations. Hospitals were needed too to meet the requirements of welfare legislation. At the very beginning of the Fifties only just under half of British households had a bathroom.

In contrast to the past, however, new housing contained inside toilets, bathrooms, separate bedrooms for family members and gardens, even though small in size. Modern housing estates were built, often a mix of houses and high rise blocks of flats. The latter were seen as a good way of dealing with the housing demand and initially such high-rise accommodation was viewed favourably by its new tenants; but problems, such as isolation and supervising children at play, began to be revealed later.

A feature of this housing progress was the establishment of new towns, such as Corby, Harlow, Peterlee, Basildon and Crawley, with housing separate but near to factories, and the demolition of slums and older housing.

With the more general availability in the home of such appliances as electric washing machines, vacuum cleaners, electric and gas cookers, refrigerators, and water heaters, household work was made less of a chore. In the home, wartime utility materials and design gave way to new materials and more modern designs.

Britons had learned to live with the rationing of food and other goods during the Second World War but it took a further nine years before food rationing finished completely in 1954. Another vestige of the war years, the identity card, had been abolished in early 1952.

Although mass produced and cheaper than before the war, the consumer goods of the Fifties could only be afforded by some people by using a form of credit known as hire-purchase, by which the cost of goods was spread by regular payments over a number of weeks or months. Also known as the "never-never", it was important in allowing young people, for example, to buy a guitar and perhaps later an electric guitar and amplifier.

However, while life became easier in all sorts of ways, some attitudes were slow to change: for example, as regards women in society (this was the decade that launched the Miss World contest); homosexuality (the recommendation of the 1957 Wolfenden Report that homosexual acts in private be legalised was rejected); constitutional reform (reservations about the concept of monarchy were not well received); and capital punishment, which was retained — the controversial hangings of Derek Bentley, Timothy Evans and Ruth Ellis would, however, lead to its abolition in the Sixties.

Alongside home-based leisure activities and hobbies, television-viewing became a new addition to such pursuits for many people in the Fifties. Television would come to be seen as one of the greatest agents for social and cultural change, and along with radio, would help promote the new

1956 And All That: Skiffle Reminiscences

I attended Swansea Secondary Technical School for Girls from 1955 to 1960 which, although offering quite an innovative curriculum for the time, was hell-bent on turning out nice middle-class gels. In 1955, the Second World War had only been over ten years, but it was felt Britain was heading for what we assumed to be a sunny and prosperous future.

My, and my schoolfriends' part in this scenario was to fill the gap between whatever path we chose and ultimately getting married. Getting married was the goal we were to achieve, regardless of whether we were destined for Woolworths or Oxbridge in between. Discussion in most girls' bedrooms, the great unacknowledged social and cultural centres, revolved around whether you left work when you got married, or waited until you were pregnant.

In other girls' bedrooms, as well as the acoustically friendly toilet block at school, listening to records on the Dansette, doo-wop a cappella, jiving to hand claps and handjiving was the norm. Elvis and Everly Brothers were lovingly practised for public consumption in the toilet block. This was the atmosphere which prevailed at school and in which I was a passive watcher not a participator in the toilet culture.

I think I may have been regarded as a bit odd at school, although I can't remember anybody saying as much. I was an avid listener to Voice of America jazz programmes and had my first gig at a local jazz club in Swansea aged fourteen in 1958, where I played boogie piano in the interval. I was not of the Elvis/Everly culture, but I sorely missed not being part of the fun and noise in the toilet block. None of my classmates were interested in jazz. Outside of school, they back-combed their hair and wore layers of starched petticoats and v-necked sweaters, or toreador pants and flatties.

However, I dabbled in acoustic guitar and could perform Lonnie Donegan numbers quite adequately. With Christmas 1959 approaching, and my class anxious to participate in the school concert, I suggested a skiffle group. Looking back, I think it was purely in order that I could actually join in, or be part of, what all the other girls were enjoying in the toilet block — participating in music. Surprisingly, two or three of the girls said that they had guitars at home (I never knew) but couldn't play them. By the end of the week, three of us were managing to co-ordinate three chords and somebody had made a tea-chest bass. All the class sang "Rock Island Line" to our accompaniment.

Our efforts caused great excitement in the class and girls would bop or hand jive. I felt that I belonged. No longer a loner. Casting aside sulky silence to shout and encourage even greater, noisier participation from the rest of the group. If skiffle was what it took to achieve integration, that was OK by me. I remember the teachers being exceedingly disapproving and angry as skiffle was not in the academic mission statement of the school. We did not manage the Christmas concert, and our skiffle group fizzled out during the Christmas break. Some girls blossomed briefly in the toilet block or classroom until their light was dimmed by convention. Others went to mull things over for thirty-odd years

Jen Wilson

popular music, including skiffle. Outside the home, sport, going to the cinema, and the annual holiday, amongst other things, supplied people's entertainment and filled their leisure hours.

Most people holidayed in Britain, as foreign travel did not become popular until the Sixties, although within the UK, Jersey was a favoured destination. Many Britons, however, holidayed at camps provided by Butlins — the first at Skegness in 1936 — and Pontins, often sited at seaside locations. The aim of the holiday camp was to provide everything on site, including evening entertainment. The camp amateur talent contest provided an outlet for holidaymakers, including skiffle groups, to show their worth, and a number of successful professional performers — often on television — began their careers as holiday camp entertainers.

Television broadcasting began in Britain in 1936 but progress was delayed due to the war; ten years later there were fewer than 100,000 viewers and these were all in the London region. New transmitters in 1949 and the early Fifties meant that four in five of the population would have access to television. In 1950 the general election returns were televised by the BBC for the first time and in the same year the first television programme from the continent — a two-hour programme transmitted in Calais — was televised. It was also a year in which the production of television sets increased by 250 per cent, and the following year the first televised party political broadcast was made — on behalf of the Liberal Party.

In 1954 the Independent Television Authority was set up under the chairmanship of Sir Kenneth Clarke following the passing of the Television Act permitting independent television transmissions. ITV began broadcasting in September 1955 in the London area with programmes like *Take Your Pick*, *Michaela and Armand Denis*, and *I Love Lucy*.

In early 1957, the BBC got round to filling the one-hour broadcasting interval between six and seven each evening. This interval was known as "the Gap" or "Toddlers' Truce" and supposedly allowed parents time to put their children to bed. Programmes for this new slot included *Tonight*, *Gardening Club*, and, on Saturday night, *Six-Five Special* — an innovative popular music programme for young people.

By the end of the Fifties, television had established itself as a major influence for selling consumer goods, providing a platform for politics and affecting popular culture and social behaviour. It thus began to be held responsible for some of society's problems and changes; it clearly brought about the death of the variety theatre and reduced cinema attendance significantly, many eventually becoming bingo halls; then there was the loss of newspaper and magazine titles. Television also killed off the well attended Saturday morning "pictures" — special cheap cinema programmes put on for children.

Given the limitations of early television, radio was still a popular medium — the long-running radio serial, *The Archers*, began in May 1950.

1956 And All That: Skiffle Reminiscences

I was born in Liverpool in 1943 and grew up there. I had only a brief flirtation with skiffle in the 1950s when I first began to play the guitar as a thirteen-year-old lad — this would be around 1956.

Most young people of my age had seen Lonnie Donegan and Nancy Whiskey on the television — our nine-inch set was bought in 1953 for the present queen's coronation, as were the majority of television sets at that time — and heard them via records and radio. The guitar seemed to be a very glamorous instrument and many young kids, like myself, were strongly attracted to skiffle.

As wages were low at that time, and instruments fairly expensive, my dad made me a guitar from a kit bought from the "Hobbies" shop situated in Tarleton Street in central Liverpool. My "Hobbies" guitar wasn't a very good one, and very difficult to play, but it got me started.

I formed a skiffle group with other kids from school: David Slack on guitar, Peter Tear on drums, Roy Hetherington on tea-chest bass, plus myself doing vocals and playing guitar. We learned to play songs like "Freight Train", "Cumberland Gap" and "John Henry" from little books of lyrics and chords that you could buy from ordinary stationers. These were sold throughout the late Fifties and early Sixties and often included photographs and biographical details of the stars who were associated with the songs.

John Harper

However, Fifties radio is probably best remembered as the golden age of radio comedy, although the BBC was making some efforts to respond to the demands for popular music by young people. As recounted in a later chapter, skiffle was to be among the starting points for this development.

By the end of the Fifties, teenagers — of whom there were about five million at the close of decade — were healthier, better educated and more secure economically and socially. They had money, less material worry than earlier generations of young people, and time, and could therefore respond to the excitement and changes going on around them. As today, there were problems of the generation gap and the difficulties of personal relationships that beset the teenager. For the first time, perhaps, young people could establish their own separate identity through their choice of clothes, hairstyle, language, music and dance, and make themselves heard about their likes and dislikes. Teddy boys in Edwardian-style clothes, others in jeans and jumpers; girls in blouses and full skirts with many petticoats and wide waist belts. Boys' hair cut in a DA (duck's arse) or Tony Curtis hairstyle; girls with ponytails or, later in the Fifties, back-combed "beehive" hairstyles. Then there was teenage talk: "dig" — "square" — "crazy man, crazy" — "go, man, go" — and an energetic, exhausting dance style — jiving. Young people, with money and time

became the targets of fashion, broadcasting, films, records, comics and magazines.

Teenage magazines began with *Marilyn* in 1955 and grew in number and circulation and were to become dominated by pop stars and the pop world. *Mirabelle*, a new romantic picture-story weekly, first appeared in September 1956 and included amongst its picture-realism stories features on film, television and record stars, as well as hit parade news. The first issue included a David Whitfield song book supplement but in July 1957 it offered "the low-down on skiffle", with items, for example, on how to form a skiffle group, Lonnie Donegan, and skiffle fashion — skiffle hair, dress and beauty.[4] Lonnie Donegan also appeared as the subject, with "exciting glamour photos", of a booklet (No.12 in the series) in the Amalgamated Press's Fans' Star Library.

There was, however, a darker side to teenage life in the Fifties: "The violence among young people was growing. More crimes were committed by teenagers than ever before. This was believed to be caused by boredom in the young and so ways were sought to redirect their energies. These included youth clubs and the Outward Bound courses which gave youngsters a taste of adventure and taught them self-reliance."[5] Another approach was the "short, sharp shock" juvenile detention centre, the first opened in

Skiffle group formed by five members of the 48th Field Regiment serving with the British Army in Malaya, performing in front of an audience in the field, November 1957. (Courtesy Imperial War Museum.)

1952. More positively, given the concern for young people, was the Duke of Edinburgh's Award Scheme, announced in February 1956. Awards could be gained in many different pursuits, the first awards being presented at Buckingham Palace in June 1958.

National Service, which continued through most of the Fifties, was an inescapable feature of the late teenage years, although deferment was possible for various reasons: "like it or not, you had to spend two years in the Army, Navy or Air Force. If you'd left school at fifteen you faced three years at whatever job you could get, knowing that it would come to an end on your eighteenth birthday when your call-up papers arrived in the morning post."[6] National Service brought together young men from all walks of life and provided opportunities for them to form skiffle groups, performing for their fellow servicemen in the NAAFI, at ships' concerts and elsewhere.

Skiffle — the music of many teenagers — found a home in youth clubs and coffee bars and generated a demand from young people for guitars and other skiffle instruments, as well as sheet music and tutors. Skiffle came to encroach on a number of aspects of society, including, as surprising as it may seem, church music, and existed side by side with rock 'n' roll.

If Donegan's "Rock Island Line" recording marked the point in early 1956 when skiffle became public property rather than a small element of the jazz world, then the attention attracted in 1955 to "Rock Around the Clock", performed by Bill Haley and his Comets, did much the same — and to more lasting effect — for rock 'n' roll. For a while skiffle and rock co-existed, but it was rock 'n' roll that survived skiffle's commercial demise in late 1958. They had shared musical origins and, like skiffle, rock 'n' roll had a short recording history before bursting on the popular music scene.

Bill Haley was originally a country and western musician who after working in various groups formed Bill Haley and his Comets in 1953, recording "Crazy, Man, Crazy" which made the American charts because of teenage interest. In 1954 Haley signed with Decca and had a million seller with "Shake, Rattle and Roll", which was also the first of Haley's songs to make an impact in the UK in December that year. However, it was "Rock Around the Clock", featured in the film, *Blackboard Jungle*, that brought the Comets both greater fame and notoriety. The film was released in the States in February 1955 and by May the "Clock" was in the Top Ten there and stayed five months. In Britain the film and its song put "Rock Around the Clock" amongst the top sellers in October that year and the Comets' success was strengthened by the later release of a quickly and cheaply made film in which they appeared, also called *Rock Around the Clock*.

The film was released in Britain in 1956, opening in the West End. On general release "it was taken by Teddy boys, students and others as an excuse to let off some youthful high spirits. There was jiving in the streets, cases of hooliganism and overtime for the police... As a result the showing of *Rock Around the Clock* was banned in certain towns."[7] With a further entry of the "Clock" in the hit parade, as a result of the later film of that name, and of other songs, such as "See You Later, Alligator", "Razzle Dazzle", and "Rip It Up", Haley dominated the UK charts during the mid-Fifties. In February 1957 he and his Comets arrived in Britain as part of a tour that was also to take in Manila and Australia.

Haley's success was said to be based on "a lifetime finding out what the public wants — especially that powerful teenage section of the public."[8] If that was the case, he was one of the first to write popular songs expressly for teenagers. However, his age, chubby face, and kiss curl did not reflect teenage fancies or fantasies and, with the arrival of Elvis Presley in 1956, he and his Comets were soon replaced by the "King" and other rock 'n' rollers.

A sign of the times was the changed nature of the coverage of the *Melody Maker* which, once subtitled "for the best in jazz", became more orientated towards popular music. There was also journalistic competition from the *New Musical Express*, which launched the first UK pop charts.

Although teenagers had money to spend, there was little entertainment aimed at them in the early Fifties. Youth clubs and organizations, like the Scouts, were popular and it was said that: "four out of ten British teenagers belonged to some kind of club."[9] Many churches had youth clubs that met of a weekday evening or after the Sunday evening service.

However, the National Association of Mixed Clubs and Girls' Clubs, with 2000 clubs and 150,000 members, were not happy with the relevance of youth clubs of the day nor the way they were organised and run, and clubs were beginning to lose members. In 1958 it launched an appeal for £250,000 to provide one-purpose youth clubs (for specific interests); coffee-bar clubs to bring youngsters off the streets; youth workers, visiting clubs (clubs without walls); house groups (to listen to records); and bridge-builders — those linking youngsters and the official organisations that deal with them. A *Daily Herald* reporter conducted his own survey around the country as to why young people preferred coffee-bars to youth clubs and found that youth clubs were too much like school. His conclusion was that youth clubs "could be a success if the people running them forgot about education and social reclamation and provided an informal meeting-place where youngsters can hear their favourite records and music in a carefree, possibly exciting atmosphere."[10] It was this change that the Association was trying to achieve with its experimental programme.

What is not usually appreciated is that Lonnie Donegan founded a number of skiffle and folk music clubs around the country in towns such as Bristol, Cardiff, Birmingham, Liverpool, Manchester and Leeds. There was also a Shrewsbury club in a college for the blind.

In fact whenever Donegan played a new town he liked to form a club there. Because of his regard for his fans, he preferred doing this to the usual fan club approach. Amongst other activities, such as learning to play the guitar, and learning about American jazz and folk, the clubs ran their own talent contests and visited local hospitals. They were thus rather like the single-interest type of club that the NAMCGC had proposed in its programme of change.

As organised in 1958, the skiffle clubs each had their own committee, which was responsible to the main London office, and which met monthly or fortnightly. Each club member paid a shilling a week subscription to meet expenses. As most of these clubs had not been in existence long in 1958, Donegan paid for the hall hire and intended to do so until the clubs could pay their own way.

When Lonnie Donegan was in one of his club towns, he held an informal meeting and all the club members were invited. New Donegan releases were also sent to each club for it to build up a library of his recordings.[11] Mick Groves of the well-known Spinners folk group "was secretary of the Liverpool branch of Lonnie's club at the Cavern, which at one time even numbered Paul McCartney and George Harrison among its members."[12]

Playing skiffle made its mark there in the ordinary youth club too, reversing the process whereby adult leaders decided and provided activities. Apparently welcomed by many youth leaders and often encouraged, the challenge to develop music-making as a youth club activity which skiffle had begun, was nonetheless not taken up.[13]

Teenagers who were too young for the pub, frequented milk bars and coffee bars, drinking milkshakes, coffee or a bottled drink like Coca-Cola. A common decor of cane furniture and potted plants would be dominated by a juke box and the Gaggia machine hissing frothy coffee into perspex cups. Happy the coffee bar owner with a basement that could be used for live

Cartoon from *Punch*, 20 November 1957. (Courtesy *Punch*.)

musical entertainment, although even without such a space, a solo artist or duo might be accommodated in the coffee bar proper at certain times such as a Saturday night.

In lieu of live music, the coffee bar juke box offered a numbered and regularly changed selection of the latest pop records. Putting the appropriate money in allowed either a single or multiple choice of tunes.

Three contemporary views of the fashion for coffee bars and their music have been culled from Fifties issues of the humorous magazine, *Punch*, which looked at the phenomenon generally and at Soho in particular.

Following comments about decor, staff and catering, *Punch's* 1956 writer notes that coffee-bars "are an unstable form of business and tend not to remain coffee bars for long." If the owner is not careful, they can easily turn into a restaurant, caff, jazz club or youth hostel. The jazz club will be the inevitable result of hiring an Old Etonian with a guitar but: "The very first evening he fails to turn up (having gone to his sister's coming-out dance) endless offers of substitutes will pour in, from another Old Etonian to a four-piece skiffle-group. One should engage the skiffle-group; they play for fun and do not need the money as much as the Old Etonian. They can be housed in the cellar and two shillings entrance-fee charged to customers wanting to go and hear them. Also coffee in the cellar can be a shilling instead of ninepence."[14]

A later issue of *Punch* prints the lyrics for "Coffee-House Rock", in which a daughter replies to her mother's accusation that she's going "To mix with the riffraff in the coffee-bar" by supposedly singing: "Don't knock the coffee-bars, Momma, / No, / Don't knock the coffee-bars, Momma! / They give the modern generation the same old lift / That they once gave squares like Addison and Swift..."

Momma decides to investigate the coffee-bar fashion herself and then responds: "I won't knock the coffee-bars, Baby, / No, / I *won't* knock the coffee-bars, Baby! / I've discovered it's the same old basic old squeal / If you give it for Sir Richard or for Tommy Steele. / Comparing Lonnie Donegan with Garrick, / It's Lonnie makes my old heart ache; /... So I won't knock the coffee-bars, Baby, / 'Cause this is what I aim to do — / Going to buy a scarlet sweater and a second-hand Lambretta / And hit that old Expresso till I'm coffee solid through, / And I'll never knock the coffee-bars, Baby, / For I guess I belong there too!"[15]

Another *Punch* writer visited several coffee bars in Soho in January 1958 and, like a latter-day Mayhew, commented on their cramped, ill-lit premises, filled with continuous loud music rendering conversation nigh impossible. The writer found that the frequenters of these places were mainly between fourteen and twenty, seventeen being the most usual age. Coffee at a shilling a cup was consumed slowly and music was often provided by a juke-box. "At other times the music emanates, through loud-speakers, from some dim, hidden recess in the coffee-house where a party of musicians are performing upon stringed instruments and howling,

2 I's Coffee Bar, Old Compton Street, London, c. 1956-7. (Courtesy Topham Picture Library.)

in a nasal, unmusical fashion difficult to define, snatches of a rhythmic ballad, the name of which I was unable to ascertain... These 'numbers', as they are called, had their origin many years ago... in the United States of America; recently, however, a claim seems to have been made out that they are part of the 'folk music' of Finchley, Walsall, Birkenhead, or East Croydon."

This coffee-bar crawler's last visit was to one with a basement, accessible on payment of three shillings and sixpence, and accommodating about one hundred young people in a hot, low-ceilinged room of thirty by twelve feet, full of pounding music. The writer unappreciatively views (and listens to) the scene: "upon a small rostrum, two wild-eyed musicians were savagely belabouring a guitar and a double bass, while a third shrieked into a microphone... The resulting bedlam of rattling din crashed and rebounded from every wall out of at least four amplifiers; so that the tiny cavern seemed likely to burst asunder at any moment from the very pressure of sound... It was now ten o'clock at night." He concludes: "In all my investigations of the night life of London I have observed no scene more harmless: and yet, for a reason which I am at loss to explain, I found it infinitely sad. I can but hope that they gain some temporary happiness during their mysterious rites; for their lives must be drab indeed if they are driven to seek release in such surroundings."[16]

Wally Whyton is quoted as describing the 2 I's coffee bar as being "remarkably small. Upstairs you could get ten people sitting along the front of the counter. Downstairs, it was a long narrow room, 12 feet wide and 20 feet long. It was run like a variety theatre (we sometimes had two houses) where we sang from 7 'till 9, and then from 9.30 'till 11.30. People would queue round the block to see us."[17]

Sometimes the playing of music in coffee-bars met with local opposition when licences were requested. *The Times* recorded in 1957 that the Witch's Cauldron, a coffee-bar and restaurant in north-west London, had met with such opposition. Objectors complained that it would cause noise and attract noisy people, with one indicating that they did not want "'squiffle' or other variants of rock 'n' roll." The coffee-bar owners (who were granted a licence with certain restrictions) "thought their enterprise would have a beneficial effect and take young people off the streets."[18]

In the early Fifties dance halls were not aimed at teenagers and only allowed the established ball room dances but gradually jiving was permitted, as was skiffle and rock 'n' roll. For a variety of reasons, the days of the dance band and dancing at the local palais were in decline in the post-war era. However, ballroom dancing was still a formal event in the early Fifties and men and women dressed up for the occasion and endeavoured to follow the stylised movements of dances like the waltz, foxtrot, quickstep, rhumba and tango. Such dances, while never entirely disappearing, began to be replaced among young people by the less formal styles of the decade.

Ken Mackintosh wrote and recorded the "Creep" in early 1954 which started a short-lived dance craze. The end of 1954 saw the arrival of rock 'n' roll and the mambo, with the mambo initially triumphing over rock on the dance floor. *Rock Around the Clock* and other films demonstrated to British teenagers how to jive to rock music, as later did *Six-Five Special*. In 1957 a newspaper reported that Nottingham school children spent their lunch hours at 3d rock 'n' roll sessions and came back late and exhausted to school. "Stop-the-rock" circulars were sent to parents by three head-masters but in one batch of replies only 20 parents out of 140 respondents were in favour.[19]

Jiving to rock music brought teenagers, including school children, into the dance halls and delayed their decline. Jiving was not a new form of dance — similar dances had been danced since the Thirties — but, while eschewing the acrobatics of the professional dancer, most people could master the basic movements of this energetic and enjoyable dance. Dancers also found that jive could be adapted to suit both the rhythms of skiffle and the trad jazz boom of the late Fifties.

However, before the Twist was launched in the USA in 1960, becoming a short-lived fashion in the UK, many young people tried to learn some of the steps of the Cha Cha which became fashionable in late 1958. With the advent of the Twist, the necessity to touch your dance partner (or of even having a partner) disappeared and not touching became the norm.[20]

Listening to skiffle groups in coffee bars, however, it was usually impossible to dance and so someone came up with a dance that you could do sitting down — the hand jive — which consisted of a series of hand and arm movements orchestrated as a routine.[21] Out of the one routine others developed each with its own movements and name, such as "Coffee Bar Hand Jive", the "Juke Box", the "Espresso", and the "6.5 Hand Jive". Television spread the craze to its many young viewers.[22]

By December 1956 "skiffle" guitars were being offered for sale. At Stanley Lewis, Edgeware Road, they could be bought outright from £5. 17. 6d. or as special lines of top quality from £10, or 3/9d. weekly. Thus amongst those things that could be bought on the "never-never" was that increasingly fashionable teenage accessory, the guitar. In February 1957, the Paramount Musical Instrument Co. of Shaftesbury Avenue announced the arrival of fifty skiffle guitars, costing from £6. 6. 0d. to £6. 12. 6d. The Headquarter and General Supplies company were regular advertisers of guitars for sale by post. An early March 1958 advertisement offered a guitar (said to be recommended by Lonnie Donegan) at £6. 6. 0d. or it would be sent for 5/-down (plus 5/- postage and packing) and twenty-two fortnightly payments of 6/6d. — there was a free gift of a coloured skiffle sash. Woolworths, ever conscious of a trend, offered an almost as cheap, but not necessarily viable alternative, as witness this 1956 testimony: "they had [guitars] in the window at Woolies and they were £6 19s 6d. It was your wildest dream until you got it home and you started to press down those three strings to make an A. Goodness me, I remember it actually shredding your fingers. What do you expect with a guitar that cost £6 19s 6d?"[23] In fairness to Woolies it must be said that sensitive fingertips took time to harden-up, whatever the quality of the guitar, when getting use to playing all-steel strings. If skifflers had the money, then cello guitars in a variety of models were available but more expensive at, for example, £16. 16. 0d. The Zenith Josh White guitar ("ideal for skiffle groups"), and available in late 1957, was even dearer at £24. 15. 0d.

If you wanted to make your own Spanish guitar ("star of any skiffle group"), then Hobbies Ltd of Norfolk would send you a kit for 50/6d. complete. If the best possible strings were wanted, then Cathedral, manufacturer of guitar strings, offered skiffle guitar strings at 8/- a set — "built especially for robust skiffle rhythms".

The popularity of the guitar had begun in the early Fifties and had blossomed beyond all expectations by the approach of the Sixties. In 1954 guitar sales were double that of 1953 and 1955 sales were up 150 per cent on those for 1954. Sales for 1956, however — the year skiffle burst on the scene — were five times greater than 1955. By 1957 the demand for the guitar had reached boom proportions both in the United Kingdom and the rest of Europe.[24] Even *The Times* in 1957 acknowledged its popularity when a correspondent wrote that his teenage daughter was learning the guitar

1956 And All That: Skiffle Reminiscences

I'm a Fulham lad who left school at fourteen, beginning work in 1956 at the age of fifteen in a laundry. I was a record buyer and Frankie Laine fan since I was about ten. Then came Donegan, "Rock Island Line", and the attraction of the guitar. I had to have a guitar and went to the West End and bought one instead of saving for a motor bike. Someone taught me to tune it and I began to play old songs like "Show Me the Way to Go Home". Then came skiffle.

Once in North End Road, Fulham in 1956 I saw a group of bearded, corduroyed young men thrashing away on guitars and the energy they let off made me want to do the same.

My first skiffle group was called Duffy Howard and the Amigos and consisted of my brother and a couple of other kids. We had a tea-chest bass, a barrel as a drum and a guitar which I played. My proper name is Ray Howard but I was nicknamed Duffy after the screen star Howard Duff — the surname Power came later.

By the spring of 1957 we were playing for money outside pubs round Fulham (as we were underaged and unable to play inside), and sometimes in the walkway under Putney Bridge because of the lovely echo there.

After a skiffle session I would go to bed that night and my head would be filled with the sound of skiffle guitars and in my dreams I would still be strumming and singing. I loved the smell of new guitars, albeit they were cheap ones and later the sheer magic of an old guitar. I remember that the only guitar strings you could buy back then were called Cathedral. The Amigos were superseded in February 1958 by the Dreamers Skiffle Group, with my brother and John Maycock — my first real guitarist.

Duffy Power

Below: guitar adverts, 1957.

along, it would seem, with every other youngster. He noted that their musical aspirations may be either towards skiffle or Segovia but that guitarists took their music seriously. The correspondent suggested there was a direct correlation between guitar-playing and the post-war young person's lack of interest in politics; in an unsatisfactory world the young turn their energies to music-making. "If, in fact, they are merely strumming while Rome burns, they do no better than their elders who call neither for guitars nor the fire brigade." [25]

A similar boom story had unfolded in the USA. In 1952 Americans spent eleven and a half million dollars on guitars and by 1957 this had risen to twenty-two million dollars. In the late Fifties there were reckoned to be four and a half million amateur guitarists in the States and annual sales of the instrument totalled 350,000. Credit for this interest in the guitar was given to factors as diverse as rock 'n' rollers (especially Elvis Presley); the folksong renaissance; the press attention given to popular singers like Ricky Nelson; Arthur Godfrey and his ukulele (good for ukuleles too?); television; big beat exponents, and the wide acceptance of country and western music. [26]

Thus the guitar established itself in the Fifties, to become thereafter, in the words of Ivor Mairants: "a household musical instrument second only in number of players to the piano and perhaps rising to become the world's most popular?" [27] For the demand for the guitar carried on into the Sixties and beyond to the present day. In his biography of the Beatles, Philip Norman gives some idea of the demand for the guitar in the skiffle-crazed Fifties in his description of Hessy's, the central Liverpool music shop, where: "Frank Hessy, the owner, was sending a van regularly down to London to buy up every one to be found in the Soho street markets. Jim Gretty, his showroom manager, was selling roughly one guitar a minute

from the hundreds festooned along the narrow shop wall. Jim was himself a guitarist, Western-style, and each week held a beginners' class in an upstairs room, chalking huge elementary chord-shapes on the wall."[28]

In the early to mid-Sixties, the guitar was claimed to be the biggest selling instrument in the world with, according to Ivor Mairants, American sales of around five million and British sales approaching the million.[29]

In an internal 1962 BBC memo, offering information to support the suggested return of *Guitar Club*, producer John Kingdon notes that Selmers were selling twenty thousand guitars a year (with monthly sales of twelve thousand pounds) and estimated that some fifty thousand were sold yearly. "Staggering figure, eh?" was Kingdom's final comment,[30] although the last figures seems a rather low estimate, if Selmers alone was selling twenty thousand.

Figures for the Nineties, supplied by the Music Industries Association, guestimate that 273,700 acoustic and electric guitars were sold in 1994. No longer as high as earlier estimates but outstripping all other instruments with the exception of the portable keyboard.

Other instruments offered for sale in the Fifties for playing skiffle included the skiffle bassello, mentioned earlier, the skiffle board (from Len Wood, Shaftesbury Avenue, at 37/6d.) complete with drum, sticks, hooter, cowbell, washboard, etc, and, from Lovells of Peckham, a skiffle drum set (full-size, glitter finish drum, cymbal and high-hat) at £29 or £3 deposit and twelve monthly payments of £2. 11. 9d.

Not only did would-be skifflers need guitars and other kit, but they also needed guidance about music and how to play skiffle, in order to try to reproduce the songs they heard on records. Many young people knew absolutely nothing about the guitar and music and, while taking down the words from a record could be done, it was time-consuming and the vocal clarity of the singer sometimes left something to be desired.

To cater for these song needs, both sheet music for individual tunes and song albums were produced by the music publishers. Ken Colyer (Dash Music), Lonnie Donegan (Essex Music), Chas McDevitt (Lawrence Wright), Alan Lomax and the Ramblers (Feldman), the Vipers (Essex Music) and others all had song albums issued, usually covering their recorded repertoire. Skiffle even got the arrangement treatment when Campbell and Connelly announced two brand new arrangements suitable for skiffle groups — "Mama Don't Allow It" and "Honeycomb" — at 4/- per set.

A number of song compendiums were also published, one *Skiffle Galaxy* (Essex Music), featured songs performed by six of the leading skiffle groups, while *Skiffle Hit Parade* (Essex Music) gave the buyer eighteen skiffle songs for 3/-. Another collection, *Album of Music for Skiffle Groups* (Francis Day & Hunter) was an obvious culling of eleven songs from the firm's back catalogue, only three of which, according to the *Melody Maker*, might conceivably be adapted to skiffle: "Frankie and Johnny" (recorded by Donegan), "Steamboat Bill", and "Turkey in the Straw". As the *MM* explained: "A new feature [of the album], however, is the washboard part with hints on loud and heavy 'hits' and 'strokes' across the corrugated surface." Tongue-in-cheek, it adds: "This alone might commend the book to would-be skifflers anxious to wrestle with the complexities of this most basic of all instruments."[31] Writing in the same paper later in the year, Steve Race reported details of a recent letter in *Weekend*, where a reader had enquired about how to tune a washboard for use in a skiffle group. Steve commented: "Poor reader: someone must have sold him an F sharp washboard."[32]

Steve Race's *Weekend* reader sounded as if he was in need of Bob Cort's booklet, *How to Play Skiffle Successfully*, which claimed not to be a music or guitar tutor but an introduction to skiffle, with practical answers to all the most frequently asked questions put to Bob Cort about playing skiffle. The booklet described what instruments were needed, how to buy them and learn to play them, and how to play some well-known songs as a group, with tips on their presentation.

Cort emphasised that it was "the spirit which gave the skiffle group its essential flavour" not particular tunes or sound, that skiffle was party music and should be entertaining. Folk songs with their choruses allowed people to join in, which is what they want to do at parties, and that scout, student, boat and rugger club songs could make skiffle material. A feature of the booklet was its simply laid-out songs with words below chord names and

1956 And All That: Skiffle Reminiscences

I was given my first guitar, a Bells-Napoli, for Christmas in 1957, and with it came a guitar tutor, probably by Dick Sadler. Most tutors in those days were particularly difficult to work through, especially on your own, and really only covered such aspects of guitar playing as jazz, dance band, or classical. My playing progressed slowly until Bob Cort's book, How to Play Skiffle Successfully, *was published. Here were real and exciting songs that were great to perform, not obscure and difficult chord progressions. For though not strictly a guitar tutor, the playing instructions were easy to relate to and understand. This got me going quickly in the right direction and before long I was also in possession of a couple of Lonnie Donegan song books. I was away!*

Geoff Harrris

In the mid-Fifties I spent a year in hospital after contracting polio and, on my discharge, I had a lot of time on my hands, despite the physio and occupational therapy. I had always had an interest in popular music, and, during my teens, this had matured into an interest in jazz.

With time on my hands. I realised that I had an opportunity to learn an instrument, but my choice was limited by a lack of lung power — I had been in an iron lung for two months. However, I reckoned I could cope with a guitar and I purchased an acoustic guitar and a book of chords, nearly driving my mother mad in attempting to master "Home on the Range" and its three chords. Eventually I got there, and then Lonnie Donegan's "Rock Island Line" shot to the top of the charts and the skiffle craze had started.

I found that I had three friends who knew my three chords and, with the addition of a tea-chest bass and a snare drummer, the Crescendo Skiffle Group was born. We never did have a washboard, which meant we were considered very progressive.

Tim Mallinson

fingering symbols for guitar. Another publication issued around the same time was the *Skif-Rok Guitar Tutor* (Southern Music, 3/-).

Both of these aids for the would-be skiffler and guitarist have long since been forgotten, overshadowed by Bert Weedon's guitar tutor *Play in a Day* published by Chappell. This tutor, first published in 1957, and meant for would-be jazz, skiffle and dance band guitarists, was the one used by the likes of Paul McCartney, George Harrison, Eric Clapton and Pete Townsend. In its thirtieth anniversary edition in 1987 — its section on skiffle had been dropped earlier on — it was noted that the tutor had been published in several languages and had sold over two million copies.

Southern Music were the publishers of Jack Good's *Hand-Jive at 6.5*, (price 3/-), advertised as describing and illustrating all movements fully and including "Formation Hand Jive". Every aspect of the popular music scene however small was, it would seem, capable of exploitation.

According to Max Jones, the popularity of skiffle in 1957 was saving sheet music by reviving slumping sales. Skiffle had triggered a boom in sheet music, as skiffle albums were doing big business. A Lonnie Donegan song collection, containing "Rock Island Line" and others, had reached sales of 50,000 copies at 2/6d. each.[33]

Skiffle might be said to have really achieved recognition when it became the subject of a 125-page illustrated book on the subject, published in 1958 — Brian Bird's *Skiffle: The Story of Folk-Song with a Jazz Beat* (Robert Hale, 10s 6d), with a foreword by Lonnie Donegan. However, at the time of its publication, Bob Dawbarn in the *Melody Maker* thought it was a year too late, as by then the skiffle craze had gone the way of all other crazes.[34] This was clearly true in terms of the commercial popular music world and therefore possibly lessened the impact the book might have made. Probably commissioned in 1957, when the skiffle craze was at its height, its author felt there was an assured future for skiffle, while recognising it would branch out and develop in various directions, such as the blues, country, folk and church music. In this latter respect he proved correct but the skiffle of acoustic guitars, washboard and tea-chest bass did not live on as the major popular music force that it had once been.

Much of Bird's book is about jazz, rather than skiffle — there is even a chapter on running a jazz club. However, the author offers some advice on forming a skiffle group in one chapter and in another gives brief descriptions and photographs of the leading skiffle groups of the day. In a final section, Bird considers the attraction of skiffle, its future ("skiffle will not die"), and quite naturally as a clergyman, the jazz or skiffle mass. A more substantial review than Dawbarn's notice was that by *Jazz Journal*'s Tony Standish, who was very critical of the book's contents: "His [Bird's] observations are neither profound nor always correct... and a dangerous naiveté pervades his approach to the entire subject of jazz." Standish complains that: "In addition to the hoary clichés... the prose is spotted with descriptions of the Negro and his music that might be right out of Beecher Stowe." When it comes to Bird's descriptions of leading skiffle groups, Standish nails his colours firmly to the mast, applauding the entertainment given by the likes of Colyer, Barber, Donegan, the City Ramblers and the 2.19 and Eden Street skiffle groups, but scornful of the "corn" from Bob Cort, the Vipers, Les Hobeaux and Chas McDevitt, all of whom he saw as helping to kill off skiffle.[35] In spite of these criticisms, Brian Bird's enthusiasm for skiffle and jazz comes across and it is always difficult to be the first to write about a new subject and to do so without the perspective that is given by time.

The Fifties threw up criticism of church services, saying that the words and actions of the clergy in the sanctuary were remote and that the nature of the music did not encourage participation by the congregation. Since those days, much has changed, so that congregations are increasingly participants in, and not merely observers of and listeners to, what takes place.

It is not too fanciful, perhaps, to see skiffle as contributing towards this movement for less stuffy church services, that made use of modern musical forms and instruments with more appeal (particularly to young people), and allowed more participation by the congregation. The popularisation of amateur music-making, which began with skiffle, coincided with changes that were afoot in the Anglican Church — changes that brought the celebrant at holy communion down from the sanctuary to face the people at a nave altar and provided the congregation with rhythmic, catchy music that encouraged people to join in.

A major sign of this change was the composition, publication and recording of Geoffrey Beaumont's *Twentieth-Century Folk Mass*, considered controversial at the time. Published in 1957, the mass is interestingly sub-titled as a mass for one or more cantors and congregation.[36] Beaumont felt that church music was dated but that church music with a jazz beat — his mass became known as the jazz or skiffle mass — would attract young people to services.

Then, as now, the BBC played a major role in reflecting changes in aspects of national life, and its Religious Department approved the *Twentieth-Century Folk Mass*. It was thus televised as the setting for an Anglican service of holy communion from St Augustine's Church, Highgate at 6.30 p.m. on Sunday 13 October 1957. While the televised version used a twenty-five-piece orchestra that included drums, guitar, saxophone, trumpet, strings and the Peter Knight Singers, Beaumont had devised his mass essentially for amateurs. As vicar of St George's Church, Camberwell he had rehearsed the work with a local skiffle group; a photograph of the occasion shows Beaumont at the piano singing lustily to the accompaniment of three guitarists and tea-chest bassist, all adding their voices to the performance.[37] Indeed, it was said that the mass was written in response to East End teenagers' request for a service with their sort of music.

As might be expected, views about the jazz or skiffle mass polarised. There were those who found it nauseating, too complicated, the music inappropriate, going on for too long in places, or who called it Julian Slade rather than jazz. Others felt young people should be able to express themselves and worship in words and music they understood, that the mass was enlivening and charming. Steve Race, jazz pianist and Methodist youth leader, endorsed the aims of the composition because the church lagged behind popular taste, but did not think that Beaumont had got the relationship of words to music right: "Musically I should say the composer jumps between Ivor Novello, Gershwin and Moodie [sic] and Sankey".[38]

An American reviewer of the work, while not entirely unsympathetic, could not see how jazz, with its particular origins, could "have much to do with the 'folk' music of those making up an average parish in the Church

of England." He humbly advised any reader putting it on in his own church in the States to have a new post lined up for the Sunday after.[39]

A review of the television broadcast in the *Musical Times* reflected a battle of tradition and change that continues today. The reviewer found the work cliché-ridden and banal and said it would have been out of place and incongruous even if the folk mass had been the best of its type. The reviewer of the music score in the same issue was not enamoured of it either and at first glance had felt it impossible to review seriously. The reviewer ended a little more constructively, however, by wondering whether there was a living composer who could rise to the challenge and write something attractive to, and singable by, the ordinary churchgoer.[40] Even more scathing, snooty and high-minded was the long anonymous editorial in *Musical Opinion*: "Bad? Of course it is bad, as every church musician, every clergyman with the slightest pretensions to culture and good taste will immediately admit. But unfortunately there are those who cannot instantly recognise bad taste." Damned for its associations with music of the dance hall, the radio band and television show, the author ends by offering a couple of revisions: "Now, doesn't that go better, Mr Beaumont?" he enquires.[41]

A much more favourable view of the *Twentieth-Century Folk Mass* was taken by a writer in another issue of *Musical Opinion*, published nearly two years later in October 1959, who makes many telling points that could also be used to rebut the criticism levelled at amateur music-making, whether church music, skiffle, rock or jazz. "This is the age of do-it-your-self... Before, a few did things beautifully, and the many were content to

HARDWARE

The Music Shop

have it done, for they did little... Not only do we want to sing ourselves, we want to sing songs with which we can identify ourselves; not the songs of a past age, or an alien taste."[42]

Cartoon by Thelwell from *Punch* 24 July 1957. (Courtesy *Punch*.)

Since those days hymn books often include new popular tunes (together with guitar chords), which are aimed particularly at young people, alongside old favourites, and suggest accompaniment by instruments other than the piano or organ.

In 1957 skiffle became well and truly established in the national psyche as a genre of popular music — the Salvation Army had its Hallelujah Skiffle Group, a washboard appeared in a Boy Scout Gang Show song, and Peter Sellers recorded "Any Old Iron" with a skiffle accompaniment (the Mate's Spoffle Group featuring Fred Spoons). In May 1957 *Reveille* published a four-page pull-out featuring Lonnie Donegan (a "skiffle is my life" follow-up was promised for the following week), details of where skiffle was being played around Britain, the correct dress for skiffling ("lightly and loosely clad, Bernice and Michael find dancing is fun in a skiffle cellar"), how to play skiffle, and brief biographies of the other skiffle groups, as well as their line-ups.[43]

In August that year, readers of *Woman* magazine were offered advice on how to plan "your outdoor skiffle party", that included guidance on what to wear, making a barbecue, skiffle records and DIY music.[44] The woman's page in the *Daily Herald* for 25 September 1957 promised that the skiffle separates it described would make the reader the belle of the ball. The separates consisted of a skiffle sweater and skirt dotted with felt outlines of washboards, guitars, tea-chest basses, palm trees and maracas!

Good for the calypso as well, apparently. Everybody from the Duke of Bedford to the reader of the newspaper's kid was said to be skiffling and this was "a gay rig for those lively evenings ahead" that would stand out amongst the jeans and the T-shirts and be quickly copied by other girls.[45]

Skiffle also engaged the humorists in 1957 and 1958 and cartoonists in *Punch* and the new television magazine, *TV Times*, and elsewhere, found something to be funny about, and as might be expected, usually touching on the washboard and tea-chest bass.

There was also a children's novel by Valerie Hastings called *Jo and the Skiffle Group* published in 1958. The plot involves a skiffle group which performs at the Blue Parrot coffee bar. Don Watson, who plays guitar and sings, is the leader of the group.[46]

Advertisements too made use of the popularity of skiffle. Kellogg's Rice Crispies offered a free skiffle whistle in every packet for a short time in October 1957. The Gramophone Shop in London, under the rubric of "Siegfried or Skiffle?", advertised the range of its stock ("kazoo to Grand Opera or the keyboard to the washboard"), and the quality of its service both in-shop and postal. The makers of the Walter 303 tape recorder used a picture of young people (apparently) playing skiffle in an 1958 advertisement in the *Melody Maker* to promote the sale of the machine: "Every record you make... is a winner — skiffle, vocalising, amateur dramatics, jazz or serious."

In mid-1957, the "bands" column in the *Melody Maker* was used — at 8d. a word — to advertise the availability of the Riversiders and Sunrisers skiffle groups. Listed among advertisements for Eric Silk's Southern Jazz Band and Lou Preager's Ambassadors Band, skiffle may really be said to have come of age.[47]

Although its achievements can be recognised, by 1959 the mood, fashions and character of Britain in the Fifties were changing. John Elliot, introducing his dramatised documentary, *Roundabout*, an impression of youth of the day, wrote in the *Radio Times*: "This is a new generation. The teddy gang is out, the Italian jacket is in, the motor-scooter is in. Skiffle is on the way out, slums are on the way out. There are new tunes, new homes, new roads opening up. In spite of that, the juvenile crime rate is higher than ever, children and parents awkward as ever. Jobs are harder to find, money not quite so easy to come by. The H-bomb is still with us; life doesn't get any easier to understand, and to be adolescent is still to be uneasily between two worlds."[48] A rather pessimistic view for the end of the Fifties but indicative that not everything had stood still in a decade that was perhaps like a preparation, or dress rehearsal, for the Swinging Sixties to follow, when the cult of the teenager would intensify even more.

4 The Big Four — Skiffle in the Hit Parade

From about mid-1956 Donegan was becoming firmly established as a force in popular music through his skiffle records. A few other skiffle groups would also achieve a showing in the record charts of the period — the Vipers, Chas McDevitt and Nancy Whiskey, and Johnny Duncan and his Blue Grass Boys. Of all these artists, Donegan was to be by far the most successful commercially, finding work in variety, pantomime and television, as well as continuing to have chart successes until 1962. Because of the skiffle craze, however, all of these groups, as well as many others, achieved a certain amount of national fame through radio, television, concert and variety appearances, as well as on record.

While enjoying less popular, commercial success, the historical importance of Ken Colyer, Alexis Korner and Chris Barber to skiffle demands some account of their continuing involvement. For different reasons both Korner and Barber gave up on skiffle during the craze they had helped to start, and Colyer's brand of skiffle seemed untouched by it.

After his earlier Fifties recordings, Colyer recorded three further skiffle sessions for Decca. The first, on 25 May 1956, and without Korner this time, saw the recording of four sides — "Old Riley", "Down Bound Train", "Stack-O-Lee Blues" and "Muleskinner Blues" — the other personnel being Colin Bowden (washboard), John Bastable (banjo) and Donegan's bassist-to-be, Micky Ashman, Dick Smith having left for the Barber band. The second session, on 12 March 1957, and the third, on 11 November 1957, involved Colyer, Bowden, and Bastable, with Ron Ward on bass instead of Ashman; these last two sessions included Bob Kelly (piano), who was also featured in the only instrumental, "House Rent Stomp".

Reviewing the reissued Decca skiffle sessions of 1954-57, a writer in *Folk Roots*, contrasted the "wild'" man Donegan, and his hard-edged delivery, with the serious approach and the natural and relaxed singing of Colyer.[1] Another writer, reviewing the same reissue, perhaps damns Colyer with faint praise by calling him "a perfectly pleasant and competent singer".[2] Contemporary reviewers of the Colyer skiffle *oeuvre* in the *Gramophone* and *Jazz Journal* varied in their response, one recognising Ken's obvious sincerity and commending a particular set of songs, while two others used the Memphis Jug Band as a yardstick, with one criticising tempo, treatment, rhythm, accenting, tone and emotion. A fourth queried whether Englishmen could approach the quality of black American singing. Another, more favourably inclined, wrote: "At a time when much amateur talent is masquerading under the name of skiffle, it is a pleasure to hear this Ken Colyer group managing to capture the spirit of this popular form of jazz."[3]

Ken Colyer's Jazzmen and Skiffle Group had a regular performance venue at the Ken Colyer Club, Studio 51 in Great Newport Street. Founded around 1956 by Colyer, it was a small cellar club on the fringes of Soho, and was an important venue for traditional jazz in 1957 and 1958, featuring blues and boogie, as well as skiffle. Reviewing the Colyer band in mid-1956, John Reddihough commented on the distinctive sound of the skiffle group, with Reddihough remembering Big Bill Broonzy's appreciation of Ken's style. Reddihough wrote that Colyer sang and played guitar in the same relaxed way as his lead trumpet playing and that his delivery was soft and "lazy", as is the case, he noted, in good blues singing.[4] Soft and lazy was not, however, what seemed to appeal generally to young people, who took more to the excitement generated by Donegan.

Skiffle was also included in other Colyer band dates, such as a Sunday afternoon performance at the Adelphi Theatre, featuring also the Omega Brass Band, in March 1957, and Skiffle Session No. 5, together with the Vipers and Bob Cort, at the Royal Festival Hall Recital Room in January 1957, compèred by Ken Sykora. Ken Colyer's Jazzmen and his Skiffle Group also featured in a George Lewis concert át the Manchester Free Trade Hall in 1957.

In Hamburg, in March 1958, the Colyer Skiffle Group recorded three tracks: "Ham 'n Eggs", "Nobody Knows the Trouble I've Seen" and "Down by the Riverside". The group on this occasion comprised Colyer, Bastable, Ward and Bowden, with Ray Foxley on piano.

Colyer was still playing skiffle at the end of 1958, when commercially it was over, as an announcement in the *Melody Maker* for the Ken Colyer Jazzmen and Skiffle Group at the Poplar Civic Theatre in December, made clear.

The music press of the early Sixties recorded Colyer's continuing loyalty to New Orleans jazz (he saw himself as "keeper of the flame") and of the snubs he received. Omission from the Royal Variety Show 1961, at the height of the trad fad, and little airtime — two broadcasts in four years.[5] Ken was not one for publicity, however, and was happy as long as he and the band could earn a reasonable living and enjoy themselves playing; he could be relied on apparently to bring in a good club crowd.

In August 1964 Colyer revived his skiffle group, made up of himself (twelve-string guitar, vocals), Sammy Rimington (mandolin) and John Bastable (banjo). For the recordings the following year Bill Cole played bass but there was no percussion. Colyer restarted the group mostly because of enquiries from fans who remembered it from the Fifties, but also because of the then current interest in the blues and their origins, and because Ken himself enjoyed playing it. He reported that a twenty-minute spot by the skiffle group was performed at most shows and was going down well.[6]

Wandering, an LP featuring this latter-day Ken Colyer Skiffle Group was recorded at Twickenham in July 1965 for KC Records, Colyer's own label. It was re-issued in 1996 together with four tracks from an EP recorded on the same date as *Wandering*. There were some old favourites on the two discs, like "Muleskinner Blues" and "I Can't Sleep", but also new material such as "Drop Down Mama", "Poor Howard" and "Easy Ridin' Buggy". Four were Ledbetter numbers, four traditional songs ("Colorado Trail" has traditional words to a Colyer tune), two spirituals, and others culled from Jimmy Rogers, Montana Taylor, Sleepy John Estes, and Woody Guthrie. Colyer claimed that his versions were not carbon copies of other people's performances and, referring back to the skiffle boom, suggested it had highlighted "the spurious more than the authentic, but the authentic always manages to survive. A music critic at the time said that our brand of Skiffle sounded to him more like 'Old Time Jazz' and he hit a nail on the head."[7] Colyer recorded four other skiffle tracks in Hamburg in 1966 and 1968 as part of LPs; the skiffle numbers were also issued separately. The songs featured Colyer, Bastable and Cole; a newcomer on the 1968 recording was Malcolm Murphy on washboard, who had joined Colyer as a drummer in 1966.

Colyer continued to lead a band during most of the years up to his death in 1988. In his obituary for *Jazz Journal*, Owen Bryce wrote of Colyer's reputation and influence: "So, the Guv'nor's dead. No need to mention his name... we all knew him as just The Guv'nor. And Guv'nor he most certainly was. His influence on hundreds of musicians and followers and collectors was simply enormous... Sadly, he played little in his last few years... and often sang or played the guitar almost as much as trumpet."[8] Today the Ken Colyer Trust keeps Ken Colyer's memory and achievements alive.

Alexis Korner, Ken Colyer's former skiffle associate, predeceased him in 1984 at the age of fifty-five. By the late Sixties Korner had become known a the "Father of the British Blues" — a title he apparently detested — and at his death as: "the root of a musical tree which blossomed across traditional boundaries leaving virtually no aspect of Western musical development untouched from skiffle to new romantic."[9] However, in the mid-Fifties he was still involved in skiffle, as in November 1956, a little while before he left his full-time job at the BBC in January 1957, Korner took part in a recording of two numbers "Kansas City Blues" and "Casey Jones" made by a group known as Beryl Bryden's Backroom Skiffle. In addition to Beryl on washboard, the other musicians involved were Alexis

1956 And All That: Skiffle Reminiscences

Our song repertoire consisted of the usual "copies" of skiffle hits — and non-hits — but later we got songs out of folk, gospel and spiritual song books. Not really knowing the melody, we strummed the chords and did a skiffle version. The Vipers were the main influence on us and a lot of other groups in the basic way a song was approached — that basic strumming thrash! Later, all sorts of stuff crept in. As I was a Fats Domino fan, I introduced a lesser-known blues of his, "Going to the River" — we duplicated the original piano triplets on guitars. The bass-player hated this number and called it "rock 'n' roll"! Yes, purism certainly existed, although I was catholic in my tastes right from the start — skiffle was to me a convenient, easy way of interpreting songs I liked. We even did (just for fun) the pop-song "Lollipop" (recorded by the Chordettes and the Mud-larks) complete with finger-in-the mouth popping effects. One rival group didn't realise we didn't take this song seriously and teased us with remarks like: "The Amazons sing nursery rhymes"!

Amongst our favourites and influences, Lonnie was the hero, of course — that great voice and energy, and good choice of material. The Vipers were regarded by me as rather second division, but they had a great influence because their basic approach was easy to copy, and their vocal sound was easier to approximate. After all no-one could sing like Lonnie.

I loved (and still love) Ken Colyer's group, because of their laid-back sound. Colyer was revered by some fans as he was pure, authentic skiffle, not the commercial Donegan brand. When Lonnie recorded "Don't You Rock Me Daddy-O", all the purists said: "Of course, he's doing rock 'n' roll now." My God, there were some arguments at school about what was and what wasn't real skiffle.

Dave Illingworth

(guitar, and backing vocals), Cyril Davies (guitar, harmonica and backing vocals), Frank Clarke (bass), and Dave Stevens (piano). *Jazz Journal* thought "Casey Jones" the better side in spite of the rather "wooden" playing of the skiffle group and a ragged chorus, and, acknowledging Beryl Bryden's singing ability, looked forward to some pleasant records.[10]

Two other titles ("Rock Me" and "This Train") were recorded by this group in January 1957 but not released.[11] In early January it was announced in the *Melody Maker* that Beryl Bryden was intending to form a specially recruited skiffle group to tour the variety halls but Beryl confirms that this proposal was not taken any further.

In February 1957, Alexis Korner's Breakdown Group recorded eight numbers at the Roundhouse (*Blues from the Roundhouse*) for Dobell's 77 Records label, of which only one hundred copies were pressed. The Roundhouse was a Victorian pub on the corner of Brewer and Wardour Streets, not far from Picadilly Circus. Titles on that occasion included "Skip to My Lou", "Ella Speed" and "Boll Weevil", and the group consisted of Alexis (guitar, mandolin and vocals), Terry Plant (bass), Cyril

Davies (guitar, harmonica and vocals) and Mike Collins (washboard). All the titles were subsequently re-issued in April 1970.

Using the same LP title, Alexis went on to record *Blues from the Roundhouse, Volume One*, in July 1957, that featured the Alexis Korner Skiffle Group performing four numbers that included, "I Ain't Gonna Worry No More", a Sleepy John Estes number, and "County Jail", originally recorded by Big Maceo Merriweather in 1944. This group comprised Alexis, Cyril Davies, Mike Collins, Chris Capon (bass) and Dave Stevens (piano). Although seen as a blues disc, Tempo Records insisted that it be issued as by the Alexis Korner Skiffle Group, presumably to capitalise on the music craze of the day. The *Gramophone's* reviewer thought Korner's band a "much more praiseworthy group than the average so-called 'skiffle' bands". They sang and played the blues "in a surprisingly authentic manner", used harmonica and piano and none of the numbers were "threadbare hill-billy" songs.[12]

One previously unissued track from the February 1957 recording ("Steamline Train") and four from a March 1957 solo session recorded in Buckinghamshire, were subsequently released in November 1984.

While wishing to abandon skiffle, Alexis Korner had found it difficult to entirely forsake that music and its associated genres and went on to record American ballads with Alan Lomax in February 1958, and two Woody Guthrie songs, amongst other material, with Rambling Jack Elliott in October and November 1959. In between these recordings, Alexis' "skiffle" group line-up, with the substitution of Jim Bray for Chris Capon on bass, had recorded as Alexis Korner's Blues Incorporated (*Blues From the Roundhouse, Volume Two*) in April 1958, released in December that year. Although not recording again with his own group of that name for another four years, the foundation was being laid for Korner's special place in popular music.

While Korner would try to escape the skiffle label, his former bandleader, Chris Barber, was happy to continue to promote the music. In early June 1956, the *Melody Maker* carried an advert for the Festival Pleasure Gardens, Battersea, announcing a performance by the Chris Barber Jazz Band, with Ottilie Patterson and the Dick Bishop Skiffle Group, on Tuesday June 12th. However, Barber's replacement for Donegan was not the fort-holding Bishop but the American country singer, Johnny Duncan, who although ignorant of jazz, looked and sounded very much like Lonnie Donegan. Duncan (guitar, mandolin and vocal), along with Dick Bishop (guitar and vocal), Chris Barber (bass) and Ron Bowden (drums) recorded as the Chris Barber Skiffle Group in September 1956. Their EP featured a railroad worksong, "Can't You Line'em"; "Gypsy Davy", a folk song with both American and English influences; "Doin' My Time", a murder and prison song learned by Duncan from a group led by Lester Flatt, and a spiritual, both sung by gospel singers and played by jazz bands, "Where

THE CHRIS BARBER SKIFFLE GROUP
with Dick Bishop
and Johnny Duncan

Sleeve of the Chris Barber Skiffle Group EP. Johnny Duncan (l.), Dick Bishop (r.).

Could I Go", in which Duncan sang and played the mandolin. The *Jazz Monthly* reviewer recommended the record to collectors of curiosa and was not enamoured of Duncan's "high-pitched castrato whine" suggesting that his performance on "Doin' My Time" placed him "with Ray and Presley as one of the more eccentric manifestations of our decade."[13] *Jazz Journal* too had its bit of fun, admitting that, coming from the Barber stable, it was well produced, beautifully recorded, sentimental, corny, amusing, competent — in other words, horse manure, beautifully cooked. The reviewer suspected that Johnny Duncan was a pseudonym for a cockatoo — his nasality and falsetto were thought a bit too much.[14] Once again the jazz press refused to take skiffle seriously and judged it for what they wanted it to be rather than for what it was.

Duncan left the Barber band in early 1957 in order to form his own group. David Boulton has suggested that when he joined: "Barber's band again became the primary skiffle workshop, since Duncan's use of Western and other non-Negro material paved the way for the use of English, Scottish and European folk-song."[15] The presence of Duncan on the skiffle scene may have encouraged greater use of white music but Donegan had already travelled that path and the assimilation of non-American folk songs into

80

skiffle never took place to the extent that many hoped it would.

With the skiffle craze moving towards its height, Dick Bishop also left Barber in late 1956, initially to work with Donegan and then to lead his own group. So, after February 1957, Barber discontinued the use of a skiffle group within his band. However, a *Melody Maker* advert for the Chris Barber Band Show at Wembley Town Hall on 25 March 1957 announced both Ottilie Patterson and the skiffle group, with which Ottilie sometimes sang, as special attractions. At an Odeon, Barking venue in May that year, with the Avon Cities Jazz Band in support, Barber was apparently relying on that band's skiffle group for that kind of music.

Another small contingent from the Barber band that scored hit parade success with "Petite Fleur", the Sidney Bechet composition, was that led by Monty Sunshine on clarinet. Recorded in October 1956 for an LP, and subsequently released as a single, it had sold a million copies by 1960, the year Sunshine was asked to leave the band. Sunshine, however, was said to have been unhappy anyway over Barber's introduction of an electric guitar and the band's copying of the Muddy Water's sound.

The departure of Donegan in 1956 and then, in 1960 of Monty Sunshine, did not stop the success of the Chris Barber Band which continues to this day. Having helped establish skiffle, Barber went on to further his earlier related interest in rhythm and blues and, after it had achieved popularity in the early Sixties, extended the band's title to Chris Barber's Jazz and Blues Band and found regular work within it for rock and blues musicians such as John Slaughter (guitar) and Pete York (drums).[16] Barber's success — and survival — has been founded on extending the band's instrumentation, broadening its repertoire beyond that generally used by trad jazz bands, and tours, especially of the continent.[17] His championing of skiffle was one aspect of this open-minded approach to playing jazz.

Chris Barber had lost Donegan prior to his USA visit in May 1956, but Lonnie had to honour various commitments with the band on his return. During Lonnie's absence, however, his popularity had grown to such an extent that on his return he decided to form his own group for recording and variety appearances. What Donegan needed, it was determined, was live exposure and his agents set about securing a variety tour of the Moss Empires, the best of the variety theatre circuits. Preston and Dutton had to convince Moss Empires, however, that Donegan was good enough to top the bill and to do so persuaded the Moss Empires big cheeses and their booking agents to attend a concert at the Stoll Theatre, Kingsway, in London on Sunday 26 August 1956 at 3 p.m.

This was Lonnie Donegan's first public appearance with his new post-Barber skiffle group and this Sunday afternoon jazz show was all about promoting his future. On the bill were the Terry Lightfoot Jazzmen, a fairly new trad band, and the more mainstream jazz groups, the Al

JAZZSHOWS present

Lonnie Donegan

with his Skiffle Group

Terry Lightfoot's Jazzmen
Al Fairweather Quartet
Dill Jones Trio
Yolanda

SUNDAY, 3-0 p.m.   *STOLL THEATRE*
AUGUST 26th, 1956   *KINGSWAY*

SOUVENIR PROGRAMME — ONE SHILLING

Souvenir programme for Lonnie Donegan's concert at the Stoll Theatre, Kingsway, London, 26 August 1956. (Courtesy The Ray Mander and Joe Mitchenson Theatre Collection.)

Fairweather Quartet, and the Dill Jones Trio. Yolanda supplied the glamour that seemed to be obligatory. The second half of the show featured Lonnie Donegan and his Skiffle Group who, on the strength of their enthusiastic reception that Sunday afternoon — "Lonnie Donegan hotter than a furnace" — were offered a twelve-week tour as top of the bill, opening in Nottingham in September and ending with a fortnight at the Prince of Wales Theatre. This was extended to three weeks by Bernard Delfont even before Donegan arrived there.[18]

The *Lonnie Donegan Showcase*, his first album for Pye and recorded in late August 1956, did what was considered impossible at the time for an LP by joining the hit parade in December 1956. Some might regard this as the classic Donegan album with titles such as "Wabash Cannonball", "I'm Alabamy Bound" and "Frankie and Johnny".

The keys to Donegan's success were identified by the reviewer of his Prince of Wales Theatre performance in early December 1956. While

admitting the performance had not been to everyone's taste — "an insult to the intelligence" was overheard — the reviewer noted Donegan's uninhibited singing, dedicated intensity, sincerity, simple but often humorous announcements, his frenzied abandon and the beat. "And make no mistake, the Skifflers do generate a beat, far more beat than many more publicised and 'modern' outfits. A word here for the tasteful work of guitarist Denny Wright, who certainly does not let the fetish for amplification dominate him." Donegan was declared to be a "natural".[19]

The *Lonnie Donegan Hit Parade*, his first two singles after "Rock Island Line", were issued as an EP in January 1957, following requests from audiences during his tour to hear them. This was the first of eight hit parade compilations, the last issued in 1961.

Also in January 1957 "Don't You Rock Me Daddy-O" entered the charts, reaching number four in March and knocking out the competing version from the Vipers, whose song it was originally. It was joined in April 1957 by "Cumberland Gap" which rose to number one in May. The versions by the Vipers (Parlophone) and Dickie Bishop (Decca) looked like doing well until Donegan's recording appeared and went to number six in one week; the Vipers had more limited success and lower down the chart. These earlier successes were later followed by "Gamblin' Man" backed with "Puttin' On the Style" (number one in June 1957) and then

83

> *1956 And All That: Skiffle Reminiscences*
>
> *I was only twelve years old or so in 1957 but recall being introduced somehow or other to the sounds of Chris Barber, the Happy Wanderers, Ken Colyer and something else which emerged, at least partly, from that type of music — skiffle. A shellac single on Pye Nixa, Oriole or some other label cost five shillings and seven pence in "old" money. This was a not inconsiderable sum in those days, and it was a case of literally picking up the pieces if you dropped one on the lino. My 78s by Lonnie Donegan or the Vipers — I still have some of them — were worn white, partly through playing and partly because they were played on the family radiogram, which had a pickup arm weighing about 2 lbs and used needles bought by the boxful and which had to be (or should have been) replaced after every fifty plays.*
>
> *Mother's diary, otherwise known as the Family Archive, notes that on 16 March 1957: "Michael bought 'Cumberland Gap' — another noisy record". What were the words of 'Cumberland Gap'", I never did decipher them all? The Vipers were my special favourites because of the exciting edge to the voices, the harmonies, the tuneful solid guitar sound, and the fact that they kept faith with a washboard for so long — skiffle was never quite the same for me with a drum kit.*
>
> *Mike Waites*

in October by "My Dixie Darling", number ten in November.

At one point in his second variety tour, in early 1957, Donegan became ill and was unable to travel to Nottingham. Johnny Duncan took his place, arriving in time for a fifteen-minute rehearsal with the group. Earlier in the day, Duncan had been rehearsing his own group, which he had just set up. Donegan rejoined his own group mid-week.[20]

In April 1957 Donegan undertook his second US tour as supporting act to the Harlem Globetrotters during the interval. Donegan nearly got the bird in Los Angeles because audiences thought he was imitating Elvis Presley, who, at that time, was experiencing the peak of the "Down with Elvis Campaign". Fans and sportswriters were also put out because the Globetrotters failed to offer the usual interval comedy.[21] On return to Britain, there was a difference of opinion as to whether the tour had been cut short by a few days, Donegan denied the accusation that it had been a flop and said he hoped to return to the States. During the tour the group had travelled 13,000 miles, performed nineteen shows in cities all over the USA and had audiences of 10,000 for each show.[22]

Advertised as the "Skiffle Sensation of 1957", Lonnie Donegan starred in a Skiffle Festival in early June 1957 at the Royal Albert Hall, with Chas McDevitt, Nancy Whiskey, Bob Cort, and the Avon Cities and Cy Laurie jazz bands. He also appeared in the movie version of *Six-Five Special* in 1957, and featured "Jack O' Diamonds" which, entering the charts in December, reached number fourteen in January 1958.

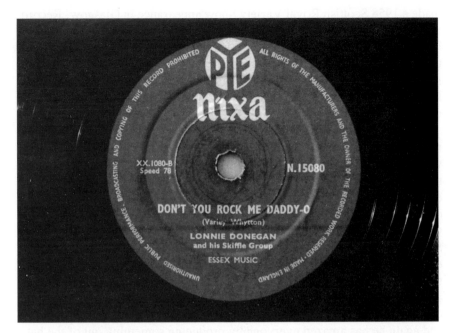

Lonnie made his first pantomime appearance in 1957 as Wishee Washee in *Aladdin* at the Chiswick Empire and repeated the part at Stockton-on Tees in 1958. In 1959 he was in pantomime for the third year running, playing Crusoe's daft brother, Billy, in *Robinson Crusoe* at the Finsbury Park Empire. In 1960 he appeared in the comedy role of Buttons at Nottingham.

During 1957 and 1958 there were personnel changes to the skiffle group. Jim Currie (guitar), previously with Tony Crombie, took over in March 1957 from Denny Wright, who had joined Johnny Duncan, and bassist Peter Huggett replaced Mickey Ashman, who left the group in May 1958.

Another song from the *Six-Five Special* film, "Grand Coulee Dam", a somewhat quieter Donegan disc, entered the top twenty in April 1958. That month the *Melody Maker* reported that the BBC had banned the other side of this record, "Nobody Loves Like an Irishman", because of the line, "Praying all night with his El Koran". The record had been released before the sheet music and the BBC accepted a substitute line and Donegan was able to perform the new song with its new line on BBC.[23] This was neither the first nor last Donegan disc to incur broadcasting problems: the "Battle of New Orleans" "Diggin' My Potatoes", and "Take My Hand Precious Lord", also offended the BBC sense of what was proper. In July 1958 "Sally Don't You Grieve" backed with "Betty, Betty, Betty" entered the top twenty at number fourteen, moving to number eleven in a seven-week stay.

In August 1958 Lonnie appeared for the summer season at the Blackpool Palace Theatre in an attraction billed as "The Teenage Show". He also made a 1958 Scottish Royal Variety Show appearance in Glasgow. Record releases in the remainder of 1958 were: "Lonesome Traveller" in September and, in November, "Tom Dooley", which beat off competition from the Kingston Trio's version in the new year. *Lonnie's Skiffle Party*, November 1958, which recycled "Puttin' on the Style" along with songs like "Knees Up Mother Brown" and "On Top of Old Smoky", reached number twenty-three in the charts.

Although skiffle was no longer in favour, Donegan continued to have recording successes in 1959, "Does Your Chewing Gum Lose its Flavour?", a comedy record, reached the charts in February and achieved big things in the USA over two years later. May 1959 saw "Fort Worth Jail" enter the charts for four weeks to be followed next month by the "Battle of New Orleans" which reached number two in July. Another hit single was "Sal's Got a Sugar Lip", in the top twenty chart for three weeks in September 1959.

December's "San Miguel" disc, a Mexican love song, only just reach the top twenty. By late 1959 it was some time since Donegan had recorded a song in a pure skiffle style and indeed that style was now no longer commercially fashionable. Skiffle had died but Donegan did not: "Again and again he has amazed everyone by producing something out of the hat, revealing new sides to his versatility and proving that, whatever musical fad happens to be in favour at the moment, he can always find something to suit his highly individual talents."[24]

In 1959 Pye launched their "Lonnie Donegan Presents" series, introducing new folk and traditional jazz performers, such as Clyde Valley Stompers, the Kenny Ball Band, and Miki and Griff. Donegan's role was as both talent scout and recording manager. Miki and Griff were UK singers of country music who were invited by Donegan to sing in his television series and continued working with him until 1964. He also produced their first records and they appeared on some of Donegan's own recordings, such as "Michael Row the Boat Ashore"

Starting in June, Donegan spent the summer season of 1959 in a show at the Royal Acquarium, Great Yarmouth. There he did a trio singing spot with Des O'Connor and Lorrae Desmond, took part in a comedy sketch, and joined O'Connor for a song and dance routine, the show closing with a thirty-minute spot by Lonnie's group. Takings towards the end of one week in July broke the theatre's box office records.

In March 1960 "My Old Man's a Dustman" entered the charts at number fifteen and the following month was number one. Because of its world-wide sales, Donegan was awarded a gold disc in October. Apparently the record had gone down well in Australia and New Zealand, (although a non-starter in the USA), and, in spite of the language difficulties, on the continent too. Capitalising on his popularity down-under, Lonnie undertook a three-and-a-half week tour of Australia and New Zealand in October and November 1960. In Australia, Lonnie and his

Opposite: Sheet music for "My Dixie Darling" (courtesy Peer Music).

group played six major cities with a programme that included the British comedian Billy Baxter, singers Miki and Griff, and a Western Australian group of singers and instrumentalists, the Four Clefs. 1960 saw Donegan's third visit to the USA.

In November 1960 he made a Royal Variety appearance with Cliff Richard and Adam Faith in the pop music segment. The same year saw another television series of *Putting on the Donegan*, and further top twenty chart hits with "I Wanna Go Home", in June, and "Lively" in December. "Have a Drink on Me", an adapted Lead Belly song (originally "Take a Whiff on Me") reached number eight in June 1961. Composed by Donegan for Adam Faith, who declined to use it, it was said to mark Lonnie's return to skiffle. Donegan was adamant that he had never left it and that all his records, even those made with string and woodwind backings, had a skiffle flavour.

By 1961 the line-up of Donegan's backing group was Les Bennetts (solo guitar) originally of the Les Hobeaux Skiffle Group, Peter Huggett (bass), and Pete Appleby (drums), replacing Nick Nichols, the last of the original 1956 group to leave.

The chart success of "Does Your Chewing Gum Lose its Flavour?" in the USA (number four in September 1961) made up for lack of UK chart success that year with "Bury Me Beneath the Willows" — Donegan's first recording failure. Another 1961 chart success, however, was "Michael Row the Boat Ashore" charting at number eleven in September.

"The Comancheros" and "The Party's Over" made the top twenty in February and May 1962 respectively, followed by Donegan's last hit single, "Pick a Bale of Cotton" in September that year. "Despite a steady flow of releases, Donegan was unable to make any further impact in a world dominated by the British Beat groups which, in part, he had helped to create."[25]

Donegan spent the 1962 summer season at Great Yarmouth and there was another TV series of *Putting on the Donegan*. At concerts he still got requests for skiffle numbers. In October 1962 he undertook another US trip — a month's booking at the night club for American folk talent — Village Gate.

A popular and newsworthy performer such as Donegan was bound to attract some adverse comment. He was accused of being conceited, cocksure and difficult. Lonnie countered by saying that success was always knocked; that his fans did not find him conceited; that he refused to be a yes-man — and, if pleasing himself by the way he sang and played had got him where he was, he would carry on. He would be dropped if he did not earn and so it was up to him to look after his career.[26]

To be fair some commentators did acknowledge his hard work, his desire to learn, his striving to do better, and his thoughtfulness towards others, exemplified by the time he devoted to his fans and the Lonnie Donegan clubs. Donegan also took pride in appearing well dressed: in

1960 the Wholesale Clothing Manufacturers named him as one of the ten best-dressed men in Britain. Donegan also found that people were copying his speech and dress, not just his music.

His hobbies were photography — he arranged for stage appearances to be filmed and used the results to help improve the act. He was also a record collector and possessed many field recordings of folk songs. Golf was a more newly acquired leisure pursuit.

Donegan's musical influence in the late Fifties and early Sixties was enormous and newer acts (Shakin' Pyramids and Terry and Jerry) were influenced by his work. Others pay more obvious respect to his significance, such as the tribute group, the Lonnigans.

Those who knocked Donegan might have been interested to know that Chris Barber reported in 1957: "that Alan Lomax, reckoned to be something of an authority on folk music, was played a Donegan record

---

1956 And All That: Skiffle Reminiscences

I think we must have formed our skiffle group in the autumn term of our fifth form year, which would have been in 1956. We played together for over a year at least, and probably disbanded sometime during the second year in the sixth form in 1958-9. Our group consisted of lead guitar, second guitar (me), banjo, tea-chest bass, and a washboard.

The only real musician was the lead guitarist, Peter Jenkins, whose group it was. I don't think we had a name, though I think of us as "The Peter Jenkins Skiffle Group". Peter could read music and could also play trad jazz trombone and piano. On various numbers he played piano, or doubled up on trombone for a solo. If we played at a venue that had a microphone, he would also solo sometimes on guitar. The rest of us were musically illiterate — the banjoist and second guitarist could only strum. We played mostly in the keys of C, D and E.

Our repertoire was wholly derivative of recorded skiffle music. Songs I can remember that we performed were: "John Henry", "Longest Train", "Midnight Special", "Ham and Eggs", "Frankie and Johnny", "Stack-olee", and "Lost John". It never occurred to us to write our own material, as skiffle was associated in our minds with "authenticity". Skiffle was drawing on "folk music" and therefore you didn't muck about with it; and since folk music was the product of somewhere else — never where you were — it could only be imitated.

John Barnie

What we sang was what we heard on popular records, and, although we did explore other possibilities in song books, I don't remember that we adopted any. On one occasion we did try to write our own number called "I've Got That Feeling I'm Blue". Almost as daft as "Don't You Rock Me, Daddy O"; but look how successful that was for the Vipers and Lonnie Donegan.

Mike Dewe

not so very long ago. *He attributed it to Leadbelly.*"[27]

Whatever the opinions of his music, critics could not deny Donegan's slick and professional presentation, his showmanship, the infectious enjoyment of music-making which he passed on to his fans, and his good use of comedy. He also showed a willingness to try any type of music, whether folk songs, comedy numbers, talking blues, or Cole Porter.

Lonnie believed his success came from his knowledge of the music — he spent some years studying folk music — his desire to appear as natural as possible, and maintaining the highest possible standard of entertainment. He saw his skiffle style as putting jazz into folk music, making the phrasing and feeling different, and improvisation — "those who can't improvise are not playing skiffle at all".[28] A little harsh on all those youngsters trying to emulate the every nuance of their "skiffle hero".

One of the most balanced and sympathetic assessments of Lonnie Donegan's achievements forms part of a review of the 1958 *Lonnie* LP in *Jazz Journal*, where the reviewer wrote: "Donegan's material is invariably excellent, consisting as it does of folk songs that, compared to the seasickness despair and tulip-time joy of most popular music, are almost absolute in their truthfulness and freshness. This fact alone puts me on his side. That he sings the songs with fire, gusto and, usually, understanding, makes me even more so.

"If we acknowledge the limitations of what he is doing, and admit that he occasionally misses the point by confusing consumption of energy with expression of feeling, we can go from there to some appreciation of the pleasing aspects of his work and the heartening fact of his continued existence in the jungle of popular music."[29]

A 1992 opinion of Donegan's importance and ability in a *Folk Roots* review of twenty-six reissued tracks, was expressed as: "a man who did more for the Folk Revival in Britain than... a lot of revivalists, anyway... what leaps from the speakers... is an enthusiastic clarity and vibrant delivery no one has matched since. How many five quid acoustic guitars this material helped to sell is anyone's guess."[30]

By 1965 Peter Leslie could write that: "Lonnie Donegan would seem to deserve the label of 'a real pro'. And the amateur banjo jazzman of yesterday appears to have earned the right to consider himself the Entertainer he always wanted to be tomorrow."[31]

Donegan's recording achievements from 1956 to 1962 were quite phenomenal for the time. He had more than twenty hits in the charts, many making the top ten. He was the first British performer to have an EP and LP in the singles-dominated charts, to get a golden disc for his debut single and to have a record ("My Old Man's a Dustman") go straight to number one. The last-named record, together with "Rock Island Line" and "Does Your Chewing Gum Lose its Flavour?" were all million-sellers, and on Monday 9 October 1961 two gold discs — to go with that held for "Dustman" — were presented to Lonnie Donegan by Bing Crosby at

Shepperton Studios.

The 1995 edition of *British Hit Singles* records those performers who spent most weeks in the charts between 1952 and December 1994, and Donegan comes twenty-second at 321 weeks. Above him were the likes of Cliff Richard, and the Beatles, and below him Adam Faith, Tommy Steele, Marty Wilde, Gerry and the Pacemakers and Billy Fury. Other statistics in *British Hit Singles* show Lonnie with thirty hits (thirty-two songs, including re-entries, in the top thirty), seventeen of those in the top ten, three of which were number one records. As regards the most weeks spent at number one, Lonnie notched up eleven weeks, a position he shared with six other artists, including Gerry and the Pacemakers.[32] Looked at solely in terms of the 1956 to 1962 period, one observer has calculated that Donegan was the fourth top artist in the UK after Elvis Presley, Cliff Richard and the Everly Brothers and that Donegan and Presley were the only two artists to score hits in each year of the seven.[33]

In spite of continuing to work and record, Lonnie did not remain in the show business limelight. Skiffle, however, is a testimony to his lasting importance to the development of popular music in Britain, even if he himself no longer enjoyed the top entertainment position of his golden years.

In 1966 Donegan recorded the official English World Cup song, and in the Seventies recorded with Barber again and with the German Leinemann Skiffle Group. The *Puttin' on the Style* album — remakes of his earlier hits, with all-star support and Adam Faith as producer — was recorded by Donegan in 1978. Paul Pelletier describes it as: "an orgy of self-indulgence, much enjoyed by all who took part (including Elton John, Ringo Starr, Rory Gallagher, Bryan May, etc.) but hardly a listening pleasure... The follow-up album, *Sundown*, featuring cajun and country music... was mercifully much better."[34]

At the Royal Command Performance of 1981, Donegan appeared with Alvin Stardust and Marty Wilde in a celebration of "25 years of Rock 'n' Roll" — not forgotten, then, and not perhaps entirely miscast. The Eighties saw Donegan involved in varied activities, such as working again with Monty Sunshine in 1986, acting on television, and performing at the *Country Music Magazine* festival in 1989. Today, although not in the best of health, Donegan continues to entertain; he toured with Chris Barber in 1995.

Reporting on Lonnie Donegan at 65 in 1996, Jane Kelly told of the King of Skiffle who now lives in Malaga, Spain, and who has survived two heart attacks, three strokes, open heart surgery, has been married three times, fathered seven children and was still recording forty years on.[35]

Forever linked, together with Nancy Whiskey, with the hit skiffle number "Freight Train", Chas McDevitt, like Donegan, was of Glaswegian origin. Born in 1934, he spent his early years, however, in London and Surrey.

Aged sixteen, and while still at school, he played banjo with the High Curley Stompers in Camberley, Surrey.

In 1955 McDevitt joined the Crane River Jazz Band as its banjoist and set up his first skiffle group within the band in 1956. The group often rehearsed during the lunch break in the basement archives at Unilever House where Chas worked. Group members with Chas were Marc Sharratt (washboard), John Summers (guitar), Ken Aggus (mandolin), Reg Linay (guitar and piano) and Ken Lovett (vocals). They played at a few Chelsea parties, sometimes at the High Holborn pub, the Princess Louise, in various coffee bars and with the Cranes. Membership of the group established itself as Chas, Marc, Denny Carter and Alex Whitehouse (guitars), and John Paul (bass), replacing Ron Ward who had joined Ken Colyer.

Bill Varley became their manager, entering them for a talent show on Radio Luxembourg in late 1956. Although winning four weeks running, the group lost the final, performing a song already recorded for Oriole, "Freight Train", with Chas taking the vocal. Another contestant, already known to them from the folk club circuit, Nancy Whiskey (born Anne Wilson in Glasgow in 1935), was asked to join the group, which she did in December 1956. At Varley's urging, "Freight Train" was re-recorded, with Nancy singing the lead, and released in January 1957. Around the same time as "Freight Train" (backed with the "Cotton Song") was recorded, the group also added "It Takes a Worried Man" coupled with "New Orleans" to its Oriole output.

Nancy Whiskey, the third prominent skiffler of Glaswegian origin, and subsequently dubbed Britain's "Queen" or "First Lady of Skiffle", attended art school and later became engaged to the Glaswegian jazz pianist,

Bob Kelly, who was to appear on some of the later Colyer skiffle recordings. In order to get money to marry, the pair came to London where, for ten bob a night, Nancy played skiffle in a club in Soho. She also became popular as a folk singer in jazz clubs. Nancy's performing name came from the Scottish folk song, "The Carlton Weaver", where the hard stuff is referred to as Nancy Whiskey. In 1956, before joining McDevitt, she had recorded an EP of six folk songs for the Topic label.

In early 1957, the Chas McDevitt skiffle group featured with the Eric Delaney and Lou Preager bands at the Hammersmith Palais, but its variety debut took place at the Metropolitan Theatre, Edgeware Road, where it featured in "The Skiffle Show of 1957" which was to run for two weeks from 21 January. Also in January 1957 Chas' group, with Nancy Whiskey, was the resident skiffle group at the Nancy Whiskey Club at the Princess Louise, Holborn.

In late April, the McDevitt Skiffle Group took part in what was announced as "London's First Big Skiffle Session" at the Royal Festival Hall. Other participants included Johnny Duncan, the Avon Cities Jazz Band with Ray Bush, and the skiffle groups of Dick Bishop and Bob Cort. April was also the month when "Freight Train" reached the top twenty in Britain, becoming number five in June, and remaining in the top twenty until July. The song also charted in the States, becoming a million-seller. According to Nancy, she learned "Freight Train" from an American friend while travelling through Hyde Park in a bubble car and used it in her London folk club. Rejected by Pye, the song as performed by the McDevitt group was taken up by Oriole, mainly because they did not have a skiffle group under contract. The success of "Freight Train" did not make Nancy wealthy, however, as the royalties were split six ways. Actually Nancy received one twelfth as she only sang on one side.[36]

In mid-1957, the McDevitt Group also toured Britain with American stars like Slim Whitman, Frankie Lymon and the Teenagers, and Freddie Bell and The Bell Boys.

In May 1957, the Music Operators of America decided they wanted the "Freight Train" singer at their annual convention for a surprise performance; the song had sold over half-a-million copies in the States. Nancy flew to Chicago for the performance and also appeared on television and was interviewed for radio. Because of UK commitments, she declined an offer to appear on the Ed Sullivan television show.

At the end of June 1957, Nancy Whiskey visited the United States again, this time with Chas McDevitt and Marc Sharratt, to promote "Freight Train". The trio appeared on radio and televison — on the Ed Sullivan Show and on the same bill as the Everly Brothers — but using three American musicians for their backing because of union rules. Nancy had certain reservations about this trip but Chas McDevitt felt it was not a waste of time and that musically it was an education because of the jazz musicians that they were able to hear. Prior to the trip, two further sides had been

recorded by the group — "Greenback Dollar" coupled with "I'm Satisfied with My Girl" that featured a new line-up. With Chas and Nancy were Tony Cohn (guitar, and formerly with the Cotton Pickers Skiffle Group), Bill Bramwell (an ex-Randall player, and a guitarist with a great feel for the blues), Marc Sharratt (washboard, who died in a car accident in 1991), and Lennie Harrison (bass, formerly of the Ray Ellington Quartet). "Greenback Dollar", however, only made the lower regions of the top thirty charts.

In spite of being part of the success story of the year, Nancy claimed in June 1957 that she hated skiffle: "The public likes it frantic and frenzied. I don't like that kind of music. But I sing it — for the money. *I'm going to make all the money I can before the kids get tired of the craze.*"[37] On achieving popular success, Nancy found that her weekly income rose from £4.10s to £400 a week.

In a *Melody Maker* interview in July 1957, Nancy indicated once again her dislike of skiffle and said that she never wanted to sing it. Her second trip to the America with Chas McDevitt had been disappointing and in a fortnight she had only sung twice. Her aim was to go back to the States alone. Nancy said she wanted to sing folk songs and complained that as a member of a group she had no say in the choice of her songs. However, she would still go on recording with McDevitt.[38] In July and August 1957 the new line-up recorded four further sides but Nancy Whiskey only appeared on one of these, "Face in the Rain".

The group appeared in the film, *The Tommy Steele Story*, in 1957 and sang "Freight Train" at the personal request of Tommy Steele. Subsequently the group decided to make music a full-time career. Not wishing to turn professional, however, three members of the group left in mid-1957, accounting for the new McDevitt line-up, and formed a new group called the Court Jesters. However, as the Old Timers Skiffle Group — Carter, Whitehouse and Paul, augmented by "Little Joey" Jonkler on washboard — it recorded two titles on Fontana in 1958 ("The Women Who Loved a Swine" and "The Lynching of Jeff Buckner") before disbanding that year.

The LP, *The Intoxicating Miss Whiskey*, by the Chas McDevitt Skiffle Group featuring Nancy Whiskey, was a mixture of material recorded earlier, like "Face in the Rain", and new items such as "Poor Howard" and "The Riddle Song". After recording a further side, "Johnny-O", with the McDevitt group — she was not on the track, "Bad Man Stackolee" that went with it — and a Moss Empire tour, Nancy Whiskey left the group for a solo career in August 1957.

A *Jazz Journal* review of two McDevitt Skiffle Group singles recognised the group's ability but commented that they lacked "that certain animal vitality which skiffle needs and which a group like the Vipers has". In the *Gramophone*, the group's recording of "Sporting Life" was recognised as following in Ken Colyer's footsteps but, when it came to the other

Opposite: Sheet music for "The Cotton Song". (©1997 Bradbury Wood Ltd., Chapell Music Ltd. Repr. by permission of International Music Publications Ltd.)

side, "Face in the Rain" with Nancy Whiskey, the comment was if this "is skiffle music, then I'm Liberace".[39]

After a national search and auditions, Shirley Douglas, who Chas later married, was picked out of hundreds of singers and taken on as a replacement for Nancy Whiskey. Douglas, born in Athlone, Ireland, in 1939, had been part of her parents' musical act and had been taught to play the guitar by her father. With her as the new vocalist the group continued to perform, appearing in variety, cabaret, dance halls, Sunday concerts and on television and radio. Shirley's first record with the group, in August 1957, was a skiffle version of "Across the Bridge", a film theme-song, with an original composition "Deep Down" on the B-side. This pop song given the skiffle treatment was part of a deliberate attempt to broaden the group's repertoire. In December 1957 it was announced that the McDevitt group would take part in a seven-concert, 1,000 mile tour — "Skiffle Jamboree" — with Don Lang and his Frantic Five, the City Ramblers, Les Hobeaux, the Cotton Pickers and the Eden Street Skiffle Group.[40]

After the 1957 Christmas holidays, the group began a series of one-night venues in Scotland, commencing with Perth. In January 1958 they began a second tour with the young, but short-lived rock star, Terry Dene, starting at the Gaumont, Taunton. The latter half of 1958 saw the Oriole recording of "Juke Box Jumble" backed with "Real Love" which were not considered as skiffle performances and in that year Chas McDevitt opened his Freight Train coffee-bar in London.

In 1959 the group disbanded and reformed with two former members of the Les Hobeaux Skiffle Group, Red Reece (drums) and Les Bennetts (lead guitar) and unsuccessfully tried rock 'n' roll, recording "Teenage

Letter" for Oriole. McDevitt and Douglas later performed as a duo in the Sixties and Seventies, appearing in concert with many of the greats of the time, and continued to broadcast and record. More recently, in the Eighties, Chas returned to his skiffle roots, but the re-formed original skiffle group, with John Paul and Marc Sharratt, came to an end with the tragic death of Marc. Today Chas performs solo and from time to time fronts a group that might include daughter Kerry and Jason Sharratt.

Backed by Sonny Stewart and his Skiffle Kings, Nancy Whiskey sang "Johnny O" in the 1958 film *The Golden Disc*. In that year — no longer part of the McDevitt group — Nancy Whiskey changed her act to include ballads with a big band backing. She still had strong views on skiffle but was *for* Ken Colyer, no doubt because of her husband Bob Kelly's association with that band. Nancy, who was working in variety in Birmingham at that time, had a new record out, "I Know Where I'm Going", which faced strong American competition. Shortly after the birth of her daughter, Nancy retired from show business but re-recorded "Freight Train" in 1967 and made a couple of LPs. In the early Seventies she was enjoying a cabaret career, including shows abroad and in recent years had made occasional "skiffle" appearances.

It would be easy to dismiss the Chas McDevitt Skiffle Group as largely a one-hit band, albeit an enormous hit on both sides of the Atlantic. It is true the group did not have the influence of Donegan, although like him McDevitt came from the jazz world, nor quite the same chart success as the Vipers. Nevertheless, until a change of personnel, it did confirm and consolidate that special acoustic guitar and washboard sound that was British skiffle and demonstrated that there was a leading place in the music for female performers. Like others, however, the group failed to have continuing popularity in the transition from skiffle to beat music and rock 'n' roll.

The popularity of the Vipers Skiffle Group — the "Kings of Skiffle" — and the success of their recordings, represented the only serious challenge to Lonnie Donegan's own title of "King of Skiffle". Occasionally both groups recorded competing versions of the same number. The Vipers, with its leader Wally Whyton, had its origins in folk-singers and guitarists meeting up at the Breadbasket coffee-bar, forming a group and playing for pleasure. In spite of the group's success on record and in performance, and later attempts to move away from skiffle, as a force in popular music it was relatively short-lived.

Wally Whyton was born in London in 1929 and developed an interest in jazz and swing. He saw Josh White at the Shepherds Bush Empire and got to hear records by Muddy Waters, Lead Belly, Woody Guthrie, Burl Ives and Big Bill Broonzy. On leaving school he joined a commercial art studio and at eighteen did his national service with the RAF.

In the Fifties (possibly 1955), he bought a guitar for £1 from a local

Skiffle with

The Vipers

Two Terrific Titles on their new 78 ...

Streamline Train
Railroad Steam Boat

R4308 (78 & 45 r.p.m.)

*and
Four 'Greats'
on their
first EP ...*

'Skiffle Music'

*The Cumberland Gap
Hey Liley, Liley Lo
Don't You Rock Me
    Daddy-O
It takes a worried man
    to sing a worried song*

GEP8615
(45 r.p.m. EP)

**PARLOPHONE
RECORDS**

THE PARLOPHONE COMPANY LIMITED,
RECORD DIVISION.

The Vipers. Press advert from 1957.

publican — it had been left against a drink — and joined other budding entertainers in the Breadbasket coffee bar five minutes from his home. In a few weeks a nucleus of a group had formed but with changing personnel — Tommy Steele was an irregular member. Wally was also involved in the Cavemen, a group with Tommy Steele, Lionel Bart and Mike Pratt, which did not last very long.

Another group playing in coffee bars, busking on the streets and sharing personnel, was the Chas McDevitt Skiffle Group. The Vipers, the Chas McDevitt group and Jim Dale were captured on tape by Roy Tuvey and Bill Varley at a coffee bar session but nobody was interested in the music until Donegan's "Rock Island Line" hit. Bill Varley became involved in the management of both the Vipers and Chas McDevitt groups.

Wally found that he had been bitten by the music bug and enjoyed the skiffle sessions at the Gyre and Gimble and the Breadbasket. The Vipers came up with their group name — considered slightly menacing — when a name was required for participation in a Moscow youth festival. Along with Wally, the group consisted around this time of Jean Van Den Bosch, Johnny Martyn (Booker) and Johnny Armstrong. On the 14 July 1956, after performing on the streets for the Soho Fair, and coming to the attention of the owners of the 2 I's coffee bar, the group was invited to play there regularly. Entry to the coffee bar basement cost 1/-and there were places for eighty and a small stage.

Presumably because of demand, it was announced in October 1956 that the Vipers would play at the new 2 I's Club at 44 Gerrard Street, yearly membership cost 2/6 at the door or at the coffee bar in Old Compton Street.

In December 1956, the *Melody Maker* announced that the Vipers had been signed for their first concert appearance, at the Odeon, Guildford. A successful record — "Don't You Rock Me Daddy-O" — also earned them an invitation in February 1957 to star for two weeks with the Bob Cort Skiffle Group at the Prince of Wales Theatre, London. During this appearance, members of the Vipers worked all day, played in the evening at the 2 I's after the theatre, and recorded at night. Other venues played by the Vipers included the Humphrey Lyttleton Club and the Cat's Whisker coffee bar.

In his autobiography, George Martin, the noted producer of such stars as the Beatles, tells how he came to offer the Vipers a recording contract. Aroused by the buzz going around the record business about youngsters playing in coffee bars, Martin and Noel Whitcomb, a *Daily Mirror* journalist went to the 2 I's to see Tommy Steele and the Vipers. Both dismissed Steele as "a blond cardboard imitation of Elvis Presley" and Martin admits to the mistake of passing on him. Steele was then promptly signed by Decca who made a star of him.[41]

George Martin liked the Vipers, thought they had great guts, and signed them up as an answer to Lonnie Donegan. He recognised that they were amateurs with their tea-chest bass, washboard and acoustic guitars but that they made "the most enormous sound. The style... in a way the precursor of the Beatles."[42]

Martin also recounts how he developed two-track recording, starting with Jim Dale, moving through the Vipers to the Beatles: "I could concentrate on getting a really loud rhythm sound, knowing that I could always bring it up or down afterwards to make sure the voices were coming through."[43] This technique was just right for the strong rhythm, and solo and ensemble singing style of the Vipers.

Their first recording on Parlophone, made in October 1956, was "Ain't You Glad", backed with "Pick a Bale of Cotton", also recorded some years later by Donegan. This was followed by "Don't You Rock Me, Daddy-O", written by Bill Varley and Wally Whyton (based on an old song) and recorded in November, which entered the charts at number twenty-four in January 1957, rising to ten in early February. This achievement was outdone by Donegan who also got there with his version of this song in January, lasting to March and rising to number four in February. Wally Whyton claimed that Donegan only recorded his version after hearing the Vipers play it at the 2 I's.

The Vipers turned professional in April 1957 after appearances on radio and television and making a number of successful and much imitated records for Parlophone. These included "Cumberland Gap" backed by "Maggie May", which was banned by the BBC — the group had cleaned it up, but insufficiently it seems — and "Streamline Train" which reached twenty-three in the charts in June. "Cumberland Gap" entered the charts at number twenty-five, rising to number ten but was overtaken by Donegan's version which went to number one. Following such recording success, the first of what would be three EPs of Vipers skiffle reissues

1956 And All That: Skiffle Reminiscences

Sticky weather for the first public performance of the school skiffle group. Shorts riding up thighs again. The Rev. said to be at the Fête by 5 but I decided to get the chaps there earlier so's we could rehearse the new record by the Vipers ("Don't You Rock Me Daddy O"). We never get a moment to rehearse as a rule but nobody seems to mind. The Rev. said he'd probably lend a voice to a couple of spirituals or "Green Grow the Rushes O". Waring got his tea-chest bass bashed in during some tuck-room brawl so we had to go begging to Ladey, that acneyed ass-hole who was in his study, curtains drawn, burning joss sticks. Sitting as per usual in a wicker chair gripping a cup of Nescafe with an ear an inch from his gramophone. Listening to some aged New Orleans jazz record. In the end he let us buy his waste paper box to make into a bass (you drill a hole in the bottom, pull string through, knot at one end and at the other attach a broom handle). He shouted out as we left that skiffling was ruining the true jazz cause and anyway we only knew 3 chords. He also says we don't swing. He said the same about my Bill Haley LP and my LP of the Original Dixieland Jazz Band. But I think he just prefers 78s. At least we're popular and lots of juniors, including pretty ones, would like to be like us. Even the hearties are open-mouthed. That cretin McLain has started a group too. Knows nothing about music but I'm sure he's trying to woo beauty boy Gabriel. Christ-on-a-bicycle, there'll soon be loads of groups but at least we have the advantage of genuine Jaytex check shirts. I'm going to see if I can't get my guitar electrified.

Ian Whitcomb (extract from After the Ball)

were released. Later in the year they recorded *Skiffle Party*, a mixture of songs with such titles as "Comin' Round the Mountain", "Wabash Cannonball" and "Skip to My Lou".

The *Gramophone* reviewer was as usual not well disposed towards skiffle, calling one Vipers single: "Coffee-house pseudo-skiffle music that may appeal to silly mixed-up kids, but is hardly likely to mean much to intelligent connoisseurs of jazz. To call this jazz is like saying a mutton bone is soup."[44] *Jazz Journal* was more well disposed, commenting on their first EP that: "The Vipers, with just the right amount of vigour and bounce, are to me the best skiffle group recording at the present time." The reviewer also liked their comparative relaxation, lack of deep serious-ness, and the absence of hyena-like howlings, but missed the single string guitar as "the unrelieved scuffling background becomes monotonous."[45]

In his notes to the 1957 Vipers' *Coffee Bar Session* LP, Benny Green wrote that the group "have very strong claims to the position of honour as the best group of its kind so far to appear in Great Britain." He also tried to explain the skiffle phenomenon and advanced the theory that the widespread appeal of skiffle bridged the chasm that had grown up between performer and audience in most types of jazz and offered a type of music

"to which the rising generation of adolescents could feel some affinity without ever having entered the precincts of a college of music." Green also tried to explain the success and skilled performances of skiffle recordings, mostly made by musicians "without any extensive academic training", and concluded that it has to do with sincerity and an affinity with their audience: "the skiffler has entered intimately into the social life of his time, inverting the customary gambit of thrusting between himself and those who pay to hear him a barrier of condescension." The ten LP tracks included two titles, "This Land is Your Land" and "If I Had a Hammer", both now well-known — the latter would be recorded by Trini Lopez in the Sixties. In January 1958, the *Melody Maker* described this disc as one of the best skiffle records so far, commenting on its lively handling of admirable songs.

During its most successful time, the Vipers consisted of advertising agency man and leader, Wally Whyton (guitar and vocals), coffee-house manager, Johnny Martyn and wire salesman, Jean Van Den Bosch (both guitar and vocals), brass instrument repairer, Tony Tolhurst (bass), and the journalist, John Pilgrim (washboard). Sonny Terry is reported as saying that Pilgrim was the best washboard man in the country. Tony Tolhurst had been preceded on bass by Jack Collier and Joe Muddell, a jazz bassist and freelance.

Because of the nationwide demand for the Vipers, this meant travel and variety tours for the group. On Sunday 9 June 1957, for example, they appeared at the Marina, Ramsgate and then all week at the Hull Palace in "Rock That Skiffle" with Jim Dale, other supporting artists and the skiffle contest — Stanley Dale's National Skiffle Contest. Jim Dale (no relation to Stanley Dale) and the Vipers continued to be associated with this contest for some months, performing and promoting the contest at shows in, for example, December 1957 at Finsbury Park, Birmingham and Barking. On one such tour, taking in Newcastle, Hank Marvin and Bruce Welch met the Vipers at a jazz club there. Later, when the two came to London and worked at the 2 I's, they made contact again with Wally.

Jean Van Den Bosch explained in the *Melody Maker* in April 1958 how he had got involved in skiffle and the Vipers, in spite of not really liking the music. "I used to sing folk songs in coffee houses — the '2 I's', the 'Breadbasket' and many others. Just for my own amusement. Pals would insist that I took my guitar along every time I went and it was soon the accepted thing.

"Very soon others followed... Eventually groups were formed which became the skiffle names of today.

1956 And All That: Skiffle Reminiscences

I think my first guitar was a Martin Coletti, bought in 1958, although it never really got played due to basic tuning difficulties and learning problems. I didn't come from a musical family, and, in those days, guitar lessons at school were unheard of. However, it was possible to watch and listen to those who could play, and the Family Archive records a visit on 10 July 1957 to see the Vipers at the Palace Theatre, Newcastle, now long since demolished. Dressed in what looked like blue boiler suits, they were top of the bill on one of those touring variety shows which were the main vehicle of live entertainment at that time. Of course, it was first house for me, as the second house finished a bit late for a twelve year-old with school the next day!

Mike Waites

"One day I was asked to join the Vipers and I accepted the offer quite casually. Looking back, I can't think why. I don't like skiffle and I never have.

"Perhaps I hoped vaguely that the Vipers would advance beyond that stage and lead the field instead of following it."[46]

The Vipers did eventually drop the skiffle group description and recorded two beat numbers "No Other Baby" coupled with "Baby Why?" in December 1957, followed by another single, "Make Ready for Love" in May 1958, both recording sessions unusually featuring a bass clarinet.

Given Van Den Bosch's dissatisfaction, it was perhaps not unexpected that he would leave the group in late 1957 to be replaced by Freddy Lloyd. Later, when the Vipers had a week in variety in Birmingham, Wally asked Hank Marvin to play lead guitar and Jet Harris to play bass. The Vipers' last recording — "Summertime Blues" backed with "Liverpool Blues" — included Hank, Jet, and Tony Meehan on drums, along with Whyton, and Martyn. By October 1958, Marvin and Bruce Welch were out on tour

backing Cliff Richard.

With the death of skiffle, the Vipers came to an end. Lonnie Donegan offered Wally Whyton a job, but Wally was considered too tall, and so he went off to France, busking. In 1960, the Vipers were reformed, with Whyton, Pilgrim, Ian Maclean (guitar) and a bassist, to accompany songs in the musical play, *Mr Burke MP,* at the Mermaid Theatre, London. Wally also played the part of the commentator. Four of the songs from the show were recorded on Pye with Whyton and Sally Miles as the vocalists.

Following skiffle's demise, Wally Whyton did not sink into obscurity, but enjoyed a career as a presenter of children's shows on television (Pussy Cat Willum and Ollie Beak made him more of a celebrity than skifffle did), as a recorded singer of children's songs, and as a long-serving broadcaster on radio, with programmes like *Country Meets Folk* and *Country Club.* Wally Whyton died in 1997; a celebration of his career, *A Viper's Tale,* was broadcast on Radio 2 in 1996.

Said to be born in Tennessee in 1931 — it was apparently Michigan — and with a background in revival meeting songs and country music, Johnny Duncan was not the only genuine American in Britain amongst all the skiffle performers of American blues, folk and country songs — Alan Lomax was performing here, for example — but he was the only one to make the UK hit parade. And that with a group that was not really a skiffle group after the style of the Vipers or Chas McDevitt but more like the then rockabilly group of the man he had replaced in the Barber band — Lonnie Donegan.

At thirteen, Duncan sang in a Baptist church quartet, as well as in other churches, including those for blacks. A guitarist neighbour showed him some basic chords at sixteen and the rest he taught himself. After leaving school, Johnny got a job with a roofing firm, moving with it to Texas. There he bought a guitar and formed a trio. After working around, the trio got air time on the *Saturday Night Hayride* radio show, and, on giving up their jobs, started touring.

They had some initial success, but things did not go so well and the trio disbanded until its members had earned enough money to move on. This achieved, they moved to Indiana and were given their own radio show, which really payed off until Johnny Duncan was called up in 1952.

Duncan served in the US Army in Britain, forming a country group at the camp at Molesworth, near Huntingdon, Cambridgeshire, at which he was stationed and where he entertained the troops. He married a local girl, Betty, in 1953 while at Molesworth, returning to America with her in 1954 for demobilization. Johnny Duncan's wife returned to England to visit relatives in late 1955, was taken ill, and had to have an operation. This brought Duncan back to Britain again and he decided to stay and look for work.[47]

He may not have considered a career in music — while selling clothes on his father-in-law's Huntingdon market stall — had he not recognised the opportunities of the time. A copy of the *Melody Maker* took him in the direction of Humphrey Lyttleton's club where people thought he was Lonnie Donegan. Playing that night in 1956 was the Chris Barber band, and Chris too was taken by Johnny Duncan's similarity to Donegan, who had not long left Barber to front his own group. On being told by Duncan that he could sing and play guitar, and after an audition, Chris Barber got him to join his band that weekend, playing at the Festival Hall. Duncan not only looked like Donegan he sounded like him.

Less American in manner than some British singers, and good at picking up local accents, he was labelled the Cockney Hill-Billy in the Midlands. In describing his musical background to Tony Brown in the *Melody Maker*, Johnny Duncan said that his roots were in country music, which he had listen to since he was a kid, and that he had heard jazz and skiffle "though we didn't call it that."[48]

After joining the Barber band as Donegan's replacement in 1956, he left the following year to form his own group. In addition to himself this consisted of Denny Wright (guitar, and formerly with Lonnie Donegan), Jack Fallon or Johnny Bell (bass), Lennie Hastings (drums) and Danny Levan (violin). In homage to Bill Monroe's Blue Grass Boys, Duncan gave the same name to his own group. Although seen by the fans at the time as a skiffle group, possibly because of his Barber skiffle association, Johnny Duncan and his Blue Grass Boys were a country band, as the instrumentation (Danny Levan on violin, for example) and the group's repertoire indicated. As Duncan himself said: "Don't get me wrong, I like skiffle — but I aim to introduce a broader pattern of music, After all, Country and

Western is really nothing but a modification of skiffle.

"I think British audiences are going to like it. Folk are pretty much alike all the world over."[49]

Duncan cut his first Columbia disc in late February 1957 and his variety debut with his own group took place at Leeds on March 3 1957. An EP of four songs ("Freight Train Blues" and three others), reviewed in *Jazz Journal* was described as: "A brisk performance from this American hillybilly [sic] singer, with plenty of falsetto decoration. Last track ["Out of Business"] is likeable. Really professional accompaniment, where Sandy Brown [the jazz clarinetist], in rather unusual company, provides some pleasant phrases."[50]

In August 1957, the Blue Grass Boys achieved a hit with "Last Train to San Fernando" which stayed in the charts for 17 weeks, reaching number two. Nik Cohn believed that this song was much better than anything that Donegan had recorded and that if skiffle had not died suddenly, Duncan might have gone on to do well. "Last Train" was a new arrangement by Duncan of a Trinidadian calypso; the b-side of the record, "Rock-A-Billy Baby" was also well received. Cohn nominated "Last Train" as the best British Fifties record, claiming a lack of competition meant that he was "taking no great chances" in making such "a cosmic claim".[51]

Duncan and his group appeared in variety and in a number of radio and television programmes of the period. In February 1958 it was announced that the group was booked for its second, eight-week nationwide variety tour of the Moss Empires starting in March. He introduced radio programmes for both the BBC and Radio Luxembourg and he and his Blue Grass Boys had two further minor hits with "Blue Blue Heartache" and "Footprints in the Snow", both making number twenty-seven in the last months of 1957. Later in Britain Duncan worked as a country singer in clubs and again after emigrating to Australia in 1974.

With the exception of the Vipers, who came to skiffle via the coffee-bar route, Colyer, Donegan, Barber, Korner, McDevitt and Duncan all came to it through their involvement with jazz. Duncan's association with jazz was a brief one, however, and did not seem to make much of a mark on his later independent career, while McDevitt was also caught up in the coffee bar scene. Of them all, and discounting Barber whose band gave up skiffle as his vocalists left him one by one to form their own groups, only Donegan had regular and lasting commercial success beyond the skiffle craze years with the kind of group that he set up after leaving Barber. To do so Donegan was obliged eventually to drop the skiffle description and to broaden his repertoire to include, amongst other material, comedy songs like "Putting on the Style" and "My Old Man's a Dustman" and "Does Your Chewing Gum Lose its Flavour".

With some exceptions, skiffle was not much appreciated by "serious" record reviewers of the time, who, it must be said, were probably not

LAST TRAIN TO SAN FERNANDO
Words & Music by
Randolph Padmore
Sylvester DeVere
The Mighty Dictator
Recorded by Johnny Duncan on Columbia
2/-
CROMWELL MUSIC LTD.
4 DENMARK STREET W.C.2.
By arrangement with Duchess Music Corporation New York

Skiffle events of 1957.

writing for the teenage skiffle fans who bought the records. Some of those prominently involved in skiffle — Nancy Whiskey, Jean Van Der Bosch of the Vipers, and Alexis Korner — were themselves not always fully committed to the music. Whatever *their* individual reasons, there was a view that once skiffle had entered the hit parade it went commercial. This was certainly true of Donegan, although it was precisely that commercial success that stimulated the skiffle craze. Other groups, such as the Vipers courted commercial success and, in doing so, produced an essentially British skiffle sound that was to be much imitated by young boys and men, generally outside the jazz scene. Colyer, one of skiffle's pioneers, was never commercially minded and his contribution to skiffle can get overlooked by the historian of popular music. Korner took to the blues, becoming the mentor to youngsters of a like mind, and Duncan became more country than skiffle, his whereabouts apparently unknown today. Donegan, along with McDevitt, are the "Big Four" skiffle survivors and on occasion continue to play the distinctive music of the Fifties in the Nineties.

Opposite: Sheet music for Johnny Duncan's "Last Train to San Fernando".

5 Listen to the Song I Sing — Groups Galore

The Big Four — the Vipers, and those groups led by Donegan, McDevitt and Duncan — enjoyed commercial success and in many ways they, along with Colyer, set the standard for others, particularly the amateur groups, to emulate. A number of other skiffle groups, such as the Avon Cities Skiffle Group, the City Ramblers and that led by Bob Cort, also achieved some national recognition with the skiffle audience but never quite became household names. Some of these groups, perhaps less well-known to other than skiffle fans, existed before the boom, others were formed by musicians because of it — to capitalise on a popular music fashion. Yet others, such as the Eden Street, 2.19, or Worried Men, were spawned by the skiffle craze itself and began to experience some of the same commercial exposure as musicians like Donegan and the Vipers who they had probably taken as their models. Skiffle, then gave rise to groups galore, a number of which recorded, although often not extensively.

Outside of the Colyer and Barber groups, the only other skiffle group within a jazz band to be significantly recorded was that in the Avon Cities Jazz Band, founded in 1949, when it began playing in the Bristol and Bath area. Known as Ray Bush and the Avon Cities Skiffle — Ray Bush (guitar and vocals) was the band's clarinetist — it recorded eight tracks in June 1956 that included "How Long Blues", "Green Corn" and "This Little Light of Mine". These were subsequently issued as both 78rpm couplings and two EPs. Produced relatively early on in the skiffle boom, the *Gramophone* reviewer of the first EP and a 78rpm was quite well disposed towards these numbers, although refusing to see them as proper skiffle, and in particular commended Mike Hitchings' mandolin playing. However, given a preference for the work of the Memphis Jug Band or Cannon's Jug Stompers, the same reviewer of the second EP suggested the Avons made use of harmonica and/or jug.[1] Another reviewer of the first EP in *Jazz Journal* thought the music bogus but inoffensive and more wholesome than some of the attempts at rhythm and blues he had heard. A different *Jazz Journal* reviewer of some of the numbers on the other EP thought them unobjectionable and "better than the sort of stuff that Lonnie Donegan turns out, for there is relaxation of a kind here."[2] *Jazz Monthly* too thought that two of the skiffle tracks under review bore no relationship to the original form — it was "a polite form of rock and roll". Ray Bush was thought better than Donegan but the whole thing was considered rather uninteresting. The reviewer reflected on the fact that "Huddie Ledbetter made little money in his lifetime, while today singers who give poor imitations of his vocals can reach the top of the hit parade."[3]

The guitarist, Wayne Chandler, left in 1957 to join Terry Lightfoot's band and the group recorded a further four tracks in London in April 1958, as part of an LP, with Ray Bush (guitar, vocal), Mike Hitchings (mandolin), Geoff Nichols (bass), Basil Wright (playing drums, not washboard on this occasion). The songs, "I'm on My Way to Canaan Land", "Hand Me Down My Walking Cane", "House of the Rising Sun", and "Roll 'em Pete" were briskly dismissed by *Jazz Monthly* as being as dire as most skiffle offerings and having little relation to what the reviewer considered was the genuine article.[4]

The Avon Cities Jazz Band is still in existence and plays regularly at a Bristol pub, although only two founder members remain — Geoff Nichols and Mike Hitchings.

Although previously playing skiffle in a band within a band, former Barber associate, Dickie Bishop, left the jazz band world and formed his own group, the Sidekicks, in March 1957, and played at jazz clubs, concerts and variety theatres, as well as on radio and television. Bishop wrote some of his own songs and had some success with "No Other Baby", also recorded by the Vipers and by Bobby Helm in America. The group released eight sides

Press advert January 1957.

1956 And All That: Skiffle Reminiscences

I believe that it was sometime in 1958 that we realised that skiffle was losing its appeal to audiences, so we dropped it from the programme. At the same time, the band was changing its style. Mike Hitchins was doubling on alto sax and we were playing trad jazz mixed with highly arranged mainstream.

Then Tempo Records invited us to another recording session in April 1958 and said they wanted skiffle as well as band numbers on the one LP. The result was not a success. One critic said that the record sleeve (a photo of us standing on the Clifton Suspension Bridge in the pouring rain) was as gloomy as its contents. I believe that we did four skiffle numbers on that record, but apart from "House of the Rising Sun" in 12/8, I cannot remember any of the other titles. That was the last time that we skiffled.

A short time later Jan Ridd, Wayne Chandler and my brother all left the band through pressure of their daytime jobs and were replaced by John Critchinson , Frank Feeney and Johnny Phipps. In 1963 John Critchinson and I, feeling "hemmed in" by the Avon Cities style, left the band and teamed up with another bassist to play our own style of jazz.

The Avon Cities Jazz Band is still in existence and plays on alternate Fridays at the "Old Duke" pub in Bristol. Only Geoff Nichols and Mike Hitchins of the original band remain. Ray Bush married a Mojave girl and is now living on an Indian reservation outside Los Angeles and leading a jazz band in the city.

My memory of those days is one of enjoyment: we enjoyed playing jazz and skiffle and audiences enjoyed listening. There were several of our skiffle numbers that I loved because they had nice melodies and interesting chord sequences, but they were only received politely by the listeners; yet monotonous, two chord numbers always brought the house down! During our time as a skiffle group we played many times alongside Wally Whyton, Chas McDevitt and Lonnie Donegan.

Basil Wright

during 1957 and 1958 — seven titles in all as "No Other Baby" was issued twice with different couplings.

The Sidekicks were made up of Dickie Bishop (guitar and vocals), Don Wilson (bass), Stan Belwood (drums) and Bob Watson (guitar and vocals) who was later replaced by Pete Korrison. Both Wilson and Belwood had played in jazz bands (Belwood with Mick Mulligan) while Korrison, who had recorded with Donegan, had been a founder member of a number of skiffle and folk clubs before skiffle became popular.[5]

Dickie Bishop, born in 1935, took up the banjo-ukulele at the age of fourteen and formed the Brent Valley Jazz Band. Bishop became a professional after national service and in 1955 joined Chris Barber to share vocals with Lonnie Donegan. He had also worked as a solo country singer and guitarist. At Donegan's departure from Barber, Dickie took over banjo, guitar and vocals, later joining Donegan in variety in late 1956 for six months, before branching out with his own skiffle group the following year. From summer 1958 Bishop played with Mickey Ashman, then with Kenny Ball from spring 1959, briefly leaving Ball to lead the Sidekicks again in early 1960 for a few months. Now living in Germany, Dick Bishop took part in Chris Barber's reunion tour in 1995 together with Lonnie Donegan.

Two of the founding members of the Bill Bailey Skiffle Group, Bill Bailey and Freddy Legon, also came from a jazz background. Both had played in the Original London Blue Blowers — often seen as a precursor to the skiffle movement — a trio which had a jazz repertoire (making use of the guitar, kazoo and comb-and-paper blue-blowing), and included a washboard player, Johnny Jones.

Freddy Legon, a Londoner, was given a ukulele at fourteen but sang and played clarinet on his first gigs with the Blue Rhythm Boys, a group in which his cousin Bill Bailey played guitar and sang. Later, in the Original London Blue Blowers, Freddy Legon played paper-and-comb and sang.

Dickie Bishop c. 1956. (Courtesy Cromwell Management.)

Early in 1957 both musicians decided to form a skiffle group and soon became regular contributors to the *Saturday Skiffle Club* radio programme. The original instrumentation was three rhythm guitars, tea-chest bass and drums. The six-man group eventually consisted of Bill Bailey (guitar, vocals and kazoo), Freddy Legon (electric guitar, vocals and comb-and-paper), Stan Jayne (guitar, vocals and washboard), Dave Coward (bass), Bill Powell (guitar and banjo) and John Beauchamp (drums).[6] The group broadened its scope by members playing more than one instrument and by extending its repertoire to include jazz and English and Scottish folk songs but it made no commercial recordings.

Unlike the previous three groups, the City Ramblers, seeemed to have no previous jazz band prehistory or association. Formed in 1954, before the skiffle craze had taken off, it originally took spasm music as its inspiration and began by performing on the London streets. Its founders were the red-bearded art teacher Russell Quaye and his wife, Hylda Sims. In 1956 the group successfully toured Belgium, Germany and Denmark and made its first radio and television broadcasts, as well as its first recording in September that year in Copenhagen. Later, in July 1957, it visited Moscow for a fortnight of concerts as part of the Sixth Annual World Youth Festival.

The City Ramblers boasted a repertoire of over 300 songs and instrumental pieces that covered calypsos, music hall songs, English and Scots

111

1956 And All That: Skiffle Reminiscences

Our repertoire of songs was added to from the recordings of the Vipers, Dick "Cisco" Bishop, Ray Bush and the Avon Cities' Skiffle, Chas McDevitt and Johnny Duncan. We also kept up with Lonnie Donegan's output, as well as drawing material from the Weavers, Hank Williams, Woody Guthrie, Buddy Holly and the Everly Brothers. We learned to adapt our programmes to suit particular audiences, adding spirituals for church socials and Irish and Scottish songs for the Friday night crowd flocking to the Leigh Arms, which included expat construction workers at the nearby Bankside Colliery.

In the summer of 1957, we made two 78rpm records at a local studio, which was little more than a converted front room of a large house. Western Sound Recorders was situated in Wilson Patten Street, Warrington, and was a Quaker family-run concern operating on Christian principles. We recorded " I'm Alabama Bound" backed with "Worried Man Blues" on a 10" metal disc. A second recording, on a 12" disc, featured Bob singing Hank Williams's "Wedding Bells" and a group effort on the other side, a rendition of "You'll Never Get to Heaven", popular at boy scout camp fires and with our audiences

Norman Froggatt

ballads, and jazz. With seven members it was larger than most leading groups and, along with the Chas McDevitt and Alan Lomax groups, it featured female musicians — Hylda Sims (guitar and vocals) and Shirley Bland (washboard, banjo and vocals). The other musicians were Russell Quaye (quattro — a small, four-stringed guitar — kazoo and vocals), Jim McGregor (guitar and vocals), Bob Taylor (blue-blowing, jug and snare-drum), Vic Pitt (bass) and Eric Bunyan (fiddle and mandolin). The four featured vocalists all specialised in solo songs and the group's range of instruments was somewhat different to the usual skiffle group with its jazz and country features. The bassist Vic Pitt, had played in his brother's trio in the Skiffle Cellar in 1958 and accepted the invitation to join the Ramblers, working with them until joining Kenny Ball in 1959. Prior to Vic Pitt, the group's recordings had featured either Anthony Buquet or Peter Maynard on tub-bass. They were the resident group at the Skiffle Cellar, London and had appeared at most major venues including the Royal Albert Hall and the Royal Festival Hall.[7]

Reviewing four tracks of the City Ramblers' 1956 recording made in Copenhagen, the *Gramophone's* reviewer got almost enthusiastic about skiffle for once, as the group and its performances met his idea of what skiffle was all about: "a well balanced ensemble of three *assorted* strings, washboard and two or three wind instruments, however humble, and playing numbers that don't always sound like an imitation of Tin Pan Alley's conception of mountain music." Praise was given for the fluent clarinet, the remarkable effects using the trumpet mouthpiece, imaginative washboard playing and the inclusion of an instrumental, "I Want a Girl". The fluent clarinetist featured on some tracks was Henrik Johansen, the

The City Ramblers in Europe c. mid 1950s. (Courtesy Max Jones Archive.)

trumpet mouthpiece was played by Chris Bateson, the washboard by Alan Sutton. Rambling Jack Elliott supplied guitar and vocal for "Midnight Special", also recorded on this occasion, and apparently released only on the Storyville label along with other tracks. Not everyone was pleased with the Copenhagen EP, however. *Jazz Journal's* reviewer thought it "not really up to the standard of a rather lame jug band."[8] A different *Jazz Journal* critic of the group's "Ella Speed" and "2.19 Blues" 1957 single thought them the best of the skifflers making "quite an authentic noise". In spite of some reservations about Hylda Sims' blues singing, the *Gramophone* reviewer of the same record was equally appreciative of the group: "The kazoo and blue-blower are quite exceptionally good."[9] Later *Gramophone* reviews of City Ramblers recordings, while still preferring the group to others, commented on less interesting material, made a less than satisfactory comparison with the Dixieland Jug Blowers, whose "Boodle-Am-Shake" the Ramblers performed, and noted the inclusion of hillbilly-type songs. The wish is made that the "group would record more of the out-and-out jazz numbers that I've heard them play; their version of 'Shine', for example, really moves."[10]

In December 1957, the City Ramblers seemed to be at the height of their success. They were due to fly to Stuttgart in January for a one-day television appearance, were discussing a three-week tour of Spain and Italy for the spring, had been invited to appear in the BBC's Fourth Annual Festival of Dance Music in 1958, and were to make their fourth *Saturday Skiffle Club* broadcast at the end of December. While the group was then touring in "Skiffle Jamboree", pianist Johnny Parker was leading the resident band at the Skiffle Cellar club.[11]

According to Holger Lührig, Russell Quaye kept playing skiffle and jug band music in the Sixties and Seventies and recorded in Germany in 1961. This LP, recorded in Frankfurt am Main as by the London City Ramblers, had a line-up of Russell Quaye, Bob Taylor (funnel), Terry Hennessy (spasmophone — a gramophone horn with tuba mouthpiece) and Rose Ann Law (washboard). The titles, that included "Blue Heaven" and "I Wish I Could Shimmy", indicate a jazz or spasm performance rather than a skiffle one. In the Seventies and Eighties Russell Quaye often toured on the continent with Mimi Daniels, made television and radio appearances and three LPs. He died in early 1984 after a heart attack.[12]

> **That SPASM MUSIC! The Latest!**
> **The Greatest! The Mostest!**
>
> # CITY RAMBLERS
>
> **BOODLE-AM-SHAKE** TEMPO
> **and DELIA'S GONE** No. A.165. 78 & 45 r.p.m.

Another group that, like the City Ramblers, acknowledged its roots, was the Barnstormers Spasm Band. Brian Rust, the well-known jazz discographer, joined an existing group of four other musicians known by that name in February 1957. The band comprised Jim Robinson (guitar), John Gunn (kazoo), John Wadley (harmonica) and Peter Wadley (bass); to which Brian Rust added his washboard (later the drums too), as well as singing. In the summer of that year the band was joined by John Denning (banjo), Rust's brother-in-law. In September 1957, one of their acetates was given an airing by the jazz broadcaster Rex Harris, but the band failed a Hughie Green audition.

In February the following year George Martin got the band to record two sides for Parlophone ("Whistling Rufus" and "Won't You Come Home Bill Bailey?"), issued in March as Do-It-Yourself-Jazz. A further two sides recorded at that time were rejected. The band appeared later on *In Town Tonight*, at a concert in the Queen Elizabeth Room, Royal Festival Hall, and at the annual radio show at Earls Court, and in two performances on BBC television in the last part of 1958. Rust was replaced on the second show by John R.T. Davies since, working for the BBC, Rust was not permitted by his boss to appear.

In February 1959, the band recorded four sides for Tempo, that included "Tiger Rag" and "Shine", although the pieces were not issued until October. According to Rust, two tracks appeared as one of the last 78s to be pressed in England. There were various other band engagements but pressure of work obliged Rust to leave in October 1960 and sometime in 1961 the Barnstormers disbanded.[13]

Charles Fox, in the *Gramophone*, while recognising the Barnstormers' enthusiasm, said something more was needed by a group that produced the sort of home-spun jazz likely to be found in the Lower Remove. John Oakland reviewing the first two of their recorded tracks in the same journal

114

was impressed by their "sheer joie-de-vivre, freshness and ingenuity" and in December chose it as the most interesting novelty of the year.[14] Was it better to be appreciated as a novelty rather than not at all?

Like other skiffle group leaders, Bob Cort also had something of a jazz background. Born in 1930 at Loughborough, Leicestershire, he attended Loughborough Grammar School; subsequently he studied at the Leicester College of Art and played guitar in local bands — he was originally a dixieland enthusiast. Cort then developed as a solo singer/guitarist act for cabarets and parties, later playing in coffee bars. Much of his material was of the folk kind which became familiar through skiffle, and so he was prepared for skiffle when it arrived. Cort went to London in 1954, and was later heard playing in a coffee bar by Mark White of Decca, who signed him up.[15]

Bob's first record, "It Takes a Worried Man" backed with "Don't You Rock Me Daddy-O", was issued in January 1957 and during that year his group recorded several other Decca singles, including "Freight Train", "Six-Five Special" (the signature tune of the Saturday BBC television show of that name), "School Day" and a two-part medley, "Skiffle Party". When Bob Cort's first record was released, it was announced in the *Melody Maker* that he and his group would make their concert debut at the Festival Hall on 29 January. Along with the Ken Colyer Skiffle Group and the Vipers they were to take part in a National Jazz Federation skiffle session. The Bob Cort group was then immediately booked as residents for the skiffle series organised by the NJF at the Festival Hall, where they presented party music — folk songs, nonsense songs, jazz and skiffle.[16]

In February 1957, the Bob Cort group shared the "Kings of Skiffle" show at the Prince of Wales Theatre with the Vipers. It provoked an unappreciative review from the *Jazz Journal's* diarist, who said that Cort was nervous, sang flat and suggested that his musicians — "four well-

---

1956 And All That: Skiffle Reminiscences

A lesser-known favourite of mine was Ray Bush and his Avon Cities Skiffle Group from Bristol. They came from within the Avon Cities Jazz Band and Ray Bush (clarinet) was also the lead singer in the skiffle group. They recorded an EP on the Tempo Label with great songs, all of which I performed. They were quite similar in approach to Colyer, even using a mandolin on some numbers. I also liked Russell Quaye and the City Ramblers because they embraced the jug band sound to a certain extent — we never went that far.

Our pet hates were Bob Cort and Chas McDevitt. I suppose because their male vocal leads were rather weak and female lead singers (Nancy Whiskey and later Shirley Douglas in McDevitt's group) were not really approved of. However, a McDevitt B-side, "I'm Satisfied with My Girl" became quite a favourite amongst groups, mainly, no doubt, because of its slightly suggestive lyrics.

Dave Illingworth

known jazzmen" — would probably want their names kept out of the proceedings. The diarist referred to solos on guitar and washboard that occurred at several points "before the inevitable chanting chorus was switched on again." The Vipers seemed happier, although apparently introduced as Walt Whiteman and the Vapers, and "developed quite a swing on 'Don't [You] Rock Me Daddy-O'", insufficient it would have seemed to prevent people exiting to the bar.[17]

In June 1957, Cort's group, featuring Ken Sykora on solo guitar, recorded an LP, *Ain't It a Shame (to Sing Skiffle on Sunday),* a mixture of standards and folk: "The Streets of Laredo" followed by "I Can't Give You Anything But Love". Unfortunately, the title of this LP left an opening for skiffle's less than appreciative *Gramophone* reviewer, who wrote: "it's a shame to sing this sort of stuff any time. It's even more of a shame to label it skiffle and sell it in great dollops."[18]

In adddition to making records, the Bob Cort group broadcast, appeared in the West End (the group shared top of the bill with the singer Yana for a two-week season at the Prince of Wales Theatre), at the Royal Albert Hall, and made television appearances, but refused to turn professional. At the time of the recording of the *Six-Five Special* signature tune, Bob Cort had been working in an advertising firm for six years and was loathe to give up a reliable job for music but found it difficult to turn down contracts when offered them. The group members agreed with this stance. For them, music was their hobby and if they played the same numbers constantly, full-time — they thought — the fun would go out of it.[19]

BOB CORT

is this week's visitor to

THE
Ten-Forty Club

Bob Cort, from *Radio Times*. (Courtesy BBC.)

The Cort group also topped the Skiffle and Blues concert presented by the National Jazz Federation at the De Montfort Hall, Leicester in early November 1957. In spite of the added attractions of Dickie Bishop and his Sidekicks, the Johnny Parker Band and a local group — the Betty Smith Skiffle Group — there was a small audience, possibly due to the fact that Count Basie was playing at Coventry that night. Although Cort himself thought that skiffle in a varied programme was fun, three hours of skiffle was another matter and he could not blame people for staying away.[20]

In the same month as this poorly attended concert, Bob Cort announced that the strain of two jobs was getting too much and his firm's directors had agreed to him taking six months off from his work as an advertising visualiser to concentrate on show business. At the time of this announcement, Bob said that he and his group had been signed for a Christmas pantomime and would also tour Britain with the Paul Anka Show.

Around October 1957, Cort's *Making the Most of Skiffle*, was published by Felix McGlennon at 2/6d. It provided would-be skifflers with guidance on the necessary instruments (and how to buy and play them), how to play some well known songs, as well as tips on presenting the group in a competent and professional manner.[21] A short *Melody Maker* review of the book endorsed Bob Cort's approach and concluded: "Cort believes skiffle is a healthy sign in this age of radio and television and potted amusements. Which, to me, is adequate reason for this book." And continued: "The only trouble is, practically every time I switch on the radio I get a skiffle group"[22] — which rather spoiled it.

In addition to the leader (guitar and vocals), the Bob Cort Skiffle Group's line-up was Ken Sykora (guitarist and BBC radio presenter), Nevil Skrimshire (guitarist, formerly with Humphrey Lyttleton and later Alex Welsh), George Jennings (bass) and Bill Colyer (washboard). Bill Colyer was later replaced by the Australian drummer, Viv "Clambake" Carter and the two guitarists by Vic Flick and Diz Disley. Later Ray Oliver took over on drums and Ivor Daniels replaced Diz Disley; Bryan Daly also played guitar with the group. Liz Winters provided additional vocal input on a couple of the early singles.

In 1959, following the skiffle craze, Bob Cort recorded the album, *Eskimo Nell*, a collection of sixteen songs, and later the *Barrack Room Ballads* LP. By 1962, however, Cort was combining the career of publican with that of resident singer on the BBC children's television series, *Sing a Song*, where he sang to his guitar and illustrated songs with his own drawings. He was also featured in the radio programme *Listen on Saturday* and had appeared on programmes such as *Saturday Club*, *Easy Beat* and *Ring-a-Ding-Ding*. The year 1976 marked a decade and a half of children listening to Bob Cort singing to his guitar on *Listen with Mother*, for which he had written the theme tune. Cort died in 1982 at the age of fifty-two — about a week after the BBC's decision to take off *Listen with Mother*, first broadcast in 1950.[23]

The Les Hobeaux Skiffle Group was a good example of a successful band, albeit of brief duration, that was created by the skiffle boom and of one of the many groups that played at the 2 I's. The group's title, Les Hobeaux, is the French version of the American word 'hobos', meaning tramps or wayfarers. Its members had an international background, either by country of origin, parentage or residency: Les Bennetts (guitar), was from Yorkshire, Roger Smith (vocalist) had spent five years in South Africa, Darryl Lyte (guitar and piano) was from Turkey, Keith Lardner (lead vocalist), was descended from an African chief, Brian Gregg (bass), was a Scot with a Norwegian mother, and Roy Tobin (guitar) a Londoner with a Spanish mother. Other people associated with this group were Red Reece, a drummer, who replaced Tobin when he was called up, Winky Wimbledon and Rex Rehak (bass), and Alan Jones and Dave Russell (washboard).[24] According to Chas McDevitt, "the original members of this group were still students at the Polytechnic in Regent Street, London" in August 1957, but within a short space of time jumped from "a group of busking students to a top-of-the-bill attraction."[25] At the 2 I's Les Hobeaux began by supporting the Vipers and finished by replacing them when the Vipers toured. The group recorded "Toll the Bell Easy" backed with "Oh, Mary, Don't You Weep" and "Hey, Hey Daddy Blues" coupled with "Mama Don't Allow" in 1957 for HMV, which were well received and also issued as an EP, called appropriately enough *Soho Skiffle*. It also made broadcasts and variety appearances, played concerts (replacing Donegan once when he was ill), was seen on *Six-Five Special*, and featured in the film *The Golden Disc* in which the group sang "Dynamo", its last recording in 1958. When the group split up, Les Bennetts and Red Reece joined McDevitt; later Bennett became part of Donegan's backing group.

Three other, lesser known groups, associated with the 2 I's coffee bar, were the Blue Jeans, Soho, and Worried Men skiffle groups. The Blue Jeans appeared on the *Rockin' At the 2 I's* Decca LP, performing "Lonesome Traveller" and "When I Get to Glory". The Soho Skiffle Group, led by Jimmy Bryning (guitar and vocal), recorded five tunes for Melodisc. "Give Me a Big Fat Woman" was the only unusual title among such skiffle favourites as "Midnight Special" and "Frankie and Johnny". The Worried Men played at the Skiffle Cellar and elsewhere, as well as the 2 I's, and were led by singer-guitarist Terry Nelhams (later to be re-christened Adam Faith). As far as is known, the group released no singles but was featured on two 1958 Decca LPs: *Stars of Six-Five Special* (performing "Fraulein") and *Rockin' At the 2 I's* ("This Little Light", and "9000 Miles from Home").

With exception of the Bill Bailey Skiffle Group, all the groups described in this chapter recorded for various labels: Tempo, Decca, Parlophone, HMV and Melodisc. The Esquire record label, however, particularly helped to promote the skiffle movement and its better amateur performers by recording four skiffle competition winners: the first three groups placed in the National Skiffle Contest at Bury St Edmunds in June 1957 — the 2.19, Station and Delta skiffle groups — and the Lea Valley Skiffle Group, winner of the first prize in the contest at the Ritz, Leyton. Esquire usually issued this skiffle group material as both EP collections and 78 couplings.

The 2.19 group from Gillingham, Kent, recorded sixteen titles (four EPs) for Esquire in 1957 and 1958; four titles had been recorded before the group won the National Skiffle Contest. It was led by Mik Lauder and Mike Wallace (guitars and vocals), with four different bass players on the four EPs (Vic Pitt in 1958), and a change of washboard player (from Davey Chandler to Idle Bill Smith) after the first EP. The group became well known for its concert and club appearances (at the Modern Music Club in Gerrard Street, for example) and appeared at the Festival Hall's recital room, on the BBC's *Saturday Skiffle Club*, and ATV's *Saturday Spectacular*. The numbers recorded on the Esquire label covered such songs as "Freight Train" and "Railroad Bill" as well as lesser known items like "Roll the Union On" and "Texas Lady".

From Fulham, London, the Station Skiffle Group were a group of six musicians that included a banjoist and vamp accordion player. Originally formed at a church club in early 1957, they were very active in competitions, winning the Butlins All England Skiffle Contest, coming second out of seventy-five acts in the Carroll Levis series at the Metropolitan Theatre, winning the first heat of the Carlton Ballroom Skiffle Contest and coming second in the National Skiffle Contest at Bury St Edmunds. In late June 1957, the group recorded an EP of four songs that included "Steamboat Bill" and the "Titanic".

The Station Skiffle Group's name stemmed from the fact that they played on the platform of West Kensington underground station — where the stationmaster gave them a room to rehearse in — and they became the first skifflers to perform on the tube trains when invited aboard by the guards. But the group has another claim to fame because it attracted the attention of Britain's first independent pop record producer, Joe Meek, who had been responsible for helping to make "Bad Penny Blues" by Humphrey Lyttleton into a hit record. Joe wanted to get a demonstration record together to persuade Denis Preston to give him his first official recording session as a producer. He had also composed a number with Charles Blackwell entitled "Sizzling Hot" and was looking for someone to perform it.

Press advert, September 1957.

One evening he dropped into the Boileau Arms where the Station Skiffle Group were playing. "What he was looking for was a competent skiffle band. What he found was a nutty bunch of 18 years olds [sic]: one crawling about the stage with a washboard strapped to his legs, another was standing, rocking on his beer barrel bass while the singer, guitarist and accordion player were jumping about pulling faces. And the sound was terrific! The audience were full of it and he knew that if he

119

could capture this atmosphere on disc he would be onto a winner."[26]

After their performance, Joe took the group to a coffee bar, where he learned they had made some unsuccessful records, and offered them the opportunity to do more with him as their recording and personal manager. The latter job was already taken by a girlfriend's father but the offer of recording manager was accepted, although Joe wanted a name change for the group. As the lead vocalist was Jimmy Miller, and there was a Bar-B-Cue sign on the coffee bar counter, it was decided they would be called Jimmy Miller and the Barbecues.

After rehearsals in his flat, where Joe had a cramped studio and control room, and at West Kensington station, Joe played Denis Preston a rough recording of "Sizzling Hot" and then in August they all went off to a studio. After overcoming problems of recording the washboard, the song, together with the B-side, "Freewheeling Baby" was recorded. Joe "was delighted with it and played it over and over... he had made his own little bit of pop history by becoming Britain's first producer-engineer. Until then it was unheard of for the producer to also man the controls, and he would be doing it a lot in the future."[27]

Joe recorded Jimmy Miller and the Barbecues live a week later at the Metropolitan Theatre, Edgeware Road, where they were winners in the National Skiffle Contest. Unfortunately "Sizzling Hot", released on Columbia in September 1957, got nowhere — "too much atmosphere and not enough music!" has been suggested — and the Barbecues were told their sound, based on improvised instruments, would have to change through the use of drums and a proper bass guitar. With the exception of Jimmy Miller, the Barbecues resisted a change of sound and Joe recorded his next song, "Jelly Baby", backed with "Cry Baby Cry", with Jimmy and some session men. Released in February 1958, the record did not sell and the Barbecues broke up soon afterwards.[28]

Other people, including Lonnie Donegan and Johnny Duncan, benefited from Joe's recording techniques. "Last Train to San Fernando" was engineered by Joe. He also engineered Donegan's *Showcase* LP and before 1957 was over he had had a hand in "Don't You Rock Me Daddy-O", "Cumberland Gap", "Gamblin' Man", and "My Dixie Darling". The last-named was made in the British Legion drill hall at Plymouth making use of the echo in the men's lavatory. "Cumberland Gap" had been created in a rush — eight minutes for a run-through and one take — as Donegan had played it on a live television show without recording it first and this immediately created a demand for it. Other groups got in first, losing Donegan some sales, but his version was five weeks in the charts at number one.[29] Joe Meek, known as the *"Telstar* man" from the enormous 1962 instrumental hit he created for the Tornados, committed suicide in early 1967.

Formed and led in Glasgow by Douglas Taylor (banjo, guitar and vocal), the Delta Skiffle Group played local jazz clubs and dance halls and was resident at the Mahogany Hall Jazz Club. After getting to be runners-up in the Scottish National Skiffle Championship, the group was placed third in the National Skiffle Contest. This was a five-man group — three guitars,

washboard and bass — with the guitarist and singer doubling on banjo. Six tracks were recorded for Esquire in June 1957 and these included less usual material like "John Brown's Body" and "Open Up Them Pearly Gates ", as well as tunes such as "Skip To My Lou" and "Ain't You Glad".

Reviewing the Esquire LP of songs from the three winning groups in the First National Skiffle Contest, the *Gramophone's* man wrote that it was "quite the most boring record to which I have ever had to listen." *Jazz Journal's* review was more positive: "Although this is not the most polished of skiffle music, several of the tracks are well worth hearing, and Esquire are to be commended on encouraging a contest such as this."[30]

The Lea Valley Skiffle Group from Hackney, London, formed in early 1957, had been semi-finalists in the Butlins All England Skiffle Contest and third in the Donegan Trophy Competition and though not winning a place at the Bury St Edmunds National Contest were recorded by Esquire in September 1957. The group that recorded consisted of Ron Till and Trevor Morgan (guitars and vocals), two other guitars, banjo, washboard and two-string bass. The Esquire EP comprised "Steamline Train", "Railroad Bill",and two spirituals, "I'm Gonna Walk and Talk", and "Oh, Mary Don't You Weep".

The Skiffle Craze

Opposite: Skiffle club adverts.

Other groups who recorded during the skiffle boom, usually on minor labels, and not previously mentioned in this or earlier chapters, were not numerous, and included: Johnny Christmas and the Sunspots, who recorded a Starlite Records EP in March 1958; the Coffee Bar Skifflers, probably session musicians, who recorded an EP, *Skiffle Session*, for the Woolworth Embassy label in 1958; the Eden Street Skiffle Group, responsible for a set of ten flexi-disc 78rpms distributed by Headquarter and General Supplies at 10/- an album; the Frog Island Skiffle Group, who made an EP on the 77 Records label; and Sonny Stewart's Skiffle Kings, who recorded four tracks for Phillips in 1957. No sound record seems to have survived of a number of groups known from radio broadcasts — the Cotton Pickers, the Martians, Hi-Fi and Pete Curtis groups, for example. Nor were the many amateur groups of the time recorded for posterity, although some personal sound archives of some individual groups may exist locally. This is a pity, as a record of how such groups sounded would be an important source for appreciating the development of popular music.

During 1956 to 1958, when skiffle was "in", the music business occasionally attached that label to some recorded music — jazz, folk and popular — that was not really skiffle. Jimmy Jackson, initially a country singer was marketed by Columbia under a "rock 'n skiffle" label in 1957. Alan Lomax and the Ramblers, a folk group that recorded a few songs for Decca in August 1956, and included Peggy Seeger, Ewan MacColl and Shirley Collins in its personnel, and featured a washboard player, was sometimes also seen as part of the skiffle scene. A few of the recorded jazz performances of the period, such as those by the Bob Wallis Washboard Beaters and the Clyde Valley Stompers get drawn into the skiffle canon because of instrumentation and repertoire. And one or two jazz performers deliberately adopted the skiffle tag — the Charles McNair and Betty Smith groups, for example — when no skiffle (in the British sense) was involved. Other musicians were seen as skifflers mainly by association: the trombonist and bandleader, Don Lang, a regular on *Six-Five Special*, who recorded an album called *Skiffle Special*, and the jazz singer, George Melly (together with his Bubbling-Over Four), who appeared a number of times on *Saturday Skiffle Club*.

The music industry also produced cover versions of some skiffle hits by mainstream artists: both Billy Cotton and Dickie Valentine recorded "Putting on the Style"; while "Rock Island Line" was recorded by Don Cornell and Bobby Darin. Other skiffle numbers were covered then or later by British or American performers: for example, "Freight Train" (Beverly Sisters), "Midnight Special" (Andy Griffiths), and "Hey Liley Liley Lo" (Polka Dots). Skiffle medleys were put together by Winifred Atwell and Dick James, while "Skiffling Dogs" by the Stargazers and "Skiffling Strings", an instrumental piece by Ron Goodwin, also made use of the "in" word.

Skiffle parodies were produced by Stan Freburg ("Rock Island Line") and Jim Dale with "Picadilly Line", as well as comedy numbers by Peter Sellers with a skiffle type accompaniment: "Any Old Iron" and "Putting on the Smile". Comedy was also at the heart of the Morris and Mitch songs

122

1956 And All That: Skiffle Reminiscences

A college friend called Paul Morris, who played banjo and guitar, used to take us up around 1957-58 to the Troubadour Folk Song Club in the Old Brompton Road, London, to listen to Martin Carthy, the Thameside Four, Long John Baldry, Redd Sullivan, Shirley Collins, and Rambling Jack Elliott. We (a folk trio and the Mike Howley Band) did a floor spot there each time; the club was run by Jenny Barton.

We also did a gig with the fiddle player Eric Bunyan of the City Ramblers at a barbecue at Abinger Hatch, near Dorking; "Hand Me Down My Walkin' Cane" was our best number.

Terry Potter

Skiffle Venues in and Around London 1956-57

2 I's Club, 59 Old Compton Street, W1

44 Skiffle Club, 44 Gerrard Street, W1

51 Club, 10-11 Great Newport Street, WC2

Addlestone Jazz Society, Weymann's Hall

Baker Street Jazz Club

Battersea Jazz Club, Cornet of Horse

Bedfont Jazz Club

Blues and Skiffle Club, Roundhouse Wardour Street, W1

Boleyn Hotel, Staines

Breadbasket Espresso Bar and Restaurant

Cat's Whisker Coffee Bar, Kingly Street, W1

Chiesman's Restaurant, Lewisham

Chislehurst Caves

Cook's Ferry Inn, Edmonton

Croydon Jazz Club, Star Hotel, London Road

Cy Laurie Jazz Club, Great Windmill Street, W1

Enfield Jazz Club, The Barn, Ponders End

Ewell Jazz Club, Organ Inn

Fighting Cocks, Kingston

Fox and Goose, Ealing

Gyre and Gimble Coffee Bar, 31 John Adam Street, WC2

Harringay Jazz Club, Willingdon Road

Hendon Jazz Club, Heriot Road

Hot Club of London, Shakespeare Hotel, Woolwich

Humphrey Lyttleton Club, 100 Oxford Street, W1

Kew Jazz Club, Boathouse, Kew Bridge

Kingston Jazz Club (over Burtons)

Lewisham Jazz Club

Manor House Jazz Club, N4

Modern Music Club, 5 Gerrard Street, W1

Nucleus Coffee Bar, Monmouth Street, WC2

Owen Bryce Jazz Club, Bull, Birchwood, Swanley

Park Lane Jazz Club, Croydon

Princess Louise, High Holborn

Queen Victoria, North Cheam

Railway Hotel, Epsom

Royal Forest Hotel, Chingford

Skiffle Cellar, 49 Greek Street, W1

Soho Sinners Skiffle Club, Kentish Town

Swan, Walton-on-Thames

Thames Hotel, Hampton Court

Troubadour Coffee Bar, Old Brompton Road, SW

Two Brewers, East Hill, Wandsworth

Watford Jazz Club, St Albans Road

Wealdstone Jazz Club, Trinity Hall

White Hart, Southall

Whittington Hotel, Cannon Lane, Pinner

Wimbledon Jazz Club,

with such titles as "What Is a Skiffler?", "Six-Five Nothing Special", and "The Tommy Rot Story".

With some exceptions, most of the groups mentioned so far were based in and around London. Outside the main concert, theatre and other spots, the *Melody Maker's* weekly club calendar, largely reflecting the London jazz and skiffle scene, provided details of groups and performance venues —

Playing in and Around London in 1957

Some of the independent skiffle groups — those not attached to a jazz band — are set out below. Names are taken from the Melody Maker's *Jazz Club Calendar and do not include the very well known groups who were listed.*

2.19	Footwarmers	Ramblers
Alabamy	Dony Grey's	Red Devils
Alley Cats	Greyhounds	Riverside
Anacondas	John Hasted's	Johnny Rolph's
Bentmen	Hells Angels	Saffron Valley
Black Shadows	Ken Hyne's	Saxon
Bluejeans	Jimmy James's	Sinners
Bohemians	Jubilee	Skiffle Cats
Boll Weevils	Johnny Makins'	Soho
Buck Town	Rudy Marsalis and his	Soho Sinners
Cavemen	Creole Skiffle Group	Spiders
Clerics	Ken Mount's	Pete Stewart's
Cotton Pickers	New Hawleans	Sunrisers
Pete Curtis's	Old Timers	Vampires
Delta City	Panthers	Wayfarers
Discord	Penitentiary Five	Weevils
Dave Duggan's	Phoenix City	West Five
Eastsiders	Tony Pitts's	Ted Wood's
Eden Street	Quakers	Yacka

pubs, clubs and coffee bars — for skiffle fans. The detail in the calendar announcements also gives some idea of the growth of the music from 1956. The Skiffle Cellar, Soho, opened by Russell Quaye in April 1957, presented skiffle seven nights a week and the following month a listing in *Reveille* showed that, in addition to the Skiffle Cellar, the music could be heard elsewhere every night in the London area.[31]

Although more than one commentator at the time was anticipating an assured future for skiffle, this was not to be the case. By the end of 1958 the skiffle craze was over and by March 1959 skiffle had completely disappeared from *MM* club advertising. Russell Quaye and the City Ramblers were still performing at the Cellar, Greek Street, but there is no mention of skiffle in the club announcement.

While British skiffle had no exact contemporary equivalent in the USA, the land of its origins, it was taken up elsewhere in Europe, as well as spreading to Australia and New Zealand. Although some were possibly formed later than the Fifties, skiffle groups emerged in France, Germany, Sweden and the Netherlands. In Germany, for example, the Washboard Rhythm Boys Skiffle Group recorded five titles, including "Mama Don't Allow" and "Worried Man Blues", in Hanover in October 1958. The group

> # THE BIG SHOW
>
> starring
>
> # JOHNNIE RAY
> ### ("MR. EMOTIONS")
>
> with
>
> ## Graeme Bell's Skiffle Gang
> ## and
> ## Vic Sabrino
>
> *　*　*
>
> ## Joe Martin
>
> *　*　*
>
> ## Patricia Smith
> Winner of the ATN T.V. "TALENT QUEST"
>
> # A LEE GORDON PRODUCTION
>
> The "Big Show" Orchestra under the direction of
> **DENIS COLLINSON**

Graeme Bell's Skiffle Gang supported Johnny Ray's third Australian Tour in 1957.

consisted of piano, banjo, two guitars, clarinet (on some tracks), bass, washboard and solo and group vocals.[32] These would seem to have been more Colyer than Donegan-type skiffle performances.

Australia provides an interesting case study of how skiffle music winged its way across the globe. In his history of jazz in Australia, Andrew Bisset comments on the lack of access to black records and says that Australians muddled through. He notes, however, the influence of white bands like the Mound City Blue Blowers and the California Ramblers.[33] In Australia in 1950 the Good Oh Washboard Whackers made music for a short while.[34] Writing in the late 1970s about the imbalance of airwaves content, Don Burrows states that jazz-cum-popular music was much more readily accessible in the Thirties and Forties and usually available free. Bondi Beach at the weekend would attract groups of two or three guitars, ukulele, harmonica, possibly a clarinet, snare drum and brushes.[35]

In Australia, however, skiffle was particularly associated with Graeme Bell, the jazz pianist and bandleader who did so much to promote jazz in his country in the Forties. Having established a reputation in Australia, Bell visited England in 1947-8 and again in 1951-2. In 1954 he toured Korea and Japan for the army with a six-piece band. In February 1957 he settled in Sydney where he led a piano, bass and drums trio in a residency at the Bennelong Hotel. As a *Melody Maker* subscriber, Bell noticed the attention being accorded to skiffle in Britain. Thinking it was destined to take off in Australia, Bell decided to get in quickly and recruited an old friend Vic Sabrino as the necessary singer.

In July 1957, Graeme Bell (playing celeste) with Vic Sabrino (vocals), recorded "Freight Train" backed with "Sweet Georgia Brown", and "Don't You Rock Me Daddy-O" coupled with "John Henry". The other musicians involved in these Columbia recordings were Johnny Sangster (washboard), Freddie Logan (bass), and Geoff Mack and Charlie Morrow (guitars). "Freight Train" made the top ten, skiffle became newsworthy, and Bell's group, known as the Skiffle Gang, did radio and television shows and further recordings in August 1957.

Singles were subsequently released of "The Gospel Train" and "Gamblin' Man", each coupled with one of two tunes that Graeme Bell had written himself: respectively "Come Skiffle Chicken" and "Skiffle Board Blues" (both published by Southern Music). Clarinet was added on the first of these Bell tunes and tenor saxophone on the second.

Further impetus was given to the Skiffle Gang's activities when the group was asked to be a supporting act during Johnny Ray's ("Mr Emotions") third Australian visit in 1957. Billed as Graeme Bell's Skiffle Gang — Bell played piano — with Vic Sabrino, the other musicians on this occasion included a different bassist, George Thompson, and Billy Townsend (guitar and banjo-ukulele) replacing Charlie Morrow; Geoff Kitchen played tenor saxophone. The tour was a great success — Graeme Bell thought highly of Johnny Ray's showmanship — and created more demand for the Skiffle Gang. Bell's first year in Sydney ended with the *Daily Mirror* voting the Skiffle Gang with Vic Sabrino, along with the Horrie Dargie Quintet, as top artists of the year. "Freight Train" was voted best Australian record of the year by the Sydney *Sun*.

After two years at the Bennelong Hotel, Graeme Bell's trio did a short season at a pub and then Bell took to organising professional musicians to play a series of one-night engagements at dance venues, but was still doing appearances with the skiffle group.[36]

Like most popular music forms that attract young people — jazz, rock 'n' roll or punk — skiffle had its critics. As with anything new that did not fit into the accepted scheme of things, skiffle was often mocked, but its significance was understood by some, even if only for commercial reasons. Skiffle's contemporary critics would never have believed in its importance for the development of popular culture and music but that importance became more and more obvious as the Fifties and Sixties slipped by.

Like other forms of popular music, skiffle attracted a certain amount of attention in the UK music press and elsewhere. Although David Boulton observed that none of the national newspapers "noticed the growth of skiffle during 1955 and 1956, until the rock 'n' roll wave made them music-conscious",[37] there were attempts to deride it ("music for the unmusical"), explain its popularity and worth, and ponder its musical future. An early, and somewhat caustic critic, who admitted that to him skiffle was painful in the extreme, focused in April 1956 on the trend-setting groups of Colyer and Donegan. Graham Boatfield noted that Colyer and Donegan had approached skiffle differently when it came to repertoire. Colyer imitated mainly black music, with a preference for the melancholic, while Donegan alternated between "the bouncier Leadbelly numbers and established white folk song." Religious songs were unaccountably performed by both singers, although Boatfield recognised that not all who played "The Saints" took the words literally. This divergence of repertoire accounted, according to Boatfield, for the fact that: "Colyer gives the effect of a bankrupt pier-show of black-faced minstrels, Donegan sounds like a number of intoxicated hillbillies returning from some over-lengthy orgy."

Boatfield's other criticisms were that Colyer and Donegan were far from the real skiffle groups (they were not jug bands but possibly spasm bands — paroxysm or seizure was considered more accurate by Boatfield); that it was impossible to copy "personal" black music and that white American singers did not presume to do so; that if music is transplanted it needs to be imbued with its own personality. As unsympathetic as ever, Boatfield's final sentences insisted that: "The voice, being much more individual than any instrument, cannot really be copied, and folk song — which the skiffle groups are attempting — can under no circumstances be either transplanted or copied. London voices probably best naturally employed in singing 'Knees up Mother Brown' are not quite happy with 'Midnight Special'."[38] Boatfield seems to forget that many of the skiffle folk songs had already been transplanted once — to America.

In July 1956 — with skiffle not long under way on the popular music front — a *Melody Maker* article put it under fire. One of its early protagonists, Alexis Korner, wrote a piece called "Skiffle or Piffle?", claiming that, given its origins, skiffle was rightly an instrumental music performed privately. Consequently, interval skiffle spots at jazz clubs and concert sessions were a nonsense. Korner considered that British skiffle music, except in one or two instances, bore "but a superficial resemblance to the music which inspired it". Korner admits to shame and regret at being one of the originators of the skiffle movement with a perhaps unnecessary remark about the musician who had taken "upon himself the nickname of one of the three greatest blues singers of all time."

Korner berates the generally poor standard of British skiffle, although recognising its commercial success, goes on to praise Cyril Davies (the one new person of note in his opinion), is certain that "sniffle" was there to stay, and appreciated he was unlikely to get further skiffle employment.[39]

In a postscript to Korner's piece, Ken Colyer wrote that he did not care if skiffle lasted and that he preferred to play it at parties rather than on the concert stage. In Colyer's estimation, skiffle had not produced any worthwhile talent but had encouraged record companies to reissue the original recordings.[40]

Steve Race, in "Skiffle Isn't Piffle", March 1957, came to the aid of skiffle, which he said was having a rough time in the press, and admitted he rather liked it, although as with jazz he did not like everything that was done in its name. Race liked it in the first place because it had boosted amateur music-making around Britain: "There is something intrinsically good about even a bad group of amateur players. Skiffle or Piffle, they're making music of their own." Secondly, he liked it because of Donegan's personality: he sold records, hit headlines, brought Sunday concerts to life, had an instantly recognised voice, sold British records in America, and kept worse people out of the limelight. He was also nursed on the essentials of jazz.[41]

The following week the *Melody Maker* put "Skiffle on Trial" when it asked the views of various musicians and one of its writers whether skiffle was part of jazz — was it music or menace? *MM's* Bob Dawbarn was quite clear that skiffle was "the dreariest rubbish to be inflicted on the British public since the last rash of Al Jolson imitators." Chris Barber recognised that there were those who were cashing in on skiffle but that was no reason to say it was no good, although he did not necessarily like all skiffle. Tommy Steele, once part of the skiffle movement, was supportive but said he was going to leave it to Lonnie. Lonnie was quite open about what he was doing and how the conditions he now enjoyed were right for playing and performing well. Bill Colyer said that nobody knew what skiffle would lead to in the early days but that skiffle sold to Presley and rock 'n' roll fans and that there was no reason for anyone to get smug and self-righteous.[42]

The following week, in letters to *Melody Maker*, readers gave their views on skiffle as a part of jazz. Generally dismissive, they included one from Alexis Korner, who wrote that he was not then playing in skiffle groups. He had "played a concert with Ken Colyer, two or three sessions with Jack Elliott and Derroll Adams (strictly hillbilly) and an occasional session with Bob Kelly (strictly Chicago race blues)." Korner said his main point was not that skifflers were prostituting an art but that they were musically inept and this was still the case.[43]

Early in April that year, Max Jones and Sinclair Traill recognised the great interest in American folk music since the Second World War and confessed to feeling "less hot and bothered about skiffle than a lot of chaps seem to do." They recognised that the standard of performance was often low — true also of a lot of popular music and jazz — that most skifflers would probably not move on "to an appreciation of more authentic and subtle performances in the idiom" but to other attractions, although some may be attracted to artists like Big Bill Broonzy. The two writers commented that Big Bill was tolerant of skiffle, had visited the Roundhouse in Wardour Street, and had said that he would be proud if Lonnie or others recorded his best songs. Derroll Adams, playing with Jack Elliott in clubs and cabaret, also had a rosy view of skiffle. He expressed surprise "to hear so many folk songs being sung and the large number of people interested in the authentic Negro songs and mountain music."[44]

Humphrey Lyttleton, no less, turned his attention to skiffle and its future in the *Melody Maker* in June 1957 and began by lambasting the absurd purists — players of only genuine Lead Belly and early Donegan. Humph felt that treating British folk songs like American ones — the wish of the skiffle intelligentsia — would not work. Harnessing the jazz beat to the words and melodies of American folk songs was what made skiffle popular. Folk singers had been playing their music for years without any particular interest being generally aroused. "It's the beat that counts — and American songs, often first cousins to jazz itself, lend themselves most readily to the rhythmic supercharging which popular skiffle demands."

As for the future of skiffle and its many groups, Humph believed its popularity would pass and changes in music fashion would discourage groups out of existence. However, he did not see why skiffle would not remain "part of our recreational life when all the fuss has died down."[45]

In a *Melody Maker* article in July 1957, Fred Dallas, folk singer, songwriter, instrumentalist and leader of the Original Riversiders Skiffle Group, opined that skiffle would not die, in spite of the jibes about the ability of those who made up the movement that was sweeping Britain.

Dallas admitted that his group was musically limited — but it was exciting — and, playing in the open air, attracted crowds of over one hundred. Few had turned up to hear Fred and his wife play the same songs in a folk style. Dallas reckoned that in spite of the jeers about Cockney accents and limited technique, boys were learning to play their instruments but were receiving no guidance from their detractors about adapting skiffle to British folk music — skiffle, like jazz, needed UK roots to flourish. Meanwhile, Dallas was happy for skiffle to keep its transatlantic character but argued that the critics should encourage more recordings by Guthrie and Pete Seeger, from whom skifflers could learn, and should complain about the passport problems that had kept Seeger away from Britain. Dallas ended by wondering: "Are they sorry that folk music is no longer the preserve of the select few? Because I'm not. It can't be too popular for me."[46]

In August 1957, Alan Lomax was posing the question as to why skiffle was so popular. He briefly described the history of American folk music, with its roots in an Irish-Scots-English-Welsh amalgam acted on by black influences. Lomax claimed: "It was natural that the resultant Afro-British products would become popular with the youngsters of skiffle — they had already succeeded in pleasing the racially prejudiced people of British descent in the South." Skiffle was encouraging young people to play and sing the songs they liked to sing. It was possible that the potential of the largely scorned British folk song repertoire would be realised by the citybilly skifflers.[47]

The skiffle controversy got some airing outside the music press. The *Daily Herald's* Spinning Disc column of June 1957 declared that musicians called skiffle "the three-chord trick" and said its exponents could not tell a crotchet from a quaver, and that it was bogus but sold. With little ability, and a guitar or a washboard, skiffle gave Joe Bloggs the chance of becoming a star. The article also expressed concern that skiffle, as an overnight sensation, was turning into a l-o-n-g day.[48] Alan Lomax was interviewed in the same newspaper in late 1957 about British skiffle, and said that it was different from the American product in its beat and feeling, that it had a sound of its own, and had created a new interest in both British and American folk songs, which was a good thing. His interviewer said he was less enthusiastic than Lomax about skiffle but could "hear where the performance has a characteristic British sound. Call it the Donegan touch."[49]

In February the following year, the *Herald's* television critic, Philip Phillips, wrote that he was "sick to death of Bill Brainless and his Skifflers and Charlie Clodhopper and his Rock 'n' Rollers" and wanted *Six-Five Special* taken off the air. He had also canvassed views from Ted Heath, Jack Payne, Geraldo, Joan Regan and *Six-Five Special's* producer Josephine Douglas. The result, summarised in his headline, was that: "Stars Agree on Skiffle Piffle", although Douglas had said "We have the finest artists in our programme...[it] is attacked because it makes news."[50] Later that week Phillips received hundreds of letters that, he said, needed sorting with asbestos gloves. Rock and skiffle were seen as debasements of pop music by five out of six writers — but all were in the older age group. The others were teenagers, who admitted to no time for other music, particularly classical music. A selection of readers' letters were headed with captions like "Insult", "Turn It Off", and "Morons", or "What's Wrong?", "Petty", and "Old Fogies", shewing the strength of feeling of opposing sides.[51] In March 1958, a schools inspector of music at Nottingham wrote to the *Daily Herald* to say that it was "better for children to be interested in skiffle than not to be interested in music at all."[52] The previous year the *Herald* had reported the views of a Dr Josephine Brew, a psychologist and educational adviser to the National Association of Mixed Clubs and Girls' Clubs who took a washboard to youth club meetings and, given the opportunity, played. Dr Brew had also written about rock 'n' roll in *Family Doctor*, saying there was nothing new or wrong about it.[53]

Skiffle also claimed the attention of the legal profession — a woman barrister defending it, saying it taught young people to entertain themselves and not rely on television and films. This statement was occasioned by the case of a young girl who had run away from home and was found at Southend with a skiffle group. Put under a supervision order and sent back to her parents, she was nonetheless told by the chairman that: "There is nothing wrong with skiffle groups, if they teach young people to rely on themselves."[54]

Skiffle even registered with classical musicians, for in an extempore talk on jazz by Sir Malcolm Sargent, he referred to ragtime, bee-bop, boogie-woogie and rock 'n' roll, and, without exactly mentioning the s-word, "something that I think is performed on a washboard". Sir Malcolm seemed to be of the view that these varied forms had been devised to make jazz saleable, "because it is originally a monotonous form of amusement and has to be varied almost year by year. I would say that jazz is the most successful way yet found of using the art of music to make money."[55] Flash Harry was ill-informed about jazz, as a *Listener* correspondent enlightened him, although considering him right about rock 'n' roll — "the commercial exploitation... of musical form".[56] Sargent also appeared condescending about popular music — but this was not the only occasion.

Skiffle even made the correspondence columns of the *Times*, where a writer, under the heading "Skiffle or Skiffle", complained about only being able to find "skiffle" on the three radio channels in his hotel room. He deplored this state of affairs and blamed it on the education system. A letter in response — attacking its wording rather than its message — said that the choice was not "skiffle or skiffle" but "skiffle or nothing: nothing giving ample opportunity for other pursuits, including reflection on the educational system which enabled him to make such an illogical statement."[57]

Brian Bird said that he wrote his 1958 book on skiffle because of the ignorant nonsense about it in newspapers and magazines. "It has been the fashion, in some circles, to accompany the mention of the word 'skiffle' by a hardly veiled sneer."[58] Regrettably, forty years on, this can sometimes still be the case.

Whatever the impression given by this and the previous chapter about the appeal and availability of skiffle, it would be misleading to suggest that skiffle totally dominated popular music from 1956 to 1958 or that its appeal was universal. The entertainment industry created opportunities for a number of skiffle groups to flourish and record during this period, but only a few enjoyed any real success in the hit parade and only Lonnie Donegan had more lasting commercial success. It was the personal experience of, and involvement with skiffle by young people, and those around them — in spite of the mixed views about its value and future — that constituted the real skiffle craze and raised national awareness of the music. Young people responded to and encouraged the groups described in these two chapters, with some, as we've seen, taking their place amongst them. The skiffle craze was essentially the grassroots reaction to a music-making challenge that many young people could not resist.

6 *Mama Don't Allow — Grassroots Skiffle*

First performed in Britain as interval music at jazz performances, then unexpectedly becoming a commercial success as popular music, skiffle was quickly embraced by teenagers and those just out of their teens. It became a music craze that attracted all types of young people. A maths wizard of 15 — he had A-levels in maths, physics and chemistry — interviewed by a national newspaper in September 1958, claimed not to be a swot and that his real interests were skiffle and pop. He played guitar and drums and was a fan of both Lonnie Donegan and Elvis.[1]

Teenagers, and mainly male teenagers, wanted to perform this music for themselves and their fellow teenagers were happy to listen and dance to it. While challenging the perceived passivity of the younger generation, brought up with television, the radio and gramophone records, their involvement in skiffle did not always meet with general approval by the older generation, who found the music to be too loud and energetic and insufficiently melodic.

Skiffle groups were formed all over the country, in universities, youth clubs and schools, both public and state, at the work place, and even in the army which took it across to Germany. Opportunities were looked for by the groups to perform their music, whether in their local youth club or coffee bar, or in one of the many skiffle competitions organised both locally and nationally. For a while skiffle became a popular and widespread pastime. Jazz too had encouraged young people to make music with which they identified but skiffle captured the imagination of the younger generation much more completely than jazz had done in earlier years. Weight of numbers may have made skiffle seem a craze of the teenage, male working-class but its appeal was to a much wider social spectrum of young people.

Various statistics were published about the number of clubs, groups and people involved in skiffle in the Fifties which give some indication of the perceived scale of the craze amongst young people of the time. A *Times* correspondent reckoned that there were at least 500 groups in England in July 1957 and contrasts their earnest and sedate approach with that of rock 'n' roll's hectic hysteria.[2] A writer in the American *Jazz Review* said that: "A year ago there were only about twenty groups around London. Now there are nearer 400, with one to ten groups in every English-speaking center from Glasgow to Cape Town".[3] Figures published in March 1958,

doubled this figure for London, saying that there were over 800 professional and amateur groups in that city alone.[4] The *Daily Herald* reported
in August 1958 that about 800 groups had taken part in the National Skiffle
Competition.[5] Writing ten or so years later, Nik Cohn said there were an
estimated three thousand skiffle clubs in London during the craze, and
although they closed as fast as they opened, it was still an impressive
statistic.[6] Benny Green claimed in 1957 that the latest statistics for the
country showed there nine working skiffle groups to every hundred head
of population. This meant "more or less that everybody in the country is
working in a skiffle group"[7] — no doubt a bit of tongue-in-cheek journalism
but indicative of the perceived activity. As with commercial skiffle, the
youth craze in Britain had no American parallel. This was unusual, as most
crazes and trends in popular music tended to emanate from those shores.

The skiffle phenomenon affected all sorts of young people, some destined
later in adulthood to be a national politician, a theatre director, a public
relations man, or, as shown in a later chapter, a success in popular music.
The conservative politician and former Home Secretary, Michael Howard,
was born in the early Forties, grew up in Llanelli and attended grammar
school there. He played the piano until he was thirteen but then "took up
the guitar and formed a skiffle group with friends from school. I was the
singer and we had sideburns and wore drainpipe trousers. We did all the
Lonnie Donegan numbers and later some Elvis songs but I don't think we
did many public performances."[8] Neil Kinnock, the former leader of the
Labour Party, and at one time on the other side of the House of Commons
to Michael Howard, was credited by the *Guardian* as once being a
washboard man.[9] Trevor Nunn, appointed director of the National Theatre
in 1996, was born in Ipswich in 1940, the son of a cabinet-maker. He
attended Northgate Grammar School, where he directed *Hamlet* and played
in a skiffle group.[10] Max Clifford, the publicist, born in the mid-Forties,
failed his 11-plus and went to Pelham Secondary Modern in Wimbledon.
Clifford admits to not taking up any of the academic opportunities,
preferring to play football. In his last school year a skiffle group was
formed, called the Dominoes (after Fats Domino), and Max Clifford was
its singer and a guitarist. Leaving school at fifteen, and after a couple of
other jobs, Clifford started at the EMI press office — a few weeks later he
was given the Beatles to launch.[11]

Those who made a living from playing skiffle would be used to performing
in the recording, radio or television studio, on the variety stage, in clubs
or taking part in one of the popular floating jazz fiestas (on the River
Thames or in the English Channel). Many semi-professional and amateur
groups might also have the opportunity occasionally to perform in such
surroundings. For most amateur grassroots groups, however, their performance venues were more likely to be the local youth club or coffee bar,
garden party, carnival, dance hall, pub, cinema, church hall — or skiffle

1956 And All That: Skiffle Reminiscences

The Crescendos' performance on the bus was greeted with hysterical applause and our first official booking, for the Far Headingley Young Conservatives annual dance, quickly followed. The function was held at Castle Grove Masonic Hall, Headingley, Leeds. Goodness only knows what the brothers made of the devil's music but the young conservatives seemed to love it.

Several similar gigs took place, but we shot to fame through the good offices of an old school friend, Mike Paley, a hugely talented musician. By the outbreak of the skiffle craze, he had joined the White Eagles Jazz Band, resident every Saturday night at the Grand Hotel, Harrogate — better known as the Snake Pit. Mike got us a gig to play for half an hour in the interval. We were paid ten shillings (50p) but entrance was free; we had beer money and the attention of the opposite sex, often enjoyed by stars of the stage. The Grand Hotel is now Inland Revenue offices!

The original members of the group were Derek Fleck (lead guitar), Jim Bedford and Ben Lowe (guitars), Peter Sparkes (snare drum), and me (guitar and vocals). All in all we had a wonderful time in the early days when it was all new, especially during the summer when we used to skiffle from Leeds to the Grand in Harrogate in an open-topped Riley which Jim Bedford bought for £5 and rebuilt.

My favourite memories are of being paid the compliment of a pro band refusing to play with us because we were not members of the Musicians Union, of falling off the stage whilst singing, of all things, "The Wreck of the Old 97", and of getting stuck in the back of a Sunbeam Rapier Coupé with a young lady.

Tim Mallinson

competition. Amateur groups might also play in the open air or on the streets, or supply the support for the touring big names of popular music.

Amateur groups thus appeared in the *Stars of Six-Five Special* road show, much to the annoyance of the Musicians Union who banned the Woodlanders and the Steeljacks from appearing at Plymouth in January 1958. The local MU secretary told the *Melody Maker*: "These skiffle groups, with their meagre musical ability, sprouting everywhere nowadays, and playing cheaply, are a menace to the professional musician."[12] In practice, skilled musicians (as skifflers) lacked spirit, had difficulty in playing the right kind of beat and appearing sincere. The following month, David Simpson and his Sidewinders (the resident group at the Bradford Topic Folk and Skiffle Club) were vetoed at the Bradford Gaumont but paid over £30 to join the Musicians Union.[13] The MU's policy was to try to enrol amateurs where they were in direct competition with professional musicians, ensuring they could demand the minimum union rate. According to Chas McDevitt: "in quite a few skiffle contests promoters insist on entrants being MU members — surely a sign of vigorous representations by the Union."[14]

The programmes of two London Soho clubs, the Modern Music Club and the Skiffle Cellar, exemplify the opportunities that were on offer to amateurs. The Modern Music Club provided opportunities for skiffle groups in its May 1957 programme of rock, jazz and jive — groups like the Sinners, Rudy Marsalis and his Creole Skiffle Group ("Britain's only coloured skiffle star"), the Sunrisers, Johnny Yorke's Alleycats, the Boll Weevils, and Dony Grey and his Stage and TV Skiffle Group.

The Skiffle Cellar hosted all the leading groups and soloists but also provided opportunities for amateurs. Towards the end of 1957, for example, the Spacemen, a group of five, and all members of the Wanstead Aero Modelling Club, made their third appearance at the cellar. *Jazz Journal's* diarist, Brian Nicholls, at the Skiffle Cellar in 1957 with his editor to hear the New Hawleans Skiffle Group (the group with the punny title), noted the crowds pouring in and felt the club had its good points. For instance, performers — whether groups or singers — had their names hung on a special name rack inside the door. Nicholls observed that: "During our visit, rows of earnest young people sat and listened to the New Hawleans group as though transfixed, while, behind them, the next group warmed up with a series of nervous twitches in accompaniment to the music."[15]

Another picture of the club scene was painted by Gabriel Gersh in *Jazz Review*, who noted that the Skiffle Cellar, amongst others, provided "a platform... for the hundreds of little suburban and provincial groups, making the journey to London to seek fame". Noted too was the mix of material being used — from folk songs to popular music — and that the newer skiffle groups made no distinction between skiffle and rock 'n' roll. The skiffle audience had been joined by Teds and their girls, who could not sing or play but could dance wonderfully. "So dance they do... at the back of the club, to skiffle and everything else that comes."[16]

The skiffle scene was not confined to the capital, however, but enjoyed a healthy existence in many other parts of Britain, especially if the many teenage, grassroots groups are taken into account. *Reveille* in May 1957, with the skiffle boom in full swing, provided a snapshot of skiffle music-making — both venues and groups — around the country and it is likely that the situation in Liverpool, where it was reckoned that one skiffle group or another played every night in one of it's jazz clubs or ballrooms,[17] was true to some extent in many of Britain's large towns and cities. Some amateur groups even had business cards printed to promote their musical activities.

Alongside such locations, grassroots skiffle groups around the country met and performed in a variety of venues, such as youth clubs. The Ellesmere Youth Club in Shropshire, for example, was established about 1955 at Ellesmere Secondary Modern School. By mid-1957 the club offered a variety of opportunities, such as basket-making, drama, panel games, and dancing to skiffle, and provided a place for the local group, called the Bandits, to practice and perform. The group of six teenagers consisted of two guitarists, a harmonica player, an oil-drum bassist, snare drummer

For all Social Occasions

The Shadows
'SKIFFLE GROUP'

All communications to :—
V. Petkervitch
12 South Eaton Place
S.W.1

with cymbal, and washboard player."[18] Evington Valley Youth Club, Leicestershire, was the launch pad at the end of 1956 for a newly formed eight-man skiffle group. This large group played only American folk songs (no rock 'n' roll) and consisted of three guitars, banjo, drums, washboard and two tea-chest basses.[19] Elsewhere, Paul Shepherdson recalls how he formed a skiffle group at a church youth club in Hull about 1957 known as the Sioux City Seven. He says it was not a very good group, it failed an audition for *Opportunity Knocks* in a costly expedition to Leeds, but it came first in a talent competition at the local Regal Cinema.[20]

Skifflers also made their way into the dance halls. In May 1957, the Princess Ballroom (Chorlton Palais) advertised for singing groups, electric guitarists, small bands, female vocalists — and skiffle groups. The following month the Ilford Palais announced "rock 'n' roll, skiffle and fun" every Sunday (2/9d for members), from 7.30 -11.30 p.m. In the same month, the great opening night of the Stanley Dale's Teenager, the Marina Ramsgate, was publicised in the *Melody Maker*. Non-stop dancing to Rory Blackwell, Ricky James and the London Skifflers was promised at the opening night and then nightly for the season. A notice in the local press advertised a "Skiffle Dance" at the Assembly Rooms, Market Harborough for 23 November 1957, featuring bands and the local Double Diamonds

Found in a copy of Brian Bird's book on skiffle. Is the group to the left The Shadows?

Some 1957 Skiffle Venues Outside London

Birmingham
Adam and Eve, Bradford Street
Birmingham Jazz Appreciation
  Society
Maryland Jazz Club, Old Stone
  Cross, Dale End

Bristol
Locarno Ballroom, The Glen
New Orleans Jazz Club, St
  Michael's Hall

Chesterfield
Hill's Cafe, Lordsmill Street

Glasgow
Bill Patterson Studios,
  St Vincent St.
British Legion Hall, Shettleston
  Cemetery Road
Community House

Leeds
Bob Barclays Studio 20 Jazz Club

Mecca Locarno

Liverpool
Cavern
Grafton Ballroom
Locarno

Manchester
Cumberland Gap Club,
  Thatched House Hotel, off
  Market Street
Bodega Restaurant, Cross Street

Nottingham
Victoria Ballroom

Rochdale
Carlton Ballroom

Sheffield
Blue Boar Hotel
Plumpers Hotel, Tinsley

Skiffle Group. The half-term dance at the College of Art, Hull in February 1958 — ticket 2/6d — featured the Pilgrims Skiffle group amongst jazz and other groups.[21] At a grand victory dance — Ballymena United had won the Irish Cup — at Ballymena Town Hall in May 1958, there was to be music by Dave Glover and his Showband and the Dusty Millar Skiffle Group, the All-Ireland champions. A dance the previous year in Randalstown, Ballymena was advertised as presenting the Saints with the Sinners Skiffle Group, and a rock 'n' roll competition to find Antrim's champions.[22]

Given the right audience, cinemas seemed to provide an ideal local venue for skiffle groups. In early July 1957 the *Melody Maker* reported that Ken Colyer's Jazzmen would lead an open-air procession and concert of local jazz bands at Bexleyheath as a preliminary to a series of nightly skiffle sessions at the local Odeon cinema, which was showing *The Tommy Steele Story*.[23] At the Savoy cinema, Croydon, during one week in 1958, the local Hot Rods Skiffle Group gave a series of nightly performances.[24] The introduction of a skiffle group into the Saturday evening programme was well received by the young people in Leicestershire at the Barlestone cinema in mid-1959. A twenty-minute performance was presented by the Vikings Rhythm Skiffle Group from Enderby to the whistling, shouting and singing of the younger element of the audience. Allotted five minutes,

Some 1957 Skiffle Groups Outside London

Birmingham	Red Robins	Demons
Banners'	Riversiders	Gin Mill
Thunderfoot Burton	South Siders	Hobo
Celestial Three	Spyders	Liver
Derek Watts'	Dill Taylor's	Mike McComb's
		No. 95
Bootle	**Bradford/Leeds**	Pilgrim
Ron MacKay's	Ray Allen's	Rod Vallesi's
	Calder River	Zenith
Bristol	Conway	
Tommy Allen's	Heaven and Hell	**Manchester**
Avon Cities	Morley Five	Paul Beattie's
Avonside	Rebels	Cotton Pickers
Bridge Valley	Red Barn	Mill Brow
Falcons	South Side	Wasps
Johnny McEllin's	Steeldrivers	
Midnite	White Kittens	**Nottingham**
Red Devils		Pete Sturman and his
Johnny Smith's	**Leicester**	Trentside Five
	Barry Lane's	
Chesterfield	Belgrave	**Sandiacre**
Catacomb	Cobras	**(Derbyshire)**
	Dynamics	Downtown
Glasgow	Brian Parke's	
Red Allan's	Skiffrock Boys	**Sheffield**
Clansmen		Black Diamonds
Delta	**Liverpool**	Lewis's
East Kilbride	Angel	
Kalamazoo	Brunswick	**Warrington**
Kansas City	Central	Phil Hartley's
Kinning Park Ramblers	Dark Town	

the five youngsters in the group played at least sixteen items before they were allowed to leave the stage. The Vikings — two guitars, piano, drums and tea-chest bass — who had already given their services to various local charities, were booked for a garden party and a return visit to the cinema in aid of the football league.[25] What is interesting is that this event occurred some months after the demise of commercial skiffle and that the group were in demand and featured a piano.

Skiffle had to find its sea (and river) legs, as groups came to be included in various riverboat shuffles and the like. Although often manned by the skiffle names, some amateur groups did get a look in. The Floating Festival of Jazz organised for mid-June 1956 by Jazzshows Ltd aboard the *Royal Daffodil* — a ticket cost 35/- for a River Thames journey from London to Margate and back — was advertised as featuring, amongst others, Chris

Barber's Jazz Band with the Lonnie Donegan Skiffle Group and Ottilie Patterson, and Ken Colyer's Jazzmen with the Skiffle Group. A riverboat shuffle in May 1957, starring Dick Charlesworth's Jazzmen and some unnamed skifflers, was commended by a promoter poet:

Riverboat Shuffle on the twelfth of May
Leaves Richmond at ten — on the river all day
With Charlesworth plus Skiffle we're sure
  you'll agree
Seventeen and six is a reasonable fee
Tickets are limited so now you must hurry
Send to thirty-five Halford Road, Richmond,
  Surrey.

A "Rock Across the Channel" no-passport day trip (Gravesend and Southend to Calais), presented by Club Haley and the 2 I's coffee bar, was advertised for 1 June 1957 and was to feature ten rock and skiffle groups. Amongst the skifflers were Chas McDevitt, the Cotton Pickers and the Alleycats. At £2 a ticket, Le Club de la Côte D'Azure, advertised their first "Rock Across the Channel" day excursion for Sunday 23rd June 1957. Music would be heard from ten top bands playing jazz, mambo, rock 'n' roll and skiffle. The skifflers would include the winners of the National Skiffle Contest at Bury St Edmunds.

Jazzshows Ltd organised another floating musical event from the Tower of London downstream to Margate in 1958. The general arrangement on board appearing to be of jazz on the fore-deck and skiffle in the hold. Groups included George Melly, a trad band and Sonny Terry and Brownie McGhee, whose sessions were the day's musical highspots. At Margate the two Americans "went on the sands and dispensed good music to an admiring circle — a rare event on the Kent coast and apparently not provided for in the byelaws."[26]

Given its novelty value, a skiffle group might be invited to play at a garden party, carnival or garden fête. After all, it was at a July 1957 Woolton Parish Church garden fête, at which the Quarry Men (with John Lennon) were playing, that the famous first meeting of John with Paul McCartney took place. A cabaret at the drama society's garden party in Market Harborough in mid-1957 included a skiffle group made up of boys from the local grammar school who performed several skiffle favourites such as "Cumberland Gap" and "Freight Train"[27] A Melton carnival day around 1959-60 featured a five-man skiffle group playing from a stationary carnival float.[28]

Busking is an honourable tradition and skifflers were not afraid to play on the streets or in the open air. The City Ramblers had begun by busking on the streets of London and in early 1958 it was reported that an unidentified (but definitely British) group had recently been seen playing outside cafes in Paris. One skiffler wrote that he had sung folksongs to small select groups for ten years but that open-air skiffle performances at Walton Bridge or Hampton Court on a Sunday ensured a crowd of over a hundred people.[29] Other groups met at weekends in the Chislehurst Caves and advised their audience to bring candles.[30]

The streets offered an instant and changeable venue for the under-aged and uninhibited, and there was a chance to make some small change. A

1956 And All That: Skiffle Reminiscences

Our group played at a number of venues in Abergavenny. We played in the intervals at the grammar school and girls' high school Christmas dances two Christmases in a row; also at a golf club Christmas dance; at a talent show on the stage of the Abergavenny town hall; for one or two birthday parties, for one of which we actually got paid ten shillings (50p) — worth a lot more then.

I'm not sure how many skiffle groups there were in the area at the time, but there were enough for a skiffle competition to be held in a room above a pub in the centre of town. Each group played two numbers and the winning group was chosen on a vote by the audience. Each member of the audience had a ticket which could be used to vote for one group. As I recall it, a rival group had packed the audience with family and friends, and we came second.

John Barnie

Playing opportunities at our own chapel were plentiful but unpaid. Attempts to play for money at other venues were usually turned down on the basis that: "We have our own group — thank you." Such was the skiffle craze that there was a group on every corner. In two years at it, I think the most I ever earned covered a new set of guitar strings. We did play a fair number of unpaid gigs, however, as the local chapel was still the centre of social activity and television had not taken over completely as yet. There was always the Christmas pantomime, regular Saturday socials, and a men's group that put on "concerts". We played regularly at most of these events. In addition the youth club clientele were entertained with the latest that the Six-Five Special had to offer.

Bob Brooks

Within a short time the Livewires were in demand as performers at working-men's clubs and social gatherings, accepting whatever was offered by way of a fee. Sometimes it was a straight fee of £5, or £1 each and free beer. We were easy about it — we were enjoying ourselves.

Throughout 1957, as skiffle became more popular, we played as many as four engagements a week, including church socials, rugby clubs and wedding receptions, as well as those pubs that were licensed for music.

Then in September of that year, after playing at the Leigh Arms Hotel, Newton-Le-Willows, the landlord offered us a regular Friday evening booking for a fee of £6. Mr Symonds, we liked to think, recognised our talents which in turn filled his pub with customers attracted by the rarity of live entertainment. After a couple of months our "contract" was extended to include Wednesday evenings.

Norman Froggatt

The Cockatoos Skiffle Group. L. to r. Chick Douglas, Barry Lloyd, Bud Milton and Rod Gregg. January 1957. (Courtesy Hulton Getty Images.)

Times correspondent wrote a piece in October 1958 about a young skiffle group he had encountered on several occasions playing in public and collecting money in a box. In his view, the thirteen-year-old skifflers played with the assurance of veteran troupers and succeeded in attracting a small admiring crowd but also some protests from local residents. They made use of the underground bridge for resonance, had a small repertoire, that included "Rock Island Line", and were just ordinary-looking children.[31]

As will be seen in the next chapter, radio and television provided opportunities for skiffle groups, including amateur ones, to broadcast, but probably the most important feature of the grassroots skiffle scene was the skiffle competition. This provided a challenge to perform well, to try out new material, earn some prize money and perhaps get a foot on the popular music ladder that might result in something more rewarding than publicity in the local newspaper.

The National Skiffle Contest was, given its association with *Six-Five Special*, probably the most high profile of all the skiffle craze competitions. It was launched on 19 August 1957 with the first of a series of contests at the Metropolitan Theatre, Edgeware Road, London. After London, the contest went on to theatres at Derby, Nottingham, Sheffield, Leeds, Leicester, Chiswick and Manchester. Headed by the Vipers Skiffle Group and Jim Dale, the programme also featured those amateur groups that had entered the contest. Local contest winners went on to appear in the London

1956 And All That: Skiffle Reminiscences

I round up the other 7 guitarists and we all got down to the fête at just on Tombola time. So we had lots of time to rehearse. We all tune to an open E chord, then just slide a stiff finger up or down to change. Presto! We decided to do "The Wreck of the Old 97", "This Land is My Land" and "Where Could I Go but to the Lord" but in the end we couldn't do them all because the Rev. gave a long speech about the place of skiffle in society and then there was only a few minutes till prep. Speech was quite interesting I suppose. He said skiffle was healthy everyday people music and that one could express oneself as the spirit moved one. Not everybody was Yehudi Menuhin but these young men were playing for nothing and had realized the school credo "I Too Will Something Make and Joy in the Making" by building their own instruments (cheek! I paid £12 for my Hofner). He finished by saying that he hoped to hold a Skiffle Mass in the near future when hundreds would be able to make a cheerful noise unto God. *Then he sang and clapped with us on our one number. Afterwards some flower-hat-ted lady came up and said she hadn't an earthly what we were playing but it sounded* likely *and much better than the Hakkabod arts class singing wild selections from the* Firebird Suite. *A gang of local yokels sneered at us and one said that I wasn't a bit like Lonnie Donegan and he had an electric guitar. I must get one.*

Ian Whitcomb (Extract from After the Ball)

heats, semi-finals and final which were all televised on *Six-Five Special* in 1958.

Another National Skiffle Contest, in the sense that it was open to all, rather than being organised on a national basis, took place at Bury St Edmunds, Whit Monday 1957, and was held under the auspices of the International Jazz Club and local Round Table. Cups, cash prizes, and the chance to be recorded by Esquire Records, ensured that the contest aroused a great deal of interest, and just over forty entries were received from places as far apart as Bournemouth, Glasgow, Grantham, Birmingham, Swansea, and London. Fourteen of London's many groups took part from districts like Fulham, Putney, Shoreditch and Paddington. East Anglia fielded more than a dozen groups, Ipswich contributing four of them. Rutland's only skiffle group, from Oakham, consisting of five draughts-men, also entered the contest.

A number of groups from London and the south had already been successful in skiffle competitions — the 2.19, the Saints, the Station, the Skiffle Cats, and the Lea Valley outfits. The Saints, from Fulham, had come sixteenth out of sixty-three in their first skiffle contest after only being together for four weeks and had played at various West End venues. There had been previous competition success also amongst entrants from elsewhere in Britain: Birmingham's Gator's group were winners of the Birmingham *Evening Despatch* Saturday Swingtime Challenge Trophy Competition, against over twenty Midland groups, and Glasgow's Delta group had been runners-up in the Scottish National Skiffle Championship. Of the contestants, the 2.19 had already recorded for Esquire and the Station had recently auditioned for Decca.

One competing group, The Dick Whittington Katz from Cambridge, had played at the Cambridge University Jazz Club and with Cy Laurie, its members including a bass player who was a captain in the United States Army Air Corps. Another, the Sunrisers from Barnet, were a successful group in their native Hertfordshire and in London's West End. They were the original resident band at the Modern Music Club and had played at venues as varied as Kensington Town Hall, Wood Green Jazz Club and the Cat's Whisker Coffee Bar. The Parkside group from Hendon appeared to be the only contestants who were part of a jazz band; in their case the rhythm section of the Parkside Jazzmen.[32] The contest judges were to be James Asman, the jazz commentator and record critic, Graham Boatfield, a journalist with an interest in folk music and British jazz and skiffle, and Paul Oliver, who at that time was completing a pioneering book on the blues. On the day, Johnny Duncan replaced James Asman. The rules of the contest allowed each group up to six minutes to perform two numbers and representatives of Hammer Theatres Ltd, Gerry Ambrose and the Club de la Côte D'Azure Ltd were listed in the programme as being present for offers of engagement.

Unfortunately for the promoters of the National Skiffle Contest, the day of the competition (organised as an open-air event) was wet but some thirty-four groups turned up. Most were fairly conventional and usually copied recordings of the successful commercial groups, of whom "the strongest and perhaps most pernicious single influence is that of Lonnie Donegan."[33] The judges had been asked to look for original numbers and a dozen or so were offered, otherwise the repertoire was as to be expected. The contestants varied in age from twelve — the youngest group in the contest, Keith Watts and his Skiffling Saints, had members whose ages ranged from twelve to fifteen years — to a gentleman of middle years and, with few exceptions, were lively and seemed to enjoy themselves. In spite of the rain the event attracted a large crowd.

Looking back, the contest winners provided no surprises. First was the 2.19 Skiffle Group, who sang "This Little Light of Mine" and "Trouble in Mind"; second was the Station Skiffle Group with "Don't You Rock Me" and an original number, "I Loved My Baby", and third, the Delta Skiffle Group, whose two songs included "John Brown's Body". One of the competition judges at Bury St Edmunds reflected that: "If one must categorise skiffle, it seems on this showing to be a thriving music of young workers from the towns." He recognised, however, that "There is... room here for a half-dozen anthropologists."[34]

Skiffle competitions were held at most of the holiday camps. Those held at Butlins at Ayr, Filey, Pwllheli, Skegness and Clacton, for example, as part of the National Weekly Skiffle Contest, were sponsored by the *Daily Herald*, which regularly announced the heat winners of the £25 prizes in its columns during the summer months of 1957. According to an advertisement, £175 in cash prizes was to be won weekly by holiday campers and there was a special Butlins address in London from which skifflers could obtain holiday booking forms. Contestants were usually groups of friends on holiday together or pick-up groups formed from holiday-makers, at least one of whom had probably brought a guitar with them. A pick-up group, who had never played together before, were usually obliged to use their ingenuity to create improvised rhythm instruments from items found

National Skiffle Contest Competitors, Bury St Edmunds 1957

Barnet (Herts)
Sunrisers

Birmingham
Gator's

Bournemouth (Hants)
Kapota

Bury St Edmunds
Michael O'Meara's

Cambridge
Keith Watts and his Skiffling Saints
Dick Whittington Katz

East Dereham (Norfolk)
Vampires

Elmswelll (Suffolk)
Black-Zombies

Felixstowe (Suffolk)
Riversiders

Felsham (Suffolk)
Blue Ties

Gillingham (Kent)
2.19

Glasgow
Delta

Grantham (Lincs)
Vagabonds

Hardwick (Cambs)
Rafe Kaye's

Harlow (Essex)
Matching

Hemel Hempstead (Herts)
Rhythm Seekers

Houghton-le-Spring (Co. Durham)
City Wildcats

Ipswich (Suffolk)
Cardinal
Mac Klann
Tracker
Riversiders

London

Battersea
Penitentiary Five
Belgrave Road
Eager Beavers
Fulham
Saints
Station
Hackney
Lea Valley
Hendon
Parkside
North London
Jay-Dee
Paddington
Skiffle Cats
Palmers Green
Toreadors

Putney
Harlequins
Queen's Park
Alexander
Shoreditch
Pirates
Stamford Hill
Badgers
Tottenham
Atlanta

Oakham (Rutland)
Smokey-Moke

St Albans (Herts)
Sunspots

Sheringham (Norfolk)
Ramblers

Stevenage (Herts)
Ixodes

Swansea (Penlan)
Panthers

Thetford (Norfolk)
Five Sided Squares

Trumpington (Cambs)
Rebel

Wallasey (Cheshire)
Ron McKay's

round the camp. At Skegness three boys and a girl (aged 14 and 16) teamed up as the Nose Vipers and won the heat prize. Most groups tended to be of older teenagers or people in their twenties, or a mix of the two. The names adopted by these Butlins holiday camps units included the Saints, the Mad Hatters, the GR Skiffle Group, and the Chalet Bandits.

Earlier in 1957 Butlins had organised a week-long skiffle contest at the Metropolitan Theatre, Edgeware Road. Auditions were held in the morning and winners appeared nightly alongside the Butlin Skiffle Group. The final was presented on Friday night to both houses and a free holiday at Butlins went to the winning team.

The *Daily Sketch* also organised a national skiffle competition and at the Savoy, Croydon, the seven-strong Hot Rods of Thornton Heath were runaway winners of the local finals, later came first in the district finals at Bexleyheath and qualified for the regional finals at Kingston.[35] The Little Rascals — some just schoolboys — won the Northern Ireland area final of the *Daily Sketch* competition at the Ritz cinema, Belfast, in March 1958. There were nearly 100 entries from the area and victory for the Little Rascals meant a trip to England to participate in the grand regional final.[36]

As well as national competitions, there were those of a purely local nature. One such was the competition organised at the Civic Hall, Croydon by J. Hadad Promotions, which was won by the Cellarmen. Their prize was five guineas and a recording test.[37] Others that were advertised included the *Croydon Times* skiffle contest of mid-1957; the "Battle of the Skiffle Groups" at Wimbledon Palais in February 1957 during the London Society of Jazz Music's annual jazz ball; an "All Star Skiffle Contest" at Kensington Town Hall in May 1957, and a contest during May and June

of the same year at the New Carlton Ballroom, Uxbridge Road, W.12 —
£20 in prizes plus bookings were on offer. The local contest organised by
Stanley Dale, when the Vipers and Jim Dale appeared all week at the Hull
Palace in June 1957, seemed like a forerunner of his later National Skiffle
Contest.

The talent competition was somewhat different to these competitions,
as the skiffle group was usually in competition with other types of
entertainer rather than other skifflers. Talent competitions might be purely
local affairs run by the council, for example, or more professional events
designed to choose acts, including skiffle groups, to appear on radio and

---

1956 And All That: Skiffle Reminiscences

*Later versions of the group featured, at different times, an electric lead
guitar and banjo. We gigged at pubs, youth clubs and even organised our
own "skiffle parties", hiring the hall and getting our mums to provide
sandwiches, etc. The latter were very successful but hard work for all
concerned. About fifty people would turn up and we usually broke even,
although the "skiffle parties" were not done for money but for the freedom
to play at length.*

*We also took part in skiffle contests, which were a cheap way of making
money for the organisers — lots of group took part but none were paid.
There was a lot of rivalry — none of the camaraderie amongst singers and
musicians that I later experienced at folk and jazz festivals. We complained
bitterly when we were knocked out of a heat by a group with an electric
lead guitar — these were early days — and called them "cheats"!*

*Some heats were held in jazz clubs during the interval. I hated doing
these, because most jazz fans despised skiffle and so they were hardly a
responsive audience. I imagine, however, that skiffle groups that were
known to be part of a recognised jazz band had no problems here. The
Amazon and other groups had no obvious jazz connections, so we were not
"one of them". Competitions that stick in the memory include one at the
famous Kingston Granada cinema in 1958, where about six groups
performed prior to the showing of the film,* Juke Box Jamboree, *which
starred Jerry Lee Lewis, Fats Domino, Carl Perkins, etc. The signs of the
changing times were apparent earlier at Croydon in November 1957, where
the contest was won by an out-and-out country group featuring steel guitar,
and at Mitcham Baths, where the winner was an Elvis Presley clone,
complete with Scotty-and-Bill-type backing.*

*Gradually the repertoire broadened to include lots of rock 'n' roll,
country, blues and pop — as long as they didn't have too many chords. I
suppose the skiffle group must have folded up about 1958, early 1959.
There were various reasons for the break-up: new hobbies; decline in
out-and-out skiffle gigs, and the fact we were not really geared up to play
convincingly in other styles at length. I think I was the only music freak in
the Amazons and, while skiffle was a starting point for many musicians,
some skifflers only took part in the craze as a passing fad and then gave
up playing altogether.*

Dave Illingworth

The Cobras, St. Mary's Church Hall, Ewell Village, c. 1958. They were also known as the Maryland Skiffle Group.

television talent shows. Just before Christmas 1957, George Williams of the Railroaders from Newcastle noticed the announcement of a talent competition to be held at the Granada Cinema, Edmonton, north London. The Railroaders, of whom Hank Marvin and Bruce Welch were members, entered and played well enough in the competition heats in London to gain a place in the semi-finals in January 1958 and progressed through to the finals. Following strenuous practice, they set off for London for the competition final on 6 April 1958. The Railroaders were placed third, however — after a traditional jazz band and a Malayan opera singer.

Scotland had its own All Scotland Skiffle Championship in the first half of 1957 that attracted well over 100 entries, when the Kansas City group became the Scottish national champions. In Wales no such countrywide skiffle competition seems to have taken place, although Welsh groups took part in the Bury St Edmunds and the Stanley Dale national contest — in the latter a Cardiff group (the Denson Boys) reached a televised heat on *Six-Five Special* in May 1958.

In late 1957 the *Melody Maker* reported that skiffle was spreading in Ireland and that plans were afoot to create a national skiffle organisation for all small groups. Around the same time it recorded that the proprietor of the Top Hat Ballroom, Dunlaoghaire was offering a cup for the best skiffle group in Dublin. It was proposed the contest winners would then compete against British groups. In Ballymena, Northern Ireland, skiffle might form part of a jazz or variety concert and could take the shape of a contest. In March 1958, the Satellites won a competition at a packed town hall — the Banana Boys and the Ramblers were second and third. The Satellites also won first prize (£5) at a contest a little later — the Zombies and the Dominoes coming second and third on that occasion. In October 1958 a skiffle contest and variety show at Ballymena town hall was announced, the contest to be judged by Dusty Millar, the All-Ireland champion skiffler.[38]

In Wales, skiffle (sgiffl) was one of the activities that Urdd Gobaith Cymru, the Welsh-language youth movement, encouraged in its clubs into the early Sixties to help give the organization a more modern image. A skiffle group was known as a *parti sgiffl* and some groups made use of the accordion as well as guitars. Skiffle was also played by Urdd members on more formal occasions such as at a Noson Lawen (an evening of entertainment) and at the Urdd and national eisteddfods. A group associated with the Urdd movement, was the Girls Skiffle Party from Pontypridd, formed about 1957, who performed at the annual concert in the local working men's hall and became quite well known. The girls appeared on television and took part in a Welsh radio series. The seven girls sang in Welsh, harmonized, accompanied themselves with the guitar, washboard and other "odd" instruments, and performed old folk songs and new songs.[39] The available information suggests that skiffle in Wales — where associated with the Urdd — was more closely linked perhaps with the indigenous musical heritage than elsewhere in Britain.

The personnel details available for all but three of the forty-three groups intending to participate in the National Skiffle Contest at Bury St Edmunds provide a useful guide to the make-up of amateur groups in mid-1957. At its most basic, such a group consisted of two guitars, a bass (occasionally a proper string bass) and a washboard. The solo singing might be handled completely by one of the instrumentalists or shared with others. The size of the group could be increased by extra guitarists, by having both a drummer and a washboard player, and by adding other instrumentalists on clarinet, banjo, harmonica, accordion, steel guitar or mandolin. In one there was also a second bass.

In some competing groups at Bury St Edmunds, one or more of the guitars might be replaced by a mandolin, banjo, ukulele, banjolele or ukulele-banjo. Or one of the players might have one of these instruments available as an alternative to playing the guitar. Some groups relied solely on drums rather than a washboard but on occasion the percussionist might play either washboard or drums, as required by the performance. Spoons, bones, sandpaper or bongos were used by a very small number of groups for extra percussive effects.

A couple included a pianist, in one case in lieu of a second guitar and in the other doubling on guitar and vocal. A small number of groups were already using electric or amplified guitars for one or more of their instruments. Three included female members but none were credited with also playing an instrument. In two cases they seem to have been entirely responsible for the singing, in the third it was a shared effort.

1956 And All That: Skiffle Reminiscences

I don't remember a decision to form a skiffle group only what might have been our first practice — in the Dailey's front room. I was the group's singer and also played a mandolin tuned as for a ukulele and strummed like a guitar. The mandolin had been a gift; the "my-dog-has-fleas" ukulele tuning was musical knowledge acquired from somewhere. The other members of the group contributed guitar (Brian Brind), tea-chest bass (my brother Peter) and "drums" (an upturned bread bin played with wire brushes.) Our drummer, Mike Dries, had learned his art in the Boys Brigade. This all sounds too organised to have been an impromptu skiffle session at which, if I remember rightly, "Alabamy Bound" (our only full number at that stage) was played endlessly.

Quite soon the mandolin was replaced by a guitar — a repaired job from somebody's loft — for which I paid ten shillings. The repair soon gave out under hectic skiffling and I purchased a new Spanish guitar (on the never-never) for about £13 from a music shop in Kings Street, Hammersmith. Our line-up didn't change much during our time as a group but the quality of our kit did — Brian's Gene Autry guitar (complete with cowboy picture) was replaced by an f-hole guitar, and a snare drum and high hat replaced Mike's bread bin. The tea-chest bass remained the same but its player was now Tony Hull. At some point we decided to call ourselves the Mainline Skiffle Group — probably because of all the "train" songs we sang — not perhaps a name we would choose today.

Finding somewhere to practice regularly was a challenge met by using the unoccupied basement of the requisitioned Victorian house where I lived in the Upper Richmond Road. My family, originally from Fulham, had been bombed out during the war and we were awaiting rehousing in this large house divided into two flats. The neighbours in the top flat didn't exactly complain about our basement skiffle practices but remarked to my mother that they thought she had said that I had a good voice. My singing ability as an angelic choirboy (with unbroken voice) had been boasted of a few years earlier. The key of E was a good skiffle key in terms of its volume and musical effect but my fingers would not make the necessary B7 chord that was part of the three chord trick in that particular key. Consequently I "stopped" playing when we reached it (Brian was good at the difficult bits) but continued to sing, resuming the fingering when the song required a guitar chord that I could accomplish. No one seemed to notice!

From time to time the group's line-up was augmented — by another guitarist at one point, mouth organ and clarinet. The latter instrument rarely appeared, however, in our "public" performances but at parties where we were invited to play.

Mike Dewe

Improvised instruments depended very much on ingenuity, and on preferences for a particular sound or playing method. The British version of the tub bass, for example, consisted of an upended tea-chest to act as a resonator (that is with its open end downwards) with a hole drilled in the middle of the top. A piece of string or twine was passed through the hole

Unidentified skiffle group on the *Royal Daffodil* en route to Calais, July 1957. (Photo, T. Davis, courtesy Hulton Getty Images.)

and kept in place by a knot in its end. The free end of the string was then taken up over the top of an upright — a broomstick or wooden batten — and fastened in place. The bottom of the broomstick was not fixed to the tea-chest and could be located behind a small block of wood to stop it slipping when plucked. The instrument was played by holding the tea-chest firmly down by placing the foot on one corner, grasping the top of the batten or broomstick in one hand and plucking the string with the other. Pulling the broomstick back raised the note, releasing the tension lowered it. To save wear and tear on the fingers, the player might wear a glove or use a bass-sized "plectrum" — a beer mat might do in an emergency. A fixed upright, with a "fretted" tuned string, is a more sophisticated version of DIY bass construction.

Bob Cort encouraged people to get hold of a proper string bass, even an old cracked one, as it would give a better sound. He compared playing the tea-chest bass to whistling, easy to do if you can but difficult to explain to those who can't. "To me it seems impossible, but I've heard many a man who really does get good, clear notes from his box bass."[40] The keen tea-chest bass player might be challenged to make an instrument that resembled the string bass, equipped with one or more strings. The Soho Skiffle Group had such a bass as do today's Black Sheep Skiffle Group from Leeds (see photo p.28).

In Britain in the Fifties, the washboard rhythm, or scuffle, was usually created by the player wearing metal thimbles on the fingers of each hand as they moved across the ribbed washboard surface. Other items that could be used instead of thimbles were a piece of wire, a nail, fork or other small metal object — chains sewn into gloves, for example. Various attachments, such as cowbells, woodblocks (or small cymbal) might be added to the frame, or held on a separate stand, to produce a range of additional effects. Sitting, the washboard might be played across the knees or propped against the chest. Played standing, it could be suspended across the chest by a shoulder strap or secured horizontally on some kind of stand. If the player chose to scrape both sides, then it would have to be held between the knees, possibly longways, or mounted upright on a frame. Bob Cort warned against the washboard player attempting to steal the show and playing too loudly; the washboard was only one of the instruments providing the beat and its sound had to be kept in correct relationship to the others.[41]

Like most entertainers, professional skifflers of the Fifties gave some attention to their dress, whether the cowboy outfits of Dickie Bishop and his Sidekicks, the striped trousers, jumpers, shirts and ties of the men in the City Ramblers (the two woman wore dresses of similar pattern), or the matching jumpers and trousers of the Bob Cort and Chas McDevitt groups. Pictures of the Bill Bailey Skiffle Group and Lonnie Donegan's group in action show six be-suited men in the former and bow ties and tuxedos in the latter.

Unlike their rock 'n' roll successors, amateur skifflers did not always appear to have given much thought to the question of dress and group members might all be dressed casually and differently, or display a mix of casual and more formal wear. Sometimes the effort would be made to standardize dress — white shirts, cravats and dark trousers, for example. Or the group would go a little further and have the initial letter or full wording of the group's name on its jumpers.

Bob Cort felt that members should all to wear a similar outfit — casual clothes were perfectly acceptable — as an important aspect of skiffle was its visual effect. Skifflers were thus also enjoined to look happy, even if something had gone wrong. He also suggested painting the wooden part of the washboard and decorating the tea-chest bass, which could be lettered with the name of the group. Skifflers were warned, however, against painting their guitars or screwing electrical pick-ups to them, as this could damage the tone.

Bob Cort was also concerned about song presentation and gave five examples of his approach to some well-known skiffle songs. He indicated, though, that his tips on presentation were not inflexible rules and encouraged groups to experiment.[42]

While showing some agreement with Cort's advice, Brian Bird believed that on the whole the music would speak for itself and that presentation and showmanship were therefore relatively unimportant — the "act

1956 And All That: Skiffle Reminiscences

We had camp fire sessions in the late Fifties, playing and singing what was recognisably skiffle. Bill, a few years older than me, could play a few chords on the guitar, whilst another friend, Alan, had a ukulele. He had been taught the G, C and D7 chords by our local vicar! The music was played mainly to try and impress the local girls, although I seem to remember that whilst it was great fun to try, it was not very successful!

Eventually, I obtained another guitar, but first I was presented with a tea-chest bass (costing ten shillings and made by a DIY acquaintance), as a birthday present in 1958 or 1959. The camp fire gatherings had led to more formal "practices" and, as mother notes in the Archive on 15 October 1960: "Michael just coming home with skiffle bass from youth club." The normal venue was Bill's garage, where we chalked proposed programmes on the walls, and tried desperately to master the change from G to D7 and back again. "Tom Dooley" was a favourite at this time, as all you needed were those two magic chords.

When things needed livening up, it was usual to augment the skiffle sound with an old World War Two air raid siren. My dad would always say: "What are you practising for?" There was no logical answer to this but we did eventually get some bookings at local events, such as the Women's Institute Garden Party in July 1961.

We had no form of amplification, of course, but we made up for this by sheer weight of numbers and instruments. Just as a chameleon changes colour, so the Riding Mill Skiffle Group changed shape. Anyone who turned up was accommodated. At one time or another there would be a guitar, banjo, ukulele, homemade drum and brushes, jar of beans, cello, trombone, and tea-chest bass. The music was something of a mixed bag: "Green Grow the Rushes, O!" jostled "Maggie May", whilst Lonnie Donegan stood next to Hank Locklin. But, of course, to be able to pick and mix was half the pleasure of it all. As far as I've been able to find out, the final appearance of the Riding Mill Skiffle Group was in the village pantomime in February 1963.

After such a late flowering, it was perhaps inevitable that the bloom would quickly fade.

Mike Waites

natural" school of thought. This is perhaps to misjudge the role that entertainment plays in the presentation of popular music. A role that both Donegan and Cort clearly identified and gave thought to.

As regards the music itself, Cort suggested that groups should aim for a light, lively beat and emphasised the need to take the beat seriously. "Always remember that one of the hallmarks of a really amateur group is the speeding up or slowing down of the rhythm." Skifflers were reminded to be certain that their instruments were in tune, and to show a concern for tone and varied rhythms. While admitting the need to care about technique, Cort was aware of the danger of sacrificing the simplicity appeal of skiffle.[43] Nevertheless, simplicity did not mean a disregard for quality

Duffy Power with the New Vagabonds, 1958.

in performance.

A fairly constant theme from commentators was that amateur skifflers should find their own songs — remember the British folk song heritage — and not always copy commercial skiffle recordings. This seems to have happened in only a small way. For those on the lookout for other American songs, however, W.E. Harrison & Sons Ltd, Ipswich (importers of American books and magazines) advertised in the programme of the National Skiffle Contest at Bury St Edmunds details of ballads and blues books of interest to groups looking for new material. The titles included *Best Loved American Folk Songs*, collected, adapted and arranged by John

155

1956 And All That: Skiffle Reminiscences

You could buy sheet music of the rock 'n' roll songs that we wanted to play, and, though none of us could read music, we could copy the records by using the sheet music's lyrics and chord symbols (in conjunction with a guitar chord book). In this way we learned to play the newest songs, as well as expanding our chord vocabulary. I can remember the lyrics of many of the songs to this day, whereas I couldn't tell you the name of pieces that I played last week, never mind playing them from memory.

John Harper

After nearly forty years it's almost impossible to imagine what the group I played in sounded like, but given our level of control over our instruments it can't have sounded very good? What amazes me is that we had the nerve to get up and sing in public time and time again. But public performance was part of the skiffle ethos. It wasn't good enough just to play in somebody's front room. Perhaps the truest comment on our group was one I overheard at the Abergavenny Golf Club ball, where, as we pressed through the crowd to get to the bandstand for the second interval set, someone groaned audibly, "Oh no, not them again!"

John Barnie

and Alan Lomax; *A Treasury of Railroad Folklore*, edited by Botkin and Harlow; *American Folksongs of Protest* by John Greenway; *American Mountain Songs* collected by Ethel Richardson and edited and arranged by Sigmund Speath; and *A Treasury of Mississippi River Folklore*, edited by B.A. Botkin. The British side of things was represented by the Scottish *Border Ballads*, edited by W. Beattie and a collection of industrial folk ballads edited by Ewan MacColl called *The Shuttle and the Cage*. Also on offer was a collection of twelve international folksongs with guitar accompaniments. Skifflers might seek out new songs in other publications, such as Francis & Day's *Hill-Billy Albums* or the Lomaxs' *American Ballads and Folk Songs*.

The experience of Derek Mason, from Fulham, London, and the Black Cats from Leicester, illustrate some of the different aspects of amateur skiffle. Derek, who began on washboard with a group called the Ravens, later joined the Saints, considered the best group in the area, as their washboard player. Gigs included the Odeon cinema, Tooting, that put on regular Sunday evening shows. The Station Skiffle Group, of Bury St Edmunds fame, split up in 1957 and Mike Jarvie formed a new group, the New Station Skiffle Group, which Derek Mason later joined to replace the washboard player who had gone over to guitar. The group played regularly on a Friday night at the Constitutional Club, Shorrolds Road, Fulham, and Thursday and Sunday at the Prince of Wales pub, Ravenscourt Park, Hammersmith.

The New Station Skiffle Group took over the original group's placing in the National Skiffle Competition, winning through to the July semi-final on *Six-Five Special* but were beaten by the Saxons from Barking. With the onslaught of rock 'n' roll, and the marriage of the group's leader Mike Jarvie, the group broke up in 1959.[44]

The story of the Black Cats also exemplifies the importance of the competition as well as illustrating the changing face of skiffle during the group's career. From Granby Road Youth Centre, the Cats were formed at Easter 1957 as the Black Jacks, changing their name because of the black cat's face painted on the drummer's bass drum. They found appreciation early on as the winners of the Leicester Diocesan Youth Fellowship skiffle competition organised by Leicester's youth chaplain at St George's Hall in June 1957. The winners were invited to perform later in the week at another church venue and were promised a cash prize and a certificate.[45]

The Black Cats then took part in Carroll Levis television auditions in August 1957 and gained first place in the first house and third place in the second at the Palace Theatre. This gave them two chances in the area finals and if they won they would appear on ITV. The group was in the process of composing its own signature tune, "Black Cat Blues".[46] In September 1957, they took part in a local final of the World Skiffle Championship, along with other local groups like the Dynamics, the Foresters, the Johnny Denver Group and the Skiffabillies. The Black Cats went on to win the area final of this championship (and £15) held at the Leicester Palais, beating another local group, the Dynamics (awarded £10), by two points. As their performance was of almost professional standard, the Cats were offered a contract by the BBC to do a series on *Six-Five Special* but turned it down, as it would have meant some of them giving up their jobs in order to turn professional which would make them liable for national service.[47]

The Black Cats were originally a five-man group with three guitars, drums, and tea-chest bass. With the addition of a washboard player, the enlarged group had functioned from the latter half of 1957. However, by the time they had participated in and won through to a televised heat of the National Skiffle Contest on *Six-Five Special*, they travelled to London in early April 1958 in the company of £300's worth of instruments. Gone were the acoustic and improvised instruments: in their place there were a proper double bass and electric guitars. Skiffle was changing. The Black Cats sang "Streamline Train", hoped to win a big money prize and become the nation's champion skifflers[48] but unfortunately lost their heat to the Double Three Skiffle Group from Colchester.

In *Pop from the Beginning*, Nik Cohn wrote disparagingly that skiffle — Teddy-boy jazz — was "knockabout American folk song thumped out any old how on guitar and washboard. Its major attraction was that any musical ability was entirely irrelevant. All you needed was natural rowdiness."[49] No doubt some young people jumped on the skiffle bandwagon only to find they had no talent or that for them the skiffle craze was just that — a craze that passed. For many others it was different. They took care over their music-making and its presentation, emerging from the skiffle craze to go on to other kinds of popular music — skiffle being the departure point for a variety of musical journeys. Amateur groups became more professional and almost self-contained when later, like the Beatles, they began to write their own material.

In the beat music era early in the next decade, attention was drawn to Britain's large, grassroots popular music network. This did not happen overnight, nor was it entirely a result of British beat music itself but was the natural development of the network created by the skiffle craze. As Mick Houghton puts it: "skiffle... was too limited and unsatisfying to last, but it did create a guitar/group consciousness that long outlived the boom. The significance of the skiffle craze lay not in the charts but in the coffee bars, church halls and other temporary venues where thousands of kids formed skiffle groups and were hooked on playing this ersatz form of rock & roll. The essential flaw in skiffle was its lack of power."[50] Electric guitars, amplifiers and proper drum kits would change all that.

Skiffle rolls on! The Riding Mill Skiffle Group playing in July 1961 at the Women's Institute Garden Party, Riding Mill, Northumberland.

7 Over the Points —
Skiffle Takes to the Airwaves

A common view of the BBC in the Fifties is that the corporation did little to cater for popular music, in particular the music needs of young people, and the specialist music audiences for jazz, folk and skiffle. An examination of the decade's BBC radio output, however, especially from its Light Programme, shows that the BBC was conscious of the requirement to provide popular music, was trying to cater for specialist music audiences and becoming increasingly aware of the need to respond to the music interests of the teenage audience. With a single television channel, the BBC was in a less strong position to respond to the many demands made on it in the Fifties but, with *Six-Five Special*, it created a successful popular music show enjoyed by teenagers and one that also provided a skiffle showcase, especially for amateur groups.

If the BBC's heart was roughly in the right place, what might be the complaints that could be levelled against it? First, that its output for specialist audiences was too small. Secondly that it was broadcast at inconvenient times, and lastly that it was often safe and old-fashioned in its approach. On television, it would seem, popular music could not be allowed initially to stand on its own but had to be accompanied and supported by variety performers or sporting personalities. For, even when being innovative, the BBC could be conservative in its treatment of innovation. This is not to say that changes and improvements did not occur in the late Fifties, but they were insufficient to prevent the wholesale reorganisation of BBC radio in the next decade, sparked off by the competition from the pirate stations.

Part of the Fifties problem was that the BBC had a monopoly of radio (although not of television broadcasting from 1955) and, while obliged to try and please everybody, there was no doubt about where its cultural biases (and inhibitions) lay, particularly in the field of popular music. This lack of challenge to its approach (other than from continental stations like Radio Luxembourg), perhaps hindered significant change.

Recognition of the BBC's need to cater for a wide range of tastes was reflected in its own late-Fifties statement about recent programme developments: "A number of programme series were developed as vehicles for a wide variety of the best popular musical entertainment, including jazz,

'skiffle', popular songs and dance music. The annual Dance Music Festival
was held at the Royal Albert Hall, again with great success. The appeal of
gramophone record programmes was undiminished, and *Housewives
Choice* and *Family Favourites* continued to attract audiences that were very
large indeed by present-day standards."[1]

The annual Festival of Dance Music, begun in 1955, was later joined
by an annual Jazz Saturday, both broadcast on the BBC's Light Programme
from the Royal Albert Hall. The dance music festival ran until 1959 —
each usually consisted of three concerts broadcast at fortnightly intervals
around March-April time — and presented a mix of bands, instrumentalists
and vocalists. The third annual festival in 1957 in its first concert featured
"today's sensation", Tommy Steele and his Steelmen, while the second
and third concerts presented Nancy Whiskey and the Chas McDevitt Skiffle
Group and the Bob Cort Skiffle Group respectively. New developments in
popular music were thus being recognised and taken on board.

The first of three Saturday night concerts in connection with the Fourth
Annual Festival of Dance Music was broadcast in March 1958 and Johnny
Duncan and his Blue Grass Boys were among the performers. In the two
subsequent concert broadcasts, Russell Quaye and the City Ramblers, and
the Chas McDevitt Skiffle Group with Shirley Douglas, were on the
respective bills.

The following year the first Saturday concert of the Fifth Festival of
Dance Music — and called "Down-Beat" — included the Oscar Rabin and
Bob Miller bands, the Jazz Couriers and the Bobcats, a threesome (two
aged twelve and one fourteen) on guitar, banjo and tea-chest bass. Other
than an appearance by Don Lang (and Johnny Duncan in a later Saturday
festival concert), the Bobcats seemed to be among the last broadcasting
vestiges of the skiffle craze.[2]

The year 1957 began auspiciously for jazz, as it was given its own *Jazz
Saturday* in February that year. Jazz had been featured in the BBC's
Festival of Dance Music as one type of "music-for-dancing" but the
demand could not be accommodated satisfactorily within the festival and
so *Jazz Saturday* was launched. In its first year, this event offered two
Saturday evening broadcasts of a six-band concert from the Royal Albert
Hall. Five of the bands were those of Barber, Brown, Laurie, Lyttleton
and Mulligan; the sixth was Lonnie Donegan and his Skiffle Group. The

Festival of Dance Music, Radio Times, 21 March 1958. (Reproduced by permission.)

festival was also visited by television's *Saturday Night Out* and Donegan and his group were featured performers in this half-hour version of the event.

On 1 February 1958 the BBC Light Programme presented another *Jazz Saturday* and skiffle was represented by Johnny Duncan and his Blue Grass Boys and Russell Quaye's City Ramblers. The *Radio Times* noted: "The BBC's first *Jazz Saturday* was put on... last year to satisfy some of the demand for jazz encountered in the Dance Music Festival. All the tickets were sold within a few days of the box office opening... This year two *Jazz Saturdays* have been arranged... but even so the demand for tickets has again exceeded supply... Jimmy Grant told us... 'There is quite a bit of skiffle, too, which after all has its roots in jazz'."[3] The second 1959 *Jazz Saturday* concert was called "Dixieland and After" and displayed the talents of the Dankworth, Lyttleton and Welsh bands and instrumentalists such as Tubby Hayes and Kathleen Stobart. There were two jazz singers, Beryl Bryden and Elaine Delmar, but, as in the first concert, no skiffle — its day had past.

Prior to any special attention given to skiffle by BBC programmers in 1957, the music had begun to be featured in broadcasts at the very end of 1956, although doubtless it was also to be heard earlier that year in various radio record programmes. A Monday evening television show called *Off the Record*, presented by Jack Payne, included the Vipers on 10 December 1956 and Lonnie Donegan on Christmas Eve. From early 1957 the BBC's radio output was beginning to reflect the greater interest in skiffle. For, as well as spots in the dance music festivals and jazz Saturdays, skiffle was broadcast in *Break for Jazz, Rhythm and Blues, Let's Have a Ball, Saturday Skiffle Club, Guitar Club*, and on television's *Six-Five Special*. Another programme, *Skiffle and Jazz*, seems to have been a radio project for broadcasting in July 1957 but never made the airwaves.

Break for Jazz was a 1.00 p.m. forty-minute programme that ran from

PORT
.onn Andrews
    Racing
results
  Webster

eports
  and interviews
grounds

ion Desk
  in which experts
tions and problems

g Sport
  administrators, and
Eamonn Andrews at
to discuss topics of

sified Football Results
ogramme includes:
  Ar~enal *v*. Manchester
   ~ity *v.* W'

THE BBC LIGHT PROGRAMME PRESENTS

JAZZ SATURDAY

Chris Barber's Jazz Band
with Ottilie Patterson

Mick Mulligan and his Band
with George Melly

Sandy Brown and his Band
with Neva Raphaello

**Johnny Duncan
  and his Blue Grass Boys**

Russell Quaye's City Ramblers

FROM THE ROYAL ALBERT HALL: 8.0—8.30: 9.15—10.0

INSTRUMENTAL STARS
Ken Rattenbury(trumpet)
Al Fairweather (trumpet)
Dill Jones (piano)

MASTER OF CEREMONIES
Brian Matthew

Produced by Jimmy Grant
and John Kingdon

6.30   JUST JAZZ
A programme of traditional
mainstream and modern jazz

11.15   EDMUNDO ROS
and his
Latin-American Orchestra
From Edmundo Ros' Club London

Jazz Saturday,
Radio Times 24
January 1958.
(Reproduced by
permission.)

March to July 1957 and showcased bands such as those of Laurie Gold, Humphrey Lyttleton, Freddy Randall, Eric Silk and Kenny Ball. It also provided air time for one or two skiffle groups, such as Bob Cort's group and the Cotton Pickers. Robin Boyle introduced the Friday morning series, *Rhythm and Blues*, between July and September. The title is a little misleading as it was a vehicle for the usual jazz bands. However, it too provided an outlet for skiffle groups such as the Cotton Pickers and those led by Bob Cort, Johnny Duncan, Russell Quaye, Chas McDevitt and Dickie Bishop. At the height of the skiffle craze, the music got the BBC's accolade of recognition when the *World of Jazz* broadcast "Thirty Years of Skiffle" in September 1957, introduced by the jazz historian, Rex Harris.

From October to December 1957, the 1.00 p.m. *Let's Have a Ball!* offered a Friday jazz and skiffle date. Each programme featured one jazz band and one skiffle group and, in addition to the more usual jazz and skiffle names, the programme provide an opportunity for the Martians, Eden Street, 2.19 and Brett Brothers' groups. Although skiffle featured on other radio and television programmes to some degree, for skiffle historians, the three key BBC programmes of the late Fifties were television's *Six-Five Special*, and radio's *Saturday Skiffle Club* and *Guitar Club*.

On Saturday 16 February 1957, BBC TV invited viewers for the first time "to take a trip on the Six-Five Special", presented by Pete Murray and Jo Douglas and jointly produced by Douglas and Jack Good. Freddie Mills, the boxer, was also involved, and responsible for talking about sport. The new programme, which took its name from its 6.5 p.m. transmission time, was described as being "designed for the young in spirit" and promised "plenty of music, in the modern manner, with rock 'n' roll, skiffle groups, traditional jazz, featuring top groups and soloists."[4] And so on successive Saturdays viewers were asked to climb aboard the *Six-Five Special*, where the vigorous jiving of the audience became something of a programme hallmark, attracting some adverse comment for its supposed impropriety.

> *1956 And All That: Skiffle Reminiscences*
>
> *During the skiffle craze, we were often called upon to judge amateur skiffle contests at Bath, Bristol, and Weston-Super-Mare, for example. At these events we were disappointed that none of the groups tried anything original, they all used Whyton, McDevitt and Donegan numbers.*
>
> *The Avon Cities' first television appearance was for the BBC probably in about March 1957, at their Bristol studios opposite Jimmy Young also making his TV debut. The band and its skiffle group also played at various times on Television Wales and the West opposite the Merseysippi Jazz Band, Sonny Terry and Brownie McGhee, and Big Bill Broonzy.*
>
> *Basil Wright*

Pete Murray it was who coined the show's opening phrase: "It's time to jive on the old 6.5".

In its fourth programme — one that included Tommy Steele and his Steelmen and Big Bill Broonzy — skiffle was represented for the first time by the Vipers. According to audience research, the Vipers scored rather poorly, as the words of their number were drowned by their instruments.[5] In subsequent weeks, the Lonnie Donegan and the Chas McDevitt skiffle groups, the latter with Nancy Whiskey, each appeared on a programme.

During May to August sports programmes (usually cricket) ousted *Six-Five Special* from the schedules or reduced its length to 15, 20 or 25 minutes, rather misleadingly altering its title, one would think, to *Extra Special*. Not everyone was happy about these scheduling arrangements and a Scottish viewer wrote to the *Radio Times*: "I feel that I must write and tell you how disgusted I am with having to put up with 'professional golf' instead of that first-class programme, *Six-Five Special* on Saturday May 18. *Six-Five Special* is the only decent programme provided for us teenagers: goodness knows there are enough sports programmes without putting off the *Six-Five Special*. Who wants to watch a man swing his 'stick' when we could be watching a 'cat' swing his 'chick'?"[6]

Throughout the second half of 1957, *Six-Five Special* regularly featured skiffle groups, such as those led by Bob Cort, Chas McDevitt, Sonny Stewart and Lonnie Donegan, and others like the Vipers, the Worried Men, Les Hobeaux, and Johnny Duncan and his Blue Grass Boys. In its final programme of the year, 17-year-old Roy Gibbs appeared; a Manchester teenager, who, after a nation-wide contest earlier that year, had become Britain's Skiffle Champion. He and his fellow teenagers were billed on the *Six-Five Special* shown on 28 December as "Roy Gibbs and the Live Jive Five". The *Radio Times* commented on the skiffle phenomenon: "Just over a year ago the word 'skiffle' meant little or nothing in this country. And when at last it crept into radio and television programmes a lot of people shook their heads and said it couldn't possibly last. Today it has been adopted by thousands — professionals and amateurs alike."[7]

One notable event in 1957 was the broadcast for 16 November, which came from the 2 I's coffee bar, where teenagers jived and listened to a bill of Don Lang's Frantic Five, the King Brothers, the Chas McDevitt Skiffle Group, the Worried Men, Wee Willie Harris and others. A film excerpt

and
THE WEATHER

6.5 SIX-FIVE SPECIAL
from the Winter Gardens Pavilion
Weston-super-Mare
with
Josephine Douglas and Pete Murray
aided and abetted by
Freddie Mills
introducing
**Ken Mackintosh
and his Orchestra**
**The Ray Ellington Quartet
with Val Masters**
Lorrae Desmond
The Avon Cities Jazz Band
Mac McCoombe
**Johnny Duncan
and his Blue Grass Boys**
Don Lang and his Frantic Five
and
Jim Dale
introducing
**Stanley Dale's
NATIONAL SKIFFLE CONTEST**
This week:
The Six Thunders of Birmingham
v.
The Moonshiners of Sheffield
Script by Trevor Peacock
Produced by DUNCAN WOOD

7,0   DALE ROBERTSON
in

The Six-five Special, Radio Times, 7 February 1958. (Reproduced by permission.)

in the programme featured Terry Dene. A memo from the Deputy Director of Television Broadcasting to the television Head of Light Entertainment expressed approval of this outside broadcast and applauded it as "first class television as well as first class entertainment."[8] Commenting on the undoubted success of *Six-Five Special*, one newspaper called it "the hunch that clicked" and "the BBC's touch of genius". It noted that it did not patronise or talk down to its young audience — claimed to be four-and-a-half million — and that no other programme had similar viewing figures for that time of day.[9]

In November 1957, Stanley Dale wrote to BBC Television offering his National Skiffle Contest as part of a package show or as a "gimmick" on *Six-Five Special*. In the event, the BBC went for the latter option, to be introduced by Jim Dale, and broadcast as a fortnightly, six-minute feature, during which two amateur skiffle groups from different towns would play one number apiece. Jim Dale would then ask viewers to vote for the group they preferred. Skiffle groups would be eliminated by the voting until a final round led to a winner. It was suggested that the corporation would give prizes of £100, £75 and £50 to the winners.

At the end of January 1958, the BBC contracted Stanley Dale for thirteen fortnightly skiffle contest programmes from 1 February to 19 July and Dale was to pay the skiffle groups concerned at not less than agreed minimum union rates. The competition did not quite stick to this fortnightly timetable and went on until 23 August. In the last heat, two semi-finals and finals, three groups, rather than two, played on each occasion; in the semi-final for the 9 August, however, four groups were involved. The first edition of *Six-Five Special* for 1958 offered a typical mix of performers, with a bill made up of the Worried Men Skiffle Group, Don Lang and his Frantic Five, the Downbeaters, Johnny Worth, the Five Dallas Boys, Rosemary Squires, and Johnny Dankworth and his Orchestra. Later programmes continued to feature skiffle groups from time to time, such as Johnny Duncan and his Blue Grass Boys, the Vipers, the City Ramblers, the Eden Street group, and Lonnie Donegan. Further proof that skiffle touched very many young people, even those not yet in their teens, was demonstrated by the newspaper report of the *Six-Five Special* appearance

Six-Five Special — Stanley Dale's National Skiffle Contest 1958

Competitors

Date	Competition Stage	Groups
1 February	heat	The Rebels (Leeds)* The Alley Cats (Chiswick)
15 February	heat	The Six Thunderers (Birmingham) The Moonshiners (Sheffield)*
1 March	heat	The Attic Boys (Hull) The Southerners (Reading)*
29 March	heat	The Station Group (London)* The Wild Five (Manchester)
12 April	heat	The Black Cats (Leicester) The Double Three (Colchester)*
26 April	heat	The Saxons (Barking)* The Sinners (Newcastle)
10 May	heat	The Darktown (Liverpool)* The Sidewinders (Bradford)
24 May	heat	The Casanovas (Nottingham) The Teenage Vipers (Glasgow)*
31 May	heat	The Denson Boys (Cardiff) The Woodlanders (Plymouth)* The Johnny Spencer Group (Bristol)
12 July	semi-final	The Rebels (Leeds) The Double Three (Colchester)* The Southerners (Reading)
19 July	semi-final	The Station Group (London) The Saxons (Barking)* The Moonshiners (Sheffield)
9 August	semi-final	The Darktown (Liverpool) The Vikings (Elephant & Castle) The Woodlanders (Plymouth)* The Teenage Vipers (Glasgow)
23 August	final	The Double Three (Colchester) The Saxons (Barking) The Woodlanders (Plymouth)*

* = winners

of the Imps, a group made up of five boys aged twelve, three playing ukuleles and the other two bass and washboard.[10]

However, the major *Six-Five Special* contribution to skiffle in 1958 was in the programme time (from February to August) it gave over to Stanley Dale's National Skiffle Contest. The table on page 165 lists the competing skiffle groups and demonstrates that contestants represented the wide geographical spread of skiffle in Britain. The contest was won by the Woodlanders from Plymouth, with the Saxons from Barking and the Double Three from Colchester coming second and third.

By February 1958 *Six-Five Special* was one year old and the *Radio Times* "Round and About" column had this to say about the effects of, and reaction to the programme:

"Are you one of the many millions who have learnt to jive on the Old Six-Five? Every Saturday for the past year, a considerable percentage of the population has tuned in to the *Six-Five Special*, and watched the younger generation having its fling.

"Many have protested — the squares, of course. Many have been initiated into the world of skiffle, rock 'n' roll, jazz, and the hand-jive. Stars have been created. Even a film has been made. Records have been launched by it, and Benny Hill has added it to his honourable collection of BBC scalps.

"But whatever the reactions have been, the viewing figures have soared since the Six-Five Special first came rattling over the points, and there is no doubt that this programme has been largely responsible for introducing an enormous number of amateurs to the joys of making their own music at home."[11]

The *Six-Five Birthday Special* included Russell Quaye and the City Ramblers and had Jo Douglas, Pete Murray and Freddie Mills cutting the cake. Others involved in the birthday celebrations were Mike and Bernie Winters, Denis Lotis, Rosemary Squires, The Dallas Boys, Marty Wilde, Laurie London, the Mudlarks, Jackie Dennis, Kenny Baker and the Dozen, Don Lang and his Frantic Five, Carl Barriteau, and Tommy Steele in a film excerpt from *The Tommy Steele Story*.

The BBC recognised that "the programme devised to fill the 6.00 to 7.00 p.m. period on Saturdays, was phenomenally successful with the younger and teenage audience."[12] Apparently planned at short notice, this innovatory programme had provided a debut for young singers — a number subsequently signed up by record companies — and an opportunity for small bands and groups. With a regular adult audience of some seven million adults, the "programme has become a national institution equally enjoyed by the parents" as by the young people for whom it was mainly intended.[13] Not everybody was happy with the programme, however. *Six-Five Special* was accused of encouraging and glorifying tuneless tripe, and the BBC and the record companies of capitalising on the lack of taste amongst teenagers to the detriment of good pop music.[14]

The broadcast of *Six-Five Special* for the 15 March was from Paris and later programmes in 1958 came from around the UK — from Barry,

Glasgow, Southampton and the Isle of Man, for instance. In late March 1958, a newspaper story reported that Pete Murray and Freddie Mills were to leave after that Saturday's programme and that Jo Douglas would leave in mid-May. By the transmission of 5 April Josephine Douglas was the sole presenter, Pete Murray having left the show, and from the 19 April she was joined by Jim Dale. Dale who was responsible for introducing the National Skiffle Contest part of the programme, was an impressionist and comedian and would-be all-rounder, who later had some success as a pop star but greater success as an actor.

In September 1958 the BBC were being advised by a newspaper columnist to bury *Six-Five Special*, as it suffered by contrast with ITV's *Oh Boy!*. After thirteen weeks, ITV claimed that *Oh Boy!* — produced by former BBC employee, Jack Good — was attracting more than five million adult viewers. The Deputy Director of Television Broadcasting, no less, declared that the *Six-Five Special* of 22 November was a reminder of the sad state of a once excellent programme. In November 1958 the news was put out that the show would be taken off and given a new look, as the BBC was said to have no intention of ending it, although it would be shortened to thirty minutes. The BBC admitted in early December that its over-sixteen audience (twelve million at its peak) was down to four million.[15] Later in the month, however, the *Radio Times* officially announced that the *Six-Five Special* had reached the end of the line; the last programme, *Six-Five Special Party*, would go out on 27 December and then: "A new programme called *Dig This!* takes over — a swift moving, up-to-the minute show with all the latest pop music presented in a new streamlined manner, with Bob Miller and the Millermen as the resident band."[16]

This big change in programme came into force on Saturday 3 January 1959. *Dig This!*, subtitled "The new Six-Five Show", was hosted by Gary Marshal. In the first week in April, *Dig This!* was replaced (perhaps re-titled is more accurate) by *Drumbeat* — "beat" apparently being the "in" word. *Drumbeat* too featured Bob Miller and the Millermen and Adam Faith was one of the regulars on the programme.

The last *Drumbeat* — of what was thought by the BBC to be a highly acceptable successor to *Six-Five Special* — was, however, heard on 29 August 1959. Without ceremony, *Drumbeat* was replaced by the well established *Juke Box Jury* at 6.50 the following Saturday. Moved from its Monday slot, and with David Jacobs in the chair, the opinions were sought of a panel of four celebrities on the latest popular records. However, *Drumbeat*'s official successor, according to the *Radio Times*, was a programme called *Flying Standards*, which was broadcast at 7.30 on a Friday evening from October 1959, and subtitled "The All-Time Hit Parade". The programme was as short-lived (it was last broadcast on 18 December) as its title was mysterious.

Six-Five Special rightly deserves to be remembered but its lesser known successors were probably a little closer to the kind of programme that was wanted by teenagers. While *Six-Five Special* was not a major showcase for the professional skiffle group (though many appeared on the programme), it provided a marvellous opportunity for amateur skifflers through its hosting of the National Skiffle Contest and in that way perhaps helped maintain the popularity of skiffle at a time when it was beginning to wane commercially. Sadly, *Six-Five Special* and its successors were largely overshadowed by their commercial television rivals. Not until *Top of the Pops* in 1964 did BBC television regain the advantage that it had largely conceded to its rival in the late Fifties, although there were other, but different successes along the way, such as *Juke Box Jury*.

Skiffle Session, a fifteen to twenty minute programme consisting of two or three singers with accompanying skiffle group, was a suggestion for a new radio programme from producer Jimmy Grant in January 1957. Grant cited in support of his proposition the increasing popularity of skiffle, its wide repertoire, and a growing number of groups of professional standard.[17]

Following up this proposal, the BBC held a skiffle group audition on 11 March 1957 and listened to the groups of Cy Laurie, Chas McDevitt, with Nancy Whiskey, Johnny Duncan and Dickie Bishop, as well as the Cotton Pickers. The first to be auditioned, the Cy Laurie Jazz Club Skiffle Group, was considered the least satisfactory, while Chas McDevitt's group got the top marks.[18] After these auditions, Jimmy Grant put forward another, slightly different proposal in April 1957, for a longer programme (thirty-minutes), to be called *Skiffle Party*, at an estimated cost of just over £82. Grant had been involved in judging a skiffle competition at the Streatham Locarno and the fact that the place was packed, even on a Monday, seems to have confirmed his belief in the need for such a standard length programme.[19] Later in April, a series of eight thirty-minute programmes for the Light Programme, at a cost of £55 per programme, was confirmed at the BBC. Jimmy Grant was to produce and the programme was to be recorded.[20]

Having realised that there was an enormous interest in skiffle, the BBC launched its new radio programme, to be called *Saturday Skiffle Club*, on 1 June 1957. The first programme was, like its successors, broadcast after the morning's 10 o'clock Greenwich Time Signal, and on that groundbreaking occasion featured the Chas McDevitt Skiffle Group with Nancy Whiskey, and the Danny Levan Trio. No presenter of this first recorded programme was noted in the *Radio Times*, although Brian Matthew became its regular voice. Brian Matthew had been a broadcaster with the British Forces Network in the late Forties, at the same time that Alexis Korner worked in its gramophone library. He subsequently trained as an actor at the Royal Academy of Dramatic Art and was then employed as a broadcaster for the English Department of Dutch Radio in Hilversum. Matthew was then offered a post as a trainee announcer with the BBC, ending up at the Light Programme when "Jimmy Grant... devised a programme [*Saturday Skiffle Club*] quite unlike anything that had been heard on BBC radio before. It was very much by way of an experiment and he asked me if I would like to introduce it."[21] Brian Matthew did not know what skiffle was but liked the idea and so took over the new 10 o'clock Saturday spot previously occupied by cinema organ music. In due course *Saturday Skiffle Club* came to feature all the successful skiffle recording artists of the period, as well as many of the lesser known groups.

Not long after its inception, there was criticism from "on high" in the BBC that the programme contained too much American material. In response it was said that thought and effort had gone into looking for British material but that it did not suit the skiffle beat. Nevertheless, in the first four programmes approximately one in three songs had been British and some very rhythmic Scottish folk music was planned for the programme from Glasgow in July.[22] In that month, Jimmy Grant auditioned three more skiffle groups and found them "up to broadcasting standards and worthy for consideration for programmes, bearing in mind that they are new and therefore inexperienced broadcasters." The groups were the 2.19 Skiffle Group, the Brett Brothers (the addition of Jack Fallon on bass was suggested for this country group), and the Eden Street Skiffle Group. The following month the responsibility for the administration of the auditioning of jazz and skiffle groups was passed from Grant to a colleague.[23]

The programme did not stick strictly to skiffle music as practised in the UK but included, right from its early broadcasts, artists such as the jazz singer George Melly (usually with his Bubbling Over Four); singers, Neva Rapaello and Beryl Bryden; the jazz pianist, Dill Jones; Syd Chalmers (fiddle music); the Ken Sykora Trio (guitar music); the boogie pianist Cyril Scutt; saxophonist and vocalist, Betty Smith with her Quintet, and folk singers Shirley Bland and Jim McGregor.

By November 1957, *Saturday Skiffle Club* had a weekly audience of over two and a half million listeners. From the start of the programme its producer, Jimmy Grant, had received lots of requests from groups to be auditioned but he found many amateur skiffle groups lacking in basic musicianship. The average audience for the show in mid-1958, expressed as a percentage, was 7.29 per cent and the only other popular music programmes that came anywhere near this figure were those of Victor Silvester (5 per cent) and Ted Heath (4.14 per cent).[24]

In 1958 the radio skiffle club went on much as before and continued to feature less well known groups, such as the Hi-Fi, Peter Curtis, Martians, and Creole skiffle groups. Music other than skiffle came from former contributors, such as, George Melly, Dill Jones, Shirley Bland and Jim McGregor, and from new ones like Al Meek and his Rio Ranch Boys, the folk singers, Steve Benbow and Isla Cameron, and the Joe Gordon Folk Four, as well as the pianist, Johnny Parker. Brian Matthew explained: "As the programme developed... Jimmy [Grant] started to diversify from the original concept and introduced more folky elements... while many of the groups began to introduce more sophisticated instruments, electric guitars for instance. Skiffle was on its way out and rock and roll on its way in."[25] Truth to tell, *Saturday Skiffle Club* had never been a pure skiffle programme from its earliest days.

Real recognition of the popularity of skiffle, however, was perhaps confirmed by the programme of 17 May 1958. This was a one-hour show (Johnny Duncan and his Blue Grass Boys and the Pete Curtis Folk and Blues Quintet), with guest appearances from Bob Cort, Lonnie Donegan,

Chas McDevitt, Russell Quaye, Nancy Whiskey and Wally Whyton, whose groups had all appeared in past programmes, and who were asked to choose their favourite skiffle record. Other groups featured in past programmes included those led by Colyer, Bishop, Bill Bailey, as well as the Delta, Avon Cities and Worried Men outfits.

On August Bank Holiday Monday that year, there was an extra half-hour of skiffle in the shape of *Bank Holiday Skiffle Club*, introduced as usual by Brian Matthew and featuring Russell Quaye's City Ramblers (with Hylda Sims, Shirley Bland and Jimmie McGregor), and the Terry Renn Skiffle Group. However, the following Saturday's programme perhaps indicated a subtle change of direction — neither participating group (the Steve Benbow and Jimmy Jackson quartets) used the word "skiffle" as part of their group title. The following week the programme featured Johnny Duncan and his Blue Grass Boys and the Vipers, the latter, a leading skiffle group, no longer using "skiffle" as part of its group title.

Subsequent programmes were a further development of this trend, with some programmes much as before, while in others some groups dropped the skiffle appellation (Chas McDevitt, and the Soho Group, for example), and folk singers continued to appear, such as Fionna Duncan and the Joe Gordon Folk Four, and Gerard Campbell. The final *Saturday Skiffle Club* on Saturday 27 September 1958 featured the Pete Curtis Folk and Blues Quintet, Al Meek and his Rio Ranch Boys, and Roy Guest.

> ...ews Summary at 9.30
>
> **9.55   FIVE TO TEN**
> A story, a hymn, and a prayer
>
> **10.0   Greenwich Time Signal**
> **SATURDAY SKIFFLE CLUB**
> Dickie Bishop and his Sidekicks
> Leonard Hill's
> Eden Street Skiffle Group
> Introduced by Brian Matthew
> Produced by Jimmy Grant
> (BBC recording)

Saturday Skiffle Club, Radio Times 14 February 1958. (Reproduced by permission.)

On 4 October 1958, *Saturday Skiffle Club* was replaced by *Saturday Club*, also produced by Jimmy Grant, with Brian Matthew continuing as presenter. The demise of *Saturday Skiffle Club* could be seen as a signal that the skiffle craze, at least from a broadcasting point of view, was largely over. The replacement programme advertised itself as a new two-hour show (a big increase in air time) for "skiffle, jazz and 'pop' music". This first programme — described as "the best of today's 'pop' and entertainment" — showcased Terry Dene and the Dene Aces; Humphrey Lyttleton and his Band; Gary Miller (the week's recording artist); Johnny Duncan and his Blue Grass Boys (country and western); and Russell Quaye's City Ramblers (folk and spasm). It also had "Cats Call" (disc stars requested by listeners) and "First Time Round"(newest releases).

Brian Matthew has recounted how the change to *Saturday Club* came about. "Delighted with the unexpectedly big success of this experimental half hour the head of the department, Jim Davidson, then asked Jimmy if he could come up with a formula to fill the two hours on Saturday mornings. He did so and a programme was born that was destined to run for ten years, certainly the first and far and away the most important breakthrough for pop music on British radio."[26]

Saturday Club was preceded at 9.00 a.m. by *Children's Favourites* —

170

1956 And All That: Skiffle Reminiscences

We learnt most of the numbers as they emerged, week after week, via the ever increasing number of professional groups, and amassed about thirty songs and all of seven or eight chords. We even had an audition for Saturday Skiffle Club *but by then we had suffered numerous changes of personnel and what had started as great fun was becoming rather a chore. Also by now my rehabilitation was ending and I was told to find a proper job. And so, what had by then become the Tim Mallinson Skiffle Group, fizzled out in early 1958, although we still played at a few parties until we all went our various ways.*

Tim Mallinson

After the milk round on a Saturday morning, it was home for Saturday Skiffle Club *from 10.00 to 10.30 am. Within that half-hour one could catch not only the big names but lesser lights like the Cotton Pickers (always good value) and also jazz influences like the boogie pianist, Cyril Scutt. The late Fifties and early Sixties were heady days, as popular music as we know it was just beginning to get off the ground, and lads of my generation were mostly keen to get in on the act somehow. Skiffle provided an ideal opportunity to try.*

Mike Waites

record requests presented by Rex Palmer — and followed at midday by *Top of the Form*, a general knowledge contest between competing schools. The *Radio Times* noted that *Saturday Club* "completes a Saturday morning devoted to children and teenagers."[27]

The second *Saturday Club* offered "Folk, skiffle and spasm music" with appearances under this rubric by the Terry Renn Group and the West Five Skiffle Group. The next programme had a slot called "Rock and Skiffle" with music from the Soho Group and the Martians. The following week *Saturday Club* was back to "Folk, skiffle and spasm music", this time from Glasgow and played by Joe Gordon and his Folk Four and Fionna Duncan, and Lonnie Donegan and his Skiffle Group. Skiffle, usually in association with folk, spasm or rock music, continued to be a *Saturday Club* category until the last programme of the year, a programme that included Cliff Richard and the Drifters, the Johnny Dankworth Orchestra, and Joe Gordon and his Folk Four with Fionna Duncan.

Skiffle survived into the new year but after the programme announcement for the *Saturday Club* of 10 January in the *Radio Times*, which listed the Terry Renn Group, there was no further mention of the genre in later programme details, except for one throw-back on 14 February. Sometimes under the heading of "folk music with a beat" however, skiffle artists who had appeared in *Saturday Skiffle Club* or elsewhere occasionally appeared, such as the Vipers, the Soho Group, the Pete Curtis Folk and Blues Quintet, the Joe Gordon Folk Four, Steve Benbow, and Johnny Duncan and his Blue Grass Boys, as well as new names, such as the Wanderers.

By mid-1959, *Saturday Club* was credited with three-and-a- half million listeners, although audience research did not include young people under

> *1956 And All That: Skiffle Reminiscences*
>
> *My first musical memories are of singing in Horsham parish church choir from 1942 to 1949 and performing Handel's* Messiah *and Brahms'* Requiem — *all by ear as I didn't read music. Having got hold of a mouth organ in 1950, I played on church coach outings, but I was told I played it back to front, i.e. the wrong way round, the low notes being on the right. I still play the same way!*
>
> *I was influenced musically in the period 1948 to 1954 by the band of Edmundo Ros, the singers Guy Mitchell and Alma Cogan, and Eddie Calvert and his golden trumpet — I even bought one and practised in a "sound-proof" room at RAF Waterbeach, Cambridgeshire during my national service. I was a great fan of the Basil and Ivor Kirchin Band too, a small jazz/latin combo. I liked their rhythm and beat.*
>
> *In December 1956, I was demobbed from the RAF and in 1957 I started listening to the new skiffle music, especially to all the groups on* Saturday Skiffle Club, *often whilst at the barber's shop. The Chas McDevitt Skiffle Group with Nancy Whiskey, and Marc Sharratt on washboard, was my favourite group. My idol was their guitarist, Bill Bramwell. The Vipers, the Eden Street and 2.19 skiffle groups were also favourites of mine. The City Ramblers, with Vic Pitt (now with Chris Barber) on bass, were well to the fore of the skiffle groups I admired. I knew them from their records and attendance at a few gigs.*
>
> *Terry Potter*

sixteen, who wrote most of the letters to the club. Much of the show's success was put down to Brian Matthew's breezy informality. The programme's scope was widened to include all forms of pop music and jazz, with an emphasis on the big beat. Jim Dale resurfaced and did holiday duty for Brian Matthew in August 1959. Most of the show was live but recordings were an important part. Visitors to the studio included Cliff Richard, Marty Wilde, Lonnie Donegan and Chris Barber. *Saturday Club* claimed to have changed the Saturday-morning listening habits of millions[28] and, in spite of its new title, it did not completely reject skiffle but allowed it gradually to fade away.

Although the Light Programme had already responded to the enormous interest in skiffle, in mid-1957 it launched another initiative — *Guitar Club* — to help cope with the scale of that demand and also with the interest that had been awakened in the guitar and its music. The genesis of the programme went back to October 1955, when the BBC mooted the idea of a guitar programme featuring the many types of guitar music from classical to Latin-American, though not skiffle at that date. Ken Sykora was suggested as a pleasant and authoritative presenter for the programme. The impetus for the programme was the feeling that the guitar was enjoying a renaissance in the USA and that this was having an effect in the UK. In May 1957 the Light Programme scheduled a series of eight programmes of *Guitar Club* — for transmission on a Monday, 6.00-6.45 p.m. — with a weekly budget of 75 guineas.[29]

SATURDAY CLUB

10.0 to 12.0

THE BEST OF TODAY'S 'POP' ENTERTAINMENT

Terry Dene
and the Dene Aces

Humph's Jazz Cellar
Humphrey Lyttelton and his Band

THIS WEEK'S RECORDING ARTIST
Gary Miller

COUNTRY AND WESTERN MUSIC
Johnny Duncan
and his Blue Grass Boys

'Cats Call'
Disc stars you've requested

FOLK AND SPASM MUSIC
Russell Quaye's
City Ramblers
with Hylda Sims
Shirley Bland and Jim Macgregor

★

'First Time Round'
Spinning the newest releases

Introduced by Brian Matthew
PRODUCED BY JIMMY GRANT

6.30 Big Ben; News Summary

12.0 Round the British Isles with
TOP OF THE FORM
' general knowledge

1.10 THE
RE
Jack P
popular gra
here, the

1.40 1,500 m.:
247 m. and

1.45 MOVI
A
sound-track
popular fir
The Ran
' Re
from the nov

Jeannie C

Basil De
Prog
Desmond C

2.10 The
THE
T

Produced by John Kingdon, the programme was first broadcast on Monday evening 15 July 1957 and Ken Sykora invited listeners "to a session of music from 'Spanish to Skiffle'." This first session displayed the talents of Ike Isaacs (guitar), with a resident group, and the guests included Bob Cort and Dorita y Pepe. The following week's guests were Nancy Whiskey, Francisco Cavez and John Williams, and Johnny Duncan appeared on the 12 August programme. Ken Sykora, the deviser of *Guitar Club*, and later voted Britain's number one guitar player by the *Melody Maker*, was a lecturer in economics and geography, a writer, and disc jockey, as well as a guitarist. Sykora was, of course, one of the guitarists called upon to play in Bob Cort's group, although he himself was an acoustic jazz guitarist playing and improvising in the style of Django Reinhardt.

On 5 October *Guitar Club* moved from a Monday to an early Saturday evening slot at 6.00 p.m. and was shortened to half an hour; there was also a change of presenter to Roy Williams. The club's guests included Nancy Whiskey and Rory McEwen. Programmes in 1957, while featuring skiffle, seemed to prefer the skiffle group leaders to their groups and there were appearances from Johnny Duncan, Wally Whyton, Jimmy Jackson, Chas McDevitt, Dickie Bishop, Ken Colyer and Bob Cort. As far as can be judged, not all editions of *Guitar Club* lived up to the promise of "Spanish to Skiffle" and indeed towards the end of 1957, skiffle was neither a regular nor a strong feature of the series, although folk singers and Latin-American music (regularly provided by Dorita y Pepe) had their place.

News of *Guitar Club* reached *Jazz Journal* diarist, Brian Nicholls, who

Saturday Club, Radio Times, 26 September 1958. (Reproduced by permission.)

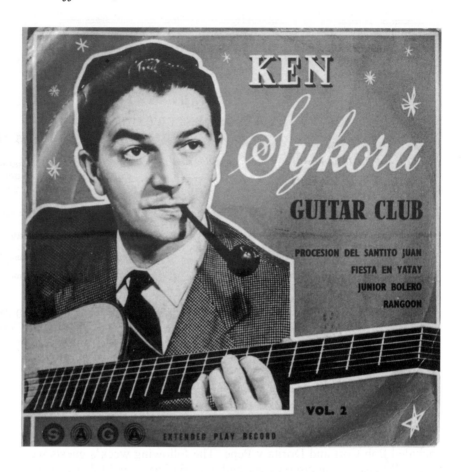

Ken Sykora Guitar Club, Saga EP.

went along to the BBC's Piccadilly Studio to see what would be made of its "Spanish to Skiffle" brief. "As it turned out, there was no real skiffle — only a Scottish skiffle singer called Jimmy Jackson — but there were some Spaniards and a lot of Django Reinhardt type jazz."[30]

The last programme for 1957 — Saturday 28 December — was billed as: Ken Sykora, Ike Isaacs and the Guitar Club Group, Steve Benbow, Archie Slavin, Jimmie McGregor and Shirley Bland, and Bert Weedon, and was now described as "A session of rhythmic music from 'Spanish to Skiffle'." Ken Sykora seems to have had only a playing role on this and earlier transmissions, as the programmes continued to be introduced by Roy Williams.

Guitar Club continued on into 1958 with only the very occasional skiffle contributor, such as Bob Cort and Nancy Whiskey and, through late 1957 to early 1958, it had a listening figure of 2 per cent (it began with 1 per cent). The programme disappeared from the schedules in May, however, to allow for cricket and other sports coverage in the early Saturday evening period. It returned to the air on Saturday 6 September 1958 in its usual 6.00 p.m. slot and, as Roy Williams had not been considered entirely successful, it was hosted once again by Ken Sykora. *Radio Times* commented that: "the Guitar Club Group provid[es] the musical framework for an impressive list of guests. Invited along to the first session are Nancy Whiskey, the skiffle singer, Dorita y Pepe, those rousing Latin-American-style pair, and K Boundy — the 'K' is his name, not an initial — making his second appearance with the Club."[31] By this time, however, the "Spanish to Skiffle" description of the series had been dropped and for the rest of its broadcast life it had no apparent connection with skiffle, although Bob Cort appeared on the show in the first programme of 1959.

Guitar Club continued on into 1959 — by the summer it had notched up thirty-eight programmes and had been only expected to last six — and in re-introducing the programme in September 1959, the "Round and About" column in the *Radio Times* had this to say: "'Skiffle is dead. There may be a few groups still working out in the sticks — with washboards and tea-chests and all — but you certainly won't see it billed in programmes.' We are indebted to this obituary on a short-lived but memorable form of entertainment to producer Johnnie Kingdon, who is quick to add that 'this is my very personal opinion.' He then told us what type of music is still very much alive: 'Rock and folk-beat — folk-singing with a beat: the sort of thing that Lonnie Donegan has done in "The Battle of New Orleans".'

"What we had actually started to talk... about was *Guitar Club*... And on this he had no doubts: 'The guitar is as popular as ever, though it has to be played really well: the days of the three-chord trick are over.'

"The range of styles in the Club will be as wide as ever this season — from flamenco to modern jazz... Famous guitarists visiting Britain will again be welcomed, and the Club will resume its visits to regional centres like Bristol and Manchester to exploit the considerable local talent. Similar visits last season produced some of the Club's most successful programmes."[32]

As far as *Guitar Club* was concerned skiffle had been "dead" — or at least not part of its programming — for some time. However, interest in the guitar continued and thus so did *Guitar Club* — although there was a decline in listening figures from the second series in 1959 to early programmes in 1960, which were later on a Saturday[33] — the last programme going out in April 1960. Johnny Kingdon lobbied for the return of *Guitar Club* in August 1962 but to no avail. This was a pity, given the enormous and continuing interest in the guitar in the Sixties, the programme could have gone in many new directions to its original brief of "Spanish to Skiffle".

Skiffle also appeared from time to time in various other 1957 television programmes. *Come Dancing*, presented by Paul Carpenter from the Locarno Ballroom, Streatham, on 11 November 1957, included in its programme the finals of the World Skiffle Championship. Lonnie Donegan appeared once again in the *Off the Record* television programme on 29 November 1957. In the same month, Bernard Hollowood in *Punch* complained that the BBC was giving too much "of its space and time to the deadbeat rhythm of skiffle." Hollowood did have some good words to say about skiffle and skifflers but hoped that they would move on to jazz and swing and take the BBC with them.[34] In spite of Hollowood's lobbying, the Chas McDevitt Skiffle Group with Shirley Douglas appeared in December on *Off the Record*, which was shown rather irregularly in early 1958 but occasionally included skiffle groups, such as Sonny Stewart and his Skiffle Kings, the Bob Cort group, and Les Hobeaux. Lonnie Donegan was not completely forgotten, however, and appeared with his skiffle group as the guest star on the *Billy Cotton Bandshow* on television in late May 1958.

Broadcasting in the last half of 1958 seemed to demonstrate the public decline of skiffle. Johnny Duncan and his Blue Grass Boys appeared in radio's *Blackpool Night* in early July, and Lonnie Donegan was among the artists appearing in the charity Royal Performance at the Glasgow Alhambra, of which recordings were made during the performance and broadcast on the Light on Sunday 6 July. However, the bill for the Royal Variety Performance broadcast in November that year contained neither Duncan nor Donegan or any other skifflers.

A Cockney's Day Out, a radio broadcast on the August Bank Holiday, (aiming to provide an impression of a Londoner's Bank Holiday), included amongst its musical interludes, however, the Travellers Skiffle Group. And *Midday Music-Hall* the following month presented the Chequers Skiffle Group amongst other items from the Midlands. An edition of the *Carroll Levis Talent Show* for late October included a group called the Skifflelettes.

Whatever the state of skiffle at this time, Lonnie Donegan was apparently still in demand and in November appeared in Alan Melville's *A-Z through the world of entertainment*, dealing with the letter "D" that week.

For radio in 1959 it was almost as if skiffle had never existed. Apart from Donegan, the only other survivor seems to have been Johnny Duncan and his Blue Grass Boys, who appeared in various programmes throughout the year, beginning with *London Lights* and *Nightride* in January, with later appearances in *Bandbox*, the *Fifth Festival of Dance Music*, *Swingalong*, and four transmissions of *Saturday Club* beginning in April. Johnny Duncan and his group also appeared on television in June 1959, in a programme called *Hank's Round-Up*.

A visitor on radio's *Ten-Forty Club* in August and early October had been Bob Cort, while Lonnie Donegan seems to have confined his few broadcast appearances to television. He appeared as a guest star, along with the King Brothers on *Drumbeat* in May and in excerpts from his Great Yarmouth *Lonnie Donegan Show*, that included contributions from Des O'Connor and Mikki and Griff. There was also an appearance in the children's television show, *Crackerjack*, in October. It was commercial television, however, that would keep Donegan more fully in the viewer's eye by giving him his own series in 1959.

The BBC had given skiffle a reasonably good crack of the whip during its rise and fall. How did the music fare on the commercial television channel, which began broadcasting in the London area in September 1955? This new ITV channel soon became identified with a whole raft of popular British and American programmes such as the *Adventures of Robin Hood*, *Gunsmoke*, *Emergency-Ward 10*, and *Dragnet*, and quickly gained recognition for the drama output of its *Armchair Theatre and Television Playhouse* series.

On the popular music front in 1956 there were a number of regular programmes, such as the *Jack Jackson Show*, which featured performers and personalities from the record world, and the trendily titled *Cool for Cats*, a record programme introduced by Kent Walton and networked in 1957. Musical fare in 1958 included the musical quiz, *Spot the Tune!*, a non-stop selection from the hit tunes of the day, *Top Numbers*, and in 1958, an half-hour programme of western-style music set against the background of a Canadian dude ranch and called *Melody Ranch*. Music was also a major component of the ITV variety shows — *Sunday Night at the London Palladium*, Val Parnell's *Saturday Spectacular* and similar weekday productions. None of these musical programmes measured up to *Six-Five Special* until *Oh Boy!* — "an explosion of beat music" — entered the lists of a Saturday at 6.00 p.m. in September 1958, a spot that earlier had been allocated to the *Jack Jackson Show*.

In comparison with the BBC, which also had a radio output, evidence in the *TV Times* suggests that skiffle did not feature as much. Lonnie Donegan, with his skiffle group, was a regular performer on such programmes as the Saturday, Sunday and weekday evening variety shows from the Palladium, Prince of Wales or elsewhere, and also appeared several times on the *Jack Jackson Show* between late 1957 and early 1959. He also showed up on *Oh Boy!* a couple of times, along with newer names like Marty Wilde, and Cliff Richard and the Drifters. The Vipers Skiffle Group also appeared on Val Parnell's *Saturday Spectacular* in May 1957 — a climax to their recent record successes.

In 1959 Lonnie was given his own series, *Putting on the Donegan* — a showcase for Lonnie, his songs, his guitar and his show business friends — regulars were Miki and Griff. Given its success with the family audience as well as teenagers, a second series was recorded in late 1959 for transmission early in 1960. Lonnie saw the popularity of these series as proving that he was a worthwhile entertainer and not solely a singer.

The other main skiffle groups seemed to have fared less well. The Bob Cort Skiffle Group appeared on the *Jack Jackson Show* in early 1957 along with Tommy Steele and others. The Chas McDevitt Skiffle Group appeared in *Palais Party* in April 1957, on the *Jack Jackson Show* in March 1958 and, with Shirley Douglas, on Jack Hylton's *Thursday Show* later in the same month, together with Tessie O'Shea, Max Miller, Buddy Holly and the Crickets. A bit of a mixture, even for a show sub-titled *See You, Soho*.

Both Cort, McDevitt, Shirley Douglas and Johnny Duncan appeared occasionally in a 6.15 p.m. religious programme, launched in 1958, called *Sunday Break*. It was described in the first instance as a programme for young men and women, using the newest methods of entertainment. Presumably skiffle was seen as such. Later it was billed as a Sunday club

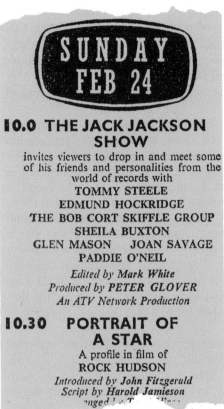

SUNDAY FEB 24

10.0 THE JACK JACKSON SHOW

invites viewers to drop in and meet some of his friends and personalities from the world of records with
TOMMY STEELE
EDMUND HOCKRIDGE
THE BOB CORT SKIFFLE GROUP
SHEILA BUXTON
GLEN MASON   JOAN SAVAGE
PADDIE O'NEIL

Edited by Mark White
Produced by PETER GLOVER
An ATV Network Production

10.30   PORTRAIT OF A STAR

A profile in film of
ROCK HUDSON

Introduced by John Fitzgerald
Script by Harold Jamieson
~nged ' ~ T   ~''~

The Jack Jackson Show, TV Times 22 February 1957. (Reproduced by permission.)

for teenagers.

With the exception of Lonnie Donegan, Johnny Duncan and his Blue Grass Boys fared slightly better than the other main groups, appearing at least four times on ITV from 1957 to 1958: the *Christmas Eve Show* for 1957 and three times on the *Jack Jackson Show* in 1958. A late evening *Jazz Jive Gala* in November 1957 featured the Barber, Laurie and Charlesworth bands and the less known Jubilee Skiffle Group.

Where skiffle perhaps got more of a look-in, albeit at an amateur level, was on the Sunday afternoon children's programme, *Carroll Levis Junior Discoveries*, a talent feature for young people aged twelve to fifteen — later broadened to the under-fifteens. Groups that appeared on the show between July 1958 and April 1959 were the Malestrum, Avro, Viscounts, Comets, and Panthers skiffle groups. Others included the Skifflettes, the David Luther's Skiffle Group, and the Barbara Denman Girls' Skiffle Group — the latter, an all-girl group, something of a rarity.

In early 1957 and 1958 there was an evening adult version of this programme — the *Carroll Levis Show* — where he presented the pick of his discoveries. It is known that skiffle groups auditioned for Carroll Levis but, unlike the junior version, *TV Times* published no details. In 1956 Hughie Green was presenting *Opportunity Knocks*, another amateur talent show, but this may have been too early to have provided opportunities for amateur skifflers, although later series and the talent show, *Bid for Fame*, did so.

Through the late Fifties — when the BBC took up, and subsequently dropped skiffle, provided some broadcasting opportunities for the new teenage pop stars, and rightly judged the immense popularity of and interest in the guitar and its music — the corporation showed that it had made a number of efforts to respond to the demands of the teenage market. At the end of the decade, the BBC could rightly claim that it was "the foremost musical provider in the country." Although talking about serious music (of which there was an average of 45 hours a week, i.e. 2340 hours a year), it went on to note that "the network sound radio services presented some

2300 hours of light music, over 1300 hours of dance and 'pop' music."[35] The latter music category, and one most likely to appeal to the younger audience, was, numerically at least, apparently treated less favourably by the programmers.

It says something for the scale and impact of the skiffle craze — although its association with jazz may have helped to give the music respectability in the eyes of the BBC — that even that rather conservative institution featured it in its radio and television output and was prepared to dedicate one programme — *Saturday Skiffle Club* — to the genre. In reality, however, even the programme supposedly given over to skiffle was rarely allowed to be devoted solely to it, as skiffle items were usually accompanied by other sorts of music. While the BBC would only employ skiffle groups of broadcasting standard, groups that developed during the craze were given an opportunity to audition and to prove themselves suitable, and some did so.

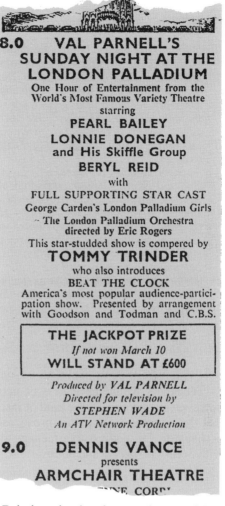

Saturday Night at the Palladium, TV Times 15 March 1957. (Reproduced by permission.)

Other amateur groups from around Britain gained a chance of recognition through the national contest broadcast on *Six-Five Special* and the talent competitions fronted by Carroll Levis.

Out of the skiffle craze came a better awareness on the part of the BBC of the music needs of young people. *Saturday Club* was a step in the right direction but even here the mix of jazz, folk, popular music and pop was not properly targeted at the teenager. While it might use the word "rock" in its description of 1959's *Go Man Go*, no programme seems to have been devoted to rock 'n' roll in the way that skiffle had been treated, even though the two musics co-existed at the time. Skiffle was acceptable, rock 'n' roll had yet to gain acceptance. However, British teenage products from a combination of the skiffle and rock experiences began to emerge in the late Fifties — Tommy Steele, Marty Wilde, Adam Faith and Cliff Richard — and found a place on the radio and television shows of the period. Other results of these musical developments would arise in the Sixties, notably the Beatles.

1956 And All That: Skiffle Reminiscences

On the 6th January 1958, we auditioned for Hughie Green's television talent programme, Bid For Fame, at the television studios in Didsbury, Manchester. Boarding the train at Warrington, lugging our instruments, including the tea-chest bass, we felt confident of our launch to go national. Mr Green had other ideas and we were told that we had not been successful through "lack of originality". We also received a bit of free professional advice — that Bob should be given the lead singer role. We had always taken turns to sing solo and, in spite of this well meant advice, we continued to do so.

Our continuing seriousness of purpose was shown by our entering the National Skiffle Contest sponsored by the Daily Sketch. A successful audition gained us entry to the local heat, which took place at the Ritz Cinema in Warrington on Thursday 13th March, with Jim Dale heading the panel of judges. We were floored when we were told we could not sing either Buddy Holly's "Oh Boy" or the Everly Brothers's "Bye, Bye, Love" since they were not in the tradition of skiffle, although songs like this were beginning to form part of the skiffle group repertoire. Reluctantly, we performed "You'll Never Get to Heaven", sung in the best skiffle fashion with a nasal twang and three-part harmony. Jim Dale was unimpressed and we bowed to the superiority of the winning group, the Memphis Five from Widness, who gave a superb rendering of "Ella Speed".

Norman Froggatt

Teenagers would have to wait until the advent of Radio 1 in 1967, however, in order to get the kind of instant and constant access to the music that they wanted from public broadcasting. The BBC had taken too long, perhaps, to fully adjust to a teenage audience that it had first catered for with *Six-Five Special* and *Saturday Skiffle Club* ten years earlier, in 1957.

8 Oh Boy! — Skiffle Goes Pop

The BBC's transformation of *Saturday Skiffle Club* into *Saturday Club* in October 1958 seemed to mark the end of skiffle as a commercial music, although it was reckoned that the BBC axe had fallen late. Rumours about the death of skiffle had begun, however, by January 1958, when Carroll Levis of ITV's *Discoveries* show, claimed that bebop, skiffle and rock 'n' roll were on the way out and would be replaced by the ballads and sweet music of the Thirties within the next twelve to eighteen months. Levis said that he was in constant touch with young people and that ballad singers and musicians were beginning to win his contests.[1]

However, the following advertisement in a January *Exchange and Mart*, gleefully reproduced in *Jazz Monthly* in March 1958, showed that skiffle was still attracting would-be practitioners: "Must sell: Owner abandoning music (forming own skiffle group): B. and H. Regent trumpet and case (excellent condition) £12.10.0."[2]

In April 1958, the *Punch* Diary, prompted by newspaper reports of the resignation of key people from *Six-Five Special*, asked whether skiffle was dying and hinted that skiffle and rock were on their way out. The diarist had been informed by a BBC spokesperson, apparently agreeing with Carroll Levis, that there would be a return to the ballad.[3]

Skiffle's demise may in some instances have been helped by disillusionment. For in April also, the former Vipers' member, Jean Van Den Bosch, explained in the music press why he had left the group and thrown up an income of £100 a week. He felt the public would take anything provided it got enough publicity.[4]

The next month, the *Melody Maker's* front page headline was "Skiffle on the Skids". It reported that the term "skiffle", which had guaranteed success a few months back, was now being dropped from group titles, such as the Vipers and the Soho Group, and some outfits were in difficulties. Bob Cort had returned to his old job with an advertising agency, and would only play occasional Sunday concerts; Dickie Bishop had disbanded his group and gone solo as a folk singer, and the Vipers, who had packed Britain's theatres, had come near to breaking up. The Skiffle Cellar was now just the Cellar and its proprietor, Russell Quaye, indicated that it presented most types of jazz as well as skiffle but "that skiffle — in the sense of just guitars and vocalising — is definitely out." A representative of the Cy Laurie Agency, which handled a number of groups, stated that "Skiffle is all finished."[5]

However, an advertisement in the same issue of the *Melody Maker* for the 1958 Floating Festival of Jazz in mid-June announced the participation of Les Hobeaux, Dick Bishop and his Sidekicks and the City Ramblers, as well as jazz bands that had skiffle groups. It was later reported that nineteen bands and skiffle groups played to over 3000 fans on that June Sunday aboard *Royal Daffodil* and *Royal Sovereign* on the Thames journey to Margate and back, even if the music was reputedly on the skids.[6]

In a kind of turn-back-the-clock letter to the *Melody Maker*, which also smacked of disillusionment, Brian Jackman of the Eden Street Skiffle Group blamed the fact that skiffle was skidding on electric guitars, drum kits and rock numbers. He urged that skiffle should be kept simple — singing was the most important thing — and that it should leave commercialism behind and return to the jazz clubs and coffee bars. While recognizing that the word skiffle had been outgrown — its repertoire had broadened — he seemingly could not accept the other changes that had occurred.[7]

In the *Daily Herald* in late August 1958, Chas McDevitt and his manager and agent, Bill Varley, blamed the death of skiffle on the many amateur groups who attracted too much attention in dance halls, variety theatres and on television. Jim Dale, however, in the same newspaper report, said that of the many amateur groups who took part in the National Skiffle Competition (which was coming to an end that month on *Six-Five Special*), most had about three or four dates a week and this suggested that skiffle was not dying: "In the smaller towns in the country it is the big attraction." Yet Chas McDevitt was so certain his skiffle days were over that he decided to re-form his group to cover ballads, rock, rhythm and blues and country and western. In Varley's view: "Agents and bookers are frightened to touch anything labelled skiffle now."[8]

Commenting on the winding up of *Saturday Skiffle Club*, a newspaper headline of September 1958 splashed the fact that "Skiffle Kings Are All Washed Up". It reported that Chas McDevitt was using a smaller, cheaper band and augmenting his earnings from his coffee-bar takings. Whereas he used to hire out his group for £250 a week, it was now much less. Elsewhere, the Vipers' manager, Johnny Jack, was washing up cups and glasses in a so-called dive and remarking that the group was getting three ballroom jobs a week but did not charge as much as before.

In the skiffle groups' efforts to transform themselves by playing other kinds of music, it was the washboard players who were usually given their cards. John Pilgrim, the Vipers's washboard player (and described by Sonny Terry as the best washboard player in the country), was running a paperback stall in the West End and making more money than he did as a musician. He was off to study percussion at the Guildhall School of Music in 1959. Even diversifying Donegan had not brought in as much money as expected at the Blackpool Summer Season that year: "He was hot when we booked him [last winter], but cold by the time he got to Blackpool."[9]

Although skiffle was dead or dying, it was clear by the last two or three years of the Fifties, however, that its participants had begun to be a force

> *1956 And All That: Skiffle Reminiscences*
>
> *Then skiffle went on the wane and it seemed that my dream of actually joining in had gone. Just a little too young for it all to happen to me. But no, the flame was kept alive in the small village of Riding Mill in Northumberland where I lived. Before the tidal wave of the Beatles and the Stones, there were three or four years when popular music offered very little new to grab hold of. Buddy Holly had died in 1959, and Elvis was singing ballads. Yes, there were Cliff and the Shadows who were up and running, but what inspiration was there in the Twist? So, although skiffle as a commercial music had died out in late 1958, home-made music in our neck of the woods still meant skiffle up to the early Sixties. This doesn't mean it started late, just that it never gave up the ghost and faded out before then.*
>
> *Mike Waites*

in British popular music, as the rapid transition of some skifflers from musical obscurity to stardom demonstrated. For some talents this fame has endured in a big way until the present day, although not always entirely in the field of popular music. This skiffle legacy would become even more apparent in the Sixties when the popular music scene was full of successful artists who had begun their musical life in grassroots skiffle groups of the previous decade. Of all those who rose to fame in the late Fifties, however, the names of three solo artists and one instrumental group, deserve special consideration: Tommy Steele, Cliff Richard, the Shadows and Adam Faith. Apart from chart and other successes, they all had two things in common, skiffle and the 2 I's coffee bar. The careers of Richard and Faith were also helped by regular appearances on television's pop music programmes, such as *Oh Boy!* and *Drumbeat*.

Tommy Steele — born Thomas Hicks in Bermondsey in 1936 — was Britain's first home-grown rock star, the first example of an overnight teenage success and one that set the pattern for marketing new pop music talent. In December 1956, the *TV Times* described this lightning-quick, star-making process — from completing a voyage as cabin-boy on a large passenger liner to topping the bill — as from "Bell-Boy to Star — in Ten Weeks".[10] All this just before his twentieth birthday. Tommy was probably the very first to reap the advantages of an involvement with skiffle — although his was seemingly a brief flirtation — and of the 2 I's venue, even if he speedily moved on to a career in rock 'n' roll.

Wally Whyton recalled that whenever Tommy was home from the sea he would come to the Breadbasket coffee bar and that he and Steele as guitarists developed a "kind of loose band" with Mike Pratt on piano and Johnny York on packing case bass, playing Sunday lunch times at an East End pub.[11] Again with Mike Pratt, Steele, plus Lionel Bart on washboard, got together in 1956 as a skiffle trio, the Cavemen, and wrote a pop song take-off called "Rock with the Cavemen". Later, as Tommy Steele, Hicks recorded the song for Decca and it went to number three in November that year.

WATER, WATER

(From the film "THE TOMMY STEELE STORY")
Words & Music by · LIONEL BART · MICHAEL PRATT & TOMMY STEELE

TOMMY STEELE
THE ROCK 'N ROLL SENSATION
ON DECCA RECORDS

2/-

George Martin has owned up to making a mistake in failing to sign up
Steele — subsequently signed by Decca — when he visited the 2 I's one
evening in 1956 to see Steele and the Vipers Skiffle Group. "We sat with
our coffee and watched this genial young man bounce on to the stage with
his guitar over his pelvis, and my immediate impression was that he was
a blond cardboard imitation of Elvis Presley... Tommy had a lot of energy,
but his voice didn't sound too great — what little I could hear of it: for the
Vipers were extremely loud and he wasn't.

"By today's standards the act was positively matronly, but for those
days it was quite shocking, rather like musical masturbation; the pelvic
gyrations quite turned me off, especially as I was still thinking only in
terms of voices... so I let Tommy Steele pass."[12]

The man who discovered Tommy Steele in a coffee-bar, and set him
off on his successful career, was John Kennedy. Kennedy had gone along
to the 2 I's in September 1956 at the invitation of its ex-wrestler owner,
Paul Lincoln, to listen to the Vipers Skiffle Group, who Kennedy thought
very good but unlikely "to bring a crisis to Tin Pan Alley".[13] In a skiffle
interval, Tommy Steele sang Presley's "Heartbreak Hotel" and two other
numbers to the acclaim of the young audience, especially the girls.

184

Afterwards Tommy shouted his thanks to the Vipers, who had accompanied   Cliff Richard.
him, and made his way out to Old Compton Street and on to another
coffee-bar where skiffle was also played. John Kennedy followed. Once
again Tommy performed and "was cheered until the kids were hoarse and
still calling for more as he packed up and left."[14] Kennedy talked to Steele
over tea in a Macclesfield Street cafe and, together with his partner, Larry
Parnes, took Tommy under his wing. Although he made no skiffle records,
Steele had a number of hits in the late Fifties, some of which featured in
the 1957 film, *The Tommy Steele Story*, which, planned as documentary
about rock 'n' roll in Britain, included skiffle, calypso and traditional jazz.

If George Martin thought Tommy Steele a blond cardboard imitation
of Presley, Cliff Richard — born Harry Webb in Lucknow, India in 1940
— was popularly seen in the late Fifties as Britain's answer to the King.
In contrast to Tommy Steele, Cliff Richard, together with Hank Marvin,
Bruce Welch and Adam Faith, all had a more typical skiffle background
— playing local venues, entering skiffle competitions, auditioning for
Saturday Skiffle Club, and perhaps an appearance on *Six-Five Special*.

It was through the agency of a friend, Terry Smart, that Cliff Richard
joined the Dick Teague Skiffle Group in September 1957. Not because he
particularly liked skiffle, although he had bought Donegan records, but
because of the opportunities it gave him to perform. His real loves were
Elvis, the Everly Brothers and the Platters. As Cliff confessed: "I unasham-
edly used it [skiffle] to further my own ends."[15] The Dick Teague group
played regularly at various local venues and was managed by Teague's
father, Walter. Cliff's debut as the group's lead singer took place on 4
October 1957 at the Friday evening jazz night at the Flamstead End Youth
Club.

In the coming months the group played on average twice a week, their

185

fee being £1 rising to £3.5s for grander events, such as a function at Waltham Town Hall. The group entered a number of local talent competitions, including a skiffle contest at Haileybury Boys' Club, Hoddesdon. Cliff, however, was consciously introducing aspects of rock 'n' roll into his performance[16] and by December 1957 he was asking for his own spot to sing Presley numbers. This appalled Dick Teague, a skiffle purist of the strictest sort. Unknown to his sons, Walter Teague had obtained an audition for *Saturday Skiffle Club* for 13 January 1958, but, towards the end of January, the Teague group heard from the BBC that they had not passed.

More committed perhaps than Cliff Richard to skiffle were Hank Marvin (Brian Rankin) and Bruce Welch (Bruce Cripps). Hailing from Newcastle-Upon-Tyne, and both born in 1941, they were eventually to come together in the Railroaders Skiffle Group in 1957 after membership of separate outfits. Hank (on banjo) had formed what was to be known as the Crescent City Skiffle Group in 1956 with his brother Joe and four others and later entered a contest run by the South Shields Jazz Club in May 1957 and won. Bruce, inspired by the skiffle craze, had bought a cheap guitar and formed the Railroaders Skiffle Group. Even though its members were under age, it had a go at local pub talent competitions which offered prizes of five, three and two pounds to the successful entrants. The Railroaders performed the usual skiffle songs and "also browsed through catalogues and old files in libraries looking for ethnic material to perform."[17]

In summer 1957, Hank's group disbanded, and Bruce asked him to join the Railroaders, then playing working men's clubs and similar venues. Hank agreed. In addition to Bruce and Hank, there was another guitarist, a drummer, and a tea-chest bassist. Not long after Hank Marvin joined, the group appeared in a week's variety at the Newcastle Palace.

Seen at the time as something of a rival to Cliff Richard, Adam Faith (Terence Nelhams) was born in Acton in 1940. London-based and working in the city's centre, he was particularly well placed to take part in the skiffle craze and its aftermath. Adam and his friend Hurgy (Roger Van Engel) first became aware of skiffle when they frequented a YWCA mixed youth club that held record dances where a skiffle group performed as an extra attraction. This inspired Adam, together with Hurgy, to form a group from among his messenger boy acquaintances at Rank Screen Services and elsewhere and the group had lunchtime sessions in the cellar at Rank.

According to Adam: "The first gig we did, when we mistakenly thought we'd got the band together enough to perform, was a free concert for the staff at Rank. They'd let us practise in the screening-room at 11 Hill Street, off Berkley Square in our lunchtimes and after work. This was our way of saying thank you."[18]

The group's first paid date was at a Wandsworth boys' club, for which the fee was ten shillings each, Adam doing the vocals as usual. In spite of being a bit hazy about some of the chords and unsure of all of the words, the group was a success. Successful enough it was thought to venture into the heart of skiffle — Soho. With this as a goal, it was decided the group should be better organised and that it needed a good name. Adam was appointed manager, because he now worked in Soho and could make contact with clubs and coffee bar owners, and it was decided to call the group the Worried Men and use "Worried Men Blues" as a signature tune.

Before long the group was playing in places like Mars, the Cat's Whisker, Orlando, the Skiffle Cellar and the 2 I's. Eventually the Worried Men replaced Les Hobeaux as the resident group at the 2 I's, as Les Hobeaux had moved on to bigger things. As a response to this opportunity the group reorganised, with a new addition, Charlie McDonnell, on electric guitar. At the 2 I's, the Worried Men played to audiences of two or three hundred a night from seven to eleven, six nights a week, and Paul Lincoln started paying the group thirty shillings a week each, thought to be good money for a skiffle group. During their time at the 2 I's, the big name was Terry Dene, and the Worried Men appeared on bills with him, which was all extra money.

With his day job, his night job and extra concerts, Adam was bringing home twelve pounds a week. Not without some wear and tear, however, because he went directly from work to the 2 I's, played with his group until one in the morning and had to be up at seven for his day job. Burning the candle at both ends his health suffered and he had to decide whether he wanted to edit films or play skiffle. Just before Christmas 1957 he handed in his notice at the cutting room and stayed on at the 2 I's for a bit.

At the end of 1957, by which time Tommy Steele was well known as a rock 'n' roll star, the other stars-to-be were still unknowns and involved in skiffle. The following year or so would, however, see a change in all their fortunes. As a member of the Dick Teague Skiffle Group, Cliff had argued for the inclusion of rock 'n' roll in the group's repertoire but the others, with the exception of Terry Smart, were not to be swayed. Without any unpleasantness being felt, Cliff and Terry left the group in January 1958, after the BBC audition, and together with guitarist Norman Mitham, formed a rock group called the Drifters, which played dance and youth club venues and at the Five Horseshoes pub in Hoddesdon. There they were heard by John Foster, who offered to be their manager. Foster had no experience of show business but had been to the 2 I's and knew Tom Littlewood, who arranged bookings. Guided by Foster, the Drifters went by Green Line bus to the 2 I's for an audition. They performed two songs for Littlewood, were asked to play that night and given a two-week residency in April 1958.

During their first week they were asked by Ian ("Sammy") Samwell if they needed a lead guitarist and after an audition, he joined the group. Sammy was about to finish his national service, had played in the Ash Valley Skiffle Group, but really wanted to play rock 'n' roll. During their second week at the 2 I's the Drifters were offered work at the Regal Ballroom, Ripley, and it was then that Harry Webb and the Drifters became Cliff Richard and the Drifters. During the interval between two unpaid Saturday morning appearances before screaming kids at the Gaumont, Shepherd's Bush, the Drifters recorded a demo disc, which reached Columbia Records, where producer Norrie Paramour auditioned the group and offered a record contract.

In August 1958, just prior to the release of his debut single "Move It", Cliff turned professional, and was asked to join a tour headlined by the American Kalin Twins, who had reached the UK number one position with "When" in that month. However, Cliff and the Drifters needed new musicians for their act on the Kalin Twin's tour and Hank Marvin, who had already agreed to play on the tour for the Most Brothers, accepted a place if one could be found for his rhythm guitarist friend, Bruce Welch. The Kalin Twins tour opened on Sunday 5 October 1958 at the Victoria Hall, Hanley and while it was under way, "Move It" became a hit parade success, Cliff received a better reception on *Oh Boy!* than at earlier appearances, and he and his group outshone the Kalin Twins during the tour. When the tour ended, both Hank and Bruce rejoined the Chesternuts, a group they had played with earlier, but were soon back with Cliff on *Oh Boy!* and some Sunday concerts. It was Jack Good, the producer of *Oh Boy!*, who persuaded Cliff to ditch the guitar and sideburns — the Elvis thing — and just sing.

In Newcastle the previous year — and thus some time before first supporting Cliff Richard — the two future Drifters, Hank Marvin and Bruce Welch, were also making the move away from skiffle. Donegan had inspired Bruce to play the guitar and make music but now Presley was exciting him to play rock 'n' roll and gradually, after some resistance from

---

1956 And All That: Skiffle Reminiscences

I can remember the day in mid-1956, as if it were yesterday, when I was asked to join a skiffle group, the Zeniths, made up from a bunch of kids from Quarry Bank School, Liverpool — the same school as John Lennon attended. The only reason they asked me to join was because I knew more chords than them and could play a bit of lead guitar.

When I say more chords, I mean I knew six — C, F, G7 and A, D, E7. You may not think this was anything to shout about but in 1956 this was a lot more than the rest of the groups of the day knew. One group at the time, as I remember, tuned up the six strings of the guitar to sound like a chord and played it by placing their fingers across the frets, forming a moveable one-finger chord. This was in a talent show at the Pavilion Theatre in Liverpool in 1957.

We tried to get a gig in the Cavern Club in 1956 by taking an audition. They told us to come back when the singer knew the words, the guitars were in tune, and the bass player could afford to buy a proper bass to replace that stupid tea-chest he was using.

Eventually we progressed to rock 'n' roll in late 1958 and carried on playing that great stuff until the band dispersed in 1963. I then went on to play in country music with a band called the Saddlers until 1983, playing on Radio Merseyside, at the Empire Theatre, and many more great venues. But it was never exciting as your first skiffle group. Lonnie Donegan started it all and we had a good time playing it. Rock 'n' roll was yet to come.

Peter Rice

the more purist Hank, numbers by Elvis and Fats Domino entered the The Shadows.
Railroaders' repertoire. According to Hank: "By late '57 we were becoming pretty popular around the local clubs and actually starting to make a
bit of a name for ourselves."[19] Even though there were many other
Newcastle groups, the Railroaders played two or three nights every week
in socials and working men's clubs, sometimes making £6 or £7 a week
each. The group were also auditioned for *Saturday Skiffle Club* but were
turned down.

In April 1958 the Railroaders were placed third in the London final of
a talent competition. However, following it, the group folded and while
the others returned to Newcastle, Hank and Bruce decided to stay on in
London becoming part of Pete Chester's Chesternuts. But the Chesternuts
made few appearances, and a recording venture and a television appearance
on *Six-Five Special* failed to get them anywhere, so Hank and Bruce began
working in the 2 I's coffee bar to earn some bread-and-butter money —
"alternating between playing in the basement and working the orange
machine."[20] At the 2 I's Hank's guitar ability was acknowledged and he
and Bruce played and harmonised well together, becoming known to
regulars as the Geordie Boys. Cliff was already singing at the 2 I's when
Hank and Bruce arrived in London in April 1958 but they did not catch
up with him there until July.

Following the successes of late 1958 and early 1959 as Cliff Richard's
backing group, the Drifters became the Shadows in July 1959, and by that
time consisted of the now classic line-up of Hank, Bruce, Jet Harris and
Tony Meehan. Bassist Jet (Terence) Harris was born in Kingsbury in 1939
and he too migrated to the 2 I's, working the Coke machine by day and
playing with whoever was in the basement at night. One night he was asked
by Wally Whyton to team up with the Vipers and, "although skiffle was

on the wane, they were a big name earning good money and I jumped at the chance when Wally asked me to join them."[21] It was Jet who found the group's new drummer, Tony Meehan, before Christmas 1958. Meehan was born in Hampstead in 1943, and at twelve, playing washboard and side-drum, formed a skiffle group with two other lads. Tony went to Soho, where he heard skiffle and, in 1958, was at the 2 I's, where he heard Hank, Bruce and Jet playing and was allowed to sit in for a couple of numbers — this was the first time Tony had heard a British rock 'n' roll group. Tony took up the offer to be the 2 I's' house drummer for fifteen shillings a night and went on to play for the Worried Men (formerly Adam Faith's group) and the Vipers. Later Tony started backing Cliff Richard on some of his recordings for radio shows and towards the end of 1958 became a member of the Drifters.

The Drifters were independently offered a record contract by Norrie Paramour and released three singles without much success but continued to back Cliff Richard on record and tour. The dilemma of whether to be an instrumental or vocal group was decided by "Apache", the guitar instrumental which was the group's first number one as the Shadows in September 1960. This was the earliest of a number of strongly melodic instrumentals, featuring Hank's tremolo guitar, that peppered the charts in the next few years.

Adam Faith's chance for fame came when *Six-Five Special* was broadcast from the 2 I's in November 1957 and the Worried Men, as resident group, began and ended the programme. Adam Faith, however, remembers skiffle's decline and his fear that his group would not be able to cope with the changes taking place in popular music: "We could hardly help noticing that the crowds at the 2 I's were dwindling. We all had the cold feeling in our guts that the days of the skiffle craze were well and truly numbered. Rock 'n' roll was taking over. None of us could do rock 'n' roll; that kind of music wasn't our thing and we weren't up to it. In our hearts we understood that our days of playing together in a skiffle band were coming rapidly to an end. And it wasn't long before they did. As quickly as it started this weird form of music, that had done its job of breaking the teenage ice, went into a rapid decline. Nobody wanted it anymore."[22]

While skiffle's impending demise seemed to mean the end of the Worried Men, Adam was invited to do a solo spot on *Six-Five Special* — it was then he changed his name — and on the strength of that performance was offered a recording contract with EMI. However, unlike Tommy and Cliff, whose careers seemed to take off relatively smoothly, things did not go well for Adam until he got a regular spot on the 1959 television programme, *Drumbeat*, and a manager, Evelyn Taylor. His first hit was "What Do You Want" at the end of 1959, followed by five more in 1960.

Displacing Marty Wilde (a London skiffler who became a popular rock star and appeared on *Oh Boy!*), surviving the rivalry of Adam Faith, and hailed with greater enthusiasm by the fans than Tommy Steele at the height of his popularity, Cliff Richard has now been a major recording artist for

1956 And All That: Skiffle Reminiscences

After singing Elvis, Chuck Berry and Little Richard songs at the Greyhound, a music pub with tables and piano, things went quiet for a while. I gave up skiffle in 1958 and, after seeing Marty Wilde at the Chiswick Empire without a guitar, I dropped that as well.

I was then asked to join as a singer what was really a skiffle group, called the New Vagabonds, although we did rock songs, such as "Mean Woman Blues", a Jerry Lee Lewis number. The group included an amplified guitar and snare drum, as well as tea-chest bass and acoustic guitars. Then we did a spot at the Shepherd's Bush Gaumont, augmented by the Greyhound's pianist, that impressed the rock 'n' roll impresario, Larry Parnes.

I was 17 when Larry changed my name to Duffy Power (after Tyrone Power), had my hair cut, clothed me, and fixed me up with a recording contract with Fontana.

I then went on to tour in package shows, topped by the likes of Billy Fury and Marty Wilde, recorded half-a-dozen singles between 1959 and 1961, although none made the charts, and appeared on a couple of programmes in the Drumbeat *series.*

Duffy Power

close on forty years. As for Faith, he made the charts twenty-four times before retiring from a seven-year singing career. He has acted in films and on television, produced records, and also became a successful business man.

As has been seen, Steele, Richard, Marvin, Welch and Faith all found fame in their late teens and thus much earlier than the people they had taken as models, whether Donegan or Presley. They and others were a new phenomenon in popular music, deserving of comment, although not always taken seriously. As early as October 1957, and largely it would seem with Tommy Steele and Terry Dene in mind, *Punch* was commenting on the nature of "pop-mongering". Apparently the fans of '57 liked their pop idols to be aged between eight and seventeen, which was why pop songs were teen-slanted. The lad — they were all lads, it would seem — would issue his first record to coincide with his sixteenth birthday and publication of his life story in the *New Musical Express*. His first film usually came later when the idol had begun shaving. Would-be-idols, in skiffle clubs and espresso bars, were discovered by a manager or a man who knew a manager and then fed, clothed and generally made-over. Once recorded, promotion began: "so that by the time the tots actually get their first hearing of the new idol they are already fully familiar with his fictitious history, the size of his shoes, the colour of his bedspread... the title of the film he may make... A few months later, with any luck, he's in a steady job in a factory... and nobody even cares who he was."[23]

While not the transitory pop-idol of *Punch's* caricature — the Shadows have many fans today — they, like Donegan and skiffle, were the model for a host of groups that imitated their line-up, dress, movements and sound, note for note. Young Sixties guitarists who could reproduce Hank's solos were kings in their own backyards. If Donegan had helped create interest in the guitar, then the Shadows helped sustain that interest and oversaw the transition from acoustic to electric guitar in the music of popular culture. They also helped perpetuate the skiffle idea of the "group". The orderly, conforming, reassuring behaviour of the Shadows, that was so earnestly copied would soon, however, be in sharp contrast to the irreverent and outrageous behaviour of the Beatles and other Sixties groups. As Dave McAleer put it: "Their Shadows Walk became an essential part of every youth club group's stage presentation, and their many foot-tapping instrumental hits were staples in the repertoires of thousands of wanna-sound-alike combos complete with identical Fender guitars and Vox amplifiers. The Shadows were without doubt the most successful British group of the pre-Beatles era yet, despite their enormous popularity in the UK, they have never had an American chart record on their own."[24] During 1958-68, the Shadows were Britain's top instrumental group: in November 1960 they gained the *NME* poll award for Top British Small Group. They went their separate ways in 1968, sometimes reforming for recording and touring. Although at one time seen as unfashionable, many musicians cite them as an influence — an influence with its roots firmly grounded in Newcastle skiffle.

Pop music was not, however, the only music to benefit from the skiffle legacy. Skiffle had begun in the jazz world and, at its demise, those jazzmen involved in it (some perhaps only in a part-time capacity) — Dickie Bishop, Diz Disley, Bill Bramwell, Nevil Skrimshire, for example — returned to playing jazz. The skiffle experience, however, added some new names to the roll of jazz musicians, such as Dave Green, Danny Thompson, and Harvey Weston on double bass, Ian Howarth and John Stevens on drums, and Roy James, guitar and banjo. Their choice of instrument was no doubt the direct result of that skiffle experience. While such a development — from skiffler to jazz musician — was perhaps unlooked for at the time, another much desired outcome did occur — a British folk revival.

A fairly constant theme during the skiffle boom years was that skifflers should incorporate British folk songs into their repertoire, but on the whole groups seemed satisfied with their American material. In July 1957, for example, Fred Dallas, a folk musician turned skiffler, wrote that, like jazz, skiffle needed UK roots if it was not to be a dead end.[25] Colin Ward, in May 1958, looked to the skiffle groups ("which are still very much with us, despite all prophecies to the contrary") not just for folk music but for new, topical and popular songs of social comment. However, while recognising that some had brought new life to the folk song movement, "few of the skiffle groups seem to have got beyond their chain-gang-railroad complex, except as far as American union and gospel songs."[26] In his memoirs, folk singer John Hasted wrote: "All along I had a rather ambivalent attitude to skiffle. What I really dreamt of was a folksong revival, but the skiffle craze was the next best thing. I called my group a 'Skiffle and Folksong Group', in the hope that a folksong revival would

1956 And All That: Skiffle Reminiscences

However, it wasn't long (perhaps only a year) before American rock 'n' roll records became available and we were much more attracted to this new music. We listened to Bill Hayley, Elvis Presley, Paul Anka, and later the Everly Brothers and very quickly gave up playing skiffle and carried on as a rock 'n' roll group. Fats Domino provided us with "Blueberry Hill" and both Eddie Cochran and Gene Vincent were big influences on our singing styles. We imitated British stars as well as American performers: Tommy Steele gave us "Singing the Blues" and Cliff Richard "Living Doll".

By the time I was sixteen plus, I became interested in modern jazz, and by the time I had reached eighteen I was working as a semi-professional guitarist in dance bands becoming a full-time guitar player, who could read music (which was unusual during the early Sixties) in 1962. My first decent, semi-professional dance band job was playing with a quartet in the working men's club of the Metal Box Company in Speke in the south of Liverpool. None of us were full-time musicians but I earned more doing Saturday and Sunday at this club than I did from my full-time job. The fee was about £3. 10s. 0d for the two nights, which was worth more than my week's wages as an electrical apprentice.

My first professional dance band job was in France with Ronnie Hilton's (not the singer) Quartet, playing on the American base at Fontainebleau, when I was twenty. On coming home, I joined Johnny Hilton's Band at the Locarno Ballroom, Liverpool, where I stayed for two years before taking a musical director's job at the Shakespeare Theatre Cabaret Club in Liverpool.

Since the Sixties, I have worked with John Arran as a guitar duo called Contrasts, been a session musician, composer, and free-lance arranger and performer. In the early Sixties, I began teaching guitar and, in various capacities, have continued to teach music into the Nineties. I gave up full-time lecturing in September 1995 to opt for semi-retirement, recommencing full-time freelance playing for, among others, the Halle Orchestra and jazz gigs in Wales and the north-west England. I also work with my own guitar trio.

John Harper

In late 1957, or possibly early 1958, my family was rehoused in another part of Wandsworth. This move away led eventually to the discontinuation of my skiffling activities, although the other lads transformed themselves into a rock group, complete with proper string bass. I had no aptitude for rock and roll and my music interests went briefly in other directions — blues, folk music, country and western before settling on jazz. Over the years I've played rhythm guitar in a couple of groups for a short while — one college group was called the Grooves of Academe — but now, because of this book, it looks as though skiffle calls once more.

Mike Dewe

grow out of skiffle. It did."[27]

The extent of the folk song revival that emerged from the skiffle craze can be judged by the estimated figures for folk clubs from the late Fifties to the Seventies: 1958, not more than 20; 1966, maybe 300, and at the end of the Seventies about 1700.[28] Skifflers who made the transition to folk included groups like the Spinners and the Ian Campbell Folk Group and performers such as Johnny Handle, Louis Killen, Mike Harding, Bert Jansch, Roy Harris, Shep Woolley, Martin Carthy, Roy Harper and Tony Rose. Some artists returned to folk music after being part of the skiffle scene, for example, Steve Benbow and Jimmie McGregor. Members of the Alan Lomax and the Ramblers group, often associated with the skiffle boom, such as Shirley Collins, Peggy Seeger and Ewan MacColl, continued to perform and further the British folk revival. As Fred Woods commented: "It is significant that most of the early young folk singers came into the movement through their involvement with skiffle, and a large proportion of the audience went with them."[29] One example from Liverpool of the skiffle to folk transition was the Spinners, who, formed in 1958, and originating in the Gin Mill Skifffle Group, went on to perform together for thirty years.

The Gin Mill Skiffle Group was founded on Merseyside by Tony Davis, his wife Beryl, and Mick Groves. In addition to Tony and Mick (guitars) and Beryl (who plucked a cello in bass-like fashion), the group had a fluctuating membership and instrumentation that included another guitar, banjo, tuba, drums, clarinet, and bass. The Gin Mill became a successful group that played regularly at clubs, hotels and the Cavern, appeared at the Liverpool Empire and the Manchester Hippodrome with name music stars and bands of the day, and played interval spots for Mick Mulligan's jazz band and others.

At the Cavern, the Gin Mill became residents, alternating with the Ron Mackay Skiffle Group; other skiffle groups, such as the Quarry Men, would play their guest spots.

The Gin Mill was different to other Cavern groups, who usually covered the chart hits, in that it extended its repertoire with unfamiliar American folk songs and British ones. These departures from the charts were not completely successful, as Cavern teenagers preferred the latest Donegan song and, with schoolday memories, reacted against folk music.

There then came a point when Gin Mill, like other skiffle groups "found themselves facing two options — either to ride the crest of an uncertain wave and be swallowed up in the great pop and beat revolution that was gathering pace, or retreat to the minority stream of folkies, after only scratching the surface of a rediscovered sound. Interest in folk music was devoted but minimal in Britain at that time."[30]

The Gin Mill Skiffle Group took the decision to disband but in May 1958 reformed — with Tony, Beryl, Mick and his fiancée Margaret, and Stan Francis, whom they had met at Lonnie Donegan nights at the Cavern — to play for a Conservative Party fête at the Aigburth cricket ground, Liverpool. Their reception at the fête encouraged them to look for a new club base and a new name and so they became the Spinners. The

1956 And All That: Skiffle Reminiscences

As the skiffle craze died down in 1958, the group began to break up. This was not because of disagreement or lack of friendship, but rather that as young men in our late teens we had careers to pursue. In 1958 I bought my first proper guitar, which cost £5 from a second-hand shop and was, in fact, little better than my own efforts. This is not a compliment on my abilities as a luthier but rather a commentary on the standard of instrument available in those days. I also bought my first Django Reinhardt LP — I had by now become the owner of a portable electric record player. I did two other things that year: I found a guitar teacher and became a regular reader of B.M.G. (Banjo, Mandolin and Guitar) magazine. Both improved my playing far beyond the three chords of skiffle.

Now in my late fifties I still play the guitar, mainly in the jazz idiom. I have at times played in traditional jazz bands, Hot Club Quintet-style groups and other smaller combos. Since my enforced early retirement in late 1992, I have taken additional lessons and I have just finished studying for a HNC in Jazz Studies (with my guitar) at a college in Manchester.

Bob Brooks

In the autumn of 1958, I moved up to my secondary school and my guitar playing and singing took second place to many things and skiffle slowly faded away. Over the next two or three years varying friendships developed and naturally some of these included a mutual interest in making music. The problem for several of us was that we could not afford electric instruments and the paraphernalia that went with them. However, skiffle had been replaced by folk music, blues and bluegrass — Cy Grant, Robin Hall, Jimmy McGregor, Robert Johnson, Leadbelly, Johnny Duncan — and groups like Peter, Paul and Mary, the Limeliters and the Kingston Trio were popular. So that was the route that some of us followed and, by 1962, we were performing at school concerts. The material included songs that had their roots firmly in skiffle, such as "Darling Corey", "Ballad of the Alamo", and "Aunt Rhody", some a little more bluegrass, and a smattering of English traditional songs, like "Royal Oak", the "Riddle Song", and "The Keeper".

By the time I left school in the summer of 1964, at the age of seventeen, I was performing in the emerging and increasingly popular Essex folk clubs at Brentwood, Chelmsford, Colchester and Romford. Some of the material was still based on those original skiffle songs. Over time those faded away, as different songs and tunes caught people's interest and imagination, particularly British traditional music. Those of us who were aware, or gave the subject some thought, could see the continuing thread linking this varied array of music, and that is why I still regularly sing songs from my skiffle days, such as, "Darling Corey", "Freight Train", "Frankie and Johnny", and "Tom Dooley".

Geoff Harris

newly-named group found a home in the basement of Samson and Barlow's restaurant in the London Road, Liverpool, which opened in September 1958.

Hughie Jones, a former member of the High Society Skiffle Group, brought his guitar along to the Spinners' club, was persuaded to perform and asked to replace Stan Francis, who wanted to leave the group. Cliff Hall, an expatriate Jamaican, joined the Spinners in the late Fifties; his particular interest was country music and he sang to his own strummed guitar.

In 1961, after Jacqui McDonald left to go solo, the Spinners decided to continue as an all-male group and that is how this very popular Liverpool folk group will no doubt be remembered. With "In My Liverpool Home" as one of their well-known songs, the Spinners often broadcasted on radio and television, and their live concerts were regularly sold out. They attracted some criticism from the folk purists, though it was felt that their performances encouraged people towards folk music. With the exception of Cliff Hall, born in the Twenties, the other three were born in the early-

---

1956 And All That: Skiffle Reminiscences

After leaving Parnes and the Fontana label in 1961, further singles and touring followed, but by that time I had discovered the blues and was also writing songs. In the 1965 I began to work with Alexis Korner, including a series of Five O'Clock Clubs *for ITV. I was the singer, electric guitarist and harmonica player in Blues Incorporated and worked with Alexis as a duo. Later, in January 1966 I got together a band called Duffy's Nucleus that included Danny Thompson, John McLaughlin and Terry Cox. I continued playing the blues and made a few albums in the early Seventies but nothing came of them.*

Duffy Power

We were aware in a vague way that we were imitating an imitation, but in the mid-Fifties there was hardly any option. It was only possible to get glimpses of the music behind skiffle. Two of the most influential records in my life were Murderers' Home *and* Blues in the Mississippi Night — *Alan Lomax field recordings from 1948 made at Parchman Prison Farm in Mississippi and in Chicago, respectively. They were issued here on LP by Pye/Nixa. I probably acquired these in 1958, along with LPs of Blind Lemon Jefferson on London and Lead Belly on Capitol, and their acquisition had a large part to play in my turning away from skiffle to the blues. Donegan, Colyer, the Vipers, Nancy Whiskey, had seemed powerful figures in 1956-57; but eighteen months or so later, when I began acquiring the above LPs and what few blues 78s were available here, their music began to take on the aura of the inauthentic! (Ironically, listening to Donegan now, I'm impressed again by the vitality of his performances and his ability to internalise much of the spirit of his black and white American sources. Especially the white. His slightly nasal, sharp voice is very close to that of down-home white country singers).*

John Barnie

to mid-Thirties and so were neither teenage skifflers nor teenage folk music stars. However, their instrumentation as the Spinners — guitar, banjo, tin whistle, kazoo and harmonica — reflected their skiffle background and in concert it was often augmented by the addition of bassist John McCormick, known as the fifth Spinner. The Spinners released a number of albums between 1962 and their *Final Fling* album of 1988.

Britain's folk revival seemed to evolve quite naturally from skiffle but while the outbreak of rhythm 'n' blues in the charts did not occur until 1964, it also owed much to two original skiffle performers, Alexis Korner and Cyril Davies who had transferred their allegiance to the blues and formed their own band, Blues Incorporated in 1961. The rhythm 'n' blues groups identified by Nik Cohn as constituting "R&B England", and whose hit recordings peppered the charts in 1964 and 1965 in particular, were the Rolling Stones, the Pretty Things, the Animals, the Yardbirds, Manfred Mann, and the Kinks. Members of some of these groups had performed with Korner's Blues Incorporated before going on to succeed with their own bands and some had been caught up earlier in the skiffle craze. For instance: the five-man group, the Animals, contained at least two former skifflers, Chas Chandler (bass guitar) and Hilton Valentine (lead guitar); the singer with Manfred Mann, Paul Jones, remembers being fourteen when "Rock Island Line" was a hit, buying a guitar and learning the three chords; blues fan, Ray Davies of the Kinks, listed Big Bill Broonzy and Lonnie Donegan as his biggest influences in a *New Musical Express* life-lines profile of September 1964,[31] and his brother Dave's earliest interest had been in skiffle and folk. Of those performers making up the Rolling Stones — Jagger, Richards, Watts, Wyman and Jones — only Brian Jones, who died in 1969, seems to have been involved with skiffle.

In his book about those who are, or have been associated in one capacity or another with the Blues Band (founded by Paul Jones of Manfred Mann in 1979), Roy Bainton, draws attention once again to the importance of Lonnie Donegan: "One name cropped up every time we talked about the roots of British Blues... Lonnie Donegan, that's who."[32]

The Sixties rhythm 'n' blues bands were not the only groups to make the charts, as there were many rock and pop groups and solo performers who were successful in the Sixties and who represented a major part of the skiffle legacy — The Beatles, Gerry and the Pacemakers, Joe Brown, the Spencer Davis Group, Jeff Beck, Freddie and the Dreamers, Joe Cocker, and others such as Eden Kane, Johnny Kidd and the Pirates, the Brook Brothers, Chris Farlowe, Wayne Fontana, the Fortunes, Alex Harvey, Billy J. Kramer and the Dakotas, and the Swinging Blue Jeans. Some skifflers did not come fully into their musical inheritance until the Seventies or later: Gary Glitter (unsuccessful in the Sixties as Paul Raven); Van Morrison, whose early Seventies albums are considered some of the best rock music of the decade; and Chas Hodges (whose hit successes as part of the Chas 'n' Dave duo were in the charts in the early Eighties).

Much the same kind of transition happened to those whose achievements remained solely at grassroots level. Many skiffle groups seemed to progress quite naturally to other forms of popular music, although more often than not developing into a rock 'n' roll band covering songs in the charts and perhaps gaining something of a local reputation. Such groups usually made a considerable investment in instruments, sound equipment and clothes, and could be very professional in their musicianship, stage presence and the skill with which they reproduced the work of a variety of name performers and groups. David Lister's *Bradford's Rock 'n' Roll* chronicles the "golden years" of 1959-65 and provides an example of the range of talent (some with skiffle antecedents, like Clay Martin and the Trespassers) to be found in just one of Britain's towns and cities. Talent overshadowed — and perhaps overlooked for that reason — by the might of the Birmingham, Manchester, Belfast, Newcastle, Glasgow, London and Liverpool bands of the Sixties.

The home of popular music in that decade was not as London-centered as in the Fifties and the music was distinguished as much by the number of bands as by solo performers — an under-acknowledged development, perhaps, of the skiffle group tradition. Those performers with a skiffle background who became successful in the Sixties shared similar experiences and sources of inspiration with those who achieved fame in the previous decade. Accounts of skiffle groups from Liverpool, London and Belfast, who provided future Sixties stars, demonstrate once more the ubiquity of skiffle in Fifties Britain, the dedication to playing music that it inspired, the extreme youth of some of those who got involved, the financial rewards it could sometimes attract, and the possibility it offered of considerable success in the world of popular music.

The story of the Beatles provides the classic and perhaps most quoted example of the way a teenage skiffle group went on to become a rock 'n' roll band. John Lennon, Paul McCartney, George Harrison and Ringo Starr (Richard Starkey — the only member of the Beatles not to perform under his own name), all began their music careers with skiffle.

John Lennon, born in Liverpool in 1940, decided in early 1957 to form a skiffle group, the Quarry Men. Its line-up consisted of John Lennon (guitar and vocals), Colin Hanton (drums), Eric Griffiths (guitar), Pete Shotton (washboard), Rod Davis (banjo) and Bill Smith (tea-chest bass). Bill Smith was soon replaced by Ivan Vaughan, who alternated with Nigel Whalley. The group covered the usual repertoire but, inspired by rock 'n' roll, John introduced hit songs by Buddy Holly, Carl Perkins, Elvis Presley, Jerry Lee Lewis and Gene Vincent.

On 9 June 1957, the Quarry Men, after having won their audition heat, unsuccessfully took part in an afternoon audition at the Empire Theatre for the Carroll Levis *Discoveries* show. Between June and July 1958, the six-man line-up had Len Garry on tea-chest bass.

On 6 July 1957, Ivan Vaughan invited Paul McCartney (born 1942), a friend from the Liverpool Institute, to the Quarry Men's gig at Woolton Parish Church garden fête. In September 1994, an amateur recording of the Quarry Men Skiffle Group, made at the fête and the reel-to-reel machine on which it was recorded, was sold at a Sotheby auction for £78,500. The recording, an amazing survival, and bought by EMI for storage in the company's archives, was made by Bob Molyneaux, now a retired policeman, and featured Lennon singing Donegan's "Putting on the Style" and Presley's "Let's Play House".[33]

After they had played at the fête, Ivan introduced Paul to the group, who were impressed by his ability to tune a guitar. He particularly impressed John with his knowledge of the lyrics of rock 'n' roll numbers. Subsequently Paul McCartney made his debut with the Quarry Men at the New Clubmoor Hall, a Conservative Club, on Friday 18 October 1957, a venue they played on two further occasions. The Quarry Men also made a couple of appearances at the Rialto Ballroom during 1957 and, without Paul, appeared at the Cavern on 7 August that year, where they were taken to task for playing rock 'n' roll numbers like "Hound Dog".

Between early 1958 and early 1959, the Quarry Men experienced various personnel changes and during this time it recorded "That'll Be the Day" and "In Spite of All the Danger" (a McCartney composition) at the Kensington Recording Studios. The Quarry Men were among the groups who appeared at the opening night on 13 March 1959 of the short-lived Morgue Skiffle Club.

George Harrison, the youngest of the Beatles, was born in Liverpool in 1943 and in 1954 he became a pupil at the Liverpool Institute. With an interest in music aroused by skiffle, he bought a damaged guitar from a school friend, and apparently attended all of Donegan's Liverpool Empire shows and even got his autograph. According to Bill Harry, George was to say: "Lonnie Donegan was the first music star to make a big impression on me. Donegan and skiffle music just seemed made for me." Harry also notes that: "His mother helped him to obtain a proper guitar and he formed a group called the Rebels with his brother Peter and best friend Arthur Kelly, although the skiffle group only appeared for a single gig at the local British Legion club."[34]

The Beatles (early '60s?), number 54 in a series of 60 photos in a bubble gum promotion.

Leaving the Institute and with a job at a department store, George failed an audition to join the Raving Texans (later Rory Storm and the Hurricanes, but initially a skiffle group, and known until January 1957 as Al Caldwell's Texans). Through friendship with another Institute pupil, Paul McCartney, he attended Quarry Men gigs and, although not formally a member of the group, would be allowed to sit in if a guitarist failed to turn up, eventually

1956 And All That: Skiffle Reminiscences

Soon it was the Beatles' time and the Riding Mill Skiffle Group, now known as the Konkords, began appearing on the Tyne Valley weekend dance circuit. By this time the skiffle group had mutated into a four-piece rock and roll band. Our first booking was in late 1963 at the Vickers Armstrong Foremen's Club, Scotswood, Newcastle. We had to load all the equipment on the train to Newcastle and then carry everything from Scotswood Station to the club — and back, of course. The group records show that were paid £4. 2s. 6 ½d. for that gig — no fee as such but a whipround. Our main musical influences were Elvis, Little Richard, Eddie Cochran, Chuck Berry, the Rolling Stones and, of course, the Liverpool sound.

The Konkords ran from 1963 to 1968 — a demo LP and a lot of happy memories are what remain from that time. After this we all went our separate ways. My musical career laid dormant until 1973, when I joined a folk group in the Lancaster area called Home Brew, which is still going strong and of which, over twenty years later, I'm still a member. Once again, with everything, or nearly everything, thrown in, you could call it musically "a reet nasty mixture." Now and again, it's been suggested that we introduce a skiffle selection into the repertoire, but nothing of this sort has materialised as yet.

Mike Waites

becoming a full member. The Quarry Men appeared in several local talent competitions, such as those held at the Grafton Ballroom and the Pavilion Theatre, but had few other engagements.

Ringo's involvement in skiffle was entirely separate to that of the other three Beatles. He was the drummer in the Eddie Clayton Skiffle Group formed in early 1957 from employees at Henry Hunt and Sons. Their first performance was at the Labour Club, Peel Street; they appeared at skiffle contests, like those held at St Luke's Hall, and performed regularly at the boys' club at the Florence Institute. There was no eponymous Eddie Clayton but the group broke up when Eddie Miles left to get married. Ringo's stepfather, Harry, bought him a secondhand set of drums and he became a member of the Darktown Skiffle Group, although he also sat in with other bands. In March 1959 he made his debut with the Raving Texans at the Mardi Gras Club before joining the Beatles in 1962.

Another Liverpudlian to make it big in the early Sixties, as the leader of Gerry and the Pacemakers, was Gerry Marsden, born in 1942. Gerry's first proper job on leaving school at fifteen was — believe it or not — at the Kardomah tea factory in the centre of Liverpool, helping to make tea-chests. After a few months he left Kardomah, worked at Woolworth's and then got a job as a railway-van delivery boy. "Working most nights with my skiffle group, I didn't get home until about two o'clock in the morning, and I had to be on the wagon at the railway depot at six o'clock. I was so tired that the driver let me grab a sleep in the back of the van during deliveries!"[35]

The skiffle group consisted of another guitarist, brother Fred playing drums on an adapted biscuit tin, a tea-chest bass and washboard. Gerry's father acted as manager and the group's first engagement was at the Peel Street Labour Party Club, the Dingle, for which they were paid fourteen shillings and sixpence. They also played at the nearby Florence Institute boys' club and before the Lord Mayor of Liverpool. The group usually travelled by bus to youth clubs all around Liverpool and Gerry's dad helped with the big tea-chest bass, often having arguments with bus conductors who would rather not have it onboard as luggage. Although they earned very little money — they were lucky to cover their bus fares — they enjoyed playing skiffle. A certificate of excellence was awarded to the Gerry Marsden Skiffle Group in 1957 at the Youth Music Festival run by the Liverpool Advisory Committee.

Many skiffle groups had formed in Liverpool, including the Quarry Men, and Gerry's group played the same circuit. He thought that his group was better than the Quarry Men, although he recognised the special talents of John Lennon and Paul McCartney. John and he, unknowingly at the time, shared the two inspirations that shaped their musical lives: Lonnie Donegan and Elvis Presley. When he heard Presley, Gerry said to himself "Cor that's good, and it's *not skiffle!*"[36]

London, as might be expected, had its share of Fifties skifflers, such as Joe Brown and Chas Hodges, who later made the limelight. East-ender, Joe Brown (born in fact in Lincolnshire in 1941), was twelve when he bought an old guitar for a pound from a neighbour. Still at school, Joe joined a youth club skiffle group called the Ace of Clubs Rhythm Group and, while playing with them, was asked by Pete and Tony Oakman to join them in the Spacemen Skiffle Group. This six-man group, consisting of guitars (later amplified), tea-chest bass (later double bass), and washboard, practised in the small storeroom in the Oakman parents' shop.

Joe's first full-time job was as an electrician's apprentice; he then went on to the packing department of a Covent Garden printers and from there to the railway, rising from cleaner to fireman. It was through the skiffle group's drummer that Joe heard there was a job going on the railway. Being on shifts meant he had more time for playing, and the railway also let him have much appreciated unpaid leave, especially in his second year of employment, because the Spacemen were getting more and more engagements.

As Joe put it: "The Spacemen Skiffle Group started off good and got better all the time. Playing around the local pubs and clubs and appearing in talent shows we were earning quite a name for the group even if we weren't earning much money. But nobody cared about money as long as we were enjoying ourselves."[37]

Another Londoner to get the music bug was Chas Hodges, born in Edmonton in 1943, and now known as a singer, bass player and pianist. Smitten by the music of Little Richard, Chas tried the piano without success. He was also excited by — and wanted desperately to emulate — other rock 'n' rollers such as Fats Domino, Chuck Berry and Eddie Cochran. Equally exciting in his own way to Chas was Lonnie Donegan, in whose wake came guitars and skiffle groups. If not a pianist, Chas thought, he might make a guitarist and his mum got hold of an old Spanish guitar from his Uncle Alf. With help from a book of guitar chords, and after several false starts and advice on chords from a banjo-playing neighbour, he practised until he began to get quite good.

Chas says that: "I learnt to play guitar while I was at school and my first attempt at skiffle was also at school. Me and Brian Juniper used to have a few sessions round his house."[38] However, Chas's first group was the Horseshoe Skiffle Group and he did his first "playing job" with them in a hall above the Britannia pub, Edmonton, for which the group was paid. As a member of the Horseshoes, Chas was a Carroll Levis junior discovery at the Finsbury Park Empire.

Skiffle in Northern Ireland was also the launch pad at a very young age for someone who would later be revered as one of the best singer/song-writers of the era. It was the eclectic contents of his father's record collection — Muddy Waters, Howlin' Wolf, Hank Williams, Mahalia Jackson and Charlie Parker — that gave the young Van Morrison (born George Ivan Morrison in Belfast in 1945), an exceptional grounding for a career in popular music. Then in 1956 along came Lonnie Donegan, popularising the very music Van had been used to hearing at home. In the same year he acquired a guitar and learned the basic chords from *The Carter Family Style*, edited by Alan Lomax.

In 1957, Van Morrison formed his first group, the Sputniks, with friends from around Hyndford Street. In addition to washboard, guitars and tea-chest bass, one member played a homemade wind instrument christened the "zobo". The Sputniks played at Women's Institute meetings, school concerts and youth clubs using the recorded material of people like Donegan and Chas McDevitt. During 1958 the group also played at a couple of local cinemas during the intervals at children's matinees.

For those who were to become well-known performers in the Sixties or later — for example the Quarry Men, Gerry Marsden, Joe Brown, Chas Hodges and Van Morrison — the transition from skiffle to pop group was usually a somewhat lengthier apprenticeship compared with Fifties stars like Tommy Steele and Cliff Richard. Often that apprenticeship involved a stint abroad, usually in Germany.

By January 1959 the Quarry Men had ceased to operate as a group, though later, in August 1959, guitarist Ken Brown, George, Paul and John played as the Quarry Men at the Cashah Club in Liverpool. After several gigs at the club, Ken Brown left and between October 1959 and January 1960 the remaining three functioned as a trio, calling themselves Johnny and the Moondogs. During this period, in November 1959, the band made its second, and once again unsuccessful Carroll Levis *Discoveries* attempt.

After using the Jacaranda Club (as the Quarry Men) for rehearsal purposes from October 1959, the group made about a dozen appearances there as the Silver Beetles between May and August 1960.[39] In that month they became the Beatles after various personnel changes and tryouts with similar names such as the Silver Beats. The band, now comprising Lennon,

McCartney, Harrison, Stuart Sutcliffe (bass guitar), and Pete Best (drums), secured a club residency in Hamburg which ended in December 1960. They then gave regular performances in Liverpool's Cavern Club, and briefly returned to Germany, where Sutcliffe remained, McCartney taking over bass. In November 1961, the Beatles were seen by Brian Epstein at the Cavern and he subsequently became their manager. Major record companies were not impressed by Epstein's advocacy of the Beatles until signed by George Martin for the Parlophone label. In August 1962 Ringo Starr replaced the sacked drummer, Pete Best, and towards the end of that year "Love Me Do" was in the charts. With three number one single hits and a number two hit in the charts in 1963, amongst other record achievements, the Beatles were on their way to their unique and pivotal place in the history of popular music.

Former skifflers, Gerry Marsden, Joe Brown, Chas Hodges and Van Morrison, all found fame in popular music in their own way. Gerry Marsden, as the leader of Gerry and the Pacemakers (the second group to be signed up with Brian Epstein) and Joe Brown (with the Bruvvers) both having hit records in the early Sixties. For Chas Hodges, the Horseshoe Skiffle Group became a rock group called the Horseshoes and he went on to play with various musicians (including Gene Vincent and Jerry Lee Lewis), as well as appearing on many Sixties records. Today he is well known for his Chas 'n' Dave partnership with Dave Peacock (born London, 1945), which began in 1972. In Belfast, Van Morrison moved from skiffle to rock, eventually becoming part of the Monarchs Showband. In 1965 he was part of a band called Them that had two hit singles, but he then moved to the USA. The series of albums that turned him into the major star he still is today began in 1968 with *Astral Weeks*.

Skiffle thus provided a forcing-ground for many who moved on to other forms of popular music, particularly rock 'n' roll, sometimes with considerable and lasting success. Simon Frith sums up the importance of skiffle to rock, however, as not just a link in a musical chain, but as a form that "gave young British musicians the chance to develop their own ideas... outside the framework of the industry; skiffle gave them the folk confidence to play without polish, without show business, without advice, without capital." He also points up one of the significant aspects of the Beatles: "The most immediately noticeable thing about the Beatles... (and Lennon and McCartney had begun their musical lives in skiffle groups) was their detachment from Tin Pan Alley — they wrote their own songs."[40]

Those who played skiffle were often accused of performing a restricted range of songs, much influenced by available UK recordings, and not extending that range to include other American as well as British folk songs. Groups also faced criticism for extending their repertoire, as many amateur groups did (including the Quarry Men), by adding current rock 'n' roll numbers. Yet to them this probably seemed to be a natural progression of the skiffle craze, as did the desire to create their own songs. Is it too fanciful to suggest that self-taught skifflers (who picked up their playing ability by trial and error and their influences and repertoire from

recorded performances, whether Donegan or Presley) received an unstruc-
tured musical education which encouraged a freedom of action in Lennon
and McCartney (and others) that brought out their innate talent for
songwriting in the pop idiom? Fanciful or not, the nature of the popular
song and the manner of its composition would never be quite the same
again. The example set by the Beatles and others meant that the performer
as song-writer would become a major trend in pop music in the second
half of the twentieth century.

9 I'm Alabamy Bound — Skiffle Today

The skiffle craze was subsequently to lead its participants in a number of different directions from folk to pop music. In particular, cross-pollinated with rock 'n' roll and rhythm 'n' blues, skifffle gave rise to a new breed of young recording stars in the Fifties and Sixties who between them caused many changes to the world of popular music and the industry that supported it. However, having acted as the agent of change, skiffle itself, as a commercial popular music, was dead or dying according to the pundits in the months between January to August 1958 and that seemed to be clearly the case by October that year. While commercial skiffle was much derided by certain purist elements, there seems no doubt that a period of commercialism was absolutely essential for the teenage skiffle craze to take off and spread rapidly throughout the UK and elsewhere. Outside the world of commercial popular music, however, skiffle's demise appears not to have been so clear cut. Beyond London and other major centres of population, its decline seems to have been more gradual, the skiffle ethos lingering on into the early Sixties and, in fact, never entirely disappearing.

In the world of popular commercial music today, nobody makes a living solely out of playing skiffle, although the occasional number may get trotted out in performance for nostalgic reasons or as a musical novelty or curiosity. "Midnight Special", for example, was featured by Joe Brown in his contribution to that nostalgia-on-wheels event, the touring Solid Gold Rock 'n' Roll Show '96. Along with Joe Brown, the Show included Marty Wilde, John Leyton, Eden Kane, and the Vernon Girls — Fifties and early Sixties pop names to conjure with, three of whom (Brown, Wilde and Kane) were ex-skifflers.

At grassroots level, however, skiffle survives and a few groups have had an almost continuous history stretching back to the Fifties. Two examples are the Zephyrs from East Anglia and Hogia Llandegai (The Boys from Llandegai) of North Wales.

The Zephyrs, from Walsham Le Willows, got together in 1957 and took their name from a Hank Williams song, "California Zephyr". The group stopped playing for a while but reformed with the same members for the Queen's Silver Jubilee in 1977. However, the "Zephyrs" became the "Zephers" due to an unspotted spelling mistake made when the group's name was painted on its tea-chest bass.

The group line-up today consists of banjo and harmonica player, Bryan Debenham, singer-guitarist Albert Largent (whose first guitar cost ten shillings), his brother Jack on the tea-chest bass, lead guitarist and singer, Nev Ellis, and the washboard and spoons player, Bill Harris: two pig farm workers, a butcher, a retired chauffeur-gardener and an engineer. Roots and continuity are the strengths of the group: all were born in Walsham with the exception of the senior member of the group, Bill Harris, who moved to Walsham from Ingham well over forty years ago. They have only ever had two tea-chest basses in the entire life of the group.

In the early days, the Zephyrs played in pubs and at the American bases and always took a coach full of fans with them. They were successful in an Ipswich competition, with Jim Champion playing washboard on that occasion, and were hits at the Round Table fête in Bury. The group had a chance to play at the 2 I's coffee bar but turned it down because its members all had jobs and it would have meant taking a day off work and travelling up to London. In recent years the Zephyrs have raised money for charity. When they reformed in 1977, they were part of a sell-out show at Walsham village hall and to their great pleasure the group have been in demand ever since.[1]

Hogia Llandegai, taking its name from the village near Bangor in North Wales, was formed like the Zephyrs in 1957 with eight members. The group's first performance was at the Dyffryn Ogwen School, Bethesda. After many concerts in north and mid-Wales and several radio and television appearances, four of the group dropped out in 1964, leaving the remainder to soldier on until 1973. During the late Sixties, Hogia Llandegai were much in demand in Wales, as they were able to provide a full evening's entertainment (Noson Lawen) of singing, whistling, mimicry and short sketches.

Following a five-year break, three of the group — Neville Hughes of Bethesda, Ronnie Williams of Rachub and Now (Owen Glyn) Jones of Bangor — were persuaded to reform in connection with a book launch. A further seventeen years of performing together followed until their final public concert in Bethesda — where it all began — in 1996. Hogia Llandegai made a number of records, that included skiffle, chart hits and other tunes, and songs in Welsh; in the late Sixties they were the first to make a pop LP in Welsh, *Caneuon Gorau Hogia Llandegai* (Best Songs of Hogia Llandegai). It was so well received that it stayed in the Top Ten of the Welsh-language newspaper *Y Cymro* for several weeks.

At their final 1996 concert, compèred by the actor, John Ogwen, the trio were each presented with a golden disc for their record, "Hogiau Ni" ("Our Boys") and a young fan was given the group's battered old spoons used for accompaniment over the years. Clearly, in its later period, the group were loved as much for their general entertainment value as for their music, which had broaden in scope since their skiffle days.[2]

As well as the continuity of skiffle, there is also the question of its revival — and indeed its active promotion — as exemplified by developments of recent years. A skiffle revival, albeit on a small-scale, has been brought

Hogia Llandegai, the cover of their EP on Cambrian records.

about by the re-emergence of some of those who played the music the first time round, and its discovery by a later generation of musicians. Both age-groups are thus helping to save the music from dying out and possibly attracting new fans and would-be performers. The revival and promotion of skiffle has been made easier — and the music made more accessible — by the formation of the North of England Skiffle Preservation Society and the Southern Skiffle Society and a significant number of skiffle record re-issues by specialist companies.

Long before this, however, in response to demand, Ken Colyer had revived skiffle in the mid-Sixties, but this did not seem to stimulate others to follow suit. Thirty years later, the Ken Colyer Trust appears to keep the Guv'nor's attachment to skiffle going, as at its autumn 1996 Jazz Parade at Pontins, Hemsby on Sea, Norfolk, it promised skiffle, hymns and spirituals in addition to the music of a number of jazz bands.

In 1967 rumours circulated that the Kinks had featured skiffle on their recent German tour. Questioned by the *Melody Maker* about this — it being fearful that beards and tub basses would be let loose again — Ray Davies agreed that they had tried skiffle out and that the Germans seemed to like it. Davies did not think, however, that this meant that skiffle was coming back but added he had been a big Lonnie Donegan fan.[3] Three

NORTH OF ENGLAND SKIFFLE PRESERVATION SOCIETY

AT THE ALBION HOTEL ARMLEY ROAD LEEDS 12 NEAR COMET STORE

ON THE FIRST WEDNESDAY OF EACH MONTH

8·30 PM

FREE ADMISSION

Advert for the North of England Skiffle Preservation Society's regular gigs.

decades later, however, the situation is somewhat different.

Until recently the North of England Skiffle Preservation Society met at the Cardigan Arms, Leeds, on the first Wednesday of each month, after previously getting together in various pubs around Yorkshire. Regrettably, since June 1997 the society has been temporarily in abeyance until a suitable new venue can be located. Founded in the Eighties, the society's monthly meetings were presided over by the entertainment agent, John Wall, who felt the music was being played much better the second time around. As one Preservation Society skiffler put it: "It's really just an excuse for a jolly good old ding-dong... where else can middle-aged men let their hair down?"[4]

Opposite: The Black Sheep (top) and the K.C. Moaners (btm). (Photos: Mike Dewe.)

Resident groups were the Black Sheep and K.C. Moaners, both playing acoustically. The K.C. Moaners, founded by John Wall, a former Fifties skiffler, features three guitarists (one who also plays ukulele and tenor guitar), tea-chest bass, and washboard, affixed horizontally to a folding

1956 And All That: Skiffle Reminiscences

Skiffle seemed true to "real" experience — escaped convicts, train wrecks, railroad navvies, gamblers, hard men and women — whereas our life was dull and safe, tucked under the foothills of the Black Mountains. Its other great attraction was that it was a music anyone could play and was encouraged to play. You may not be as good as Donegan, but skiffle was an inexpensive, home-made music; the music that made the guitar seem such an enticing instrument. Haley played electric guitar — something none of us had ever seen in Abergavenny — but the skiffle men (mostly) played acoustic — and that we could afford, and we could get hold of, with a little difficulty.

John Barnie

Forty years on, and I still can't read music. Without the skiffle spirit of "do-it-yourself music," I don't suppose I would actually make music at all. There must be hundreds of us still around for whom skiffle was a springboard to all sorts of musical experiences. But, for those of us who lived through it, it had also a special meaning all of its own. Just listen to "Rock Island Line" or the Vipers's Coffee Bar Session to find out why.

Mike Waites

Skiffle was great fun and played a big part in my rehabilitation. I have a lot to thank Lonnie Donegan and the skiffle movement for. I once saw him in a cafe in Leeds and almost went to tell him my story, but felt it was perhaps an intrusion.

Tim Mallinson

To me the importance of skiffle is that it was the starting point for a lot of professional and amateur musicians who grew up in the 1950s. And, as skiffle was closely related to rock 'n' roll, it wasn't a giant step for many to make from one music to the other.

John Harper

Sometimes I look back and think: "If I had not dismantled that wind-up HMV gramophone that cost me two shillings to make a guitar, I could be the owner of a very lovely (and valuable) antique piece of furniture". On the other hand, I would never have acquired a passion in life that has given years of pleasure. Overall, I think it's a big 'thank-you' to Lonnie Donegan, Wally Whyton and the other skifflers for pushing me in to doing it.

Bob Brooks

stand, and equipped with various sound effects. Between them, group members also play kazoos, harmonica, and the mouthpiece and funnel and most take turns at singing. The Moaners play a wide repertoire of skiffle, blues and jazz, have featured on Radio 2's history of skiffle programme, appeared on Yorkshire Television, and on Bourbon Street, New Orleans. In spite of the temporary cessation of the North of England Skiffle Preservation Society, the K.C. Moaners continue to play regularly at various venues.

The Black Sheep's usual line-up is two guitars, banjo, homemade one-string double bass and washboard. It sings the standard skiffle repertoire but does some of the less performed numbers, such as "Easy Rider", the "Cotton Song", and "Wabash Cannonball". The original Fifties Black Sheep group, from which the present one draws some of its members, had four guitars, banjo, washboard, bass, and a mouthpiece on a gramophone horn. Known also as the 12.30 Skiffle Group, because its players met during the lunch break at Waddington's, the Black Sheep played at the Leeds Empire, the Alhambra, Bradford and, like the Beatles and many other groups, auditioned for Carroll Levis.

Former skifflers also emerged in July 1997, when the *Times* recorded that a reunion performance of the Quarry Men would take place on the 6th of that month to celebrate the momentous day, forty years earlier, when John Lennon met Paul McCartney at the skiffle group's engagement at the fête at St Peter's church, Woolton. The non-Beatle members of the former Quarry Men line-up went their separate ways after leaving the group and had never all played together since. The reunion band consisted of Colin Hanton (drums), Pete Shotton (washboard), Rod Davis (banjo), Eric Griffiths (guitar) and Len Garry (tea-chest bass). The event at St Peter's Church attracted a crowd of around 2,500 and telegrams of support were received from, among others, Paul McCartney, Yoko Ono, Cynthia Lennon, Tony Blair and the Queen. "In an interview to mark the reunion, Sir Paul McCartney said of that first encounter with Lennon: 'I can remember him now, singing in a kind of checked shirt, this guy with the slightly curly hair...[and thinking] He looks good. I wouldn't mind being in a group with him.'"[5]

Another group that has re-emerged after nearly forty years is the Maryland Skiffle Group, also known as the Cobras, following the Vipers' choice of a snake name. One of its members, Terry Pamplin (reader in Musical Instrument Technology at London Guildhall University), was asked by Channel 4's *Big Breakfast* show to appear and demonstrate a musical instrument likely to interest teenage viewers.[6] Terry chose to show how to make a tea-chest bass — his own Fifties skiffle instrument — and the producers asked him to provide supporting musicians to play skiffle. Terry managed to round up some of his original skiffle group and they performed "Worried Man Blues" on the show.

Given the item's success with the teenage audience, Terry Pamplin was contracted to appear regularly on Tuesdays demonstrating the making of musical instruments. He also managed to trace the other members of the group and it is now back on the road again. Its members, having graduated through dance and rock 'n' roll bands, have thus returned to their skiffle roots.

Skiffle may also occasionally be revisited, rather than revived, for nostalgic reasons or to experience its special excitement once again or indeed for the first time. In early 1997 skiffle was back in town in Penarth, South Wales, when its Folk and Blues Club decided to revisit the Fifties and hold a skiffle night. Members of the club formed a group (with a genuine bass on this occasion, however), mainly to sing Donegan numbers which, given members' ages, were songs everybody seemed to know. This one-off skiffle night was an event that might well be repeated in the future.

A TRIBUTE to LONNIE DONEGAN

Paul Leegan, Lonnie Donegan tribute performer.

The essence of skiffle is also being revived through the imitative performances of Paul Leegan, who, on and off for the past twenty-five years, has sung Lonnie Donegan songs and played banjo and guitar in pubs and clubs. People told him that he both looked and sounded like Donegan and, on meeting him and singing a song with him in the Eighties, Paul decided to recreate the skiffle era. Producers of the television talent shows, *Opportunity Knocks* and *New Faces*, said, however, that he would never get anywhere precisely because he sounded too much like the King of Skiffle. Now, with the advent of *Stars in Their Eyes*, a show in which people perform as famous singers, there is a strong chance that Paul will be given the opportunity to pay his tribute to Lonnie Donegan before a television audience.

Paul Leegan also performed his Donegan tribute in a skiffle and rock 'n' roll show that toured theatres in the summer of 1997. The show, *Rockin' at the 2 I's*, mixed former stars such as Karl Denver and Chas McDevitt with tribute performers such as Leegan and Danny White (as Cliff Richard) and the Runaways (as the Shadows). Backing Paul Leegan was a band called Skiff-a-Billy, with Lonnie Donegan's son, Tony (aged thirty-one) on drums. Paul Leegan has had the strange experience of having Donegan in the audience, while at the same time being backed by his son. Donegan was apparently impressed with Paul's portrayal of him.[7]

Skiff-a-Billy, Paul's backing group, and performers in their own right, is led by Robbie Mac, who has been involved with music since the Fifties. Mac rejects the idea of a skiffle revival, saying, as this chapter demonstrates, that it has never really gone away — "there have always been little pockets of skiffle groups" — and that it is particularly important to people brought up in the Fifties.[8]

1956 And All That: Skiffle Reminiscences

I suppose that, like a lot of people, I got increasingly interested in singing more non-skiffle material — jazz, blues, country, etc. — and the instrumental framework became more sophisticated as I discovered new chords. But I never stopped playing skiffle completely. An informal session today may often include a blast of "Lost John", "Bring A Little Water, Sylvie" and others.

In 1977, I joined an acoustic pub band in Sheerness, Kent, called the Pandemonium String Band. The lead singer was Ted Higham, who played banjo and had a loud voice that really gave some welly to our Donegan songs. The off-shoot group, Brahms, Liszt and Legless, also kept skiffle songs in its pub repertoire until we folded up in 1982. Later, in 1985, I joined an acoustic comedy-folk group called Aunt Fortescue's Blues-Rockers, and, although we didn't play skiffle as such, we did do "Worried Man". It was noticeable that a two-guitar Vipers thrash often materialised on the livelier numbers. More recently I have been performing both as a solo act and as a duo with John Clachan known as Old Friends. In both guises skiffle may appear alongside blues, jazz and country and original compositions.

Dave Illingworth

We continued to enjoy ourselves at the Leigh Arms and many other local venues. We moved on musically, discarding the tea-chest bass and adding banjo, on which Jack and I doubled, and later an auto-harp and mandolin. By 1959, skiffle was on the wane, Tom had less time, due to shift work, and Bob, who was now an ambulance driver, went on to sing on his own in a local pub.

Jack and I brought in younger brother Colin, who at seventeen, was a fine guitarist. We performed as the Froggatt Brothers, using three guitars, and made a 45rpm recording of "How Long Blues" backed with "Sinner Man" at the Western Sound Recorders studio.

Gradually our interest in folk song developed and, influenced by the songs of Woody Guthrie, the Weavers, Guy Carawan, Pete Seeger, and the Kingston Trio, we became a folk group and part of the massive revival that swept the country in the early sixties. Later we explored the English folk song heritage through the influence of people like Ewan McColl and Martin Carthy. We founded our own folk club in Warrington, called the Minor Bird, and it ran for almost twenty years at different venues in the town. We still play and sing together on various occasions, and include the odd skiffle song.

Norman Froggatt

Given that element of continuity and the scale of current activity, "revival" may not be quite the right word for what is happening in skiffle today, but there is no doubt about the renewal of interest, and in the popular music of the Fifties in general. The Southern Skiffle Society, with Chas McDevitt as president, aims to promote skiffle in all its forms. The society, which publishes a quarterly magazine, *Skiffle Party*, is self-funding and relies on subscriptions and money-making events to support its work.

It has organised a number of gigs at former skiffle venues, such as the Princess Louise pub, High Holborn and the Skiffle Cellar, Greek Street. The society's most ambitious event was the Skiffle Party held at the 100 Club, Oxford Street, 5 March 1997, to celebrate over forty years of the music. Compèred by Chas McDevitt, the evening provided an opportunity for many of the old skiffle stalwarts to perform once more: Chas himself, with Shirley Douglas, accompanied by Steve Benbow, John Pilgrim (the Vipers' washboard player) and others; Beryl Bryden; Duffy Power, with James Hunter; Jack Fallon; Chas 'n' Dave; Bill Colyer; and 2 I's rock legends, Wee Willie Harris, Terry Dene and Tony Sheridan. Original members of the Quarry Men, the skiffle group that gave birth to the Beatles, were also present in the shape of Rod Davis and John Lowe, who along with other musicians, performed "Worried Man Blues" and "Puttin' on the Style".[9] Lowe had revived the Quarry Men in 1992.

The Skiffle Party's proceedings began energetically with the Lonnigans, whose numbers included "Dead or Alive" and "Lost John". The band comprised the Lonnigan Brothers — Ronnie, Johnnie and Donny — and featured washboard veteran Derek Mason, who had played in the National Skiffle Contest on *Six-Five Special*. The Lonnigans were the youngest group at the Skiffle Party and featured on this occasion harmonica and mandolin, as well as guitars, drums, washboard, and a female singer — Bonnie Lonnigan — on numbers such as "Freight Train". The Lonnigan Brothers Skiffle Group has been in existence since autumn 1996 but has had previous incarnations since 1972, with various line-ups and names — the Square Peg Skiffle Band and Loose Chippings, for example. Repeated playings of Donegan's "Cumberland Gap" in 1959 on their grandmother's gramophone is blamed for setting them off on the skiffle path.

As a follow-up to the earlier occasion, a Christmas Skiffle Party at the 100 Club in December 1997 featured performers who played at the earlier event — like the Lonnigans, Chas McDevitt, Beryl Bryden and John Pilgrim — as well as new attractions. These were Ray Bush, formerly leader of the Avon Cities Skiffle Group and making a rare UK appearance from his home in California; Diz Disley, jazz guitarist and one-time member of the Bob Cort group; Stéphane Dambry, billed as "Le Roi du Skiffle Français", and Donegan doppelgänger, Paul Leegan, performing "Railroad Bill", "Grand Coulee Dam" and other favourites at what was once one of Donegan's old haunts. The evening's events were kicked off by the reunited and augmented Saxons Skiffle Group, the winners in second place of the National Skiffle Contest televised on *Six-Five Special* in 1958.

Opposite: Southern Skiffle Society presents...

The continuity, revival and preservation of skiffle, may on the whole seem

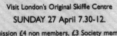

Visit London's Original Skiffle Centre
SUNDAY 27 April 7.30-12.
Admission £4 non members, £3 Society members.

THE

SKIFFLE CELLAR

49 Greek Street, Soho, W.1.

Worksongs ★ Blues ★ Spirituals ★ Ballads ★ Stomps ★ Jazz

CHAS McDEVITT

THE LONNIGAN BROTHERS SKIFFLE GROUP

PLUS SPECIAL GUESTS INCLUDING

HYLDA SIMS

FREE ADMISSION if you book a table for dinner. To reserve please call the Casa Rossini 0171 439 4159

During the late 50's, the Skiffle Cellar was the London home of skiffle. Run by Hylda Sims of the City Ramblers, presented music seven nights a week and featured the likes of Chas McDevitt, The Vipers, Dickie Bishop, Johnny Duncan, in fact every skiffle band of the day.

(vertical side text, both sides:) BAR AND RESTAURANT LONDON'S SKIFFLE CENTRE

SOUTHERN SKIFFLE SOCIETY PRESENTS

SKIFFLE PARTY

1957

CELEBRATING OVER 40 YEARS OF SKIFFLE

CHAS McDEVITT
THE LEGENDARY SKIFFLE GROUP
THE LONNIGAN BROTHERS

WITH GUEST APPEARANCES BY

BRYDEN (LONNIE DONEGAN) • STEVE BENBOW
E KINGS) • DUFFY POWER (ALEXIS KORNER)
LEY DOUGLAS (CHAS MC DEVITT) • JIM BRAY
COLYER, ALEXIS KORNER) • RAY FOXLEY (KEN
ER) • JOHN PILGRIM (VIPERS) JACK FALLON •
Y WINKLER (COTTON PICKERS) BILL COLYER
COLYER, BOB CORT) • WEE WILLIE HARRIS •
DDY LLOYD (WORRIED MEN, VIPERS) • HYLDA
S (CITY RAMBLERS) • BRIAN GREGG (LES HOBEAUX)
CK RICHARDS (WORRIED MEN)....AND MANY MORE

US A FEW SURPRISE SKIFFLE LEGENDS

WEDNESDAY
5TH MARCH 1997

100 CLUB

OXFORD STREET • LONDON • W1
7.30 - MIDNIGHT
MEMBERS £6, NON MEMBERS £8

SOUTHERN SKIFFLE SOCIETY PRESENTS

CHRISTMAS SKIFFLE PARTY

As a follow-up to our March Skiffle Party, we are presenting another EVENING NOT TO BE MISSED. March sold out and the doors closed by 9 O'Clock...
ARRIVE EARLY! OR ORDER TICKETS IN ADVANCE FROM:
DEREK MASON ON 0181 546 2713.

WITH

LONNIGAN BROS. SKIFFLE GROUP
avec STEPHANE DAMERY LE ROI DU SKIFFLE FRANÇAIS
FREIGHT TRAIN, FREIGHT TRAIN...

Chas McDevitt

THE QUEEN OF THE WASHBOARD

BERYL BRYDEN
AND THE LEGENDARY

DIZ DISLEY
RARE U.K. APPEARANCE FROM THE LEADER OF THE AVON CITIES

Ray Bush

PLUS A TRIBUTE TO LONNIE FEATURING DONEGAN DOPPLEGANGER

MR PAUL LEEGAN

PLUS MANY SKIFFLING GUESTS AND A FEW SURPRISES

100 CLUB OXFORD STREET
LONDON W1N 9FB
Between Oxford Street and Tottenham Court Road tube stations.
0171 636 0933

WEDNESDAY 10th DECEMBER
Admission: £9 non members, £7 members
DOORS OPEN AT 7.30 MUSIC FROM 8.30PM UNTIL MIDNIGHT

Please Y'Self . . .

the band that defies description!

WEIRDER than the Legendary Stardust Cowboy,
HEAVIER than Napalm Death,
more **RHYTHMIC** than the Flying Scotsman and
more **MELODIC** than Nana Mouskouri . . .

PLEASE Y' SELF shatter all preconceptions about "skiffle" bands

The only way to describe PLEASE Y' SELF is "indescribable"
See them soon . . . . then tell your analyst!
if you can find the words . . . .

FOR PLEASE Y' SELF ALBUM SALES / GIG GUIDE ETC. WRITE TO
' LAST GASP RECORDS PO BOX 38 MATLOCK, DERBYS, DE4 3YY'.

Please Y'Self, "the band that defies description..."

to be the province of men in their mid- to late-fifties and over. But, as with the Lonnigans, there are younger performers who acknowledge skiffle and its antecedents in their music. One such group, from Derbyshire, is called Please Y'Self, and developed from the remnants of the Ragbag Spasm Band in 1992. The group is made up of two brothers, John and Rob Gill, and sister Chris, who have been playing their own brand of skiffle for 25 years, both in the UK and Europe. The trio work solely with a line-up of guitar (John), washboard (Chris) and tea-chest bass (Rob) and write many of their own songs.

They have long since ceased to be imitators of Lonnie Donegan and like to feel that there is no musical genre which they cannot arrange for their three instruments, including glitter, punk and indie. The skiffle purists generally hate Please Y'Self ("Call that skiffle!") and in self-defence the Gills have penned a song called "Gonnie Donegan", the chorus of which repeats the exhortation (constantly made to them) to: "Play Lonnie Donegan".

As their publicity material puts it: "With their parents and grandparents in Music Hall, the Carter Family on the gramophone at home in the '50's and wild imaginations that pull in influences from skiffle roots to psychobilly it's no wonder it's so difficult to find the words to describe a... performance."

Please Y'Self have appeared at the Glastonbury Festival, on national and local television and radio, and have played alongside Jools Holland, Dire Straits and Donegan himself. Tours have taken them to the Falklands, Holland and Germany and the trio have made several singles and albums, of which, *Joan's Babies*, featuring additional musicians on some tracks, is a fine sampler of their own compositions, musicianship (Rob can really make a tea-chest bass perform) and varied styles.

Al Boden, "once seen, never forgotten..."

Other skiffle groups of today, or groups that feature skiffle as part of their overall repertoire, and whose members are not always old Fifties skifflers, include House Party Skiffle from Essex, the Bon Temps Playboys, the Mighty Smithereens from London, Al Boden, the Del Rios, and Wang Dang Doodle, formerly the Armpit Jug Band.

House Party Skiffle is led by Brian Mayes, a former trad jazz trumpeter, on electric bass. It is, however, essentially an acoustic group, with guitars and banjo and ex-Viper, John Pilgrim, on washboard. Singing is shared by group members and the repertoire includes railroad, music hall and gospel songs, and the blues.

Al Boden started playing skiffle in the Fifties in Kidderminster after his national service. He moved on to rock 'n' roll, country, blues and bluegrass but recently returned to his skiffle roots and is vocalist, harmonica player and guitarist with Bodey's Washboard Band, in which his son plays lead guitar. In addition to electric bass and washboard the band features a homemade noise-maker called a drumphoneam. The band has a varied repertoire that includes skiffle and comedy numbers. Over the years Al Boden has appeared on radio and television and as a support act to Ken Dodd, Karl Denver and the Bachelors, as well as acting on television as a drunk, but more usually as a tramp.

The Armpit Jug Band, using the same four musicians, had been playing its mixture of jug band songs, Twenties hits, ragtime, blues, ballads, bop and cajun since 1969. Recently the band reformed and restructured as Wang Dang Doodle, adding Doctor Groove Green, on electric piano, who had played with Birmingham area blues bands, including the Climax Blues

1956 And All That: Skiffle Reminiscences

Tony Wales and I opened Horsham Song Swappers Club in 1958 and we also formed our barn dance band, the Derrydowners. I played amplified mouth organ from the first day. I also played with the Benacre Band (1957-1960) to whom I owe much of my repertoire.

From these early beginnings, I went on to play with the bass guitarist Ashley Hutchins, of Steeleye Span, Fairport Convention, and now the Albion Band — touring, doing concerts, recordings and even television. The folk singer Shirley Collins sang with us in the Etchingham Steam Band (1974-76). Martyn-Wyndham-Read formed his Australian Bush Band in 1970 and his recordings featured my mouth organ playing.

Since the late Fifties there have been lots of folk dance bands along the way: Pandemonium String Band (1960); Country Cousins (formed in 1963 with my cousin, Ian Holder on accordion, and my wife Margaret on washboard); Country Players Band; Potters Wheel, led by Vic Gammon, which toured Sweden in 1978; the Tuthrie Band, a five-piece unit led by Ian Holder, and Cousins and Sons, formed in the late eighties — all stemming from the skiffle era. The current band, Cousins and Sons, consists of my cousin, Ian Holder (accordion) and his son, Gary (electric/acoustic bass), and my own son James (drums and percussion). I play electric harmonica — and, when I run out of puff, I play some guitar and sing. Our venues are folk and barn dances and parent/teacher association events the length and breadth of Sussex.

I've had lots of fun, met many musicians, visited many places (I never would have got to) if it had not been for the music — about 40 years of musical activity now. I have my father (who I watched, listened to and copied) and skiffle to thank for my start in music as a hobby.

Terry Potter

Band. Wang Dang Doodle now describes itself as playing acoustic and electric jazz, blues and boogie. John Stringbean Cumming is the band's vocalist, and also plays kazoo, jew's harp and sundry percussion instruments, including the washboard. The band is renowned for using a vast array of instruments: the orthodox, such as the guitar, banjo, saxophone, trumpet and mandolin; the unorthodox, like the jug and swannee whistle, and the unrecognised — the teapot and vacuum cleaner tube, for example. The band, influenced by the early jug bands, as well as those of the Sixties revival, has made radio and television appearances and has recorded.

The Del Rios, an acoustic band — two guitars, washboard, tea-chest bass, and sometimes fiddle — play a mixture of skiffle, swing, rockabilly and railroad boogie-woogie The bass player, who also plays harmonica, plucks an unusual tea-chest bass, the broom-handle is fixed upright and its single string tuned to an E. The group have been in existence for around five years and have a varied repertoire that includes traditional Southern ballads such as "Stackolee" and Chas McDevitt's "I'm Satisfied".

Opposite: The Armpit Jug Band, now the Wang Dang Doodle Band.

218

Railroad Bill, performing outside the Old Library, Cardiff.

In Wales, the skiffle tradition is continued by Railroad Bill, a band begun in 1986 when Dan Nichols, Chris Walker and Andy Baillie — equipped with washboard, tea-chest bass and ukulele — started busking on the streets of Aberystwyth. Dan has a skiffle lineage. His uncle is Geoff Nichols, bassist with the Avon Cities Jazz Band (and Fifties Skiffle Group) who stills plays in the band. On moving to Cardiff, where they regularly busk, Railroad Bill's line-up increased with the addition of Dave Jones (guitar, kazoo, blues harp) and Geoff Haynes (guitar) and Dom G. Wilson (drums). The band has recorded, appeared on television and radio, at various festivals in the UK and abroad, and has busked all over Britain and France. Advertising themselves as Britain's hottest skiffle band, the group usually eschew modern electrical music and use acoustic, improvised and home-made instruments coupled with the sheer power of their own lungs. Their display of gurning and bizarre choreography, however, may be less than usual in such bands. Railroad Bill do not confine themselves to skiffle nor acoustic instruments, however, and in electric mode admit to music influences as varied as folk, punk, pop, world and indie.

Other groups associated with the jazz, blues and folk scenes would seem to have much in common with skiffle and the music of its origins. Reet Petite and Gone are a four-man acoustic band, using guitar, mandolin and washboard that plays folk and good-time blues. The quartet made a recent appearance at the Southern Skiffle Society's "Night of the Washboards" event at the 100 Club. Kid Tidiman's Paradise Rhythm Boys (cornet, clarinet, tuba, banjo and washboard) hail from Essex, and Joe Le Taxi

Opposite: The Juggernaut Jug Band.

1956 And All That: Skiffle Reminiscences

Although we hear of the excitement of the burgeoning new world of popular culture of the Fifties and Sixties, for young teenage girls growing up in this period, particularly in the mid-Fifties, life was bound by restriction, the rigid socio-cultural identity of feminine behaviour, discrimination and, of course, being groomed for our ultimate destination of Wife and Mother. Our music lessons were restricted to singing in rounds and Welsh folk tunes. I played solo saxophone for the school concert, a Gerry Mulligan number, to complete silence except for cheering from two sixth form girls. My music mistress said afterwards that on no account was I to lower the decorum of the school in such a manner again. Similar disapproval had been evoked by a foray into skiffle at school.

Recently, I have been researching for a dissertation on women in jazz ("Syncopated Ladies: British Jazzwomen 1880-1995 and Their Influence on Popular Culture") and on its completion in 1996 gained my MSc (Econ)in Women's Studies. I am the founder and curator of the Women's Jazz Archive, formerly in the Department of Adult Continuing Education, University College of Swansea but currently in my own home until a new location is found.

Jen Wilson

A few years ago (1993) we formed a skiffle group at the Dartmouth Yacht Club for a one-off performance as part of a variety show staged to entertain the members. The group consisted of harmonica, two guitars, tea-chest bass and drums and there are mutterings that the group will be resurrected for further occasional performances at the club.

Basil Wright (Avon Cities Skiffle Group)

(guitar, bass guitar, accordion, drums and washboard) from the Welshpool area of mid-Wales.

Brett Marvin and the Thunderbolts, from Crawley, have been together as a group for around thirty years and have been described as a skiffle-cum-jug band act. They offer a unique style of music and, as well as standard instruments, make use of such improvised ones as the zobstick and the electric ironing board.[10]

The Famous Potatoes, playing "soil music", began in 1979 as the Folk Pistols and play cajun, skiffle, hillbilly and western swing. Most of its members sing and a wide variety of instruments are played — string and wind instruments, bass, accordion, drum and washboard. Founded by folk musicians in the late Sixties, the Pigsty Hill Light Orchestra's music, derived from the jazz and blues of the Twenties and Thirties, has employed various non-standard instruments — paraffin funnel, ballcock sections from a toilet, a jug, and so on — to obtain its individual sound. Following changes to personnel and instrumentation, the orchestra disbanded in 1979, was revived in the late Eighties and reverted to its former jug band style in the early Nineties.[11]

In the USA, jug bands — one of the band types associated with the origins of skiffle — have not died out. Two noted jug bands of the Sixties were the Even Dozen Jug Band and the Jim Kweskin Jug Band, the latter using washboard, kazoo, and washtub bass alongside guitar, banjo, fiddle and harmonica. Both were cited as influences by Britain's Wang Dang Doodle.

In the Nineties, American jug bands are still to be found, for example, the Juggernaut Jug Band, from Louisville, Kentucky, and the Last Chance Jug Band hailing from Memphis, Tennessee. The Juggernaut was founded in 1965 and has been performing "its strange concoction called jug band music" on and off for over thirty years. Its four members, who all take part in the vocals, adopt stage names: "Roscoe Goose" (jug, washboard and various other instruments); "Gil Fish" (acoustic bass, washtub bass and noseflute); "Jim Bayala" (guitar and kazoo); and "Tin Pan Alan" (guitar, violin and other instruments). The Juggernaut Jug Band has a programme of cover songs and originals and aims to be both entertaining and musical; given its multi-instrumentalists it has been described as an orchestra rather than a band.

The Last Chance Jug Band, was formed in late 1989, although various members had played together since the mid-Eighties. The Last Chance draws much of its repertoire from the blues but its vocalist, the blues expert David Evans (also guitar and kazoo), arranges some numbers and adds verses of his own to some of the songs. The band's four other musicians between them play jug, piano, drums, one-string bass, washboard and percussion. As with skiffle both past and present, the American jug bands of today are white performers seeking much of their material and inspiration from the music of black Americans. And no doubt this will continue to be the case.

In his own book on skiffle, Chas McDevitt draws attention to the existence of a number of other jug and washboard bands in the USA, as well as the Sunshine Skiffle Band. He also points out that the skiffle groups of Germany, France, Sweden, Holland and elsewhere owe more to the influence of British skiffle than to the American roots from which it developed and that, as in the UK, skiffle in Europe today has a small body of fans and performers.[12] Two such fans have endeavoured to document the European skiffle scene: Holger Lührig by listing some continental and other groups at the end of his publication on British skiffle, and Hans Heunks in his brief overview of skiffle in the Netherlands and Flanders.[13]

Skiffle may never have entirely disappeared but how to explain the current revival of interest in the music? Some of this is no doubt due to forty years having elapsed since its boom time. For men today in their late middle-age, the skiffle craze years are now as far away in time as the First World War would have been when they were teenage skifflers. The passing of forty years and the strong contrast between everyday life in the Fifties and the Nineties, has developed perhaps a sense of history and, as regards popular music, a realisation of skiffle's importance. This sense of history (and of skiffle's place) is reflected in recent radio programmes, the reissue of skiffle music on EP, LP and CD, and by this book and other publications.

The late Wally Whyton of the Vipers presented a series of three, hour-long autobiographical programmes on Radio 2 during December 1995 and January 1996, called *A Viper's Tale*, which had much to say about skiffle and his subsequent music and broadcasting career. Around the same time, January and February 1966, Joe Brown presented four half-hour radio programmes on Radio 2 on the history of skiffle called *Rock Island Line*. Re-isssues of skiffle recordings on CD have come from Lake Records (Ken Colyer, the First National Skiffle Contest), Roller-coaster Records (Chas McDevitt) and the German company, Bear Family Records (Lonnie Donegan, Johnny Duncan, the Vipers).

This rediscovery and active promotion of skiffle has provided a number of people with the chance to recapture some of the sights and sounds of their youth — the thrash of acoustic guitars, the metallic click of the washboard, the plonk of the tea-chest bass behind a voice singing a skiffle song. Half-forgotten memories have been revived and sometimes that original urge to play the music has been reawakened and acted upon. The act of looking back demonstrates what all those Fifties teenagers involved with skiffle were getting into — a movement, a craze no less, destined to change the face of popular music and one that helped create the idea of a distinctive teenage culture. Impossible for teenage skifflers to have known the significance of what they were doing at the time, they just enjoyed themselves and got on with playing the music.

And if the train don't stop
and turn around,
I'm Alabamy bound...

References

Preface

1. C. McDevitt, *Skiffle: the Definitive Inside Story*, London, Robson, 1997.

2. B. Bird, *Skiffle: the Story of Folk-Song with a Jazz Beat*, London, Hale, 1958.

Chapter 1

1. "This 'Royal' was Certainly a Dish Fit for a Queen", *Melody Maker*, 21 May 1960, 12.

2. M. Burman, 'What *Does* Lonnie's Dad Do?', *Melody Maker*, 16 April 1960, 6.

3. J. Godbolt, *A History of Jazz in Britain, 1950-70*, London, Quartet, 1989, 7.

4. D. Boulton, *Jazz in Britain*, London, Allen 1958,130.

5. B. Nicholls, 'A Jazzman's Diary', *Jazz Journal* 8 (4) April 1955, 13.

6. Godbolt, 13.

7. K. Colyer, *When Dreams Are in the Dust*, Ryarsh, Kent, Milbury, 1989, 138.

8. K. Colyer, 'P.S ... from Ken Colyer', *Melody Maker*, 28 July 1956, 5; B. Bird, *Skiffle: the Story of Folk-Song with a Jazz Beat*, London, Hale, 1958, 78.

9. Godbolt, 17.

10. Colyer, 1989, 104-5.

11. R. Coleman, 'Ken Colyer — Forgotten Man of Trad Jazz!' *Melody Maker*,14 October 1961, 3.

12. J. Long, 'Ken Colyer — Thanksgiving Service', *Footnote*, 20 (2) 1988/89, 25.

13. Colyer, 1989, 239.

14. Colyer, 1989, 238.

15. A. Korner, 'Skiffle or Piffle?', *Melody Maker*, 28 July 1956, 5.

16. B. Nicholls, 'A Jazzman's Diary', *Jazz Journal*, 6 (7) July 1953, 4.

17. 'Skiffle on Trial', *Melody Maker*, 9 March 1957, 3.

18. Colyer, 1989, 240.

19. Colyer, 1989, 240.

20. Colyer, 1989, 241.

21. Colyer, 1989, 241.

22. Colyer, 1989, 243.

23. H. Shapiro, *Alexis Korner: the Biography*, London, Bloomsbury, 1996, 40.

24. Shapiro, 47.

25. Shapiro, 48.

26. Shapiro, 48.

27. Shapiro, 49.

28. J. Collis, 'It's Back to the Old Washboard Days', *Radio Times* (Welsh edition), 242 (3144) 11 February 1984, 13.

29. P.R., 'Chris Barber's Jazz Band' (Columbia SEG7568), *Jazz Monthly*, 1 (1) March 1955, 18.

30. J. Vincent, 'The Banjo in Jazz', *Jazz Journal*, 30 (3) March 1977, 21.

31. Boulton, xvi.

32. T. Brown, 'The Amazing Success Story of Chris Barber', *Melody Maker*, 5 January 1957, 3.

33. Collis, 13.

34. T. Brown, 'Conceited? — They Always Say That When You're Successful, Says Lonnie Donegan', *Melody Maker*, 4 May 1957, 3.

35. *New Musical Express Annual 1962*, London, NME, 1962, 48.

36. Brown, 4 May 1957, 3.

37. J. Asman, 'Jazz Reviews', *Musical Opinion*, 108 (1291) June 1985, 238.

38. B. Dawbarn, 'The Scots-Born Irish Hill-Billy from London', *Melody Maker*, 19 May 1956, 11.

39. Dawbarn, 11.

40. Burman, 7.

41. D. Rees and L. Crampton, *Guiness Book of Rock Stars*, 3rd edition, London, Guinness, 1994, 172.

42. 'Beryl Bryden', *Jazz Journal*, 5 (9) September 1952, 18.

43. P. Leslie, *FAB: the Anatomy of a Phenomenon*, London, MacGibbon and Kee, 1965, 57.

44. Leslie, 56.

45. C. Welch, 'Puttin' on the Seventies Style', *Melody Maker*, 21 January 1978, 14.

46. Dawbarn, 11.

47. B. Nicholls, 'A Jazzman's Diary', *Jazz Journal*, 6 (7) July 1953, 4.

48. 'Round the Clubs with Mary Lou Williams', *Jazz Journal*, 6 (9) September 1953, 18.

49. B. Nicholls, 'A Jazzman's Diary', *Jazz Journal*, 7 (8) August 1954, 11.

50. J. Hasted, *Alternative Memoirs*, Shipton Green, Itchenor, West Sussex, Greengates, c.1992, 135.

Chapter 2

1. *Illustrated London News*, 231 (6178A), 8 November 1957.

2. D. J. Epstein, *Sinful Tunes and Spirituals: Black Folk Music to the Civil War*, Urbana, University of Illinois, 1977, 158.

3. H. Courlander, *Negro Folk Music, U.S.A.*, New York, Columbia University Press, 1963, 205-6.

4. Epstein, 343.

5. Courlander, 206.

6. P. Oliver, *Savannah Syncopators: African Retentions in the Blues*, London, Studio Vista, 1970, 42.

7. Courlander, 207.

8. Courlander, 207.

9. Epstein, 156.

10. H. Panassié and M. Gautier, *Dictionary of Jazz*, London, Cassell, 1956, 243.

11. F. Ramsey, *Been Here and Gone*, London, Cassell, 1960, 53-4.

12. S. B. Charters, *The Country Blues*, London, Joseph, 1960, 154.

13. W. Broonzy, *Big Bill Blues: William Broonzy's Story*, as told to Yannick Bruynoghe, London, Cassell, 1955, 8.

14. B. Olsson, *Memphis Blues and Jug Bands*, London, Studio Vista, 1970, 74-5.

15. Olsson, 76.

16. D. Barker, *A Life in Jazz*, edited by A. Shipton, London, Macmillan, 1986, 59.

17. Barker, 35-41.

18. Olsson, 22-6.

19. P. Oliver, *Conversation with the Blues*, 2nd edition, London, Cassell, 1965, 178.

20. Olsson, 82.

21. O. King, *Blue Blowing Jazz*, Mound City Blue Blowers, (EP JEL1), *Gramophone*, September 1958, 170.

22. R. M. Lawless, *Folksingers and Folksongs in America: a Handbook...*, New York, Duell, Sloan and Pearce, 1960, 103.

23. C. T. Brown, *Music U.S.A.: America's Country and Western Tradition*, Englewood Cliffs, New Jersey, Prentice-Hall, 1986, 30.

24. A. Korner, 'Skiffle or Piffle?', *Melody Maker*, 28 July 1956, 5.

25. B. Bird, *Skiffle: the Story of Folk-Song with a Jazz Beat*, London, Hale, 1958, 51,

26. R. Marsalis, 'Because He Couldn't Pay the Rent', letter to *Melody Maker*, 23 March 1957, 4.

27. F. Ramsey and C. E. Smith (eds.), *Jazzmen*, London, Sidgwick and Jackson, 1957, 183; R. Blesh, *Shining Trumpets: a History of Jazz*, 4th edition, London, Cassell, 1958, 303.

28. P. Oliver, *The Story of the Blues*, Harmondsworth, Middlesex, Penguin, 1972, 83-4.

29. Panassié and Gautier, 208.

30. Blesh, 295, 303.

31. Broonzy, 42-3.

32. Ramsey and Smith, 200.

33. Blesh, 337, 304.

34. Oliver, 1972, 164.

35. S. Leigh, *Halfway to Paradise: Britpop, 1955-1962*, Folkestone, Finbarr, 1996, [29].

36. C. McDevitt, 'The Story of Skiffle', *Radio Times* (Welsh edition), 137 (1774) 8 November 1957, 11.

37. Decca Record Co. Ltd., *Jazz on 78s: a Guide to the Many Examples of Classic Jazz...*, London, Decca, 1954, 26.

38. S.B. Charters, 'Hunting Music in the South', *New York Times*, 15 November 1959, 5.

Chapter 3

1. B. Bird, *Skiffle: the Story of Folk-Song with a Jazz Beat*, London, Hale, 1958, 104.

2. A. Langley, *A Family in the Fifties*, Hove, Wayland, 1986, 13.

3. D. Rogers, *Rock 'n' Roll*, London, Routledge and Kegan Paul, 1982, 8.

4. 'The Low-down on Skiffle', *Mirabelle*, 22 July 1957, 1-8.

5. J. Pascall, *Growing Up in the Fifties*, Hove, Wayland, 1980, 52.

6. Rogers, 7.

7. 'Hail, Haley!', *New Musical Express Annual, 1957*, London, NME, 1957, 89.

8. 'Hail, Haley!', 89.

9. T. Stacy, *Decades: the Fifties*, Hove, Wayland, 1989, 30.

10. M. Nevard, 'Coffee Society', *Daily Herald*, 1 April 1958, 4.

11. *Lonnie Donegan*, London, Amalgamated Press, 1958, 61 (Fans' Star Library No.12).

12. D. Stuckey, *The Spinners: Fried Bread and Brandy-O!*, London, Robson, 1985, 19.

13. S. Bunt and R. Gargrave, *The Politics of Youth Clubs*, Leicester, National Youth Bureau, 1980, 130.

14. B. A. Young, 'Coffee-Bar Theory and Practice', *Punch*, 5 December 1956, 672.

15. B. A. Young, 'Coffee-House Rock', *Punch*, 8 May 1957, 589.

16. A. Atkinson, 'Night in a London Coffee-House', *Punch*, 28 January 1958, 179.

17. Quoted in: D. McAleer, *Hit Parade Heroes: British Beat before the Beatles*, London, Hamlyn, 1993, 44.

18. 'Extra Charms for Witch's Cauldron', *Times*, 12 September 1957, 12e.

19. *Daily Herald*, 19 January 1957, 3.

20. McAleer, 75-79.

21. P. Brand, 'On the Soho Beat', *Melody Maker*, 26 July 1957, 9.

22. M. Nevard, 'Hand Jive!', *Daily Herald*, 29 January 1958, 4-5.

23. P. Everett, *You'll Never be 16 Again: an Illustrated History of the British Teenager*, BBC, 1986, 26.

24. I. Mairants, *My Fifty Fretting Years: a personal History of the Twentieth Century Guitar Explosion*, Gateshead, Ashley Mark, 1980, 75, 77.

25. 'Skiffle or J. S. B', *Times*, 26 August 1957, 11c.

26. 'Guitar Looking to Pluck Piano off its Perch; $22,000,000 Lute in 1957', *Variety*, 24 December 1958, 35.

27. Mairants, 380.

28. P. Norman, *Shout!: the True Story of the Beatles*, London, Penguin, 1993, 22.

29. Mairants, 103.

30. BBC Written Archives Centre R19/1, 676/1, 2 August 1962.

31. 'Scored for Washboard', *Melody Maker*, 11 May 1957, 7.

32. S. Race, 'How Do You Tune a Washboard?', *Melody Maker*, 12 October 1957, 7.

33. M. Jones, 'Skiffle Saves the Sheet Music', *Daily Herald*, 15 August 1957, 7.

34. B. Dawbarn, '"Skiffle" is Twelve Months too Late' *Melody Maker*, 6 December 1958, 10.

35. T. Standish, review of *Skiffle* by Brian Bird, *Jazz Journal*, 12 (2) February 1959, 11.

36. G. Beaumont, *Twentieth-Century Folk Mass for One or More Cantors and Congregation*, London, Weinberger, 1957.

37. O. Hunkin, 'A 20th-Century Folk Mass', *Radio Times* (Welsh edition), 137 (1770) 11 October 1957, 13.

38. A. Eperon, 'The Jazz Mass', *Daily Herald*, 11 October 1957, 3.

39. B. H., 'Jazz Folk Mass Now Available on English-Disc', *Diapason*, 1 December 1958, 25.

40. 'A Twentieth-Century Folk Mass' (editorial), *Musical Times*, 98 (1378) December 1957, 660; A.H. Morris, 'A Twentieth-Century Folk Mass', *Musical Times*, 98 (1378) December 1957, 671-2.

41. 'From Minerva House: A 20th Century Folk Mass', (editorial), *Musical Opinion*, 81 (963) December 1957, 149-150.

42. C. Cleall, 'The Master of the Choir', *Musical Opinion*, 83 (985) October 1959, 49.

43. *Reveille*, 23 May 1957, 9-12.

44. *Woman*, 8 August 1957.

45. J. Maiteny, 'Skiffle Separates', *Daily Herald*, 25 September 1957, 6.

46. V. Hastings, *Jo and the Skiffle Group*, London, Parish, 1958.

47. 'Bands', *Melody Maker*, 15 June 1957, 14.

48. J. Elliot, 'A Generation Adrift', *Radio Times* (Welsh edition), 143 (1852) 8 May 1959, 7.

Chapter 4

1. D. Peabody, *The Decca Skiffle Sessions 1954-57*, (Lake LAS007), *Folk Roots*, 9 (9) March 1988, 45.

2. M. G. Myer, *The Decca Skiffle Sessions 1954-57*, (Lake LA5007), *English Dance and Song*, 50 (2) July/August 1988, 15.

3. P. Tanner, 'Ken Colyer's Skiffle Group', (Decca F10926), *Jazz Journal*, 10 (11) November 1957, 14.

4. J. Reddihough, 'Ken Colyer's Jazzmen', *Jazz Journal*, 9 (7) July 1956, 6.

5. 'After 13 Years Ken is still Loyal to N.O.', *Melody Maker*, 4 March 1961, 12; R. Coleman, 'Ken Colyer — Forgotten Man of Trad Jazz!', *Melody Maker*, 14 October 1961, 3; 'The Strange Case of Ken Colyer', *Melody Maker*, 3 March 1962, 3.

6. R. Coleman, 'Colyer Revives "Skiffle Piffle"', *Melody Maker*, 22 August 1964, 12.

7. K. Colyer's Skiffle Group, *Wandering*, (Lake LACD68). (Colyer's 1966 sleeve notes to original recordings.)

8. O. Bryce, 'Ken Colyer', *Jazz Journal International*, 41 May 1988, 20-1.

9. E. Buchanan, 'Too Little, Too Late', *Times Educational Supplement*, 9 March 1984, 29.

10. G. Boatfield, 'Beryl Bryden's Backroom Skiffle', (Decca 45-F-J-10823), *Jazz Journal*, 10 (1) January 1957 .

11. H. Shapiro, *Alexis Korner: the Biography*, London, Bloomsbury, 1996, 232.

12. O. King, 'Alexis Korner Skiffle Group', (EP EXA76), *Gramophone*, June 1958, 34-5.

13. P. Russell, 'Chris Barber Skiffle Group', (Nixa NJE1025), *Jazz Monthly*, 3 (1) March 1957, 23.

14. G. Boatfield, 'Chris Barber Skiffle Group', (Nixa NJE1025), *Jazz Journal*, 10 (3) March 1957, 14.

15. D. Boulton, *Jazz in Britain*, London, Allen, 1958, 132.

16. B. Kernfield, (ed.), *New Grove Dictionary of Jazz*, Macmillan, 1988, 68-9.

17. J. A. Godbolt, *History of Jazz in Britain*, 1950-1970, London, Quartet, 1989, 132.

18. P. Leslie, *FAB: the Anatomy of a Phenomenon*, London, MacGibbon and Kee, 1965, 62-5.

19. L. Henshaw, 'Mr Donegan...' *Melody Maker*, 8 December. 1956, 8.

20. 'Donegan Ill: Quick Solo Debut for Duncan', *Melody Maker*, 2 March 1957, 4.

21. A. Carthew, 'They've No Love for Lonnie', *Daily Herald*, 18 April 1957, 3; 'Spotlight on Skiffle', *Melody Maker*, 13 April 1957, 6.

22. 'Lonnie, the Skiffle King, Denies Tour Flop', *Daily Herald*, 22 April 1957, 3.

23. 'Lonnie Donegan Disc is Banned by BBC', *Melody Maker*, 10 May 1958, 1.

24. 'Lonnie Tries a New Way into the Hit Parade', article reproduced in H. Lührig, *British Skiffle Groups 1954-1958*, Unna, Germany, The author, 199?.

25. P. Pelletier, 'Lonnie Donegan', 29. Article reproduced in Lührig.

26. T. Brown, 'Conceited? They Always Say That When You're Successful, Says Lonnie Donegan', *Melody Maker*, 4 May 1957, 3.

27. 'Skiffle on Trial', *Melody Maker*, 9 March 1957, 2.

28. C. Bayne, 'Putting on the Donegan', *TV Times*, 15 (190) 19 June 1959, 10.

29. T. Standish, *Lonnie*, (Nixa NPT 19027), *Jazz Journal*, 11 (12) December 1958, 19.

30. R. Reliant, *Rock Island Line*, (KAZ CD21), *Folk Roots*, (112) October 1992, 45.

31. Leslie, 73

32. P. Gambaccini, T. Rice and J. Rice, *British Hit Singles*, 10th edition, Enfield, Guinness, 1995.

33. J. F. Tanner, *Hits Through the Years, the Rock 'n' Roll Era*, 1956-1962, Whitley Bay, JFT-Valid Records, 1992, 244.

34. Pelletier, 30.

35. J. Kelly, 'Three Wives, Two Heart Attacks', *Daily Mail*, 10 May 1996, 9.

36. J. Stone, 'Nancy, Queen of Skiffle, Helped Pave the Way for Engelbert', *Leicester Mercury*, 10 May 1972, 17.

37. N. Banks-Smith, 'Miss Whiskey Sloshes Skiffle', *Daily Herald*, 29 June 1957, 4.

38. T. Brown, 'I'm Sick and Tired of Skiffle, Says Nancy Whiskey', *Melody Maker*, 20 July 1957, 7.

39. G. Boatfield, 'Chas McDevitt Skiffle Group', (Oriole CB 1357), *Jazz Journal*, 10 (6) June 1957, 20-1; J. Oakland, 'Miscellaneous and Dance' (Oriole CB 1386), *Gramophone*, November 1957, 247.

40. 'Chas McDevitt Tops 1,000-Mile Package', *Melody Maker*, 23 November 1957, 4.

41. G. Martin with J. Hornsby, *All You Need Is Ears*, London, Macmillan, 1979, 58-9.

42. Martin and Hornsby, 101.

43. Martin and Hornsby, 142.

44. O. King, 'Vipers Skiffle Group', (Parlophone R/45R/4261), *Gramophone*, May 1957, 470.

45. G. Boatfield. 'Vipers Skiffle Group', (Parlophone GEP8626), *Jazz Journal*, 10 (10) October 1957, 22-3.

46. T. Tremayne, 'The Hell of Skiffle', *Melody Maker*, 19 April 1958, 5.

47. D. Griffiths, 'Johnny from the US Has a Cockney Accent', *TV Times*, 9 (103) 18 October 1957, 16.

48. T. Brown, 'Johnny Duncan: the Cockney Hill-Billy', *Melody Maker*, 2 November 1957, 3.

49. Brown, 3.

50. G. Boatfield, 'Johnny Duncan and His Blue Grass Boys', (Columbia SEG 7708), *Jazz Journal*, 10 (7) July, 1957, 24

51. N. Cohn, *Pop from the Beginning*, London, Weidenfeld and Nicolson, 1969, 63.

Chapter 5

1. O. King, 'Ray Bush and the Avon Cities Skiffle', (Tempo 45 EXA40), *Gramophone*, November 1956, 229; 'Ray Bush and the Avon Cities Skiffle', (Tempo EP EXA50), *Gramophone*, February 1957, 349.

2. S. Traill, 'Avon Cities' Skiffle', (Tempo 45 EXA50), *Jazz Journal*, 9 (11) November 1956, 17; G. Boatfield, 'Ray Bush and the Avon Cities Skiffle', (Tempo EXA50), *Jazz Journal*, 10 (2) February 1957.

3. A. McCarthy, 'Ray Bush and the Avon Cities' Skiffle', (Tempo A146), *Jazz Monthly*, 2 (10) December 1956, 23,

4. A. McCarthy, 'Avon Cities' Skiffle Group', (Tempo TAP19), *Jazz Monthly*, 5 (2) April 1959, 13.

5. B. Bird, *Skiffle: the Story of Folk-Song with a Jazz Beat*, London, Hale, 1958, 76.

6. Bird, 74-5.

7. Bird, 77-8.

8. O. King, 'City Ramblers Skiffle Group', (Tempo EP EXA59), *Gramophone*, August 1957, 112; G. Boatfield, 'City Ramblers Skiffle Group', (Tempo EP EXA59), *Jazz Journal*, 10 (9) September 1957, 14.

9. S. Traill, 'City Ramblers Skiffle Group', (Tempo 45/A158), *Jazz Journal*, 10 (7) July 1957, 24; O. King, 'City Ramblers Skiffle Group', (Tempo A158/45A158), *Gramophone*, June 1957, 31.

10. O. King, 'City Ramblers Skiffle Group', (Tempo EP EXA71), *Gramophone*, October 1957, 197; 'City Ramblers Skiffle', (Tempo A165/45A165), *Gramophone,* February 1958, 381; 'City Ramblers', (Tempo EP EXA77), *Gramophone*, September 1958, 167.

11. 'Skiffle Page', *Melody Maker*, 14 December 1957, 6.

12. H. Lührig, *The British Skiffle Groups 1954-1958*, Unna, Germany, The author, 199?.

13. Brian Rust quoted in Lührig.

14. C. Fox, 'Original Barnstormers Spasm Band', (Tempo EP EXA95), *Gramophone*, February 1960,

442; J. Oakland, 'Miscellaneous and Dance: Barnstormers Spasm Band', (Parlophone R4416), *Gramophone,* May 1958, 519; J. Oakland, 'Critics' Choice-1958', (Parlophone R4416), *Gramophone*, December 1958, 292.

15. B. Dawbarn, 'Cort Takes a Holiday', *Melody Maker*, 9 November 1957, 8.

16. 'Skiffling Along', *Leicester Mercury*, 14 February 1957, 12.

17. B. Nicholls, 'Jazzman's Diary', *Jazz Journal*, 10 (3) March 1957, 13.

18. O. King, 'Bob Cort Skiffle: *Ain't it a Shame*', (Decca LP LK4222), *Gramophone*, February 1958, 381.

19. 'Cort at the Crossroads', Undated newspaper cutting, [1957?].

20. 'Small Audience — and Skiffler Bob Explains', *Leicester Evening Mail*, 4 November 1957, 7.

21. 'Leics. Man Gives A.B.C. of Skiffle', *Leicestershire Evening Mail*, 18 October 1957, 6.

22. J. N. S., 'Making the Most of Skiffle', *Melody Maker,* 12 October 1957, 8.

23. 'Return of Skiffler Bob', *Leicester Mercury*, 11 April 1974, 28; 'Listen with Mother... to Bob Cort', *Leicester Mercury*, 13 October 1976, 16; 'Composer Dies', *Loughborough Echo*, 17 July 1982, 1.

24. Bird, 83; 'Leading Line-up', *Reveille*, 23 May 1957, 12.

25. C. McDevitt, *Skiffle: the Definitive Inside Story*, London, Robson, 1997, 82.

26. J. Repsch, *The Legendary Joe Meek: the Telstar Man*, London, Woodford House, 1989, 51.

27. Repsch, 52.

28. Repsch, 59-60.

29. Repsch, 320-1.

30. O. King, 'First National Skiffle Contest', (Esquire

LP 20-089), *Gramophone*, January 1958, 337; S. Traill, 'First National Skiffle Contest', (Esquire LP 20-089), *Jazz Journal*, 11 (1) January 1958, 22.

31. 'Spotlight on Skiffle', *Melody Maker,* 13 April 1957, 6; 'Where to Skiffle in London', *Reveille* 23 May 1957, 10.

32. A. J. McCarthy, *Jazz Discography... January-December 1958*, London, Cassell, 1960, 222.

33. A. Bisset, *Black Roots, White Flowers: a History of Jazz in Australia*, Sydney, Golden, 1979, 17-8.

34. W.H. Miller, 'Australia Sends You Dick Hughes', *Jazz Journal*, 5 (7) July 1952, 2.

35. Bisset, [ii].

36. G. Bell, *Graeme Bell, Australian Jazzman: His Autobiography*, Frenchs Forest, Child, 1988, 246-55, 423; Bisset, 168.

37. D. Boulton, *Jazz in Britain*, London, Allen, 1958, 173

38. G. Boatfield, 'Skiffle Artificial', *Jazz Journal*, 9 (4) April 1956, 2, 4.

39. A. Korner, 'Skiffle or Piffle?', *Melody Maker*, 28 July 1956, 5.

40. K. Colyer, 'P.S ... from Ken Colyer', Melody Maker, 28 July 1956, 5.

41. S. Race, 'Skiffle Isn't Piffle', *Melody Maker*, 2 March 1957, 6.

42. 'Skiffle on Trial', *Melody Maker*, 9 March 1957, 2-3.

43. 'Readers Give Their Verdict on Skiffle', *Melody Maker*, 16 March 1957, 5.

44. M. Jones and S. Traill, 'Rosy View of Skiffle', *Melody Maker*, 6 April 1957, 5.

45. H. Lyttleton, 'Skiffle Purists Are Worried', *Melody Maker*, 29 June 1957, 5.

46. F. Dallas, 'Skiffle Won't Die', *Melody Maker* 6 July 1957, 3.

47. A. Lomax, Skiffle: 'Why Is It So Popular?', *Melody Maker,* 31 August 1957, 3.

48. 'Skiffle? They Call It — the 3-Chord Trick', *Daily Herald*, 6 June 1957, 9.

49. M. Jones, 'The Man Who's Heard It All Before', *Daily Herald*, 8 November 1957, 7.

50. P. Phillips, 'Stars Agree on Skiffle Piffle', *Daily Herald*, 11 February 1958, 2.

51. 'Don't You Mock Us, Daddy-O!', *Daily Herald*, 15 February 1958, 4.

52. 'No Sniffle at Skiffle', *Daily Herald*, 10 March 1958, 9.

53. 'Meet Dr Skiffle', *Daily Herald*, 31 January 1957, 3.

54. 'Skiffle Gets a Legal Boost', *Daily Herald*, 19 July 1957, 3.

55. 'Did You Hear That?', *Listener*, LX (1539), 25 September 1958, 453.

56. P. B. Checkland, 'The Origins of Jazz', (letter), *Listener*, LX (1541), 9 October 1958, 571-2.

57. R. H. S. Tremlett, 'Skiffle or Skiffle' (letter), *Times*, 8 January 1958, 9d; A. M. S. Smith, 'Skiffle or Nothing' (letter), *Times*, 11 January 1958, 7g.

58. Bird, ix.

Chapter 6

1. 'Skiffle Fan is Maths Wizard at 15', *Daily Herald*, 22 September 1958, 8.

2. 'The Skiffle Group's Success in Young England', *Times*, 17 July 1957, 5c.

3. G. Gersh, 'Britain's Skiffle Intelligentsia', *Jazz Review,* 2 (7) August 1959 17.

4. J. Rodker, 'Skiffle', *Mademoiselle*, 46, March 1958, 128.

5. D. Nathan, 'Skiffle's Dead, Says Skiffler No 1', *Daily Herald*, 23 August 1958, 3.

6. N. Cohn, *Pop from the Beginning*, London, Weidenfeld and Nicholson 1969, 63.

7. Vipers Skiffle Group, *Coffee Bar Session*, (Parlophone PMD1050), [1957]. Sleeve note by B. Green.

8. R. Lewis, 'I Was Such a Rebel I Became a Conservative', *Evening Standard*, 16 January 1996, 12.

9. 'Diary', *Guardian*, 14 June 1996.

10. M. J. Ellison, 'Stand and Deliver', *Guardian 2* supplement, 7 March 1996, 12.

11. J. Sale, 'Passed/Failed: Max Clifford', *Independent Education* + supplement, 3 April 1997, 7.

12. 'Fighting Fred in Skiffle Row', *Melody Maker*, 25 January 1958, 4.

13. '£30 "Fines" on 6-5 Skifflers', *Melody Maker*, 8 February 1958, 5.

14. T. Brown, 'Skiffle', *Melody Maker*, 25 January 1958, 3.

15. B. Nicholls, 'Jazzman's Diary', *Jazz Journal,* 10 (9) September 1957, 11.

16. Gersh, 17.

17. '*Reveille* Puts Skiffle on the Map', *Reveille*, 23 May 1957, 10-11.

18. M. A. Price, 'The Old Scholars' Association has Found New Interests for the Young People of Ellesmere', *Shropshire Magazine*, 8 June 1957, 27.

19. 'Rhythm and Blues on Washboard and Two Tea Chests', *Leicester Evening Mail*, 29 December 1956, 4.

20. L. Dex (ed.), *Hull Jazz and Jazzmen*, Hull, Beck Books, 1991, 92.

21. Dex, 110.

22. *Ballymena Observer*, 2 May 1958, 7; 21 June 1957, 1.

23. 'The Roving Spotlight', *Melody Maker*, 6 July 1957, 4.

24. I. King and J. Rickard, *60 Years of Jazz in Croydon — and Beyond, 1930s-1990s*, Croydon, Kings Jazz Review, 1995, 45.

25. 'Skiffle at Barlestone Cinema', *Hinckley Times*, 5 June, 1959, 4.

26. G. Boatfield, 'On the Waterfront', *Jazz Journal*, 11 (9) September 1958, 26.

27. 'Shakespeare, Skiffle, "Rock" and Calypso at this Party', *Market Harborough Advertiser*, 4 July 1957, 9.

28. 'Skiffling on Melton Carnival Day', *Melton Times*, 15 August 1991, 20.

29. F. Dallas, 'Skiffle Won't Die', *Melody Maker*, 6 July 1957, 3.

30. Gersh, 17.

31. 'Skiffle in the Streets: Young Musicians in a South-Western London Suburb', *Times*, 22 October 1958, 12f.

32. National Skiffle Contest, Hardwick, 1957. *Programme*. Includes judges, rules and list of competitors.

33. G. Boatfield, 'An Eye Upon the Skiffle', *Jazz Journal*, 10 (8) August 1957, 5.

34. Boatfield, 6.

35. King and Rickard, 44.

36. 'Skiffle Group's Win', *Ballymena Observer*, 21 March 1958, 12.

37. King and Rickard, 44.

38. 'Satellites Were Top Skifflers on Tuesday Night', *Ballymena Observer*, 28 March 1958, 12; 'Skiffle Contest at Rathkenny', *Ballymena Observer*, 4 April

1958, 9; *Ballymena Observer*, 10 October 1958, 12.

39. 'Merched y Sgiffl', *Yr Aelwyd*, 20 (1) January 1960, 1.

40. B. Cort, *Making the Most of Skiffle*, McGlennon, 1957, 12.

41. Cort, 12.

42. Cort, 13, 15.

43. Cort, 5.

44. D. Lonnigan, 'New Station Skiffle', *Two I's* [Newsletter of Southern Skiffle Society], 1958 edition, [2-4].

45. 'Skifflers Rock the Chaplain-O', *Leicester Mercury*, 13 June 1957, 6.

46. 'Skiffle Lads Get I.T.V. Chance', *Leicester Evening Mail*, 16 August 1957, 9.

47. 'Black Cat Skifflers Refuse B.B.C. Offer', *Leicester Evening Mail*, 9 September 1957, 9.

48. 'City Skifflers Will Be on the 6.5 Special', *Leicester Mercury*, 8 April 1958, 14.

49. Cohn, 62-3.

50. M. Houghton, 'British Beat', in J. Collis (ed.), *The Rock Primer*, Harmondsworth, Penguin, 1980, 151.

Chapter 7

1. British Broadcasting Corporation, *Annual Report and Accounts for the Year 1958-59*. London, HMSO, 1959, 45.

2. 'Fifth BBC Festival of Dance Music', *Radio Times* (Welsh edition), 142 (1844) 13 March 1959, 11.

3. 'Round and About in Sound.' *Radio Times* (Welsh edition), 138 (1785), 24 January 1958, 18.

4. 'Bridging the Gap', *Radio Times* (Welsh edition), 134 (1735) 8 February 1957, 3.

5. BBC Written Archives Centre, T12/360/6, 5 April 1957.

6. 'Points from the Post', *Radio Times* (Welsh edition), 135 (1751) 31 May 1957, 51.

7. 'On the Six-Five', *Radio Times* (Welsh edition), 137 (1780), 20 December 1957, 11.

8. BBC Written Archive Centre, T12/360/11, 18 November 1957.

9. '6.5 Special: the BBC's Hunch that Clicked', *Daily Herald*, 7 October 1957, 3.

10. H. Fielding, 'Five Little Imps Give Out Those Washboard Blues', *Daily Herald*, 1 February 1958, 2.

11. 'Round and About', *Radio Times* (Welsh edition), 138 (1788) 14 February 1958, 5.

12. British Broadcasting Corporation, *Annual Report and Accounts for the Year 1957-58*. London, HMSO, 1958, 46.

13. British Broadcasting Corporation, *BBC Handbook 1959*. London, BBC, [1958], 99.

14. P. Phillips, 'This Gives Me the Pip', *Daily Herald*, 10 February 1958, 3.

15. '"Dig This" is the Answer to "Oh Boy!"', *Daily Herald*, 3 December 1958, 3.

16. 'End of the Line', *Radio Times* (Welsh edition), 141 (1832) 19 December 1958, 11.

17. BBC Written Archives Centre, R/19/1540/1, 8 January 1957.

18. BBC Written Archives Centre, R19/1540/1, 11 March 1957.

19. BBC Written Archives Centre, R19/1540/1, 2 April 1957.

20. BBC Written Archives Centre, R19/1708/1, 15 April 1957.

21. B. Matthew, *This is Where I Came In*, London, Constable, 1991, 121.

22. BBC Written Archives Centre, R19/1540/1, 25 June 1957.

23. BBC Written Archives Centre, R19/1708/1, 8 August 1957; 14 August 1957.

24. 'Saturday Skiffle is the Tops', *Melody Maker*, 23 November 1957, 4; BBC Written Archives Centre, R19/1708/1, 5 June 1958.

25. Matthew, 123.

26. Matthew, 123.

27. 'British Sound Services: Innovations and Alterations', *Radio Times* (Welsh edition), 140 (1820) 26 September 1958, 9.

28. D. Wedge, 'An Invitation to Join Saturday Club', *Radio Times* (Welsh edition), 144 (1864) 31 July 1959, 6.

29. BBC Written Archives Centre, R19/1676/1, 7 October 1955; 6 May 1957.

30. B. Nicholls, 'Jazzman's Diary', *Jazz Journal*, 10 (10) October 1957, 11.

31. 'Round and About', *Radio Times* (Welsh edition),

140 (1816) 29 August 1958, 4.

32. 'Round and About', *Radio Times* (Welsh edition), 144 (1870) 11 September 1959, 5.

33. BBC Written Archives Centre, R19/1676/1. Audience research reports of various dates.

34. B. Hollowood, 'On the Air: Cool for Cats', *Punch*, 27 November 1957, 642.

35. British Broadcasting Corporation, *Annual Report and Accounts for the Year 1959-60*. London, HMSO, 1960, 12,15.

Chapter 8

1. 'Knock-out for the Rock?', *Daily Herald,* 15 January 1958, 3.

2. 'Honesty in Advertising', *Jazz Monthly*, 4 (1) March 1958, 4.

3. 'Punch Diary', *Punch*, 9 April 1958, 472.

4. T. Tremayne, 'The Hell of Skiffle', *Melody Maker*, 19 April 1958, 5.

5. 'Skiffle on the Skids', *Melody Maker*, 17 May 1958, 1, 20.

6. 'Aboard the Sunshine Skiffle', *Melody Maker* , 21 June 1958, 9.

7. B. Jackman, 'Why Skiffle is Skidding', *Melody Maker*, 24 May 1958, 12.

8. D. Nathan, 'Skiffle's Dead, Says Skiffler No.1', *Daily Herald*, 23 August 1958, 3.

9. M. Nevard, 'Skiffle Kings are All Washed Up', *Daily Herald*, 20 September 1958, 2.

10. 'Bell-Boy to Star — in Ten Weeks', *TV Times*, 5 (59) 14 December 1956, 34.

11. P. Pelletier, *1000 Years Ago: Wally Whyton and the Vipers Skiffle Group*, 1996, 10, 12. Booklet accompanying boxed set of 3 CDs (Bear Family Records BCD 15954 Cl) with same title.

12. G. Martin and J. Hornsby, *All You Need is Ears*, London, Macmillan, 1979, 58-9.

13. J. Kennedy, *Tommy Steele*, London, Souvenir, 1958, 15.

14. Kennedy, 16.

15. S. Turner, *Cliff Richard: the Biography*, 2nd edition, Oxford, Lion, 1994, 80.

16. Turner, 81.

17. B. Welch, *Rock 'n' Roll — I Gave You the Best Years of My Life: a Life in the Shadows*, London, Viking, 1989, 38.

18. A. Faith, *Acts of Faith: the Autobiography*, London, Bantam, 1996, 33.

19. M. Read, *The Story of the Shadows*, London, Sphere, 1984, 13-14.

20. Read, 28-9.

21. Read, 42.

22. Faith, 39.

23. B. Bothroyd and A. Atkinson, 'Manual for Popmongers', *Punch*, 30 October 1957, 506-9.

24. D. McAleer, *Hit Parade Heroes: British Beat before the Beatles*, London, Hamlyn, 1993, 96.

25. F. Dallas, 'Skiffle Won't Die', *Melody Maker*, 6 July 1957, 3.

26. C. Ward, 'Sing Me a Song of Social Significance', *Jazz Monthly*, 4 (3) May 1958, 30.

27. J. Hasted, *Alternative Memoirs*, Shipton Green, Itchenor, West Sussex, Greengates, c. 1992, 138.

28. F. Woods, *Folk Revival: the Rediscovery of a National Music*, Poole, Blandford, 1979, 58.

29. F. Woods, *The Observer's Book of Folk Song in Britain*, London, Warne, 1980, 34.

30. D. Stuckey, *The Spinners: Fried Bread and Brandy-O!*, London, Robson, 1985, 20.

31. J. Savage, *The Kinks: the Official Biography*, London, Faber 1984, 6.

32. R. Bainton, *Talk to Me Baby: the Story of the Blues Band*, Poole, Firebird, 1994, 5.

33. L. Donegan, 'Early John Lennon Tape Auction for £78,500 will go into EMI Archives', *Independent*, 16 September 1994, 2g.

34. B. Harry, *The Ultimate Beatles Encyclopedia*, London, Virgin, c. 1992, 204, 292.

35. G. Marsden and R. Coleman, *I'll Never Walk Alone: an Autobiography*, London, Bloomsbury, 1993, 11.

36. Marsden and Coleman, 12.

37. J. Brown and G. Wright, *Brown Sauce: the Life and Times of Joe Brown*, London, Willow, 1986, 47-8.

38. C. Hodges, *The Rock & Roll Years of Chas before Dave*, Wheathampstead, Herts, Lennard, 1987, 36.

39. G. Pawlowski, *How They Became the Beatles: a Definitive History of the Early Years: 1960-1964*, London, Macdonald, 1990, 5; Harry, 336.

40. S. Frith, *Sound Effects: Youth, Leisure and the Politics of Rock*, revised edition, London, Constable, 1983, 96.

Chapter 9

1. J. Buss, 'Still a Breeze for the Tea-chest Rockers', *Bury Free Post*, 22 November 1991, 24, 97.

2. 'Skiffle Veterans Head Home for Nostalgic Final', *Daily Post* (Liverpool), 8 January 1996.

3. 'A Touch of Skiffle, Kink-Style', *Melody Maker*, 11 February 1967, 10-11.

4. M. Kelner, 'Things Couldn't Get Any Worse', *Independent*, 24 September 1993, 17.

5. C. Midgley, 'Band that Gave Birth to Beatles Plays Again', *Times*, 5 July 1997, 3.

6. 'Skiffle on Toast', *Independent: Education Supplement*, 20 March 1997, 5.

7. S. Pratt, 'Skiffle King's Seal of Approval for Paul', *News* (formerly *Portsmouth Evening News*), 17. July 1997, 31.

8. S. Pratt, 'Music Fad Turns Full Circle', *News* (formerly *Portsmouth Evening News*), 17 July 1997, 31.

9. D. Peabody, 'Skiffle Turns 40!', *Folk Roots*, 18 (11) May 1997, 22- 3.

10. C. Larkin (ed.), *Guinness Who's Who of Blues*, 2nd edition, Enfield, Guinness, 1995, 51.

11. C. Larkin (ed.), *Guinness Who's Who of Folk Music,* Enfield, Guinness, 1993, 94-5, 228-9.

12. C. McDevitt, *Skiffle: the Definitive Inside Story*, London, Robson, 1997, 222-3.

13. H. Lührig, *British Skiffle Groups 1954-1958: a Discography with Biographies, Photographs and Background Material*, Unna, Germany, The author, 199?; H. Heunks, *A Short View on Skiffle in the Netherlands and Flanders*, Boekel, Netherlands, The author, [1998].

Select Bibliography

Books

Bainton, R., *Talk to Me Baby: the Story of the Blues Band*, Poole, Firebird, 1994.

Barker, D., *A Life in Jazz*, edited by A. Shipton, London, Macmillan, 1986.

Beaumont, G., *Twentieth-Century Folk Mass for One or More Cantors and Congregation*, London, Weinberger, 1957.

Bell, G., *Graeme Bell, Australian Jazzman: His Autobiography*, Frenchs Forest, New South Wales, Child, 1988.

Bird, B., *Skiffle: the Story of Folk-Song with a Jazz Beat*, London, Hale, 1958.

Bisset, A., *Black Roots, White Flowers: a History of Jazz in Australia*, Sydney, Golden, 1979.

Blesh, R., *Shining Trumpets: a History of Jazz*, 4th edition, London, Cassell, 1958.

Boulton, D., *Jazz in Britain*, London, Allen, 1958.

Bradley, D., *Understanding Rock 'n' Roll: Popular Music in Britain, 1955-1964*, Buckingham, Open University, 1992.

Briggs, A., *The History of Broadcasting in the United Kingdom: Volume 5, Competition* [1955-1974], Oxford, OUP, 1995.

British Broadcasting Corporation, *Annual Report and Accounts for the Year: 1954-55; 1955-56; 1957-58; 1958-59; 1959-60*, London, HMSO, 1955, 1956, 1959, 1960.

British Broadcasting Corporation, *BBC Handbook 1959*, London, BBC, [1958].

Broonzy, W., *Big Bill Blues: William Broonzy's Story*, as told to Yannick Bruynoghe, London, Cassell, 1955.

Brown, C. T., *Music U.S.A.: America's Country and Western Tradition*, Englewood Cliffs, New Jersey, Prentice-Hall, 1986.

Brown, J. and Wright, G., *Brown Sauce: the Life and Times of Joe Brown*, London, Willow, 1986.

Brunning, B., *Blues in Britain*, London, Blandford, 1995.

Bunt, S. and Gargrave, R., *The Politics of Youth Clubs*, Leicester, National Youth Bureau, 1980.

Carey D. and McCarthy, A. J., *Directory of Recorded Jazz and Swing Music (Including Gospel and Blues Records)*, vols 1-4, Fordingbridge, Hants, Delphic, 1949-52; vols 5-6, London, Cassell, 1955, 1957.

Charters, S., *The Country Blues*, London, Joseph, 1960.

Chilton, J., *Who's Who of British Jazz*, London, Cassell, 1997.

Clarke, D., *The Penguin Encyclopedia of Popular Music*, Harmondsworth, Penguin, 1989.

Clarke, D., *The Rise and Fall of Popular Music*, London, Viking, 1995.

Cohn, N., *Pop from the Beginning*, London, Weidenfeld and Nicolson, 1969.

Collis, J., (ed.), *The Rock Primer*, Harmondsworth, Penguin, 1980.

Colyer, K., *When Dreams are in the Dust*, Ryarsh, Kent, Milbury, 1989.

Connolly, R., *John Lennon 1940-1980*, London, Fontana, 1981.

Cort, B., *Making the Most of Skiffle*, McGlennon, 1957.

Courlander, H., *Negro Folk Music, U.S.A.*, New York, Columbia University, 1963.

Davies, H., *The Beatles: the Only Authorised Biography*, London, Arrow, 1992.

Decca Record Co. Ltd, *Jazz on 78s: a Guide to the Many Examples of Classic Jazz on Decca, Brunswick, Vocalion, and London 78 r.m.p. Records*, London, Decca, 1954.

Dex, L., (ed.), *Hull Jazz and Jazzmen*, Hull, Beck Books, c.1991.

Doncaster, P. and Jasper, T., *Cliff*, updated and revised edition, London, Pan, 1993.

Epstein, D. J., *Sinful Tunes and Spirituals: Black Folk Music to the Civil War*, Urbana, University of Illinois, 1977.

Everett, P., *You'll Never Be 16 Again: an Illustrated History of the British Teenager*, London, BBC, 1986.

Faith, A., *Acts of Faith: the Autobiography*, London, Bantam, 1996.

Faith, A., *Poor Me*, London, Four Square, 1961.

Frith, S., *Sound Effects: Youth, Leisure, and the Politics of Rock*, revised edition, London, Constable, 1983.

Gambaccini, P., Rice, T., and Rice, J., *British Hit Singles*, 10th edition, Enfield, Guinness, 1995.

Geddes, G., *The Shadows: a History and Discography*, Glasgow, G. and M. Geddes, 1981.

Gillett, C., *The Sound of the City: the Rise of Rock 'n' Roll*, London, Souvenir, 1972.

Godbolt, J. A., *A History of Jazz in Britain, 1919-50*, London, Paladin, 1986.

Godbolt, J. A., *A History of Jazz in Britain, 1950-1970*, London, Quartet, 1989.

Goodrich, J. and Dixon, R. W., *Blues and Gospel Records 1902-1942*, second edition, London, Storyville, 1969.

Harris, N., *The Forties and Fifties: an Illustrated History in Colour, 1945-1959*, London, Macdonald, 1975.

Harry, B., *The Ultimate Beatles Encyclopedia*, London, Virgin, c. 1992.

Hasted, J., *Alternative Memoirs*, Shipton Green, Itchenor, West Sussex, Greengates, c. 1992.

Hastings, V., *Jo and the Skiffle Group*, London, Parish, 1958.

Heunks, H., *A Short View of Skiffle in the Netherlands and Flanders,* Boekel Netherlands. The author, [1998].

Hodges, C., *The Rock & Roll Years of Chas Before Dave*, Wheathampstead, Herts, Lennard, 1987.

Hogg, B., *The History of Scottish Rock and Pop: All That Ever Mattered*, Enfield, Guinness, 1993.

Kennedy, J., *Tommy Steele: the Facts About a Teenage Idol and 'Inside' Picture of Show Business*, London, Souvenir, 1958.

Kennington, D. and Read, D. L., *Literature of Jazz: a Critical Guide*, 2nd edition, London, Library Association, 1980.

Kernfield, B., (ed.), *New Grove Dictionary of Jazz*, London, Macmillan, 1988.

King, I., and Rickard, J., *60 Years of Jazz in Croydon — and Beyond, 1930s-1990s,* Croydon, Kings Jazz Review, 1995.

Langley, A., *A Family in the Fifties*, Hove, Wayland, 1986.

Larkin, C., (ed.), *Guinness Encyclopedia of Popular Music*, 6 vols, Enfield, Guinness, 1995.

Larkin, C., (ed.), *Guinness Who's Who of Blues*, 2nd edition, Enfield, Guinness, 1995.

Larkin, C., (ed.), *Guinness Who's Who of Fifties Music*, Enfield, Guinness, 1993.

Larkin, C., (ed.), *Guinness Who's Who of Folk Music*, Enfield, Guinness, 1993.

Larkin, C., (ed.), *Guinness Who's Who of Sixties Music*, Enfield, Guinness, 1992.

Lawless, R. M., *Folksingers and Folksongs in America: a Handbook of Biography*, Bibliography, and Discography, New York, Duell, Sloan and Pearce, 1960.

Leigh, S., *Halfway to Paradise: Britpop, 1955-1962*, Folkestone, Finbarr, 1996.

Leslie, P., *FAB: the Anatomy of a Phenomenon*, London, MacGibbon and Kee, 1965.

Lewis, P., *The Fifties*. London, Heinemann, 1978.

Lister, D. A. J., *Bradford's Rock 'n' Roll: the Golden Years (1959-1965)*, Bradford, Bradford Libraries and Information Service, 1991.

Lonnie Donegan, London, Amalgamated Press, 1958. (Fan's Star Library, No. 12).

Lührig, H., *British Skiffle Groups 1954-1958: a Discography with Biographies, Photographs and Background Material*, Unna, Germany, The author, 199?.

McAleer, D., *Beatboom!: Pop Goes the Sixties*, London, Hamlyn, 1994.

McAleer, D., *Hit Parade Heroes: British Beat Before the Beatles*, London, Hamlyn, 1993.

McAleer, D., *Warner Guide to UK & US Hit Singles*, London, Carlton/Little Brown, 1994.

McCarthy, A. J., *Jazz Discography 1: an International Discography of Recorded Jazz... for the Year January-December 1958*, London, Cassell, 1960.

McDevitt, C., *Skiffle: The Definitive Inside Story*, London, Robson, 1997.

Mairants, I., *My Fifty Fretting Years: a Personal History of the Twentieth Century Guitar Explosion*, Gateshead, Ashley Mark,1980.

Marsden, G. and Coleman, R., *I'll Never Walk Alone: an Autobiography*, London, Bloomsbury, 1993.

Martin, G. and Hornsby, J., *All You Need Is Ears*, London, Macmillan, 1979.

Matthew, B., *This Is Where I Came In*, London, Constable, 1991.

Melly, G. *Revolt into Style: the Pop Arts in Britain*, London, Allen Lane, 1970.

Murray, P., *One Day I'll Forget My Trousers*, London, Everest,1975.

New Musical Express, *Annual, 1956; 1957; 1959; 1960; 1961; 1962*; London, NME, 1956, 1957, 1959, 1960, 1961, 1962.

Norman, P., *Shout!: the True Story of the Beatles*, London, Penguin, 1993.

Oliver, P., *Conversation with the Blues*, 2nd edition, London, Cassell, 1966.

Oliver, P., *Savannah Syncopators: African Retentions in the Blues*, London, Studio Vista, 1970.

Oliver, P., *The Story of the Blues*, Harmondsworth, Penguin, 1972.

Olsson, B., *Memphis Blues and Jug Bands*, London, Studio Vista, 1970.

Palmer, T., *All You Need Is Love: the Story of Popular Music*, London, Futura, 1977.

Panassié, H. and Gautier, M., *Dictionary of Jazz*, London, Cassell, 1956.

Pascall, J., *Growing up in the Fifties*, Hove, Wayland, 1980.

Pawlowski, G., *How They Became the Beatles: a Definitive History of the Early Years: 1960-1964*, London, Macdonald, 1990.

Pelletier, P., *10000 Years Ago: Wally Whyton and the Vipers Skiffle Group*, 1996. Booklet accompanying boxed set of 3 CDs, BCD 15954 C1, (Vollersode, Germany, Bear Family Records) with same title.

Platt, J., *London's Rock Routes*, London, Fourth Estate, 1966.

Ramsey, F., *Been Here and Gone*, London, Cassell, 1960.

Ramsey, F. and Smith, C. E., (eds.), *Jazzmen*, London, Sidgwick and Jackson, 1957.

Read, M., *The Story of the Shadows*, London, Sphere, 1984.

Rees, D., and Crampton, L., *Guinness Book of Rock Stars*, 3rd edition, Enfield, Guinness, 1994.

Repsch, J., *The Legendary Joe Meek: the Telstar Man*, London, Woodford House, 1989.

Richard, C., *It's Great to be Young: My Teenage Story and Life in Show Business*, London, Souvenir Press, 1960.

Richard, C., *Which One's Cliff?*, revised edition, London, Hodder and Stoughton 1990.

Rogers, D., *Rock 'n' Roll*, London, Routledge and Kegan Paul, 1982.

Rust, B., *Jazz Records: 1897-1942*, 2 vols, New York, Arlington House, 1969.

Rust, B., *My Kind of Jazz*, London, Elm Tree, 1990.

Savage, J., *The Kinks: the Official Biography*, London, Faber, 1984.

Scott, P., *When I Was Young in the Fifties*, London, Watts, 1993.

Shapiro, H., *Alexis Korner: the Biography*, London, Bloomsbury ,1996.

Shapiro, N. and Hentoff, N., *Hear Me Talkin' to Ya: the Story of Jazz as Told by the Men Who Made It*, New York, Dover, 1966. (Originally published in 1955).

Shaw, A., *The Rock Revolution*, London, Collier-Macmillan, 1969.

Stacy, T., *Decades: the Fifties*, Hove, Wayland, 1989.

Stambler, I., *Encyclopedia of Pop, Rock and Soul*, revised edition, London, Macmillan, 1989.

Stuckey, D., *The Spinners: Fried Bread and Brandy-O!*, London, Robson, 1985.

Tanner, J. F., *Hits Through the Years, the Rock 'n' Roll Era, 1956-1962*, Whitley Bay, JFT-Valid Records, 1992.

Taylor, P., *Popular Music Since 1955: a Critical Guide to the Literature*, London, Mansell, 1985.

Turner, S., *Cliff Richard: the Biography*, 2nd edition, Oxford, Lion, 1994.

Turner, S., *Van Morrison: Too Late to Stop Now*, London, Bloomsbury, 1993.

Van der Merwe, P., *Origins of the Popular Style: the Antecedents of Twentieth-Century Popular Music*, Cambridge, Clarendon, 1989.

Vansittart, P., *In the Fifties*, London, Murray, 1995.

Weedon, B., *Play in a Day: Guide to Modern Guitar Playing*, 30th anniversary edition, London, Chappell, 1987.

Welch, B., *Rock 'n' Roll — I Gave You the Best Years of My Life: a Life in the Shadows*, London, Viking, 1989.

Whitcomb, I., *After the Ball: Pop Music from Rag to Rock*, Harmondsworth, Penguin, 1972.

Woods, F., *Folk Revival: the Rediscovery of a National Music*, Poole, Blandford, 1979.

Woods, F., *The Observer's Book of Folk Song in Britain*, London,Warne, 1980.

Periodicals and Newspapers

Articles and other items providing contemporary news and opinions about skiffle used in the preparation of this book were mainly taken from: *Daily Herald, Gramophone, Jazz Journal, Jazz Monthly, Melody Maker, Punch, Radio Times* (Welsh edition), *The Times*, and *TV Times*. Other sources included: *Daily Mail, Diapason, English Dance and Song, Evening Standard, Folk Roots, Footnote, Guardian, Illustrated London News, Independent, Jazz Review, Listener, Mademoiselle, Mirabelle, Musical Opinion, Musical Times, New Musical Express, New York Times, Reveille, Skiffle Party Magazine* (Southern Skiffle Society), *Times Educational Supplement, Two I's* (Southern Skiffle Society newsletter), *Variety, Woman*, and *Yr Aelwyd*. In addition information was culled from a number of local newspapers and magazines. Full citations for individual items are listed in the References on pages 227-234.

Archives

BBC Written Archives Centre: R19/1,676 (*Guitar Club*, 1955-1962); R19/1,540 (*Saturday Club*, formerly *Saturday Skiffle Club*, 1957-); T12/360 (*Six-Five Special*, 1957-1959) and R19/1,708 (*Jazz*, 1956-1960).

Skiffle Discography 1954-1958
by Paul Redmond Drew

This is a *select* discography. It does not claim to be comprehensive in its coverage, but attempts to record the most important groups active in the period when skiffle was at its height of popularity. There are two exceptions to the end date of 1958. Both Ken Colyer and Lonnie Donegan were recording skiffle after 1958 so their entries include material after the cut-off date. Also included (at the end of the discography) are a few important compilations available on the Bear, Lake, and Rollercoaster labels.

Groups are arranged in alphabetical order, usually by surname if appropriate (e.g. Graeme Bell's Skiffle Gang under B, Jimmy Miller and the Barbecues under M). There then follows (where known) the personnel for the individual records shown. Details of the records are then laid out in four columns, with the record title (if there is one) shown in italics before the detailed information:

1. The matrix number of the track.
2. The track title.
3. The record number (preceded by the name of the record company).
4. The date of recording, with the place of recording shown in brackets below. (Unless shown otherwise all the rest of the tracks following will be the same location).

The order of records shown is either 78's/45's, followed by EP's and LP's. Some tracks show two record numbers (e.g. N15116/7N15116) — the first will be the 78, the second the 45rpm record. If the full recording date is not known, either the month and year or just the year are given.

The record labels that are abbreviated are as follows:

Col	Columbia
Dec	Decca
FA	Folkway
KCS	K C Records
Par	Parlophone
Pye	Pye-Nixa
77	77 Records
Sto	Storyville
Tpo	Tempo

Those who wish to consult fuller discographies will find the following of interest: *The British Skiffle Groups 1954-1958: A Discography with Biographies, Photographs and Background Material*, compiled by Holger Lührig, and the recently published *Skiffle: The Definitive Inside Story* by Chas McDevitt.

Attempting to give a full and accurate record has only been possible with the fullest co-operation of many people. The compiler would particularly like to express gratitude to Andrew Simon of the British Library National Sound Archive in London, and his colleague Paul Wilson, who assisted in providing many of the records mentioned in this discography.

American Skiffle Bands   FA 2610   1954/1956

The Mobile Strugglers

Ollie Crenshaw (kazoo, gtr, voc.); Moochie Reeves (gtr, voc.); Tyler Jackson (washtub bass, voc.)

Raise A Ruckus Tonight	18.7.1954	
Rock Me, Baby	(Mobile)	
My Bonnie Lies Over The Ocean		
Trouble Trouble's Followed Me All My Days		

Virgil Perkins and Jack Sims

Virgil Perkins (kazoo, washboard, voc.); Jack Sims (12-string gtr).

Goin' Around The Mountain	6.11.1955
John Henry	(Houston)

The Memphis Jug Band and Gus Cannon

Will Shade (harmonica, voc. (3); Charlie Burse (tenor gtr, voc. (1)); Gus Cannon (jug, 5-string banjo, voc. (2)).

Harmonica And Guitar Blues	5.12.1956
Tippin' 'Round (1)	(Memphis)
Old John Booker, You Call That Gone (2)	
Kansas City Blues (2)	
What You Gonna Do, Baby, When	
Your Troubles Get Like Mine (2)	
Take Your Fingers Off It (3)	

Avon Cities Skiffle

Ray Bush (voc, gtr); Wayne Chandler (gtr, bjo (1)); Mike Hitchings (mandolin); Geoff Nicholls (bass); Basil Wright (washboard).

VOG 894	Hey, Hey Daddy Blues (1)	Tpo A141;	30.6.1956
VOG 895	Green Corn (1)	45A146	(London)
	Fisherman's Blues (1)	Tpo A149	30.6.1956
	This Little Light Of Mine (1)		
	How Long, How Long Blues	Tpo A156	30.6.1956
	Julian Johnson		
	I Don't Know	Tpo A157	30.6.1956
	Lonesome Day Blues		
VOG 889	How Long, How Long, Blues?	Tpo EXA40	30.6.1956
VOG 892	I Don't Know		
VOG 890	Julian Johnson		
VOG 891	Lonesome Day Blues		

240

VOG 888	Fisherman's Blues (1)	Tpo EXA 50	30.6.1956
	Hey Hey Daddy Blues (1)		
VOG 893	This Little Light Of Mine (1)		
	Green Corn (Come Along Charlie) (1)		

Ray Bush (voc, gtr); Mike Hitchings (mandolin); Geoff Nicholls (bass); Basil Wright (washboard).

	I'm On My Way To Canaan Land	Tpo TAP18	26.4.1958
	Hand Me Down My Walking Cane		
	House Of The Rising Sun		
	Roll 'em Pete		

The Arthur Baird Skiffle Group (featuring Jack Taylor)

| M.3480 | Union Train | Beltona BL.2669 |
| M.3483 | Union Maid | |

Chris Barber's Skiffle Group

Chris Barber (bass); Johnny Duncan (mandolin, gtr, voc, solo voc in (2)); Dick Bishop (gtr, voc, solo voc in (1)); Ron Bowden (drs).

00.1014-A	Doin' My Time (2)	Pye NJ.2014;	14.9.1956
00.1014-B	Where Could I Go? (2)	7NJ2014	(London)
	Can't You Line 'Em (1)	Pye NJ.2017;	
	Gypsy Davy (1)	7NJ2017	14.9.1956
UU1025A	Can't You Line 'Em? (1)	Pye NJE1025	14.9.1956
	Doin' My Time (2)		
UU1025B	Gypsy Davy (1)		
	Where Could I Go? (2)		

Barnstormers Spasm Band

John Gunn (kazoo, voc.); Johnny Wadley (harmonica, voc.); John Denning (bjo); Jim Robinson (gtr); Pete Wadley (string bass); Brian Rust (drs, washboard, voc.).

CE 16027	Whistling Rufus	Par R4416	11.2.1958
CE 16028	Won't You Come Home Bill Bailey		(London)
	Stormin' The Barn	Tpo A168	3.2.1959
	That's All There Is		
	Shine	Tpo EXA95	3.2.1959
	Tiger Rag		
	Stormin' The Barn		
	That's All There Is		

Graeme Bell's Skiffle Gang

Graeme Bell (p, cel.); Charlie Morrow (gtr); Jeff Mack (gtr); Fred Logan (sb); John Sangster (wb); Vic Sabrino (voc.); Geoff Kitchen (cl (1) ts (2)).

CT3817	Sweet Georgia Brown	Col DO3872	17.7.1957
CT3818	Freight Train		(Sydney)
CT2819	John Henry	Col DO3887	
CT3820	Don't You Rock Me Daddy-O		
CT3821	The Gospel Train	Col DO3888	8.8.1957
CT3822	Come Skiffle Chicken (1)		

| CT3823 | Gamblin' Man | Col DO3875 | 8.8.1957 |
| CT3824 | Skiffle Board Blues (2) | | |

Dickie Bishop and his Sidekicks

Dick Bishop (gtr, voc.); Don Wilson (bass); Pete Korrison (gtr, mandolin); Stan Bell-wood (drums).

RSX. 1050	Cumberland Gap	Dec F.10869	1957
RSX. 1051	No Other Baby		(London)
	Please Remember Me	Dec F.10959	1957
	The Prisoner's Song		
RSX. 1051	No Other Baby	Dec F.10981	1957
RSX. 1094	Skip To My Lou		
	Jumpin' Judy	Dec F.11028	1958
	They Can't Take That Away From Me		

Blue Jeans Skiffle Group

Rockin' at the 2 I's
| DRL.3821 | Lonesome Traveller | Dec LF1300 | 1958 |
| DRL.3822 | When I Get To Glory | | (London) |

Beryl Bryden's Backroom Skiffle

Beryl Bryden (voc., washboard); Alexis Korner (acoustic gtr, voc. (1)); Cyril Davies (voc. (1), acoustic gtr, harmonica (2)); Frank Clarke (drs); Dave Stevens (piano).

| | Casey Jones (1) | Dec F-J-10823 | 9.11.1956 |
| | Kansas City Blues (2) | | (London) |

Johnny Christmas and the Sunspots

Johnny Christmas (gtr, voc.); Bob Neil (ukulele, bjo, voc); Robby Robinson (harmonica, bongos); Al Simmons (bass); John (Tubby) Hill (tea-chest bass).

I'm Gonna Sing Sing Sing
	Mister and Mississippi	Starlite	15.3.1958
	Black, Brown and White	ST EP 5	(London)
	Lost Love		
	Harmonica Train Blues		
	Sing, Sing, Sing		

City Ramblers Skiffle Group

Russell Quaye (kazoo, gtr, voc); Hylda Sims (gtr, voc); Chris Bateson (tpt-mouthpiece); Anthony " Bo Bo" Buquet (tub-bass); Alan "Little Bear" Sutton (washboard); Henrik Johansen (clt (1)); Jack Elliott (gtr, voc (2)).

	When The Saints	Sto A45 004	12.9.1956
	Mama Don't Allow (1)		(Copenhagen)
	Midnight Special (2)	Sto A45 501	12.9.1956
	I Shall Not Be Moved		
	I Want A Girl (1)	Sto A45 508	12.9.1956
	900 Miles		
	I Want A Girl (1)	Tpo EXA591;	12.9.1956
	2.19 Blues (1)	Sto SEP 327	
	Mama Don't Allow (1)		
	900 Miles		

	I Shall Not Be Moved	Sto SEP 345	12.9.1956
	Picket Line		
	When The Saints (Go Marching In)		
	Midnight Special (2)		

Russell Quaye (quattro, kazoo, voc); Hylda Sims (gtr, voc); Pete Maynard (tub-bass); Shirley Bland (washboard); Chris Bateson (jug (2), blue-blower); Jimmie McGregor (gtr, voc (1)).

VOG 1322	Ella Speed	Tpo A158;	22.1.1957
VOG 1323	2.19 Blues	45A158	(London)
	Tom Dooley (1)	Tpo A161;	11.4.1957
	Mama Don't Allow (1&2)	45A161	
	Good Morning Blues (1)	Tpo EXA71	11.4.1957
	Down By The Riverside (1)		
	Grey Goose (1)		
	Jubilee (1)		

Russell Quaye (quattro, voc (1)); Jimmie Mcgregor (gtr, voc (1)); Eric Bunyon (vln); Hylda Sims (gtr, voc (2)); Victor Pitt (bass); Chris Bateson (jug (1), blue blower); Shirley Bland (washboard).

VOG 2468	Boodle-Am-Shake (1)	Tpo A165;	29.10.1957
VOG 2465	Delia's Gone (2)	45A165	(London)
	Delia's Gone (2)	Tpo EXA77	1957
	Keep Your Pistol Good And Loaded		
	Careless Love		
	Boodle-Am-Shake (1)		

The Coffee Bar Skifflers

Skiffle Session

	River Line	Embassy	1958
	She's Solid Gone	WEP 1008	(London)
	Frankie & Johnny		
	Steamboat Bill		
	Ella Speed		
	Bad Man Stack-O-Lee		

Ken Colyer's Skiffle Group

Ken Colyer (gtr, voc.); Diz Disley (national steel gtr); Alexis Korner (gtr, mandolin (1)); Micky Ashman (bass); Bill Colyer (washboard).

Back To The Delta

	Midnight Special (1)	Dec LF 1196	25.6.1954
	Casey Jones		(London)
	K. C. Moan		

Ken Colyer (gtr, voc.); Alexis Korner (gtr, mandolin (1)); John Bastable (bjo, gtr (1); Dick Smith (bass); Bill Colyer (washboard).

DRX20969	Take This Hammer	Dec F.10631;	28.7.1955
DRX20970	Down By The Riverside	F-J.10631	(London)
DRX20971	Go Down, Old Hannah (1)	Dec F.10711;	28.7.1955
DRX20972	Streamline Train	F-J.10711	
DRX20969	Take This Hammer	Dec DFE6286	28.7.1955
DRX20970	Down By The Riverside		
DRX20971	Go Down, Old Hannah (1)		
DRX20972	Streamline Train		

Ken Colyer (gtr, voc.); John Bastable (banjo); Mickey Ashman (bass); Colin Bowden (washboard).

	Down Bound Train Muleskinner Blues	Dec F-J.10751	25.5.1956 (London)
DRX.22014 DRX.22016	Old Riley Stack- O'Lee Blues	Dec F-J.10772	25.5.1956
	Downbound Train Muleskinner Blues Old Riley Stack-o-Lee Blues	Dec DS3271/1-2	25.5.1956

Ken Colyer (gtr, voc.); Bob Kelly (pno); John Bastable (banjo); Ron Ward (bass); Colin Bowden (washboard); Ray Foxley (pno (1)).

DRX.23153 DRX.23156	The Grey Goose I Can't Sleep	Dec F-J.10889	12.3.1957 (London)
	Sporting Life House Rent Stomp	Dec F.10926; F-J.10926	12.3.1957
	Ella Speed Go Down Sunshine	Dec F-J.10972	12.3.1957
	Ella Speed (1) Go Down Sunshine (1) This Train (1) Midnight Hour Blues (1)	Dec DFE6444	11.11.1957

Ken Colyer (gtr, voc.); John Bastable (gtr, banjo); Ron Ward (bass); Colin Bowden (drs), Ray Foxley (pno); Mac Duncan (backing voc.).

The Ken Colyer Skiffle Group in Hamburg

	Ham 'n Eggs Nobody Knows The Trouble I've Seen Down By The Riverside	Dec DFE6563	3.3.1958 (Hamburg)

Ken Colyer (gtr, voc); John Bastable (bjo); Bob Kelly (pno); Ron Ward (bass); Colin Bowden (washboard).

Ken Colyer Skiffle Group

	New York Town Green Corn Casey Jones I Can't Sleep	KCS 11 EP	21.7.1965 (Twickenham)

Wanderin

	I'm Going To Walk And 　Talk With Jesus No Letters Today Colorado Trail Ella Speed Poor Howard I Can't Sleep Mule Skinner Blues Wanderin' If I Could Hear My Mother Pray Again Good Morning Blues Drop Down Baby Easy Ridin' Buggy	KCS 1001	21.7.1965

Ken Colyer (gtr, voc); John Bastable (bjo); Bill Cole (bass); Malcolm Murphy (washboard (1).

The Best Of Skiffle

	Alabamy Bound	Metronome	10.10.1966
	House Rent Stomp	200 104	(Hamburg)
	Take This Hammer (1)	Metronome	5.11.1968
	Ballad Of The Grey Goose (1)	WAM MLP	(Hamburg)
		15.399	

The Bob Cort Skiffle Group

Bob Cort (gtr, voc); Ken Sykora (gtr); Neville Skrimshire (gtr); George Jennings (bass); Viv 'Clambake' Carter (washboard (2); Bill Colyer (washboard); Liz Winters (vocal (1)).

DRX.22472	It Takes A Worried Man	Dec F.10831;	1957
DRX.22473	Don't You Rock Me, Daddy-O	F-J.10831	(London)
DRX.23280	Freight Train (1)	Dec F.10878	1957
DRX.23281	Love Is Strange (1)		
	Roll Jen Jenkins	Dec F.10892	1957
	Six Five Special		
DRX.23371	Jessamine (1)	Dec F.10899	1957
DRX.23372	Maggie May (1)		
	Ain't It A Shame	Dec F.10905	1957
	School Days		

Skiffle Party Parts 1 and 2

DRX.23844	Last Train to San Fernando (2)	Dec F.10951	1957
	Bring A Little Water Sylvie (2)		
	Rock Island Line (2)		
	Cumberland Gap (2)		
	Maggie May		
DRX.23845	Dont You Rock Me Daddy-O	Dec F.10989	1957
	Puttin' On The Style (2)		
	Ain't It A Shame		
	The Ark (2)		
	Yes Suh		

Bob Cort and Liz Winters

	Freight Train	Dec DFE6409	1957
	Don't You Rock Me Daddy-O		
	Maggie May		
	Six-Five Special		

Bob Cort (voc, gtr (1) & (2)); Ken Sykora (solo gtr (3), gtr (1)); Neville Skrimshire (gtr (1) & (3)); George Jennings (bass (1) & (3)); Viv 'Clambake' Carter (washboard (1); alt. with Bill Colyer), brushes (3)).

Ain't It A Shame To Sing Skiffle On Sunday

	Eight More Miles To Louisville (1)	Dec LK4222	28.6.1957
	Don't Stay Away (1)		(London)
	I'm Just A Country Boy (2)		
	This Land Is Your Land (1)		
	West Virginia Snow (1)		
	The Streets Of Laredo (2)		
	I Can't Give You Anything But Love (3)		
	Yes, Suh! (1)		
	The Frozen Logger (2)		
	Where'd You Get Your Whiskey (1)		
	You're Feet's Too Big (1)		
	Lulu's Back In Town (2)		
	Bouncing Around (3)		
	Ain't It A Shame (To Sing Skiffle on Sunday) (1)		

The Cranes Skiffle Group

Chas McDevitt (gtr, voc, whistling); Denny Carter (gtr, voc, whistling); Alex White-house (gtr, voc); John Paul (bass, voc); Marc Sharratt (washboard), Jimmie McGregor (gtr, voc), Jack Baverstock (biscuit tin, brushes (1).

X.6370	Don't You Rock Me Daddy-O	Embassy	3.1957
	The Banana Boat Song (1)	WB. 223	(London)
X.9003	Freight Train	Embassy	3.1957
	Cumberland Gap	WB. 238	

The Delta Skiffle Group

Douglas Taylor (gtr, voc, bjo (1); Don Finlayson, Tucker Finlayson (gtrs); Ian 'Ogg' Couper (bass); Hank Smith (washboard).

	John Brown's Body	Esquire 10-504	25.6.1957
	Skip To My Lou		(London)
	K. C. Moan	Esquire 10-507	25.6.1957
	Pick A Bale Of Cotton		
	Open Them Up	Esquire 10-517	25.6.1957
	Ain't You Glad		
	Skip To My Lou (1)	Esquire EP 162	25.6.1957
	Pick A Bale of Cotton		
	K. C. Moan		
	John Brown's Body (1)		

First National Skiffle Contest

	John Brown's Body (1)	Esquire 20-089	25.6.1957
	Skip To My Lou (1)		

Lonnie Donegan Skiffle Group

Lonnie Donegan (gtr, voc.); Chris Barber (bass); Beryl Bryden (washboard).

	Rock Island Line	Dec LF1198	13.7.1954
	John Henry		(London)
	Rock Island Line	Dec F 10647	13.7.1954
	John Henry		

Lonnie Donegan (voc, gtr); Chris Barber (bass, voc (1)); Pat Halcox (voc (1), pno (2)); Jim Bray (bjo (2); Ron Bowden (drs (2)). Recorded at the N.J.F. Traditional Jazz Concert, Royal Festival Hall.

DR20034	I Don't Care Where They	Dec LK4088	30.10.1954
	Bury My Body (1)		(London)
DR20035	Diggin' My Potatoes (2)		
	Diggin' My Potatoes (2)	Dec F-J10695	30.10.1954
	Bury My Body (1)		
	Rock Island Line	Dec DFE 6345	13.7.1954
	John Henry		
	Diggin' My Potatoes (2)		30.10.1954
	Bury My Body (1)		

Lonnie Donegan, Dick "Cisco" Bishop (gtrs, vocs); Chris Barber (harmonica); Pete Korrison (mandolin); Jim Bray (bass); Bob Watson (voc).

246

Backstairs Session

PE7014	Midnight Special	Pye JTE107;	19.5.1955
	New Burying Ground	NJE.1014	(London)
PE7015	Worried Man Blues		
	When The Sun Goes Down		

Lonnie Donegan (gtr); Dick Bishop (gtr); Chris Barber (bass); Ron Bowden (drs).

Skiffle Session

UU1017-A	Railroad Bill	Pye NJE1017	4.4.1956
	Stackalee		4.4.1956
UU1017-B	The Ballad of Jesse James		11.1.1956
	Ol'Riley		(London)
XX.1036-A	Lost John	Pye N.15036	20.2.1956
XX.1036-B	Stewball		

Lonnie Donegan (gtr, voc), Denny Wright (gtr); Micky Ashman (bass); Nick Nicholls (drums).

| XX.1071-A | Dead or Alive | Pye N15071 | 2.8.1956 |
| XX.1071-B | Bring a Little Water, Sylvie | | |

Lonnie Donegan Hit Parade — Vol. 1

	Lost John	Pye NEP 24031	20.2.1956
	Stewball		
	Bring A Little Water, Sylvie		2.8.1956
	Dead Or Alive		
	I'm Alabammy Bound	Pye N.15080	22/23.8.
	Don't You Rock Me Daddy-O		1956

Lonnie Donegan Showcase

ZZ.1012-A	Wabash Cannonball	Pye NPT19012	22/23.8.
	How Long, How Long Blues		1956
	Nobody's Child		
	I Shall Not Be Moved		
ZZ.1012-B	I'm Alabammy Bound		
	I'm A Ramblin' Man		
	Wreck of the Old "97"		
	Frankie and Johnny		

Lonnie Donegan (gtr, vocal); Dick Bishop (gtr, vocal); Chris Barber (bass, vocal); Ron Bowden (drs).

Donegan On-Stage

	Mule-Skinner Blues	Pye NEP 24075	25.1.1957
	Old Hannah		
	On A Monday		
	Glory		

Lonnie Donegan (gtr, voc), Denny Wright (gtr); Micky Ashman (bass); Nick Nicholls (drums).

| XX.1087-A | Cumberland Gap | Pye N15087 | 24.2.1957 |
| XX.1087-B | Love Is Strange | | |

Lonnie Donegan Hit Parade — Vol. 2

	Don't You Rock Me Daddy-O	Pye NEP 24040	22/23.8.1956
	I'm Alabammy Bound		
	Cumberland Gap		24.2.1957
	Love Is Strange		

Lonnie Donegan (gtr, bjo, voc), Jimmy Currie (gtr, voc); Micky Ashman (bass); Nick Nicholls (drums), Miki and Griff (backing voc (1)).

| XX.1093-A | Putting On The Style | Pye N15093 | 9.5.1957 |
| XX.1093-B | Gamblin' Man | | |

247

| | My Dixie Darling (1) | Pye N.15108 | 28.8.1957 |
| | I'm Just A Rolling Stone | | |

Lonnie Donegan Hit Parade — Vol 3

	Puttin' On The Style	PyeNEP 24067	9.5.1957
	Gamblin' Man		
	My Dixie Darling (1)		28.8.1957
	I'm Just A Rollin' Stone		

Lonnie Donegan (gtr, voc, whistle); Jimmy Currie (gtr); Micky Ashman (bass); Nick Nicholls (drums); Miki and Griff (backing voc).

XX.1116-A	Jack O'Diamonds	Pye N15116;	1958
XX.1116-B	Ham 'n' Eggs	7N15116	
	Nobody Loves Like An Irishman	Pye N15129;	4.1958
	The Grand Coulee Dam	7N15129	

Lonnie Donegan Hit Parade — Vol 4

	Grand Coulee Dam	Pye NEP 24081	11.1957
	Ham 'N' Eggs		
	Nobody Loves Like An Irishman		
	Jack O'Diamonds		

Lonnie Donegan (gtr, voc), Jimmy Currie (gtr); Micky Ashman (bass); Nick Nicholls (drums); Miki and Griff (backing voc).

| | Betty, Betty, Betty | Pye N15148 | 1958 |
| | Sally, Don't You Grieve | | |

Lonnie Donegan (gtr, voc, whistle), Jimmy Currie (gtr); Micky Ashman (bass); Nick Nicholls (drums), John Cole (harmonica), Miki and Griff (backing voc).

| | Times Are Getting Hard | Pye 7N15158 | 1958 |
| | Lonesome Traveller | | |

Lonnie Donegan (gtr, voc); Les Bennetts (gtr, voc); Pete Huggett (bass); Nick Nicholls (drums); Miki and Griff (backing voc (1)).

XX.1172-A	Tom Dooley (1)	Pye N.15172;	1958
45.XX1172-A		7N 15172	
XX.1172-B	Rock O' My Soul		
45.XX.1172-B			

Lonnie Donegan (gtr, voc), Jimmy Currie (gtr (3, 4)); Les Bennetts (gtr, voc (1, 2); Pete Huggett (bass (1, 2)); Micky Ashman (bass (3, 4); Nick Nicholls (drums); Miki and Griff (backing voc (1, 3, 4)).

Lonnie Donegan Hit Parade — Vol 5

	Tom Dooley (1)	Pye NEP 24104	11.1958
	Rock O' My Soul (2)		10.1958
	Sally Don't You Grieve (3)		11.1957
	Betty, Betty, Betty (4)		4.1958

Lonnie Donegan (gtr, voc, whistle), Jimmy Currie (gtr); Micky Ashman (bass); Nick Nicholls (drums), John Cole (harmonica), Miki and Griff (backing voc).

Lonnie

ZZ.1027-A	Lonesome Traveller	Pye NPT19027	11.3.1958
	The Sunshine Of His Love		12.3.1958
	Ain't No More Cane On The Brazos		19.3.1958
	Ain't You Glad You've Got Religion?		10.3.1958
	Times Are Gettin' Hard, Boys		12.3.1958
ZZ.1027-B	Lazy John		19.3.1958
	Light From The Lighthouse		11.3.1958

248

| | I've Got Rocks In My Bed | | 11.3.1958 |
| | Long Summer Day | | 11.3.1958 |

Lonnie Donegan (gtr, voc); Les Bennetts (gtr, voc); Pete Huggett (bass); Brian Simmons (washboard (1)); Nick Nicholls (drums).

| | Does Your Chewing Gum Lose Its Flavour (1) | Pye 7N.1518 | 13.12.1958 |
| | Aunt Rhody | | |

Lonnie's Skiffle Party
	Little Liza Jane	Pye N15165;	1958
	Puttin' On The Style	7N15165	
	Camptown Races		
	Knees Up Mother Brown		
	So Long		
	On Top Of Old Smoky		

Lonnie Donegan (gtr, bjo (2), voc); Les Bennetts (gtr, voc); Pete Huggett (bass); Nick Nicholls (drums); Miki and Griff (backing voc (1)).

| 45.XX.1198-A | Fort Worth Jail (1) | Pye 7N.15198 | 4.1959 |
| 45.XX.1198-B | Whoa Buck | | |

| 45.XX.1206-A | Battle of New Orleans (2) | Pye 7N.15206 | 5. 1959 |
| 45.XX.1206-B | Darling Corey | | 10.1958 |

Lonnie Donegan (gtr, voc), Les Bennetts (gtr, voc); Pete Huggett (bass); Nick Nicholls (drums).

| | Kevin Barry | Pye 7N.15219 | 3.1959 |
| | My Laggan Love | | 10.1958 |

Lonnie Donegan (gtr, voc); Dick Bishop (gtr, voc (2); Pete Huggett (bass); Nick Nicholls (drums); Miki and Griff (backing voc (1)).

| 45.XX.1223-A | Sal's Got A Sugar Lip (1) | Pye 7N.15223 | 9.1959 |
| 45.XX.1223-B | Chesapeake Bay (2) | | |

Lonnie Donegan (gtr, voc), Les Bennetts (gtr, voc); Pete Huggett (bass); Nick Nicholls (drums).

Relax With Lonnie
	Bewildered	Pye NEP.24017	10.1958
	Kevin Barry		3.1959
	It Is No Secret		10.1958
	My Laggan Love		10.1958

Lonnie Donegan (gtr, bjo (1), voc); Les Bennetts (gtr, voc); Pete Huggett (bass); Brian Simmons (washboard (3)); Nick Nicholls (drums); Miki and Griff (backing voc (2)).

Lonnie Donegan Hit Parade — Vol 6
	The Battle of New Orleans (1)	Pye NEP 24114	5.1959
	Fort Worth Jail (2)		4.1959
	Does Your Chewing Gum Lose It's Flavour (3)		13.12.1958
	Darling Corey		10.1958

Lonnie Donegan (gtr, voc); Les Bennetts (gtr, bass (1)); Pete Huggett (bass, vln (1)); Nick Nicholls (drums).

| | My Old Man's A Dustman (1) | Pye 7N.15256 | 4.1960 |
| | Golden Vanity | | 23.10.1959 |

Lonnie Donegan (gtr, bjo); Les Bennetts (gtr); Pete Huggett (bass); Nick Nicholls (drums).

45.XX.1267-A	I Wanna Go Home	Pye 7N.15267	1960
45.XX.1267-B	Jimmy Brown The Newsboy		

Lonnie Donegan (gtr, voc); Les Bennetts (gtr, bass (1)); Pete Huggett (bass, vln (1)); Nick Nicholls (drums); Miki and Griff (backing voc (2)).

Lonnie Donegan Hit Parade — Vol 7

VV.1134-A	My Old Man's A Dustman (1)	Pye NEP 24134	2.1960
	The Golden Vanity		23.10.1959
VV.1134-B	Sal's Got A Sugar Lip (2)		9.1959
	Talking Guitar Blues		23.10.1959

Tops With Lonnie

	Don't You Rock Me Daddy-O	Pye NPL.18034	1959
	Putting On The Style		
	Gamblin' Man		
	My Dixie Darling		
	Bring A Little Water, Sylvie		
	Cumberland Gap		
	Grand Coulee Dam		
	Does Your Chewing Gum Lose Its Flavour (On The Bedpost Overnight)?		
	Tom Dooley		

Lonnie Donegan (gtr, bjo); Les Bennetts (gtr); Pete Huggett (bass); Nick Nicholls (drums).

Lonnie Rides Again

NN. 1043-A	Fancy Talking Tinker	Pye NPL18043	22.10.1959
	Miss Otis Regrets		22.10.1959
	Gloryland		22.10.1959
	Jimmy Brown The Newsboy		23.10.1959
	Mr. Froggy		23.10.1959
	Take This Hammer		22.10.1959
NN. 1043-B	The Gold Rush Is Over		22.10.1959
	You Past Me By		23.10.1959
	Talking Guitar Blues		23.10.1959
	John Hardy		23.10.1959
	The House Of The Rising Sun		22.10.1959
	San Miguel		22.10.1959

Lonnie Donegan (gtr, bjo (1); Les Bennetts (gtr); Pete Huggett (bass); Pete Appleby (drums); Miki and Griff (backing voc).

	Michael Row The Boat Ashore	Pye 7N.15371	8.1961
	Lumbered		8.1961

Lonnie Donegan Hit Parade — Vol 8

	Michael Row The Boat Ashore	Pye NEP 24149	8.1961
	I Want To Go Home (1)		2.1960
	Lumbered		8.1961
	Have A Drink On Me		4.1961

Johnny Duncan and the Blue Grass Boys

Johnny Duncan (gtr, mandolin, voc); Denny Wright (gtr, voc); Danny Levan (vln); Jack Fallon (bass, vln); Lennie Hastings (drs).

	Kaw Liga	Col DB.3925	1957
	Ella Speed		

CA 24071	Last Train to San Fernando	Col DB.3959	1957
CA 24072	Rock-A-Billy Baby		
	Blue Blue Heartache	Col DB.3966	1957
	Jig Along Home		
	Get Along Home Cindy	Col DB.4029	1957
	Footprints In The Snow		
CA 24317	If You Love Me Baby	Col DB.4074	1957
CA 24318	Goodnight Irene		

Johnny Duncan and his Blue Grass Boys
Freight Train Blues   Col SEG 7708   1957
Press On
Johnny's Blue Yodel
Out Of Business

Johnny Duncan and his Blue Grass Boys no. 2
Last Train To San Fernando   Col SEG 7733   1957
Jig Along Home
Blue Blue Heartache
Ella Speed

Johnny Duncan's Tennessee Song Bag
Get Along Home Cindy   Col 33S1122   1957
Old Blue
Travelin' Blues
St. James's Infirmary
Calamity Mose
Just A Little Lovin
Which Way Did He Go
More And More
Mind Your Own Business
Just A Closer Walk With Thee

Footprints in the Snow
Footprints In The Snow   Col SEG 7753   1958
Kaw Liga
Rockabilly Baby
Get Along Home Cindy

The Eden Street Skiffle Group

Brian Jackman (gtr, voc.); Ron Lawrence (gtr, voc.); Hamish Maxwell (gtr, voc.); Micky Hopkins (mandolin); John Willard (bass); Bob Jones (washboard, drs).

Popular Skiffle Album no. 1
Man Taking Names   1958
Mary Don't You Weep   (London)
Gloryland
Judy Drownded
Black Girl
Old Smokey
Raise The Ruckus Tonight
Heaven
Easy Rider
Ain't It A Shame

The Frog Island Skiffle Group

The Frog Island Skiffle
House Of the Rising Sun   77 EP/4   1957
Going Down The Road   (London)
Hand Me Down My Walking Cane
Another Man Done Gone

The Hallelujah Skiffle Group with Clinton Ford

	Sweet Sixteen Eleven More Month	Oriole CB1425	1957/58
	In the Sweet Bye And Bye Jesus Remembered Me	Oriole CB1427	1957/58
O.9804 O.9805	I Saw The Light A Closer Walk With Thee	Oriole CB1429	1958

Les Hobeaux Skiffle Group

Les Bennets (gtr); Darryl Lyte (gtr); Roy Tobin (gtr); Brian Gregg (bass); Roger Smith (drums, voc.); Keith Lardner (lead voc.).

	Toll The Bell Easy Oh, Mary Don't You Weep	HMV POP377	1957 (London)
	Hey Hey Daddy Blues Mama Don't Allow	HMV POP403	1957
	Two Ships Dynamo	HMV POP444	1957

Soho Skiffle

	Hey Hey Daddy Blues Mama Don't Allow Toll The Bell Easy Oh Mary Don't You Weep	HMV 7EG 8297	1957

Jimmy Jackson's Rock 'N' Skiffle

Jimmy Jackson (gtr, voc.); Brian Horrey (gtr); Nevil Skrimshire (gtr); Alan Duddington (bass); Pete Appleby (drums).

CA23899 CA23900	California Zephyr I Shall Not Be Moved	Col DB.3898	1957 (London)
	Good Morning Blues Sittin' In The Balcony	Col DB.3937	1957
	Lonely Road River Line	Col DB.3957	1957
	White Silver Sands Build Your Love	Col DB.3988	1957

Rock 'n' Skiffle

	California Zephyr I Shall Not Be Moved Good Morning Blues Lonely Road	Col SEG 7750	1957
	Love A Love Photographs	Col DB.4085	1958
	This Little Light Of Mine Swing Down Sweet Chariot	Col DB.4153	1958

Country and Blues

	Midnight Train Western Plains Reckon I'll Go There's A Time For Moving	Col SEG 7768	1958

Alexis Korner Skiffle Group
Alexis Korner (vocal (1-3), acoustic gtr); Cyril Davies (voc (4), acoustic gtr (1 & 4),
harmonica (1-3)); Chris Capon (string bass); Dave Stevens (piano (2 & 3)); Mike Collins (washboard).

| | I Ain't Gonna Worry No More (1) | Tpo A 166 | 22.7.1957 |
| | County Jail (2) | | (London) |

Blues From The Roundhouse — Vol. 1
VOG 1931	I Ain't Gonna Worry No More (1)	Tpo EXA76	22.7.1957
VOG 1932	County Jail (2)		
	Kid Man (3)		
	Easy Rider (4)		

Blues From The Roundhouse — Vol. 2
	Sail On	Tpo EXA102	29.4.1958
	National Defence Blues		
	Go Down Sunshine		
	Death Letter		

Don Lang and his Skiffle Group

Don Lang (Gordon Langhorn) (voc); Terry Brown, Jack Llewlyn, Roy Plummer (gtrs);
Frank Donnison (bass); George Fierstone, Bobby Kevin (drs).

Skiffle Special
	Whiskey	HMV DLP1151	17.5.1957
	New York Gals		(London)
	The Cattle Train		
	Fightin' Men		
	This Train		
	By And By		
	A Rag, A Bone And A Lock Of Hair		
	Roll The Cotton Down		
	Poor Old Man		
	The Roving Gambler		
	Raccoon And Possum		
	Sarah Kelly From Plumb Nelly		

Lea Valley Skiffle Group

Trevor Morgan, Ron Till (gtrs., vocal); Brian Coford (gtr); Mike Warwick (gtr); Brian
Warwick (banjo); Sid Herbert (washboard); Brian Kohler (two string bass).

| ESQ 994-1 | Streamline Train | Esquire 10-508 | 5.9.1957 |
| ESQ 995-2 | Railroad Bill | | (London) |

| | Oh, Mary Don't You Weep | Esquire 10-518 | 5.9.1957 |
| | I'm Gonna Walk And Talk | | |

	Streamline Train	Esquire EP 163	5.9.1957
	Railroad Bill		
	Oh, Mary Don't You Weep		
	I'm Gonna Walk And Talk		

Alan Lomax and the Ramblers

Alan Lomax (gtr, voc.); Ewan MacColl (voc); Peggy Seeger (bjo, voc.); Shirley Collins
(voc).
| | Dirty Old Town | Dec 45F10787 | 2.8.1956 |
| | Hard Case | | |

	Oh! Lulu	Dec DFE6367	2.8.1956
	Railroad Man		(London)
	Dirty Old Town		
	Hard Case		

Chas McDevitt Skiffle Group

Chas McDevitt (gtr, whistling, voc.); Nancy Whiskey (gtr, voc (1)); Denny Carter (gtr, voc.); Alex Whitehouse (gtr, voc); John Paul (bass); Marc Sharratt (washboard); Jimmie McGregor (gtr, mandolin, voc (2)).

O.6175	Freight Train (1)	Oriole CB 1352	12.1956
O.6176	The Cotton Song		(London)
O.6177	The House Of The Rising Sun	Oriole CB 1357	12.1956
X.6378	Worried Man (2)		

Chas McDevitt (gtr, whistling, voc., mandolin); Bill Bramwell (gtr, voc); Tony Kohn (gtr, voc); Nancy Whiskey (voc (1); Shirley Douglas (gtr, voc. (2)); Lennie Harrison (bass); Marc Sharratt (washboard, drs); Johnny Parker (pno (3).

O.6227	Greenback Dollar (1)	Oriole CB 1371	5.1957
O.6228	I'm Satisfied		
	Sporting Life	Oriole CB 1386	7.1957
	Face In The Rain (1)		
	My Old Man	Oriole CB 1395	8.1957
	Sing Sing Sing		
	Johnny-O (1)	Oriole CB 1403	8.1957
	Bad Man Stackolee		
O.9756	Across The Bridge (2)	Oriole CB 1405	8.1957
O.9757	Deep Down		
	Juke Box Jumble (3)	Oriole CB 1457	8.1958
	Real Love (2)		

Chas McDevitt (gtr, whistling, voc., mandolin); Bill Bramwell (gtr, voc); Tony Kohn (gtr, voc); Nancy Whiskey (voc, solo gtr (1); Lennie Harrison (bass); Marc Sharratt (washboard, drs); Johnny Parker (pno).

The Intoxicating Miss Whiskey
	Poor Howard	Oriole MG.	
	The Fireman's Not For Me (1)	10018	[1957?]
	Sporting Life		
	The Riddle Song (1)		
	I'm Satisfied		
	Face In The Rain		
	Stack-O-Lee		
	Farewell (1)		
	Every Day Of The Week		

Nancy and Chas
	Freight Train	Oriole EP 7002	12.1956
	It Takes A Worried Man		(London)
	Green Back Dollar		5.1957
	I'm Satisfied		

Jimmy Miller and the Barbecues

| | Sizzlin' Hot | Col DB 4006 | 9.1957 |
| | Free Wheeling Baby | | 2.1958 |

| | Jelly Baby | Col DB 4081 | 2.1958 |
| | Cry Baby Cry | | |

Old Timers Skiffle Group

Dennis Carter (gtr, voc.); Alex Whitehouse (gtr, voc.); John Paul (bass); Little Joey Jonkler (washboard).

| AA 167002 1H | The Lynching Of Jeff Buckner | Fontana H105 | 1958 |
| | The Woman Who Loved A Swine | | (London) |

Original Soho Skiffle Group (i.e. Vipers Skiffle Group)

Wally Whyton (lead gtr, voc.); Johnny Martin (gtr, voc.); Jim Bray (bass); not known (drs).

	Sam Hall	Par T 70005	1957
	Kevin Barry		(London)
	Charlie Is My Darling		
	My Bonnie Lies Over The Ocean		
	I Know Where I'm Going		
	The Derby Ram		
	Liverpool Blues		
	The Ash Groove		
	She Was Poor But She Was Honest		
	Wild Colonial Boy		
	Spinning Wheel		
	Three Lovely Lasses		
	Greensleeves		
	Clementine		

Peggy Seeger, Isla Cameron, Guy Carawan

Peggy Seeger, Isla Cameron (vocs, gtrs); Guy Carawan (voc, bjo); Jack Fallon (bass); Eddie Taylor (drs).

Origins of Skiffle

	Cumberland Gap	Pye NJE1043	10.7.1957
	Freight Train		(London)
	Sail Away, Lady		
	Bring A Little Water, Sylvie		

Soho Skiffle Group

John Audrey (gtr, voc); Mike Naden (gtr, voc); unknown (gtr, washboard, bass).

DA 2579	Midnight Special	Melodisc 1403	1957
	Give Me A Big Fat Woman		(London)
	Frankie And Johnny	Melodisc 1421	1957
	Streamline Train		
	I Shall Not Be Moved	Melodisc	
	Give Me A Big Fat Woman	EPM7-72	1957
	Streamline Train		
	Frankie and Johnny		

Station Skiffle Group

Mike Jarvie (bjo, voc (1) & (2)); Jim Miller (gtr, voc (2)); Peter Cozens (gtr); Mike Hodge (vamp accordion); Johnnie Reid (one-string bass); Peter Hions (washboard, voc only (3)).

ESQ977-2	Don't You Rock Me Daddy-O	Esquire 10-503	1957
ESQ978-2	Hugged My Honey		(London)
	Steamboat Bill	Esquire 10-516	1957
	Titanic		
	Hugged My Honey	Esquire EP 161	1957
	Greenback Dollar		
	Titanic		
	Steamboat Bill		

First National Skiffle Contest.

	Hugged My Honey (1)	Esquire LP20-089	29.6.1957
	Don't You Rock Me Daddy-O (2)		
	Titanic (3)		

Sonny Stewart and his Skiffle Kings

Sonny Stewart (gtr, voc.); Pete Stewart (gtr, voc.); Steve O'Grady (lead gtr); Steve Benbow (gtr, voc.); Phil Ray (drums); John Ebbles (bass).

B26277H,			
AA 26277 1H	The Northern Line	Philips PB 719	1957
B26277H			(London)
AA 26277 2H	Black Jack		
	Let Me Lie	Philips PB 773	1957
	Mama Don't Allow		

2.19 Skiffle Group

Mik Lauder, Mike Wallace (gtrs, vocs); Jack McCormack (bass); Davey Chandler (washboard).

ESQ 918	Railroad Bill	Esquire 10-497	2.2.1957
ESQ 919	Freight Train Blues		(London)
	I'm A-Lookin' For A Home	Esquire 10-502	2.2.1957
	When The Saints Go Marching In		
ESQ 992-1	In The Valley	Esquire 10-509	2.2.1957
ESQ 993-2	Tom Dooley		
	Roll The Union On	Esquire 10-512	2.2.1957
	Where Could I Go?		
	This Little Light o' Mine	Esquire 10-515	2.2.1957
	Union Maid		
	Railroad Bill	Esquire EP126	2.2.1957
	Freight Train		
	I'm A-Lookin' For A Home		
	When The Saints		

(1) — Mik Lauder, Mike Wallace (gtrs, vocs); Jack McCormack (bass); Davey Chandler (washboard).
(2) — Lauder, Wallace (gtrs, vocs); Len Harris (bass); Idle Bill Smith (washboard, voc.).
(3) — Personnel as for (2), except Fred Cogger (bass) replaces Harris.

First National Skiffle Contest. London

| | This Little Light Of Mine (2) | Esquire LP20-089 | 1.6.1957 |
| | Trouble In Mind (3) | | 21.8.1957 |

	Texas Lady (3)		21.8.1957
	Freight Train Blues (1)		20.2.1957
	Union Maid (2)		1.6.1957

Mik Lauder, Mike Wallace (gtrs, vocs); Len Harris (bass);Fred Cogger (bass (1);Vic Pitt (bass (3); Idle Bill Smith (washboard, voc (2)).

Union Maid	Esquire EP146	1.6.1957
Where Can I Go?		(London)
Roll The Union On		
This Little Light Of Mine		
Trouble In Mind (1)	Esquire EP176	21.8.1957
Texas Lady (1)		
In The Valley (1)		
Tom Dooley (1, 2)		
Hand Me Down My		
Walkin' Cane (3)	Esquire EP196	21.8.1957
Oh, Mary Don't You Weep (3)		
Black Girl (3)		
Gipsy Davy (3)		

The Vipers Skiffle Group (see also Original Soho Skiffle Group)

Wally Whyton (gtr, voc.); Johnny Martyn (gtr, voc.); Jean Van Den Bosch (gtr, voc.); Jack Collier (bass); Joe Muddel (bass) (1); Johnny Pilgrim (washboard).

CE15673	Ain't You Glad	Par R4236	4.10.1956
CE15674	Pick A Bale Of Cotton		18.10.1956
			(London)

| CE15729 | Don't You Rock Me Daddy-O (1) | Par R426 | 29.11.1956 |
| CE15730 | 10,000 Years Ago (1) | | |

Wally Whyton (gtr, voc.); Johnny Martyn (gtr, voc.); Jean Van Den Bosch (gtr, voc.); Frank Clark (bass); Johnny Pilgrim (washboard).

| CE15771 | Hey Liley, Liley Lo | Par R4286 | 8.2.1957 |
| CE15772 | Jim Dandy | | 15.2.1957 |

Wally Whyton (gtr, voc., plectrum bjo, overdubbed lead gtr (1)); Johnny Martyn (gtr, voc.); Jean Van Den Bosch (gtr, voc.); Tony Tolhurst (bass); Johnny Pilgrim (washboard).

| CE15777 | The Cumberland Gap (1) | Par R4289 | 28.2.1957 |
| CE15778 | Maggie May | | |

Wally Whyton (gtr, voc, leader); Johnny Martyn (gtr, voc.); Jean Van Den Bosch (gtr, voc.); Tony Tolhurst (bass); Johnny Pilgrim (washboard (1)); Phil Seamen (drs (2)).

Coffee Bar Session

Darlin' (1)	Par PMD1050	15.4.1957
This Land Is Your Land (1)		15.7.1957
The Glory Land (1)		15.7.1957
Precious Memories (1)		15.7.1957
I Know The Lord Laid		
His Hands On Me (1)		16.7.1957
Easy Rider (2)		17.7.1957
Wanderin' (2)		17.7.1957
If I Had A Hammer (1)		5.9.1957
I Saw The Light (1)		5.9.1957
John B. Sails (1)		5.9.1957

Wally Whyton (gtr, voc., plectrum bjo); Johnny Martyn (gtr, voc.); Jean Van Den Bosch (gtr, voc.); Tony Tolhurst (bass); Johnny Pilgrim (washboard).

CE15799	Streamline Train	Par R4308	25.4.1957
CE15800	Railroad Steamboat		

Wally Whyton (gtr, voc.); Johnny Martyn (gtr, voc.); Jean Van Den Bosch (gtr, voc.); Jack Collier (bass); Johnny Pilgrim (washboard); Joe Muddel (bass (1); Frank Clarke (bass (2)).

Skiffle Music

	It Takes A Worried Man To Sing A Worried Song	Par GEP8615	18.10.1956
	Don't You Rock Me Daddy-O (1)		29.11.1956
	Hey Liley, Liley Lo (2)		8.2.1957
	The Cumberland Gap		28.2.1957

Wally Whyton (gtr, voc, plectrum bjo (2)); Johnny Martyn (gtr, voc.); Jean Van Den Bosch (gtr, voc.); Jack Collier (bass); Tony Tolhurst (bass (1); Johnny Pilgrim (washboard).

Skiffle Music no. 2

	Ain't You Glad	Par GEP8626	4.10.1956
	Pick A Bale Of Cotton		18.10.1956
	Streamline Train (1)		25.4.1957
	Railroad Steamboat (1, 2)		25.4.1957

Wally Whyton (gtr, voc., plectrum bjo); Johnny Martyn (gtr, voc.); Jean Van Den Bosch (gtr, voc.); Joe Muddel (bass); Tony Tolhurst (bass (1)); Johnny Pilgrim (washboard).

	10,000 Years Ago	Par GEP8655	29.11.1956
	Maggie May (1)		28.2.1957

Wally Whyton (gtr, voc.); Johnny Martyn (gtr, voc.); Jean Van Den Bosch (gtr, voc.); poss. Tony Tolhurst (bass); Phil Seaman (drs (1)).

CE15886	Homing Bird (1)	Par R4351	23.8.1957
CE15887	Pay Me My Money Down		16.7.1957

Wally Whyton (gtr, voc.); Johnny Martyn (gtr, voc.); Jean Van Den Bosch (gtr, voc.); poss. Tony Tolhurst (bass); Jack Peach (drs); Jim Dale (solo voc. (1); unidentified (lead gtr (1)).

Top Ten Special

CE15894	All Shook Up (1)	Par R4356	6.9.1957
	Last Train To San Fernando		
CE15895	Putting On The Style		
	Wandering Eyes (1)		

Wally Whyton (gtr, voc); Johnny Martyn (gtr, voc.); Jean Van Den Bosch (gtr, voc); Joe Muddel (bass); Johnny Pilgrim (washboard); Jack Peach (drs), unidentified (bjo).

Skiffle Party

CE15926	Comin' Round The Mountain	Par R4371	21.10.1957
	On Top Of Old Smokey		
	Rock Island Line		
CE15927	Wabash Cannonball		
	Gimme Crack Corn		
	Skip To My Lou		

Wally Whyton (voc.); Johnny Martyn (voc.); unidentified (gtrs); unidentified (bass); unidentified (drs, percussion); unidentified (bass/clarinet).

CE15978	Why Baby Why?	Par R4393	19.12.1957
CE15979	No Other Baby		

258

Wally Whyton (voc.); Johnny Martyn (voc.); unidentified (gtrs); unidentified (bass); unidentified (drs); unidentified (bass/clarinet); Michael Sammes Singers (1).

CE16058	Make Ready For Love (1)	Par R4435	5.5.1958
CE16059	Nothing Will Ever Change (My Love For You)		

Wally Whyton (voc., poss. gtr); Johnny Martyn (voc., poss. gtr); unidentified (gtrs); Jet Harris (bass); Tony Meehan (drs, percussion).

CE16147	Summertime Blues	Par R4484	22.9.1958
CE16148	Liverpool Blues		

Nancy Whiskey

Nancy Whiskey (gtr, voc.).

Nancy Whiskey

	Bonny Lad	Topic 7 T10	1956
	The Bold Fenian Men		(London)
	An Old Man Came A Courtin'		
	Poor Little Turtle Dove		
	The Trooper And the Maid		
	The Farewell Song		

Nancy Whiskey (gtr, voc.); Dis Dizley (gtr); Bryan Daly (gtr); George Jennings (bass); Bob Kelly (pno, washboard); Tony Kinsey or Alan Ganley (drs).

O.9736	He's Solid Gone	Oriole CB 1394	1958
O.9737	Ella Speed		

Woried Men Skiffle Group

Stars of the Six-Five Special

	Fraulein	Dec LF1299	1958 (London)

Rockin' at the "2 I's"

DRL.3822	900 Miles From Home	Dec LF1300	1958
	This Little Light Of Mine		

Select list of compilations

Bear Family Records

Lonnie Donegan
More than 'Pye in the Sky'. 8 CD's
(209 tracks) plus book.   BCD 15700-HI   1993

Johnny Duncan
Last Train To San Fernando. 4 CD's (115 tracks)
plus book.   BCD15947-DI   1996

The Vipers
10,000 Years Ago. 3 CD's (64 tracks) plus book.   BCD 15954-CI   1996

Lake Records

Ken Colyer
The Decca Skiffle Sessions. (19 tracks).   LA5007/LACD7   1987, 1993

Wandering. (15 tracks).   LACD68   1996

Various
The Esquire Skiffle Sessions 1957 (20 tracks).   LACD 90   1997

Features 2.19 Skiffle Group, Delta Skiffle Group, Lea Valley Skiffle Group, Johnny Christmas and the Station Skifffle Group.

Rollercoaster Records

Chas McDevitt

Chas McDevitt Skiffle Group. (32 tracks).   RCCD3007   1993

Index

As well as the main text, index entries cover the book's reminiscences and illustrations (indicated in bold type).

With some exceptions, index entries are not provided for song titles and skiffle group personnel. Skiffle groups noted in the main text receive entries; only a few skiffle venues, however, are listed. Names of other groups may be found in the tables on pages 139, 145 and 165, and of other venues in those tables on pages 124 and 138. The Discography provides personnel details, where known.

Abergavenny
  skiffle in 156, 210
Ace of Clubs Rhythm Group 201
Adams, Derroll 39, 129, 130
advertisements
  use of skiffle theme 74
Africa
  origin of musical instruments 29-30
Alleycats Skiffle Group 136, 140
Amazon Skiffle Group 23, 78, 148
American Skiffle Bands (record) 48
Animals (r&b group) 197
Appleby, Pete 88
Armpit Jug Band **219**
  see also Wang Dang Doodle
Ash Valley Skiffle Group 187
Ashman, Micky **5**, 8 **11**, 21, 23 75, 85, 111
Australia
  Donegan tour (1960) 86-8
  skiffle in 125, 126-7
Avon Cities Jazz Band 24, 81, 84, 93, 220
  advertisement for **109**
  Skiffle Group 17, 108-9, 110, 115, 163, 170
Avro Skiffle Group 178

Bailey, Bill Skiffle Group 3, 111, 153, 170
Ballymena
  skiffle in 138, 149-50
Banana Boys Skiffle Group 150
banjos 28, 29, 32, 33, 150
  homemade 31
Barber, Chris 3, 6, 7, 10-13, **12**, 14, 15, 19, 20, 84, 91 105, 129, 172
  and origin of skiffle label 46
  featured skiffle from 1952 10
  Jazz and Blues Band 81
  Jazz Band 2, 9, **11**, 16, 19, 22, 79, 140, 160, 178
  reunion tour (1995) 111
  signs Johnny Duncan 104
  Skiffle Group 12, 70, 79-81 **80**, 108
Barker, Danny 34
Barnie, John
  reminiscences 89, 141, 156, 196, 210
Barnstormers Spasm Band 114-15
Bart, Lionel 98, 183
bass guitars 26
Bastable, John 8, 23, 75, 76, 77
Battersea Pleasure Gardens 79
Beale Street Jug Band 36
beat music 27, 88, 158, 167, 172
Beatles 91, 99, 134, 158, 179, 183, 192, 198, **199**, 200, 203-4
Beaumont, Geoffrey 71
Belfast
  skiffle in 146, 202, 203
Bell, Graeme 127
  Jazz Band 3, 16

Skiffle Gang 127; concert programme **126**
Benbow, Steve 169, 170, 171, 174, 194, 214
Bennetts, Les 88, 96, 117, 118
Best, Pete 203
Bid for Fame (tv show) 178, 180
Big Breakfast (tv show) 211
Bilk, Acker 8, 17, 23
Bishop, Dickie **12**, 16, 19, 20, **80**, 81, 83, 110-11, **111**, 192
  and his Sidekicks 109-110, 116, 153,168, 181, 182;
broadcasts 162, 170, 173
  Skiffle Group 79, 93
Black Cats Skiffle Group 157
Black Sheep Skiffle Group 153, 208, **209**
Blackcaps Skiffle Group 13
Blackpool Palace Theatre 85, 182
Bland, Shirley 112, 169, 170, 174
Blue Jeans Skiffle Group 118
bluegrass music 33
blues 13, 196
  skiffle repertoire source 38
  use of homemade instruments 31
"Blues and Skiffle" (*Record Changer* column) 46
Blues Band 197
Blues Incorporated 79, 196, 197
Bobcats (skiffle group) 160
Boden, Al 217 **217**
Boland's Skiffle Group 24
Boll Weevils Skiffle Group 136
Bon Temps Playboys 217
Boozan Kings (spasm band) 34
Bowden, Ron 4, 6, 7, **11**, 19, 79
Bradford
  skiffle and rock 'n' roll in 198
Bramwell, Bill 95, 192
Bray, Jim 6, 7, 20, 79
Breadbasket (coffee bar) 25, 97, 98, 102, 183
Break for Jazz (radio programe) 161
Brett Brothers 162, 169
Britain
  life in the 50s 49-74
British Broadcasting Corporation
  and popular music provision 159-176
  Donegan records bannned by 85
British Forces Network 8, 168
broadcasting
  and skiffle 159-80
Brooks, Bob
  reminiscences 32, 141, 160, 195, 210
Broonzy, Big Bill 13, 14, 36, 39, **44**, 97, 129, 197
  and homemade instruments 31
  and origin of skiffle term 42
  British tours 38, 163
  participation in house-rent parties 43-5
Brown, Joe 201, 203, 205, 224
Bryden, Beryl 10, 15, 16-17, 161, 169, 214
  Backroom Boys 16-17
  Backroom Skiffle 77-8
Burley, Dan 43
  and his Skiffle Boys 45, 46; record advertisement **46**

Bush, Ray 17, 93, 108-9, 110, 214
busking 103, 111, **113**, 140-2, **220**
Butlin Skiffle Group 146
Butlins All England Skiffle Contest 119, 121
Butlins holiday camps 55
    National Weekly Skiffle Contest 144-6
    skiffle contest (Metropolitan Theatre) 146

Cannon's Jug Stompers 36, 48, 108
Cardiff
    skiffle in **30**, 149, 220, **220**
carnivals
    as skiffle venues 140
Carter Family 10, 42, 217
Carter Family Style 202
Cashah Club (Liverpool) 202
Cat's Whisker (coffee bar) 99, 144, 187
Cavemen Skiffle Group 98, 183
Cavern Club 188, 194, 199, 203
Cellarmen Skiffle Group 146
Chalet Bandits Skiffle Group 146
Chandler, Chas 197
channel "shuffles" 139-40
    Royal Daffodil (July 1957) **152**
Charters, Samuel B. 48
charts
    skiffle successes 11-12, 81-107
Chequers Skiffle Group 176
Chesternuts (pop group) 188, 189
Chicago
    house-rent parties 43-5
"Chicago Skiffle" 45
Children's Favourites, (radio programme) 170
Chislehurst Caves (skiffle venue) 141
Chiswick Empire iv, 85, 191
Chorlton Palais 137
Christie Brothers Stompers 6
Christmas, Johnny, and the Sunspots 122
church music 70-3
cinemas
    as skiffle venue 138-9
City Ramblers 24, 70, 96, 111-14, 115, 125, 140,
    153, 172, 182
    broadcasts 160, 161, 162, 164, 166, 170
    in Europe (c. mid-50s) 111, **113**
Clayton, Eddie, Skiffle Group 200
Clifford, Max (publicist) 134
clubs
    advertisements **123**
    as skiffle venues 24, 124, 134, 201
Clyde Valley Stompers 86, 122
Cobras Skiffle Group **149**, 211
Cockatoos Skiffle Group **142**
Coffee Bar Skiffflers 122
coffee bars 59, 60-1, 105, 115, 182
    as skiffle venues 24, 25, 61-3, 92, 97-9, 102
Collins, Shirley 24, 122, 123, 194, 218
Colyer, Bill 4, 5, 6, 8, 9, 10, 23, 117, 129, 214
    and the term skiffle 7
Colyer, Ken 3, 4-8, **5**, 15-16, 22, 38, 70, 84, 95, 97,
    105, 107, 129, 173
    informal skiffle sessions with Korner 9-10
    Jazzmen 6, 7, 76, 138, 140
    Skiffle Group 22-3, 24, 75-7, 78, 108, 115, 170,
    207, 224
"Come Skiffle Chicken" (song) 127
Comets Skiffle Group 178
Cort, Bob 70, 76, 84, 115, **116**
    broadcasts 169, 173, 174, 175, 176, 177
    How To Play Skiffle Successfully 68-9, 117
    Skiffle Group 93, 99, 115-17, 153; broadcasts 160,
    162, 163, 176, 177
Costers Skiffle Group 13
Cotton Pickers Skiffle Group 96, 122, 140, 162, 168,
    171, 181
country music 32-3, 40-2, 66, 104-5
Cousins and Sons (band) 218
Crane River Jazz Band 3, 4, 6, 9, 24, 92
Crescendo Skiffle Group 69

Crescendos Skiffle Group 135
Crescent City Skiffle Group 186
Croydon
    skiffle in 138, 146, 148
Cumming, John Stringbean 218
Currie, Jim 85
Curtis, Pete, Folk and Blues Quintet 122, 169, 170,
171

Dale, Jim 98, 99, 101-2, 122, 142, 148, 172, 180, 182
    as *Six-Five Special* presenter 164, 167
Dale, Stanley 148, 164
    see also National Skiffle Contest
Dambry, Stéphane 214
dance halls 63
    as skiffle venues 137-8
Dance Music Festival
    see Festival of Dance Music
Darktown Skiffle Group 200
Davies, Cyril 24, 78, 79, 128, 197
Davies, Dave 197
Davies, Ray 197, 207
Davis, Beryl 194
Davis, Rod 198, 211, 214
Davis, Tony 194
Del Rios 217, 218
Delta Skiffle Group 120-1, 143-4, 170
Dene, Terry 96, 164, 170, 187, 191, 214
Denman, Barbara, Girls' Skiffle Group 178
Denson Boys Skiffle Group 149
Denver, Johnny, Skiffle Group 157
Dewe, Mike
    reminiscences iii-iv, 89, 151, 193
Dick Whittington Katz Skiffle Group 144
Dig This! (tv show) 167
Disley, Diz 8, 117, 192, 214
"Does Your Chewing Gum Lose It's Flavour?" (song)
    86, 88, 90, 105
Domino, Fats 78, 134, 148, 189, 193, 202
Dominoes Skiffle Group 150
Donegan, Lonnie 7, 10, 13-22, 26, 57, 105, 107
    ability as banjoist 11
    American visits 2, 19, 81, 84, 88
    and origins of term skiffle 46
    as musical influence 13, 78, 84, 89, 90, 188, 191, 197,
    199, 201, 202, 207, 210
    as pantomime artist 85
    as solo artist 15
    at age 65 91
    banned records 85
    broadcasts 169, 172, 175, 176, 178
    criticism of 78, 88
    dress 89
    forms own band 14-15
    hobbies 89
    illustrative material about **11, 12, 15, 20, 83, 87,
    225**
    Lonnie Donegan Show 176
    "Lonnie Donegan Presents" 86
    member of Colyer band 6
    Paul Leegan as 212
    reasons for success 82-3, 86, 88-9, 90, 105, 129
    reception at first public performance 14
    recorded repertoire 27, 37, 38, 40, 42
    recording achievements 1, 20, 21, 82, 83-6, 88,
    90-1, 140, 224
    singing ability 11, 196
    Skiffle Group iv, 1, 10, 16, 20-1, 70, 82, 108, 128,
    153; broadcasts 160, 161, 163, 164, 171,
    176, 177; instrumentation 27
    sponsors skiffle clubs 59-60
    Stoll Theatre launch 81; programme **82**
    tour of Australia and New Zealand (1960) 86-8
    variety appearances 1, 82, 84, 85, 86, 88, 176,
    182
Donegan, Tony (Lonnie Donegan's son) 212
Donegan Trophy Competition 121
Dorita y Pepe 173, 174
double basses 26, 30, 33, 150, 152

as homemade instrument **28**, 33, 34
  see also tea-chest basses
Double Diamonds Skiffle Group 137
Double Three Skiffle Group 157, 166
Douglas, Josephine 131, 162, 166, 167
Douglas, Shirley 96-7, 115, 214
  broadcasts 160, 176, 177
Dreamers Skiffle Group 65
dress 51, 54, 56
  skiffle separates **72**
Drifters 171, 177, 187-8, 190
  see also Shadows
Drumbeat (tv show) 167, 176, 183, 190, 191
drums 26, 28, 29, 84, 150
Duffy's Nucleus (band) 196
Duncan, Fionna 170, 171
Duncan, Johnny **80**, 93, 103-5, **106**, 144, 195
  and his Blue Grass Boys 104-5, 108, 168, 224;
    broadcasts 160, 161, 162, 163, 164, 169,
    170, 171, 176, 178
  Barber Skiffle Group member 12, 79-81, 104
  broadcasts 173, 177
  Donegan stand-in 84
  similarity to Donegan 104
Dynamics Skiffle Group 157

Eden Street Skiffle Group 70, 96, 122, 162, 164, 169,
  172, 182
Ellesmere Youth Club (Shropshire) 136-7
Elliott, Jack 24, 39, 79, 113, 123, 129, 130
employment
  young people 49, 52
entertainment
  and teenagers 59-64
Epstein, Brian 203
Esquire Records 118, 143, 144
Europe
  guitar sales 64
  skiffle in 27, 125, 223
Even Dozen Jug Band 223
Everly Brothers 54, 91, 93, 112, 180, 185, 193
Evrington Valley Youth Club (Leicestershire) 137

44 Skiffle Club 24
Faith, Adam 1, 88, 91, 118, 179, 185
  early career 186-7, 190, 191
Fallon, Jack 104, 169, 214
Family Favourites (radio programme) 160
Famous Potatoes (band) 222
Festival of Britain 52, **52**
Festival of Dance Music (radio programme, 1955-59)
  113, 160, 161, 176
  Radio Times announcement **161**
fêtes
  as skiffle venue 100, 140, 143, 194-5, 199
fiddles 28, 32, 33
  homemade 31
Finsbury Park Empire 85
Floating Festival of Jazz 139-40, 182
Florence Institute (Liverpool) 200, 201
Flying Standards (tv show) 167
folk clubs 194, 195
folk dance bands 218
folk instruments
  in USA 28-33
folk music, 89
  broadcasting 159, 169-71, 175
  interest in American 129-30, 131
folk revival
  in UK 192, 194, 196, 197
  in USA 66
folk songs
  use of British 80-1, 111, 130, 155,
    192-3, 194, 203, 213
  use of American 155-6, 192, 194, 203
Foresters Skiffle Group 157
Foster, John 187
Foxley, Roy 76

Francis, Stan 194, 196
"Freight Train" 56, 91-5, 97, 115, 118, 122, 127,
  195, 214
  record label roundel **92**
Frog Island Skiffle Group 122
Froggatt, Norman
  reminiscences 13, 112, 141, **147**, 180, 213
Fuchs, Vivian 50
Fulham (London)
  skiffle in 65, 119, 143, 145, 156-7
GR Skiffle Group 146
Gang Show (Boy Scouts) 73
garden parties
  as skiffle venues 158, 140
Garry, Len 198, 211
Gator's Skiffle Group 143
Gerry and the Pacemakers
  see Marsden, Gerry
Gibbs, Roy, and the Live Jive Five 163
Gill Family (Please Y'Self) 216-17
Gin Mill Skiffle Group 194, 196
girls
  and skiffle 178, 150
  in the 1950s 54, 222
Glitter, Gary 197
Golden Disc (film) 97
Good, Jack 162, 188
goofus (musical instrument) 37
Goofus Five 36
Gordon, Joe, Folk Four 169, 170, 171
Grant, Jimmy 168, 169
Green Hughie 114, 178, 180
Grey, Dony, and his...Skiffle Group 136
Griffiths, Eric 198, 211
Groves, Mick 60, 194
Guitar Club 67, 172-5
  listening figures 175
guitars 5, 13, 26, 32, 33, 65, 69, 102, 150, 210
  advertisements for **65**
  electric 143, 148, 157, 158, 169, 182, 187,
    191, 192, 210
  homemade 31, 32
  kits 56, 64
  playing technique 151, 188
  sales 64-7
  strings 5, 64, 65
  tutors 68-9, 202
Guthrie, Woody 14, 20, 24, 40, 97, 112, 130, 213
  performing at New York party (1944) **40**
Gyre and Gimble (coffee bar) 25, 98

Halcox, Pat 6, 10, **11**
Haley, Bill, and his Comets 58-9, 100, 193, 210
Hall, Cliff 196, 197
Hallelujah Skiffle Group 73
Hamburg 76, 77, 203
hand jive 64, 69, 166
Hanton, Colin 198, 211
harmonicas 26, 31, 150, 172
Harper, John
  reminiscences 56, 156, 193, 210
Harris, Geoff
  reminiscences 34, 69, 195
Harris, Jet (Terence) 102, 189-90
Harrison, George 60, 69, 198, 199-200, 203
Harrogate
  skiffle in 135
Hasted, John
  Skiffle and Folk Group 24, 192-3
Hessy's (Liverpool music shop) 13, 66
Hi-Fi Skiffle Group 122
High Society Skiffle Group 196
hillbilly music
  see country music
hire purchase 53, 64, 151
hit parade
  see charts
Hobeaux, Les, Skiffle Group 70, 96, 117-18, 176, 182
  advertisement for **119**

Hodges, Chas 201-2, 203, 214
Hogia Llandegai 206, **207**
hokum music 34-5
holiday camps 55, 144
holidays 55
Home Brew (folk group) 200
homemade musical instruments 26-37, 43, 151-3, 218,
    222
"Hometown Skiffle" (blues record) 45, 46
Horsham Song Swappers Club 218
Horseshoe Skiffle Group 202
Horseshoes (rock group) 203
hot fountain pen (musical instrument) 37
Hot Rods Skiffle Group 138, 146
House Party Skiffle (skiffle group) 217
house-rent parties 43-5, 47
Housewives Choice (radio programme) 160
How to Play Skiffle Successfully (Cort) 68-9
Howard, Duffy, and the Amigos (skiffle group) 65
Howard, Michael (politician) 134
Huggett, Peter 85, 88
Hull Palace 101, 148

Ilford Palais 137
Illingworth, Dave
    reminiscences 23, 78, 115, 148, 213
improvised musical instruments 26-37, 43, 151-3, 218,
    222
Imps (skiffle group) 166
Independent Television
    and skiffle 177-8
Independent Television Authority 55
inter-university jazz contest (Liverpool, 1955) 4
Ireland
    skiffle in 149

Jacaranda Club (Liverpool) 202
Jack, Johnny 182
Jack Jackson Show 177
    TV Times announcement **178**
Jackman, Brian 182
Jackson, Jimmy 122, 170, 173, 174
Jackson, Tyler 48
jazz 36, 133
    broadcasting 159-62, 170, 172, 174, 179
    New Orleans revival 2-3
    women in 222
jazz bands
    place of skiffle group within 17, 23, 24
jazz clubs 7, 14, 16, 22, 76, 93, 124, 138, 148, 182
jazz mass 71-3
jazz musicians 54
    who began in skiffle 192, 193
Jazz Saturday 15, 160-1
    Radio Times announcement **162**
Jenkins, Peter, Skiffle Group 89
jiving 56, 63, 162, 166
Jo and the Skiffle Group (Hastings) 74
Johnson, Lonnie 13, 14, 15, 38
Jones, Brian 197
Jones, Hughie 196
Jones, Paul 197
Jubilee Skiffle Group 178
jug bands 33, 35-6, 48, 113, 128, 217, 218, 222-3
Juggernaut Jug Band 36, 223, **221**
jugs as musical instruments 29, 30
Juke Box Jury (tv show) 167, 168

K.C. Moaners Skiffle Group 208, **209**, 211
Kalin Twins
    British tour 188
Kansas City Skiffle Group 149
Kardomah factory (Liverpool) 200
kazoos 26, 31
Kellogg's Rice Crispies
    skiffle whistle offer 74

Kelly, Bob 75, 93, 97, 129
Kelvedon Hatch
    skiffle in 34
Kennedy, John 184-5
Kingdon, John 173
    lobbies for return of *Guitar Club* 67, 175
    on skiffle's demise 175
Kinks 197, 207
Kinnock, Neil (politician) 134
Konkords (rock group) 200
Korner, Alexis **5**, 7, 8-10, **9**, 22, 23, 24, 77-9, 105,
107, 196, 197
    criticisms of skiffle 128, 129
    Skiffle Group 79
Korrison, Pete 20, 110
Kweskin, Jim, Jug Band 223

Labour Club, Peel Street (Liverpool) 200, 201
Lang, Don 122, 160
    and his Frantic Five 96, 163, 164, 166
Last Chance Jug Band 36, 223
"Last Train to San Fernando" 105, **106**, 120
Laurie, Cy
    Agency 181
    Jazz Band 24, 84, 178
    Skiffle Group 168
Le Taxi, Joe 220
Lea Valley Skiffle Group 143
Ledbetter, Huddie ("Lead Belly") 4, 5, 14, 19, 20,
    38-9, 42, 90, 97, 109, 196
    Paris visit (1949) 37
    performing at New York party (1944) **40**
    performing for school children (1945) **38**
    songs used in skiffle 39-9
Leeds
    skiffle in 135
Leegan, Paul 212, **212**, 214
Legon, Freddy 111
Leicester
    skiffle in 156-7
Leicester Square Jazz Club 3
Lennon, John 140, 188, 198-9, 201, 203-4, 211
Let's Have a Ball (radio programme) 162
Levan, Danny 104
    Trio 168
Levis, Carroll (radio and tv presenter) 119, 157, 179,
    181, 211
    Discoveries 198, 202
    Junior Discoveries 178, 202
    Show 178
    Talent Show 176
Lewis, Furry (blues musician) 31
Library of Congress 22, 38, 42
    Archive of American Folk Song 39
Little Rascals Skiffle Group 146
Littlewood, Tom 187
Liverpool
    skiffle in 56, 188, 198-201
Livewires Skiffle Group 13, 112, 141, **147**
living standards 52-3
Locarno, Streatham 168
Lomax, Alan 21, 38, 39, 79, 89, 103, 156, 202
    and the Ramblers 122, 194
    field recordings 196
    views on skiffle 130-1
Lomax, John 38, 39, 155, 156
London
    list of groups in and around (1957) 125
    number of skiffle groups 133-4
    skiffle venues 124-5, 134; advertisements **121**
London City Ramblers 114
London Jazz Club 16, 22
London Skifflers 137
Lonnigan Bros. Skiffle Group 89, 214
Lowe, John, 214
Luther, David, Skiffle Group 178
Lyttleton, Humphrey 3, 119, 130, 170

Mac, Robbie 212
McCartney, Paul 60, 69, 140, 198-200, 201, 203-4, 211
MacColl, Ewan 23. 122, 156, 194, 213
McCormick, John 197
McDevitt, Chas 84, 91, 105, 107, 108, 115, 140, 182, 212, 214, 224
   broadcasts 170, 173, 177
   Skiffle Group 70, 92-7, **95**, 98, 153, 172;
      broadcasts 160, 162, 163, 168, 170, 176, 177
   views on demise of skiffle 182
   USA visit 93
McDonald, Jacqui 196
McGhee, Brownie 4, 13, 38, 42, 140, 163
   and homemade banjo 31
McGregor, Jim 112, 169, 170, 174, 194, 195
MacKay, Ron, Skiffle Group 194
McKenzie, Red (William) 36
Mad Hatters Skiffle Group 146
Malestrum Skiffle Group 178
Mallinson, Tim
   reminiscences 69, 135, 171, 210
mandolins 26, 30, 32, 33, 150
Mars (skiffle venue) 187
Marsalis, Rudy, and his Creole Skiffle Group 136, 169
Marsden, Gerry 200-1
   Gerry and the Pacemakers 91, 203
Martians Skiffle Group 122, 162, 171
Martin, George 99, 114, 184, 203
Marvin, Brett, and the Thunderbolts 222
Marvin, Hank 102-3, 149, 185
   early career 186, 188-90
Maryland Skiffle Group 211-12
Mason, Derek, 156-7, 214
Matthew, Brian 168, 169, 170, 172
Meehan, Tony 102
Meek, Joe 119-20
Melly, George 15, 19, 122, 140, 169
Memphis Five Skiffle Group 180
Memphis Jug Band **35**, 36, 48, 76, 108
Metropolitan Theatre, Edgware Road 93, 120, 142
Mighty Smithereens (band) 217
Miki and Griff (singing duo) 86, 176, 177
Millar, Dusty, Skiffle Group 138
Miller, Bob, and the Millermen 167
Miller, Jimmy, and the Barbecues 120
Mills, Freddie 162, 166, 167
Mississippi
   Saturday night skiffle dance 42
Mr Burke MP (play) 103
Mitham, Norman 187
Modern Music Club (London) 118, 136, 144
Moka (coffee bar) 25
Monarchs Showband 203
Morden
   skiffle in 23
Morgue Skiffle Club (Liverpool) 199
Morrison, Van (George Ivan Morrison) 202, 203
Moscow
   youth festival 98, 111
Moss Empires 81, 95, 105
Mound City Blue Blowers 3, 36-7, 126
Murray, Pete 162, 163, 166, 167
musical bows 29
musical instruments
   see homemade musical instruments; improvised
      musical instruments; skiffle (instrumentation);
      and names of individual instruments
Musicians Union 15, 135
"My Old Man's a Dustman" (song) 1, 86, 90, 105

National Association of Mixed Clubs and Girl's Clubs 59, 60, 131
national service 14, 58, 97, 110, 187, 217
   army skiffle group (1957) **57**
National Skiffle Competition (*Daily Sketch*) 146, 180
National Skiffle Contest (Bury St Edmunds) 143-4, 150
   recordings of winners 118-21, 224
   winners play on channel "shuffle" 140

National Skiffle Contest (Stanley Dale's) 102, 142-3, 157, 164, 166, 168, 182, 214
   numbers taking part 134
   list of tv competitors 165
National Weekly Skiffle Contest (*Daily Herald*) 144-6
New Carlton Ballroom, Hammersmith 148
New Clubmoor Hall (Liverpool) 199
New Hawleans Skiffle Group 136
New Orleans Joys (record) 16-17, 18
New Station Skiffle Group 158-9
New Vagabonds Skiffle Group **155**, 191
New Zealand
   Donegan tour (1960) 86
   skiffle in 125
New York
   house-rent parties 43
Newcastle
   skiffle in 186, 188-9
Nicholls, Nick 21, 88
North of England Skiffle Preservation Society 207, 208, 211
   advertisement for **208**
Northern Ireland
   skiffle in 138, 146, 149-50, 202, 203
Nose Vipers Skiffle Group 146
Nucleus (coffee bar) 25
Nunn, Trevor (theatre director) 134

100 Club 16
Off the Record (tv show) 161, 175, 176
Oh Boy! (tv show) 167, 177, 183, 188, 190
Old Friends (duo) 213
Old Timers Skiffle Group 95
Opportunity Knocks (tv show) 137, 178, 212
Original London Blue Blowers 3, 111
Orlando (skiffle venue) 187

Pamplin, Terry 211
Panthers Skiffle Group 178
Parker, Johnny 23, 113, 116, 169
Parkside Skiffle Group 144
Parnes, Larry 21, 185, 191, 196
Patterson, Ottilie **11**, 79 81, 140
Peacock, Dave 203, 214
Penarth Folk and Blues Club 212
Perkins, Virgil (washboard player) 48
pianists 150
piano
   in skiffle 47
   at house-rent parties 43
Pigsty Hill Light Orchestra 222
Pilgrim, John 101, 103, 182, 214, 217
Pilgrims Skiffle Group 138
Pitt, Vic 112, 118, 172
Play in a Day (Weedon) 69
Please Y'Self (trio) 216-17, **216**
pop idols
   as described in *Punch* 191
popular music
   and broadcasting 159-80
   and influence of skiffle 132, 182-204, 224
   network 158
   promoted by radio and tv 53-4
Potter, Terry
   reminiscences 33, 123, 172, 218
Power, Duffy 214
   reminiscences 65, 191, 196
with New Vagabonds (1958) **155**, 191
Pratt, Mike 98, 183
Presley, Elvis, iii, 54, 59, 66, 80, 84, 91, 129, 134, 148, 184, 185, 193
   as musical influence 188-9, 191, 198, 200, 201
Prince of Wales Theatre 82, 99, 115, 116
Princess Louise (public house) 24, 92, 93, 214
public houses
   as skiffle venues 24, 78, 124, 201, 206
Putting on the Donegan (tv series) 88, 177

Quarry Men 140, 194 198-200, 201, 202, 203
    recordings 199
    revived 211, 214
Quaye, Russell 111-14, 170, 181
    see also City Ramblers

radio 53, 55-6, 178-80, 188
    skiffle broadcasts 160-2, 168-75, 176, 206
Radio 1 179
Radio Luxembourg 105, 159
Railroad Bill (skiffle group) 30, 220, **220**
Railroaders Skiffle Group 149, 186, 189
Ramblers Skiffle Group 150
Randall, Freddie 3, 16, 162
Raving Texans 199
Ray, Johnny 80, 127
Razzy Dazzy Spasm Band 33
Rebels Skiffle Group 199
recordings of skiffle 112
    reissues 207, 224
Reet Petite and Gone 220
reminiscences i-ii, 13, 17, 23, 32, 33, 34, 54, 56, 65,
    69, 78, 84, 89, 100, 102, 110, 112, 115,
        123, 135, 141, 143, 148, 151, 154, 156,
        160, 63, 171, 172, 180, 183, 188, 191, 193,
        195, 196, 200, 210, 213, 218, 222
Renn, Terry, Skiffle Group 170, 171
rent parties
    see house-rent parties
Rhythm and Blues (radio programme) 162
rhythm 'n' blues 197
Rice, Peter
    reminiscences 188
Richard, Cliff 1, 21, 91, 171, 172, 177, 179, 183, **185**,
193
    early career 185-6, 187-90, 191
Riding Mill Skiffle Group 154, 183, 200
    at garden party (1961) **158**
riverboat shuffles 139-40
Riversiders Skiffle Group 74, 130
Roby, Milton (blues violinist) 31
rock groups 198
rock 'n' roll 27, 58-9, 63, 66, 109, 128, 129, 131,
136, 162, 166, 169, 188, 190, 193, 200, 210
    and BBC 179
    inclusion in skiffle repertoire 186, 187, 189
Rock Around the Clock (film) 58-9, 63
"Rock Around the Clock" (song) 58
"Rock Island Line" 1, 8, 10, 16-17, 19, 38, 54, 58,
65, 69, 70, 90, 122, 197, 210
    record label roundel 16
Rock Island Line (radio programme) 224
Rockin' at the 2 I's (show) 212
Rolling Stones 197, 200
Rollini, Adrian 37
Roody Doody Band 34
Roundhouse (public house) 78, 129
    Skiffle and Blues Club 24
Royal Aquarium, Great Yarmouth 86
Royal Command Performance (1981) 91
Royal Festival Hall 52
Royal Variety Performance (1960) 1, 88
Royal Variety Show (Glasgow, 1958) 86, 176
rub boards
    see washboards
Runaways (Shadows tribute band) 212
Rust, Brian 114

St Peter's Parish Church (Woolton) 211
    fête (July 1957) 140, 199
Saints Skiffle Group 143, 156
Salvation Army 73
Samson and Barlow's (Liverpool restaurant) 196
Samwell, Ian ("Sammy") 187
Sargent, Sir Malcolm 131-2
Satellites Skiffle Group 149-50
Saturday Club 170-2, 179
    Radio Times announcement **173**

Saturday Night at the Palladium (tv show)
    TV Times announcement **179**
Saturday Skiffle Club 111, 113, 118, 122, 168-70,
179, 180, 182
    audience size 169
    auditions 168, 169, 171, 185, 186, 189
    memories of 171, 172
    Radio Times announcement **170**
Saturday Swingtime Challenge Trophy Competition
(Birmingham) 143
Saxons Skiffle Group 157, 166, 214
schools
    skiffle at 54, 100
Scotland
    National Skiffle Championship 120, 144, 149
Seeger, Peggy 39, 42, 122, 194
Seeger, Pete 130, 213
Sellers, Peter 73, 122
Shadows (instrumental group) 183, **189**, 189-90
    importance for popular music 191-2
    see also Drifters
Shadows (?) Skiffle Group **137**
Sharratt, Marc 69, 92, 93, 95, 97, 172
sheet music 56, 68, 70, 156
Shotton, Pete 198, 211
Simpson, Dave, and his Sidewinders 135
Sims, Hylda 111, 112, 113, 170
Sinners Skiffle Group 136
Sinners Skiffle Group (Ballymena) 138
Sioux City Seven Skiffle Group 137
Six-Five Special 55, 63, 84, 85, 118, 131, 142, 149,
    157, 159, 162-8, 179, 180, 185, 189, 190,
        214
    Birthday Special 166
    demise 167
    Extra Special 163
    non-London broadcasts 166-7
    resignations from 167, 181
    signature tune 115, 116
Skiffabillies 157
Skiff-a-Billy 212
skiffle
    advertisements for events in 1957 **107**
    amateur recordings 112, **147**, 213
    American roots 26-48
    and broadcasting 159-80
    and church music 70-3
    and British folk music 80-1, 111, 130, 155, 192-3,
        194, 203, 213
    and US folk music 27, 80-1 155-6, 192, 194, 203
    as rock 'n' roll 109, 158
    cartoon humour **60**, **73**, 74
    continuity of 183, 205-6
    cover versions of hits 122
    criticisms of 127-32, 157; rebuttals 72-3, 129, 131
    demise 175, 181-2, 190, 205
    disillusionment with 102, 107, 181, 182
    early reception 12
    fashion 57, 73-4
    future of 130
    in the 1990s 205-24
    inclusion of rock songs 136, 148, 180, 182, 198, 203
    influence on popular music 182-204, 223-4
    label dropped 102, 105, 170, 181
    music arrangements 68
    musical importance to individuals 210, 218
    origins in UK 1-25
    parodies 122, 124
    purist views of 78, 130, 186, 189
    reasons for its success 100-1
    revival 206-214, 222, 223-4
    sources of repertoire 37-42, 68, 77, 78, 79-80, 89,
        112, 144, 154, 186, 202
    usage of the term in UK 46-8
    usage of the term in USA 42-8
Skiffle, Bill 42
Skiffle and Jazz (proposed radio programme) 161
skiffle basello 26, **66**, 67
skiffle board 67, **67**
"Skiffle Blues" 45

"Skiffle Board Blues" (song) 127
Skiffle Cats Skiffle Group 143
Skiffle Cellar 112, 114, 118, 125, 136 187, 214
    renamed "Cellar" 181
skiffle competitions/contests 135, 141, 142-50, 163, 206
    advertisements for (1957) **146**
skiffle drum sets 67
Skiffle Festival (1957) 84
Skiffle Galaxy (music album) **18**, 68
skiffle groups
    amateurs' fees 135, 141, 164
    dates per week 182
    dress 153
    drop "skiffle" tag 186, 187, 189, 201
    "first in Britain" claim 4
    "first *regular*" claim 7
    group concept 158, 198
    in and around London (1957) 125, 145
    instrumentation 13, 17, 32, 33, 34, 56, 69,
        89, 135, 148, 150-3, 154, 157, 158, 169,
        182, 191, 206, 208, 211, 213, 220
    number of 133-4, 141
    origins 35
    outside London (1957) 139, 145
    personnel 150
    practices 151, 154, 186
    presentation 153-4
    technique 89, 154-5
    where amateur ones formed 133
skiffle intelligentsia 130
"Skiffle Jamboree" 96, 113
skiffle mass 71-3
Skiffle Party (magazine) 214
Skiffle Party (gigs) 214
Skiffle Show of 1957 93
Skiffle: the Story of Folk-Song with a Jazz Beat (Bird)
    reviews 70
skifflers
    transition to blues musicians 196, 197
    transition to folk musicians 194, 195, 196, 197,
        200
    transition to jazz musicians 192, 193, 195
    transition to pop and rock musicians 183-92, 193,
        197-201
    transition to rhythm 'n' blues musicians 197
Skifflettes 176, 178
"Skifflin' Strings" (instrumental) 46-7,
    122
slaves
    music-making 27-9
Smart, Terry 185, 187
Smith, Betty 116, 122, 169
Smith, Bill 198
Smith, Dick 7, 8, 75
social attitudes 53-4
Soho 25, 186, 190
    skiffle venues 61-2, 93. 124
Soho Fair 25, 98
Soho Skiffle Group 118, 153, 170, 171, 181
Solid Gold Rock 'n' Roll Show '96 205
songwriters
    performers as 89, 203-4
Southern Skiffle Society 207, 214, 220
    leaflets **215**
Spacemen Skiffle Group 201
Spacemen Skiffle Group (Wanstead) 136
spasm bands 17, 33-4, 114-15
Spinners (folk group) 194, 196-7
Spirits of Rhythm 36
Sputniks Skiffle Group 202
Starr, Ringo 91, 198, 200, 203
Stars in Their Eyes (tv show) 212
Stars of Six-Five Special (road show) 135
Station Skiffle Group 119-20, 143, 144, 156
Steele, Tommy 21, 91, 98, 129, 179, **184**, 190, 193
    broadcasts 160, 163, 177
    early career 183-5
    not signed by George Martin 99
Steeljacks Skiffle Group 135

Stewart, Sonny, and his Skiffle Kings 97, 122
Stoll Theatre, Kingsway, London 81, **82**
string bands 35
string basses
    see double basses
Studio 51 (jazz club) 8, 76
suitcases
    used as drums 31, 36
Sunday Break (tv programme) 177
Sunrisers Skiffle Group 74, 136, 144
Sunshine, Monty 4, 6, 7, **11**, 15, 81, 91
Sunshine Skiffle Band 223
Sutcliffe Stuart 203
Swansea
    skiffle in 54
Sykora, Ken 76, 116, 117, 169, 172-4, **174**

2 I's Club 98
2 I's Coffee Bar 25, **62**, 206
    Cliff Richard and the Drifters at 183, 187, 189
    description of 62-3
    Jet Harris at 189
    Les Hobeaux at 117-18
    Hank Marvin at 189
    Tony Meehan at 190
    Six-Five Special broadcast from 163-4
    Tommy Steele at 183-5
    Vipers at 98-9, 118, 184
    Bruce Welch at 189
    Worried Men Skiffle Group at 118, 187
2.19 Skiffle Group 70, 118, 143, 144, 162, 169, 172
12.30 Skiffle Group 211
talent competitions 148-9, 186, 189, 200, 201
tea-chest basses 26, 29, 150, 151-2, 153, 154, 211, 218
Teague, Dick, Skiffle Group 185-6, 187
teddy boys 16, 59, 136
teenage magazines 57
teenagers 49, 56-64, 74
    and skiffle 133-158
    broadcasting for 159, 171, 179-80
    income 52
television 53, 66
    coronation of Elizabeth II 51, 56
    effects of 55
    in the 1950s 55
    skiffle broadcasts 162-8, 175-6, 177-8, 206
Terry, Sonny 13, 38, 42, 101, 140, 163
Thirty Years of Skiffle (radio programme) 162
Tidiman's, Kid, Paradise Rhythm Boys 220
Tommy Steele Story (film) 95, 138, 166, 185
Top of the Pops 168
Travellers Skiffle Group 176
Twentieth-Century Folk Mass 71-3

ukuleles 33, 34, 66, 150, 154, 160
United States Information Service
    American Library 37
United States of America
    cultural and political influence 50-1
    folk music 27-33, 155-6
    guitar sales 66-7
    usage of "skiffle" term 42-8
Urdd Gobaith Cymru 150

Valentine, Hylton 197
Van Den Bosch, Jean 98, 101, 102, 107, 181
Van Engel, Roger (Hurgy) 186
Varley, Bill 92, 98
    views on the demise of skiffle 182
Vaughan, Ivan 198
venues
    for amateurs 23, 141, 134-50, 156, 158
    London (1956-57) 124
    outside London (1957) 136, 138
Vikings Rhythm Skiffle Group 138-9
violins
    see fiddles

Vipers Skiffle Group 25, 70, 76, 83, 95, 97-103, **98**,
    107, 108, 115-16, 142, 148, 181, 190,
    210, 224
  and Tommy Steele 99
  at Palace Theatre, Newcastle 102
  broadcasts 161, 163, 164, 170, 171, 177
  influence 78, 84, 172
  reformed 1960 group 103
  signed by George Martin 99
Viper's Tale (radio programme) 103, 224
Viscounts Skiffle Group 178

Waites, Mike
  reminiscences 84, 102, 154, 171, 183, 200, 210
Wales
  skiffle in 141, 149, 150, 156, 206, 210, 212, 220
Wall, John 208
Wallis, Bob, Washboard Beaters 122
Wanderers 171
Wang Dang Doodle 217-18, 223
Warrington
  skiffle in 13, 112, 180
washboard bands 36, 48, 223
Washboard Rhythm Boys Skiffle Group 125
washboards 26, 29-30, 31, 33, 84, 110, 150, 153
  playing method **30**
  sheet music for 68
washtub basses 29
Waters, Muddy 13, 38, 81, 97, 202
Watson, Bob 20, 24, 110
  Skiffle Group 24
Watters, Lu 3
Watts, Keith, and his Skiffling Saints 144
Webb, George 3
  Dixielanders 3, 15, 16
Weedon, Bert 69, 174
Welch, Bruce 102, 103, 149, 185
  early career 186, 188-90
West, Five Skiffle Group 171
Whalley, Nigel 198
Whiskey, Nancy 56, 84, 91-7, 115, 172
  broadcasts 160, 163, 168, 170, 173, 174, 175

dislike of skiffle 95, 97, 107
  USA visits 93
Whitcomb, Ian
  reminiscences 100, 143
White, Danny, (Cliff Richard tribute singer) 212
White, Josh 14, 37-8, 97
Whyton, Wally 25, 37, 97-8, 101, 103, 183, 190,
    210, 224
  broadcasts 103, 170, 173
Wilde, Marty 91, 166, 172, 177, 179, 190, 191, 205
Williams, Hank 14, 42, 112, 202, 205
Williams, Mary Lou 22
Williams, Roy (radio presenter) 173, 174
Wilson, Jen
  reminiscences 54, 222
Wimbledon Palais 146
Witch's Cauldron (coffee bar) 63
Women's Jazz Archive 222
Woodlanders Skiffle Group 135, 166
Woolworth
  sale of guitars 64
World Skiffle Championship 157, 175
Worried Men Skiffle Group 118, 163, 164, 170, 187,
    190
Wright, Basil
  reminiscences 17, 110, 163, 222
Wright, Denny 21, 83, 85, 104, 108

Yerba Buena Jazz Band 3
York, Johnny 183
"Young Musicians" (painting by Molenaer) 27
young people 49-74
  and skiffle 133-58
  broadcasting for 160, 171, 179-80
youth clubs 59-60, 136-7, 201, 202
Youth Music Festival (Liverpool 1957) 201

Zeniths Skiffle Group 188
Zephyrs Skiffle Group 205-6
Zombies Skiffle Group 150